PENGUIN BOOKS

An imprint of Penguin Random House LLC

penguinrandomhouse.com

The Read-Aloud Handbook first published in Penguin Books 1982
First revised edition published 1985
Second revised edition (with the title *The New Read-Aloud Handbook*) published 1989
Third revised edition published 1995
Fourth revised edition published 2001
Fifth revised edition published 2006
Sixth revised edition published 2013
This seventh revised edition published 2019

Portions of this book were originally published in pamphlet form.

Newbery Medal acceptance speech copyright © 2017 by Matt de la Peña. Reprinted by permission of Writers House LLC acting as agent for the author.

Photo credits on page 357.

LIBRARY OF CONGRESS CATALOGING-IN-PUBLICATION DATA
Names: Trelease, Jim author. | Giorgis, Cyndi, revisor, editor. | Trelease, Jim. The read-aloud handbook.
Title: Jim Trelease's read-aloud handbook / [Jim Trelease] ; edited and revised by Cyndi Giorgis.
Other titles: Read-aloud handbook
Description: Eighth Edition, Seventh Revised Edition. | New York : PENGUIN BOOKS, 2019. | "Portions of this book were originally published in pamphlet form"--T.p. verso. | "The Read-Aloud Handbook first published in Penguin Books 1982. First revised edition published 1985. Second revised edition (with the title The New Read-Aloud Handbook) published 1989"--T.p. verso. | Includes bibliographical references and index.
Identifiers: LCCN 2019014911 (print) | LCCN 2019020114 (ebook) | ISBN 9780525505624 (ebook) | ISBN 9780143133797 | ISBN 9780143133797 (trade paperback)
Subjects: LCSH: Oral reading.
Classification: LCC LB1573.5 (ebook) | LCC LB1573.5 .T68 2019 (print) | DDC 372.45/2--dc23
LC record available at https://lccn.loc.gov/2019014911

Printed in the United States of America
1 3 5 7 9 10 8 6 4 2

Set in Bembo Std
Designed by Sabrina Bowers

PENGUIN BOOKS

JIM TRELEASE'S READ-ALOUD HANDBOOK

Before retiring from the lecture circuit in 2008, Jim Trelease spent thirty years addressing parents, teachers, and librarians on the subjects of children, literature, and the challenges of multimedia to print. A graduate of the University of Massachusetts, he was an award-winning artist and writer for the *Springfield Daily News* from 1963 to 1983.

Initially self-published in 1979, *The Read-Aloud Handbook* has had seven American editions as well as British, Australian, Japanese, Chinese, Indonesian, and Spanish editions. In 2010, Penguin Books named *The Read-Aloud Handbook* one of the seventy-five most important books it published in its seventy-five-year history.

Cyndi Giorgis has always been a proponent of read-aloud. She is currently a professor of children's and young adult literature at Arizona State University's Mary Lou Fulton Teachers College, where she promotes the importance and impact of reading aloud. She has been recognized for numerous university distinguished teaching awards and is the recipient of the International Literacy Association's Arbuthnot Award for Outstanding Professor of Children's and Young Adult Literature. She has chaired or served on numerous committees for book awards such as the Caldecott Medal, Newbery Medal, Theodor Seuss Geisel Award, and the Orbis Picture Award for Outstanding Nonfiction for children.

Jim Trelease's
Read-Aloud
Handbook

EIGHTH EDITION

Cyndi reading aloud to second graders during Read Across America Day on March 2 (Dr. Seuss's birthday)

Edited and Revised by
Cyndi Giorgis

PENGUIN BOOKS

This eighth edition of *Jim Trelease's Read-Aloud Handbook* is dedicated to the two Jims:

Jim Trelease for his passion and advocacy for reading aloud to children. I am forever indebted to you for allowing me to be a part of this incredible legacy.

Jim Kruger for your love and never-ending support over the years. You have been the best research assistant ever. I appreciate you reading, rereading, and offering your suggestions and edits for this new edition. We are a good team!

We must ensure that children's early encounters with reading are pleasurable so they will cheerfully return to the experience, now and forever. Our ultimate goal is to create lifetime readers.

Acknowledgments

W HEN you are presented with an opportunity to update one of the most well-known and respected books about reading aloud, having support and cooperation from family, friends, colleagues, children, teachers, librarians, and editors is essential. I would like to extend my deepest appreciation to:

My parents, Donna Zanetti and Glenn Martens. How I wish they were still living to be part of this incredible next step in my professional journey. While neither had formal education beyond high school, they both instilled in me and my sister, Glenda, a love of reading. My mother read aloud to us when we were children, and my father always read magazines and the daily newspaper, engaging us in discussion about a variety of topics. They modeled what is advocated in this book.

Students, past and present, who reaffirm with each read-aloud that experiencing a book together creates a bond that connects us. It's awesome when six-year-olds, nineteen-year-olds, and forty-somethings break into applause after you read aloud a picture book to them.

The many current and new friends who offered their stories to me. For this edition, I am especially grateful to Melissa Olans Antinoff, Kathleen Armstrong, Jim Bailey, Diane Crawford, Matt de la Peña, Charity Delach, Peter Delach, Christine Draper, Sean Dudley, Alma S. Baca Hernandez, Clara Lackey; Mark Lackey, Erika and Richard McCallum, Tiffany Nay, Elysha O'Brien, Jasmine E. Rich-Arnold, Scott Riley, Maria Rue, Jessica Saad, Francisco Sánchez, Megan Sloan, and Jimma Tadelech.

My amazing friends and colleagues, Nancy Johnson and Marie LeJeune, not only for your anecdotes, but also for recognizing that the opportunity to revise this book is a *big* deal. I cannot express to you how much I treasure our friendship.

Those in children's book publishing and marketing: Lori Benton,

Terry Borzumato-Greenberg, Lucy Del Priore, Lisa DiSarro, Katie Halata, Emily Heddleson, Angus Killick, Neal Porter, Lizette Serrano, Dina Sherman, Victoria Stapleton, and Jaime Wong. You are always ready with a book and a hug.

Children's book authors, Rosemary Wells and Kate DiCamillo, who have long advocated for reading aloud. Rosemary created the campaign and book *Read to Your Bunny* as a reminder to parents to read aloud twenty minutes every day. Along with being an incredible author/storyteller, Kate has served as the National Ambassador for Young People's Literature. Her constant reinforcement that reading aloud has the capacity to change lives is one that has been heard by children, parents, teachers, and librarians around the world.

My editors, Kathryn Court and Victoria Savanh. From our first conversation, I knew you loved this book as much as I do and want it to continue to impact and influence parents, teachers, librarians, and community members.

And last, but certainly not least, my husband, Jim Kruger. Thank you for the many dinners you prepared and the dozens of times you walked the dogs without me. I'm grateful for letting me read aloud to you when a sentence, phrase, or passage caught my ear.

Contents

Introduction

If you want your children to be intelligent, read them fairy tales. If you want them to be more intelligent, read them more fairy tales.

—Albert Einstein

Back in the 1960s, Jim Trelease was a young father of two children, working as an artist and writer for the *Springfield Daily News* in Massachusetts. Each night he read to his daughter and son, unaware of any cognitive or emotional benefits that would come of it. He had no idea what it would do for their vocabulary, attention span, or interest in books. He read for one reason: because it made him feel good when his father had read to him, and he wanted his children to experience stories in this way too.

As Jim was reading nightly to his children, he was also spending time volunteering in a sixth-grade classroom. To his dismay, he discovered that kids in some classes were reading a lot but not in others. What was different? When he pursued it further, he realized in nearly every one of the turned-on to reading classes, the teacher read aloud on a regular basis. Jim sought out research showing that reading aloud to children improves their reading, writing, speaking, listening—and, best of all, their attitudes about reading. There was one problem: The people who should have been reading the research weren't reading it. The teachers, supervisors, and principals didn't know it even existed. He also found that most parents and teachers were unaware of good children's books.

In order to provide research on the benefits of reading aloud and to offer recommendations of books, the first edition of *The Read-Aloud Handbook* was published in 1982. At that time, there was no internet or email, no cell phones, YouTube, iTunes, iPads, apps, video streaming, ebooks, Wi-Fi, Facebook, Twitter, or Instagram. The closest thing to an instant message was a facial expression that exasperated mothers gave their children as a warning. Texting was something you did on a typewriter. The first CD player was just going on sale, Starbucks was a coffee-bean shop in Seattle, and if you said "laptop" to people, they'd have thought you were talking about a TV-dinner tray.

Which brings us to the present time. With all the new technology in place and billions of dollars in testing administered, the National Assessment of Educational Progress (NAEP), commonly referred to as The Nation's Report Card, has reported that reading scores have been stagnant for the past two decades. Two-thirds of students across the country scored below the "proficient" level on reading tests administered in 2017.[1] This is despite the government-mandated No Child Left Behind (NCLB) that went into effect in 2002 and focused exclusively on reading and mathematics.

In addition to NCLB, there are also community, corporate, and organizational initiatives such as Reading for All, Read by Grade Three, Read Better Be Better, The Campaign for Grade-Level Reading, Children's Literacy Initiative, and Born to Read, just to name a few. They are all attempting to provide resources to parents, caregivers, teachers, and librarians that will increase children's early literacy skills.

With all the focus and support for reading, why aren't we moving the needle on childhood literacy issues? I hope this book can answer that question, as well as what we can do about it. Surely, there's a better way than what we've done in the past. And how do we tap into the resources that are currently available?

The Current State of Reading and Testing

We start with Tyler Hart of Reno, Nevada. In 2015, he was one of 583 students out of 1.7 million who scored a perfect 2400 on the SAT college entrance exam. In addition, he scored a perfect 36 on the ACT exam. When asked what his secret was, Tyler said that he gets ten hours of sleep a night and eats breakfast. What he didn't do was cram or take classes to help him prep for either test. When Tyler's mother was questioned about her son's perfect scores, she shared that she remembers reading aloud to Tyler and his brother as much as possible when they were young. They would also visit museums and cut out newspaper stories to discuss. Tyler's mother and father also constantly reiterated the importance of school with their sons.[2]

Never before in American history has so much been written about the subject of reading as in the past two decades. Never has so much money been spent on testing children in any subject, and never have so many reading rules and regulations been imposed on schools by a succession of administrations—with little or no improvements to show for it.[3]

In an attempt to provide more time for test preparation, many states and school districts eliminated recess, despite the increase in the obesity rate for children and adolescents in this country.[4] Many states have now begun to realize the effect on children having no time to play during the school day. In 2017, Florida enacted a state law mandating twenty minutes of recess each day.[5] Rhode Island and Arizona have recently passed similar laws. It seems amazing that we have to pass laws ensuring children can engage in an activity that encourages physical activity and socialization.

The time and space for childhood play seems to be shrinking every day.

Isn't This Reading Stuff the School's Responsibility?

Jay Mathews, the *Washington Post*'s longtime education columnist, looked back on all the student achievement stories he'd done in twenty-two years and observed: "I cannot think of a single instance in which the improvement in achievement was not tied, at least in part, to an increase in the amount of time students had to learn."[6] I've been saying the same thing for as many years. You either extend the school day,[7] or you tap into the 7,800 hours at home. Since the cost of lengthening the school day would be prohibitive in the places that need it most, the most realistic option is tapping the 7,800 hours at home.

Researchers from North Carolina State University, Brigham Young University, and the University of California, Irvine, evaluated data from more than ten thousand students, parents, teachers, and school administrators. They examined family social capital, which is the bond between parent and child such as trust, open lines of communication, and active engagement in a child's academic life.[8] They also looked at school social capital, which captures a school's ability to offer a positive environment for learning. The researchers found that both school and family involvement was important, but the role of family involvement is stronger when it comes to academic success.[9]

Contrary to the current discourse that blames teachers for just about everything wrong in schooling,[10] research shows that the seeds of reading and school success (or failure) are sown in the home, long before the child ever arrives at school.[11]

Research helps refine issues that are often politicized talk-show blather. But research can make for rather dry reading, so throughout the book, I've also included the personal and anecdotal to bring the research alive.

By personal and anecdotal, I mean people like Marie LeJeune who you will meet multiple times throughout this book. I've known Marie for years, first as a doctoral student and high school teacher, and now as a children's literature colleague and friend. Over the years, Marie and I have talked about the importance of reading aloud. I was curious why she believed it was so valuable. Here is her response:

I read aloud to my high school students and my own children because I had read the research on how beneficial it was for them. I knew that children who were read aloud to had stronger vocabularies, comprehension, and processing skills.

As a teacher, I recognized reading aloud was pleasurable for students. Building positive moments with books, characters, and literacy was so important. Reading aloud introduced new genres, themes, and authors to my students, and many of them expanded their own independent reading based on what I read aloud. We had amazing and deep conversations from these shared books—

sometimes the most powerful conversations of the year. I also could tailor my read-alouds easily to the particular needs of each class and what was happening in our lives at that moment. There were stories to offer comfort during difficult times, to celebrate being together, and to make us laugh when we needed to de-stress.

Reading aloud at home to my children meant we could share books and experiences together, curled up on a bed or couch before bedtime, or anytime. It gave us moments to laugh and to cry as we became attached to stories and characters. Reading aloud was a time we looked forward to reconnecting and sharing as a family.

Can We Really Change Families and Homes in America?

Suppose we ran a national awareness campaign for what parents can, should, and must do in the home. And I don't mean a polite little campaign in which the first lady runs around saying, "Be Best!" I mean a real in-your-face crusade.

For the past fifty years, an incessant antismoking campaign has been waged in this country. We informed and frightened people into changing their habits. Using all available media, we gave them statistics linking smoking to cancer and death. We offered confessions from smokers who were speaking through artificial voice boxes.

Gradually, public opinion swayed public practice and policy, forcing legislation and litigation that would affect most homes and every public space in America. Cigarette smoking has been reduced by more than half since 1964. As of 2015, the Centers for Disease Control and Prevention (CDC) reported 15.1 percent of U.S. adults smoke, down from 20.9 percent in 2005.[12] Over the years, hundreds of millions of lives and dollars have been affected or saved.

Using that model, we could change parental practices in this country. Our campaign would give parents the statistics on children's reading that you'll find in this book (to inform). There also would be information on the damage that is done to children's and grandchildren's futures if families fail to implement effective literacy practices (to frighten).

Here's a small example of the possibilities that exist for changing families and how little is done to reach them. For nearly three decades, the federal government has harped on the need for school reform. But nobody was telling parents what *they* should be doing to help.

I love this story that Jim Trelease tells of his own efforts:

> Taking some of the topics I've written and talked about, I condensed each one to a single-page trifold black-and-white brochure. I uploaded it to my website, along with a few lines on my home page stating they could be freely downloaded and printed out for parents.[13] That was it. No advertisements, no promotions, no publishers' links. Just little brochures for nonprofit schools and libraries to give away to parents looking for help.
>
> I was curious to see who, if anyone, would use them, so I put a note on the web page asking users to send me a request for permission—just a *request*. Over the next three years, I received almost two thousand requests from schools, mostly in the United States, but also from nearly every continent. The emails came from large urban districts as well as from little villages in the rural Southwest, from schools in the Middle East, from India, Korea, Japan, and the other day from Kazakhstan. Again and again, they said they had stumbled on the brochures by accident when they were surfing for something to help parents.

Imagine what could be done if someone were *pushing* to reach parents advocating the benefits of reading aloud and promoting it from the rooftops. Imagine what government could do with its reach and millions in funding if it thought parents and families were worth it. Imagine if we promoted parent education the way we endorse the Super Bowl or the newest reality show.

Is Reading Still Important in the Digital Age?

Reading is the heart of education. The knowledge of almost every subject in school flows from reading. Students must be able to read the word problem in math to understand it. If they cannot read the science or social studies textbook, then how can they answer the questions at the end of the chapter?

Because reading is the linchpin of education, one can say it's a safety belt for a long life. When the nonprofit RAND Corporation researchers examined all the possible causes of long life expectancy—race, gender, geography, education, marriage, diet, smoking, and even churchgoing—the most significant factor was education. Another researcher went back more than a hundred years to when states initiated compulsory education. She found that for every year of education, the individual lived an average of one and a half years longer.[14] When her research was applied to other countries, the same pattern appeared. Similarly, Alzheimer's researchers have found what they consider to be an immunizing effect to damage from the disease: Childhood reading and vocabulary buildup. More about that later in the book.

All things considered, reading—not video streaming or texting—is the single most important social factor in American life. Here's a formula that may sound simplistic, but all its parts have been documented, and while not 100 percent universal, it holds true far more often than not:

1. The more you read, the more you know.[15]
2. The more you know, the smarter you grow.[16]
3. The smarter you grow, the longer you stay in school.[17]
4. The longer you stay in school, the more diplomas you earn and the longer you are employed—thus the more money you earn in a lifetime.[18]
5. The more diplomas you earn, the higher your children's grades are in school,[19] and the longer you live.[20]

The opposite would also be true:

1. The less you read, the less you know.
2. The less you know, the sooner you drop out of school.[21]
3. The sooner you drop out, the sooner and longer you are poor and the greater your chances of going to jail.[22]

The basis for that formula is firmly established, as poverty and illiteracy are related—they are the parents of desperation and imprisonment:

- Over 80 percent of prison inmates are school dropouts.[23]
- Three out of five people in prison cannot read, while 85 percent of juvenile offenders have trouble reading.[24]

Why are students failing and dropping out of school? Because they cannot read well enough to do the assigned work—which affects the entire report card. Change the reading scores and <u>you change the</u> graduation rate and then the prison population—which changes the social climate of America.

Marie LeJeune reading aloud to her daughter Amelia.

Will This Book Help Me Teach My Child to Read?

This is not a book about teaching a child *how* to read; it's about teaching a child to *want* to read. There's an education adage that goes, "What we teach children to love and desire will always out-weigh what we make them learn." The truth is some children learn to read sooner than others, while some learn better than others. There is a difference. For the parent who thinks that sooner is bet-ter, who has an eighteen-month-old child barking at flash cards, my response is: Sooner is *not* better. Are the dinner guests who arrive an hour early better guests than those who arrive on time?

However, I am concerned about the child who needlessly arrives late to reading and then struggles through years of pain with books.

Not only will he miss out on large portions of what he needs to know in school; he'll connect reading with a pain that may stay with him for a lifetime. This book is about the steps that families can take as "preventive maintenance" to ensure against those pains. You've already read some examples, and you'll find more in the chapters ahead.

There should be no rush to have a child reading before age five. That's developmentally the natural time. If a child *naturally* comes to reading sooner, fine. This book is about raising children who fall in love with print and want to keep on reading long after they graduate; it's not about children who learn to read in order to perform for their parents or just to graduate. It's also a book about how you can enhance the read-aloud experience by not only savoring the time spent with your child but also developing an appreciation for the books that you share.

Do We All Share the Responsibility of Reading Aloud to Children?

There is an old African proverb: It takes a village to raise a child. While some might believe that reading aloud to children is the sole responsibility of parents and teachers, I would have to disagree. We all have an opportunity to make a difference in a child's life by reading aloud.

When I was growing up, I often read aloud to my parents, sister, pets, and dolls. I would read aloud books as well as items in the newspaper that caught my attention. I was a big fan of Ann Landers and would read her advice columns to my parents at the breakfast table. I enjoyed hearing the sound of words and the flow of sentences.

When I was twelve, my family moved to Jackson, Wyoming. An ad appeared in the local newspaper asking for volunteers to read aloud during preschool story time at the public library. I'm sure I wasn't quite who they were seeking, but the librarian gave me a chance, and my knack for reading aloud provided enjoyment to both the children in attendance as well as their parents.

When I first met my editor, Victoria Savanh, we talked about how much we enjoyed reading aloud and the importance of *The Read-Aloud Handbook*. She then shared with me this story:

I first met Milla when she was beginning fourth grade. I had volunteered through my company to participate in a program called Read Ahead, in which we were matched up with a reading buddy who we would meet once a week during the school year.

When we first started our sessions, she didn't seem particularly excited about reading, so we mostly did other activities like playing word games and drawing, though I would often ask that we please read a little bit before we did anything else. Early on, I had picked out a book from the popular Warriors series by Erin Hunter that tells the stories of rival cat clans. It didn't seem that she enjoyed them much until later on when she suggested we go back to the books, and began drawing and re-creating scenes as little pop-up books, which helped us both explore and imagine the world of the Warriors.

By the end of fourth grade, she had read several books from the series in her own time, and we were reading more together, in addition to our crafty projects. In the fifth-grade year, we read at every session and usually books from the Warriors series, which we had both become invested in. It was impressive how quickly we read them!

In June, I attended her graduation to middle school. It was such an honor to be invited. I met her parents who thanked me for my mentorship and commented on how much Milla had developed as a reader through the program. Their gratitude brought me so much joy. It was an immense privilege to make a new young friend and to be part of her reading journey.

If we are all part of "the village" that mentors and motivates children to discover the magic that books hold, possibly we could halt the declining statistics related to reading. Let's do it!

How Is This Edition Different from Previous Ones?

When Jim Trelease contacted me to inquire if I would be interested in revising and updating the contents for the eighth edition of *The Read-Aloud Handbook*, I was thrilled and honored. I recognize the significance of this book that has influenced adults around the world regarding the value of reading aloud to children of all ages.

Jim wrote this book from the perspective of a parent who was not seeing children being read aloud to on a regular basis. My background is being an educator—former first-grade teacher and school librarian. I am currently a professor of children's and young adult literature, teaching adults who want to be or who are teachers.

I have retained the format of this book. It continues to be two books in one. The first half comprises the evidence in support of reading aloud and the practices that nurture lifetime readers. Explained are the intricacies and techniques of making the read-aloud experience pleasurable.

The second half is the Treasury of Recommended Read-Alouds, a beginner's reference to titles, from picture books to novels. The Treasury is intended to take the guesswork out of book choices for parents, teachers, librarians, and community members who want to read aloud to children.

Strategies for fostering independent reading are an important aspect of this edition.

This book provides the rationale and research for why we should be reading aloud to children and when to begin doing so. The subject of children's reading is broader than reading aloud, that's why chapter 4 is devoted to sustained silent reading (SSR). One of the many reasons why we read aloud to children is to cultivate that desire to become readers themselves.

We also need to get dads on board in reading aloud, as discussed in chapter 5. They serve a vital role in the literacy learning of their sons and daughters.

Common sense tells us you cannot engage in reading if you don't have books. Children who have access to more print (magazines, newspapers, and books) have better reading scores. That's the "print climate," which is explored in chapter 6.

And you can't address the subject of books these days without confronting technology. Will ebooks replace traditional books? Are e-gadgets (and all that texting) helping or hindering literacy?

An addition to *The Read-Aloud Handbook* is a chapter encouraging you to explore all aspects of a children's book, from cover to cover. Too often we focus on the text and don't slow down to savor the illustrations in picture books and graphic novels. Chapter 8 will walk you through picture books describing design and artistic elements to enhance reading aloud. Because I'm an educator, I've incorporated strategies that are not meant to "test" the child, but rather to elevate the read-aloud experience.

Jim Trelease's Read-Aloud Handbook

Chapter 1

Why Read Aloud?

Last weekend in Spokane, I talked to a group of
teachers and parents and librarians and kids.

During the Q and A, a 14-year-old girl stood
up and said, "I just want you to know that my
fourth-grade teacher read *The Miraculous Journey
of Edward Tulane* out loud to the class, and it
changed my life. I was never a reader, and then I
became a reader. And now I'm a writer, too."

Reading aloud makes readers.

Reading aloud makes writers.

Reading aloud changes lives.

—Author Kate DiCamillo[1]

WHENEVER I'm asked, "Why should I read aloud to my child or my students?" (regardless of the child's age), it provides me with an opportunity to share why reading aloud is so important, for both reader and listener. The educational values of reading aloud are well documented: introducing vocabulary, modeling fluency, demonstrating expressive reading, developing comprehension, and assisting children in making connections. There is also the personal value of listening to a book read aloud. That experience may generate vivid memories of a story associated with a person, time, or place—a memory often remaining with us for years.

So why do we read aloud? Here are a few reasons gathered from new and seasoned parents:

♦ "When I was pregnant, the first gift my husband bought for our child was *Where the Wild Things Are* by Maurice Sendak. Although we are both avid readers, my heart was incredibly touched by this purchase. He hadn't bought the book because he hoped our child would love to read. He bought it because he already looked forward to reading it aloud. Reading aloud is one of the first ways a love of reading is fostered, and it's been a part of our children's lives before they were even born." (Marie LeJeune, mother of four)

♦ "I love reading to my children. It's a time to be quiet and snuggle. I believe that my son Jacob's verbal skills are so advanced because of it. He asks questions and is learning about inference and critical thinking. For example, he looks at pictures and wonders what is happening or asks, 'What are they doing?' It's been fun to see his growth in the last six months. My daughter, Nora, is five months old. She is captivated by the bright colors in books and touching things on the pages. I am certain the early stimulation will help her as well." (Charity Delach, mother of two)

♦ "As a father, reading aloud is a chance to experience something with your child and not having to tell her what to do or feel. When you are both behind the pages of a book, you're not parent/child, you are humans taking it in together. Your roles are shed, and you are both exposed on a deeper emotional level. It's a window into deeper conversation without knowing the right answer. My youngest daughter is a reluctant reader. For her, when it's read-aloud time with dad, it's about spending quality time that's only ours. There are no other distractions. I'm not thinking about work. She's not worried about friends. Reading aloud is something that nothing else can provide." (Scott Riley, father of two teenage daughters)

♦ "I love to read. Getting lost in a book is one of my favorite activities. Doing voices, making the books come alive, getting caught up in a story and feeling like the characters are family— I'll never tire of sharing that with my children." (Melissa Olans Antinoff, mother of two)

♦ "I read aloud because *I* enjoy it." (Elysha O'Brien, mother of three sons)

And here are some beliefs for why we read aloud to students offered by librarians and teachers:

♦ "Reading good books fills our minds and fills our hearts. Kids become mesmerized when they're invited to relax and let a story wash over them. You have to find out who your audience is and decide which books will hold them in your grasp. The choices are limitless. When kids share a poignant moment, it acts as a bridge and begins to build relationships among all who experience it." (Diane Crawford, elementary school librarian)

♦ "I read aloud:

  ▸ To build community for my students. We come together when we are listening to a shared story and relating it to our learning and to our lives.

  ▸ To provide crucial reading instruction for students. I don't make this a planned lesson, but there are *so* many reading comprehension skills that come from conversations occurring from a book.

  ▸ To demonstrate expressive reading. Kids need to hear it to do it.

  ▸ To show kids *how* to read. Modeling is going back and rereading when something doesn't make sense.

  ▸ To teach writing. When I read aloud, we celebrate the craft of writing by observing how an author begins a chapter, constructs purposeful dialogue, includes interesting language, or elaborates on an idea.

  ▸ To offer different perspectives. Books introduce kids to a variety of characters, people, and places. They also offer a mirror for kids to read about someone who looks like them or is experiencing a similar situation or problem.

  ▸ To "bless" a book. By reading aloud, we tell kids this book is worth reading.

  ▸ For pure joy! The read-aloud is my favorite time of day." (Megan Sloan, third-grade teacher)

♦ "For me, reading aloud is the quintessential connector, the ultimate relationship builder, the optimal model of engagement and care I can offer my students. Whether for my eighth graders or my college students, making time to read aloud is a conscious choice, a deliberate decision. And, *that* I read is as important as *what* I have selected to read. The first day of a read-aloud, I cite author Katherine Paterson: 'Read it to me is a test. Let me read it to you is a gift.' And then I add, 'This read-aloud is my gift to you.' By reading aloud, I'm giving my students the chance to slow down their lives, to set aside what's happening outside our classroom, and to step inside and surrender to this gift of story." (Nancy Johnson, middle school teacher and college educator)

These parents, teachers, and librarians are passionate about reading aloud. They observe and experience the impact it is making not only on children's ability to read and make connections to a story but on their capacity to feel differently about themselves, each other, and the world around them.

Does Research Support the Practice of Reading Aloud?

In 1983, the Commission on Reading was funded by the U.S. Department of Education to examine school scores. Since nearly everything in the curriculum rested upon reading, the consensus was that reading was at the heart of either the problem or the solution of declining test scores.

The commission spent two years poring through thousands of research projects conducted in the previous quarter century and in 1985 issued its report, *Becoming a Nation of Readers.* Among its primary findings, two simple declarations rang loud and clear:

+ "The single most important activity for building the knowledge required for eventual success in reading is reading aloud to children."[2]
+ "It is a practice that should continue throughout the grades."[3] The commission found conclusive evidence to support reading aloud not only in the home but also in the classroom.

In their wording—"the single most important activity"—the experts were saying reading aloud was more important than worksheets, homework, book reports, and flash cards. One of the cheapest, simplest, and oldest methods of teaching was being promoted as a better tool than anything else in the home or classroom. It is interesting to note that the findings of a study published over thirty years ago still hold true today.

Reading to children, preferably from infancy but certainly as they get older, in school and out of school, is what the Commission on Reading was begging the nation to do: to sow the seeds of reading desire.

The *Kids & Family Reading Report*, conducted and published by Scholastic, echoes the findings of the commission: "One of the most important things parents can do, beyond keeping children healthy and safe, is to read to them."[4] The report also advocates reading aloud to children even after they start to read on their own.

At school, the books teachers read aloud promote deeper understanding and interpretation of a story, allow children to take an active role in understanding text, and prompt children to start using mental activities that will become automatic as they begin reading independently.[5] Research also shows that when children reach primary grades, repeated readings of the same picture book (at least three times) increases vocabulary acquisition by 15 to 40 percent, and the learning is relatively permanent.[6]

The Organisation for Economic Co-operation and Development (OECD) is a fifty-year-old cooperative among industrial countries aimed at helping member nations work through modern growth challenges, including education. For more than a decade, the OECD has been testing hundreds of thousands of fifteen-year-olds in various school subjects and comparing scores among nations. In addition, the OECD interviewed parents of five thousand students who were part of the test-taking corps, asking them if they ever read to their children and how often the reading took place. The responses, when compared with children's reading scores on the Programme for International Student Assessment (PISA) exam, showed a powerful correlation: The more they were read to as children, the higher the scores at age fifteen, sometimes an advantage of as much as a half year's schooling. And the results were true regardless of family income.[7]

How Can Something as Simple as Reading to a Child Be So Effective?

Words are the primary structure for learning. There are only two effective ways to get words into a person's brain: either by seeing them or by hearing them. Since it will be years before an infant uses his or her eyes for actual reading, the best source for vocabulary and brain building becomes the ear. What we send into that ear becomes the foundation for the child's "brain house." Those meaningful sounds now will help the child make sense of the words coming in through the eyes later when learning to read.

We read to children for all the same reasons we talk with them: to reassure, to entertain, to bond, to inform or explain, to arouse curiosity, and to inspire. But in reading aloud, we also

- build vocabulary,
- condition the child's brain to associate reading with pleasure,
- create background knowledge,
- provide a reading role model, and
- instill the desire to read.

Let's start by examining how reading aloud presents children with an opportunity to build their vocabulary. Emergent literacy skills develop as children are introduced to rich vocabulary and language during a read-aloud. The words they hear in a story are generally not ones they hear in conversations with family or friends.[8]

Conversation is the prime garden in which vocabulary grows, but conversations vary greatly from home to home. Verifying the impact of this fact are the eye-opening findings of Drs. Betty Hart and Todd Risley at the University of Kansas. Published as *Meaningful Differences in the Everyday Experience of Young American Children*,[9] the research began in response to what Hart and Risley observed among four-year-olds attending the university lab school. With many children, the lines were already drawn: Some were far advanced and some far behind. When the children in the study were tested at age three and again at age nine, the differences held. What could have caused the disparities so early?

The researchers began by identifying forty-two families representing three socioeconomic groups: welfare, working class, and professional. Starting when the children were seven months old, researchers visited the homes for one hour a month and continued their visits for two and a half years. During each visit, the researcher tape-recorded and transcribed any conversations and actions taking place in front of the child.

Through 1,300 hours of visits, they accumulated twenty-three million bytes of information for the project database, categorizing every word (noun, verb, adjective, etc.) uttered in front of the child. The project held some surprises. Regardless of socioeconomic level, all forty-two families said and did the same things with their children. In other words, the basic instincts of good parenting are there for most people regardless of their socioeconomic status (SES).

Then the researchers received the data printout and saw the "meaningful differences" among the forty-two families. When the daily number of words for each group of children was projected across four years, the four-year-old child from the professional family had heard forty-five million words, the working-class child twenty-six million, and the welfare child only thirteen million.

All three children will show up for kindergarten on the same day, but one will have heard thirty-two million fewer words. If legislators expect the teacher to get this child caught up, she'll have to speak ten words a second for nine hundred hours to reach the thirty-two million mark by year's end. Obviously, an impossible task!

The message in this kind of research is that it's not the toys in the house that make the difference in children's lives, it's the words in their heads. The least expensive thing we can give a child outside of a hug turns out to be the most valuable: words. You don't need a job, a checking account, or even a high school diploma to talk with a child. If I could select any piece of research that all parents should be exposed to, *Meaningful Differences in the Everyday Experience of Young American Children* would be the one. And that's feasible. The authors condensed their 268-page book into a six-page article for *American Educator*, the journal of the American Federation of Teachers, which may be freely reproduced by schools.[10]

What Offers the Better Vocabulary: Conversation or Reading?

Talking with your children is vital if they are to develop vocabulary, learn about sentence structure, and acquire the ability to converse with others. But is conversation enough? Those forty-two children in the Hart and Risley study had varying degrees of vocabulary acquisition by the age of four: The professionals' children had 1,100-word vocabularies compared to the welfare children's 525. Similarly, their IQs were 117 versus 79.

Sociologists George Farkas and Kurt Beron studied the research on 6,800 children from ages three to twelve. They found that children from lower SES were far more likely to arrive at school with smaller vocabularies (twelve to fourteen months behind), and they seldom made up the loss as they grew older.[11]

Most conversation, whether it's between two adults or with children, consists of the five thousand words we use all the time, called the Basic Lexicon. (Indeed, 83 percent of the words in everyday conversation with a child come from the most commonly used thousand words, and it doesn't change much as the child ages.)[12] Then there are another five thousand words we use in dialogue less often. Together, these ten thousand words are called the Common Lexicon. Beyond that ten thousand mark are the "rare words," and these play a critical role in reading as we grow older. The eventual strength of our vocabulary is determined not by the ten thousand common words but by how many rare words we understand.

If we don't use these rare words very often in conversation, where do we find them? Printed text contains the rarest words. Whereas an adult uses only nine rare words per thousand when talking with a three-year-old, there are three times as many in a children's book and more than seven times as many in a newspaper. Picture books have, on average, around 70 percent more unique words than conversations directed at kids.[13] If we want to improve children's vocabularies, we need to be reading to them. A distinctive aspect of picture books is that they each tell a different story within thirty-two to forty pages. For example, the I Can Read It All by Myself book *Are You My Mother?* by P. D. Eastman is a classic tale of a baby bird searching for his mother. This book, using controlled and limited vocabulary, isn't likely to use the same words as

Oh, the Places You'll Go! (and not just because Dr. Seuss was fond of nonsensical vocabulary).[14] Picture books may seem brief in text but essentially contain more rare words than a conversation between parent and child.

As shown by data for printed material, the number of rare words increases significantly. This poses serious problems for children who are at risk and possess a higher probability of failing academically or dropping out of school. They hear fewer words and encounter print less often at home. Children at risk face a gigantic word gap that impedes reading progress throughout school. And that gap can't possibly be breached in 120 hours of summer school[15] or through more phonics instruction.

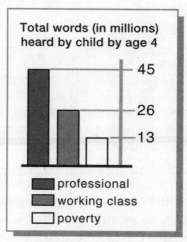

Hart & Risley, Meaningful Differences.

What Are the Skills a Child Needs for Kindergarten?

Let me make an analogy here. Inside a child's brain, there is a huge reservoir called the Listening Vocabulary. You could say it's the child's very own Lake Pontchartrain, the famous estuary outside New Orleans that overflowed because of all the water brought by Hurricane Katrina. That extra water breached the levees and tragically flooded New Orleans. We want the same thing to happen but not in a tragic way—this time the levees will be breached inside the child's brain with a positive impact.

The first levee would be the Speaking Vocabulary. You pour enough words into the child's Listening Vocabulary, and it will overflow and fill the Speaking Vocabulary pool—thus the child starts speaking the words she's heard. It's highly unlikely a child will ever say a word if she has never heard the word. More than a billion people speak Chinese—so why not the rest of us? Because we haven't heard enough Chinese words, especially in our childhoods. The next levee is the Reading Vocabulary. It's nearly impossible to understand a word in print if you've never said the word. And finally, there's the Writing Vocabulary. If a child has never said the word or read the word, how in the world will she be able to write it? All the language arts flow from the Listening Vocabulary—and that has to be filled by someone besides the child.

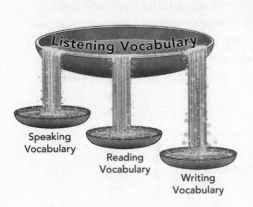

As you read to a child, you're pouring into the child's ears (and brain) all the sounds, syllables, endings, and blends that will make up the words she will someday be asked to read and understand. And through stories, you are filling in the background knowledge necessary to understand things that aren't in her neighborhood— like whales or locomotives or a rain forest.

The one prekindergarten skill that matters above all others, because it is the prime predictor of school success or failure, is the child's vocabulary upon entering school. Yes, the child goes to school to learn new words, but the words he already knows determine how much of what the teacher says will be understood. And since most instruction for the first four years of school is oral, the child who has the most extensive vocabulary will understand the most, while the child with the smallest vocabulary will grasp the least.

Once reading begins, personal vocabulary feeds (or frustrates) comprehension, since school grows increasingly complicated with each grade. That's why school-entry vocabulary tests predict how prepared a child is when she enters school.

What Happens as Children Progress Through School?

When I taught first grade, my students arrived at school on the first day filled with excitement to read. Some children were already reading, which generally could be attributed to their parents having read aloud to them. Other children possessed early literacy skills such as knowing the sounds letters make. A few children had difficulty writing their name or weren't confident in their knowledge of the alphabet. Regardless of where my students were in their literacy development, from day one and throughout the school year, all children were immersed in the stories that I read aloud. I was establishing a purpose and foundation for learning and knowing how to read.

Unfortunately, as children progress in school, we seem to whip the wonder of reading away. Reading aloud by the teacher in upper elementary, middle, and high school classrooms becomes infrequent. Children are required to respond to computerized tests about books they have read. We assign levels to books for programs such as Accelerated Reading and in turn "level" or label kids according to their reading ability. This does little to motivate children to read, especially those who are struggling to do so. Independent or sustained silent reading in many schools is limited or has been eliminated. The demands of testing students, sometimes multiple times during the school year, means that something has to go. And many times, that something is the teacher reading aloud to students.

It's no surprise that the National Assessment of Educational Progress (Nation's Report Card)[16] and other studies indicate changes in students' attitudes about reading as they get older.

+ In fourth grade, 40 percent of girls and 29 percent of boys indicated a positive view of reading, while in eighth grade the numbers dropped to 35 percent of girls and 19 percent of boys. By twelfth grade, the percentage stayed the same for girls, but increased to 20 percent for boys.

+ The Kaiser Family Foundation's longitudinal study of children eight to eighteen years of age found that 53 percent do not read any books in a given day, 65 percent do not read magazines, and 77 percent do not read newspapers.[17]

♦ In a Bureau of Labor Statistics survey from 2017, young adults between ages fifteen and nineteen (the largest concentration of high school and college students) reported spending less than eight minutes a day reading for pleasure versus two hours for watching TV and one hour a day playing games or using a computer for leisure.[18]

Let's see how the childhood figures are reflected in adulthood these days. The National Endowment for the Arts (NEA) has surveyed adult reading habits since 1982. In 2016, the NEA reported the number of adults who read literature continues to be on the decline in every age, gender, ethnic, and educational category. In 2002, only 46.7 percent of adults had read any fiction in the previous year with the rate dropping to 43.1 percent in 2015.[19] Parents' reading attitudes and behaviors appear to be shared by their children.[20] When parents read for pleasure, it impacts their child's desire to do the same.

Why Is Interest in Reading Declining?

The beginning of students' negative attitudes toward reading appears to begin in fourth grade when they must take the individual skills they have learned and apply them to whole paragraphs and pages. This juncture is famously called the "fourth-grade slump," a phrase coined from the research of the late Jeanne Chall.[21] It's where school separates the readers from the strugglers and remedials.

But—and this is a very loud *but*—if the way they have learned or been exposed to basic reading skills is so boring and joyless that they hate it, they will never read outside the classroom. Since the bulk of their time (7,800 hours a year) is spent away from school, it is imperative they use these hours to read often enough to become proficient or they will begin to fall behind. No reading outside the classroom results in low scores inside the classroom.

There are two basic "reading facts of life" that are ignored in most education circles, yet without these two principles working in tandem, little else will work.

Reading Fact #1: Human beings are pleasure centered.

Reading Fact #2: Reading is an accrued skill.

Let's examine Reading Fact #1. Human beings will voluntarily do over and over that which brings them pleasure. That is, we continually are eating at the restaurants we love, ordering the foods we relish, listening to radio stations playing music we enjoy, and visiting the neighbors we like. Conversely, we avoid the foods, music, and neighbors we dislike. Far from being a theory, this is a physiological fact: We approach what causes pleasure, and we withdraw from what causes displeasure or pain.[22]

When we read aloud, we're sending a message to the brain to condition the child to associate books and print with pleasure. However, there are displeasures connected with reading and school.

The learning experience can be tedious, threatening, and often without meaning—endless hours of worksheets, intensive phonics instruction, and unconnected test questions. If a child seldom experiences the pleasures of reading, but increasingly meets its displeasures, then the natural reaction will be withdrawal. As children's author Neil Gaiman has exclaimed, "The simplest way to make sure that we raise literate children is to teach them to read, and to show them that reading is a pleasurable activity."[23]

And that brings us to Reading Fact #2. Reading is like riding a bicycle, driving a car, or sewing: To get better at it, you must do it. Over thirty years of reading research[24] confirms this simple formula regardless of gender, race, nationality, or socioeconomic background. Students who read the most also read the best, achieve the most, and stay in school the longest.

Children will become better readers the more they hear stories read to them and the more they read independently.

Conversely, those who don't read much cannot get better at it. Why don't students read more? Because of Reading Fact #1. The multitude of displeasure messages they received throughout their school years coupled with the lack of gratifying messages in the home nullify any attraction books might possess. There is ample proof for all these hypotheses in my answer to the next question.

How Do We Fix the Reading Problem?

How exactly does a person become proficient at reading? It's a simple, two-part formula that bears repeating:

+ The more you read, the better you get at it; the better you get at it, the more you like it; and the more you like it, the more you do it.
+ The more you read, the more you know; and the more you know, the smarter you grow.[25]

In 2015, the percentage of fourth-grade students scoring at or above the proficient level in reading was 36 percent, with 33 percent at the basic level, and 31 percent below basic level.[26] The majority of students know how to read by fourth grade, but they aren't proficient at doing so. In fact, by eighth grade, 25 percent are proficient, 42 percent are at the basic level, and 24 percent are below the basic level.[27]

A 1992 landmark study conducted by Warwick Elley, *How in the World Do Students Read?*,[28] revealed two factors that produce higher achievement:

+ the frequency of teachers reading aloud to students, and
+ the frequency of sustained silent reading (SSR), or independent reading in school. Children who had daily SSR scored much higher than those who had it only once a week.

These two factors also represent the two reading facts we just examined. Reading aloud is the catalyst for the child wanting to read on his own, but it also provides a foundation by nurturing the child's listening comprehension. In an international study of 150,000 fourth graders, researchers found that students who were read to "often" at home scored thirty points higher than students who were read to "sometimes."[29] It stands to reason that the more often a child is read to, the more words are heard (bringing the child closer to comprehending more), and the more likely it is the child will associate reading with a daily pleasure experience.

Where Does Phonics Fit into All This?

There is research to validate the importance of phonics in children's reading. Children who understand the mechanics of reading—who know that words are made up of sounds and can break the sound code—have an advantage. The U.S. Department of Education's Early Childhood Longitudinal Study found that children who were read to at least three times a week had a significantly greater phonemic awareness when they entered kindergarten than did children who were read to less often. They were almost twice as likely to score in the top 25 percent in reading.[30]

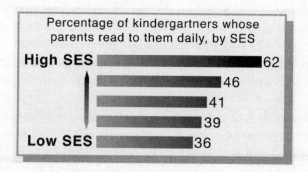

What phonics cannot do is motivate. Nobody has a favorite vowel or blend. If you ask doctors, coaches, even probation officers about the importance of motivation for the people they're dealing with, they all will tell you it's crucial. Researchers have identified instructional practices that can promote students' reading motivation.[31] However, the current emphasis on educational accountability is impacting reading. "Instruction that makes few attempts to spark children's interest and features unappealing texts can decrease intrinsic motivation."[32] It appears little actual class time is spent in pursuit of motivation, unless you think test prep is motivating.

What motivates children and adults to read more is that (1) they like the experience, (2) they like the subject matter, and (3) they like and follow the lead of people who read a lot.

How Does Reading Aloud
Create Background Knowledge?

The easiest way to understand background knowledge is to read the following two paragraphs and see if there is a difference in your understanding of each.

1.   But Sabathia, who pitched three days earlier in Game 3, gave up a leadoff broken-bat double to Austin Jackson. He struck out the next two batters, then walked Miguel Cabrera intentionally with first base open.

2.   Kallis and Rhodes put on 84 but, with the ball turning, Mark Waugh could not hit with impunity and his eight overs cost only 37. The runs still had to be scored at more than seven and over, with McGrath still to return and Warne having two overs left, when Rhodes pulled Reiffel to Beven at deep square leg.

You probably had an easier time grasping the first paragraph, a newspaper account of a baseball game in 2011. The second paragraph came from a newspaper story on the World Cricket Championship in 1999. Any confusion was because the less you know about a subject or the vocabulary associated with that subject, the slower you must read, the more difficult comprehension becomes, and the less you understand.[33] "Sounding out" the cricket paragraph phonetically wouldn't have helped much, would it?

Children who have accumulated background knowledge bring the prevalent amount of information to the learning table. This background knowledge is acquired by experiencing museums and zoos, visiting historic sites, traveling abroad, or camping in remote areas. For the impoverished child lacking the travel portfolio of affluence, the best way to gain background knowledge is by reading or being read to. (Yes, educational TV can help, but most at-risk children are not exposed to it often enough with the support of an adult.)

The background knowledge of at-risk students took a further hit with No Child Left Behind, when 71 percent of districts narrowed their curriculum to math and reading, curtailing subjects like art, music, science, and languages.[34]

The lack of background knowledge surfaces very early in a

child's school life. In a longitudinal kindergarten study, researchers found that more than 50 percent of children coming from the lowest education and income levels finished in the bottom quartile in background knowledge.[35] So once again poverty rears its ugly head as an obstacle to learning.

The Last Word on Reading Aloud, Vocabulary, and Aging Brains

Of all the endorsements for reading aloud, the following is the most unusual and perhaps most sobering. Back in the mid-1990s, two men and a woman sat talking in an office of the University of Kentucky Medical Center. One man was an epidemiologist, the other man was a neurologist, and the woman was a psycholinguist. All were involved in what would become a celebrated Alzheimer's study. Two of them had been researching an order of nuns who had consented to regular mental examinations and brain autopsies upon death and had turned all their medical records over to the researchers. The autopsies, together with autobiographical essays written by the nuns when they were about twenty-two years old, showed a clear connection: Those with the densest sentences (the most ideas jam-packed into a sentence without breaking them into separate clauses) were far less likely either to develop Alzheimer's or to show its ravages. Simply put, the larger the vocabularies and the more complex the thinking processes in youth, the less chance of Alzheimer's damage later even if they develop the disease.

Could the rich vocabulary and crammed thinking process in one's youth be an early insurance policy against Alzheimer's? As the three discussed these issues, the neurologist, Bill Markesbery, father of two, asked Susan Kemper, the psycholinguist, "What does this mean for our children?"

In his absorbing book about the study, *Aging with Grace*, David Snowdon, the epidemiologist, describes what followed:[36]

> The question caught me off guard. But when I saw the look on his face, I realized that he was speaking as a father, not as a scientist. Bill has three grown daughters, and it was clear he wanted to know whether he and his wife, Barbara, had done the right things as parents.

"Read to them," Susan answered. "It's that simple. It's the most important thing a parent can do with their children."

Susan explained that idea density depends on at least two important learned skills: vocabulary and reading comprehension. "And the best way to increase vocabulary and reading comprehension is by starting early in life, by reading to your children," Susan declared.

I could see the relief spread over Bill's face. "Barbara and I read to our kids every night," he said proudly. . . .

In the years since our study came out, I have been asked Markesbery's question many times. Parents ask me if they should play Mozart to their babies, or buy them expensive teaching toys, or prohibit television, or get them started early on the computer. I give them the same simple answer Susan Kemper gave to Markesbery: "Read to your children."

Chapter 2

When to Begin (and End) Read-Aloud

"Where's Papa going with that ax?" said Fern to
her mother as they were setting the table for
breakfast.

—*Charlotte's Web* by E. B. White[1]

PARENTS often ask, "How old must a child be before you start reading to her?" The next question is, "When is a child too old to be read to?"

The answer to the first question is easy. When a newborn is placed in her parents' arms, the natural inclination is to immediately say, "We love you! You are the most beautiful baby in the world." The baby doesn't understand the multisyllable words and complex sentences being spoken to her. Parents, grandparents, or siblings never feel crazy or even think twice about talking to that baby. And they certainly don't wait until the infant is three or six months old. But most people can't imagine reading to a newborn or infant. And that's sad. If a child is old enough to talk to, she's old enough to be read to.

Former first lady Laura Bush, who was a school librarian and continues to be a literacy advocate, has said, "As parents, the most important thing we can do is read to our children early and often. Reading is the path to success in school and life. When children learn to love books, they learn to love learning."[2]

When we begin reading aloud to our children in hopes of instilling a love of books, the tone of voice we use is essential. One of my favorite scenes from the movie *Three Men and a Baby* involves Tom Selleck's character, Peter Mitchell, reading an article about a boxing match to the baby that was left on their doorstep. When Michael, played by Steve Guttenberg, questions Peter regarding his choice of reading material, Selleck's character responds, "It doesn't matter what I read, it's the tone you use. She doesn't understand the words anyway." The point is that this was a bonding moment and not an opportunity to teach the baby about boxing.

From birth to six months of age, we are less concerned with a child understanding than with familiarizing her to your voice and the sight of books. A study published by Scholastic, titled *Kids & Family Reading Report*,[3] found that the percentage of parents reading aloud to their children from birth to the age of five increased from 30 percent in 2014 to 40 percent in 2016. The report indicated parents sought out advice from sources such as parenting magazines, websites, and blogs in addition to encouragement from friends, family, and the child's pediatrician (and hopefully this book!). Apparently, word is getting out that reading aloud to your infant, toddler, and preschooler is recommended, but that percentage still needs to be higher.

Is In Utero Learning a Myth?

Legend has it that cellist Pablo Casals began to sight-read a piece of music but soon realized he knew what was coming next, without reading it. He later learned that his cellist mother had rehearsed the piece daily in the later stages of her pregnancy.[4] Talking, reading, and playing a variety of music can help stimulate an unborn child's senses and improve brain development. These things have also been known to create a drop in the fetal heart rate if the voice is relaxed. We've long known the human voice is one of the most powerful tools a parent has for calming a child. And what many previously suspected is now firmly established in research demonstrating the voice's influence starts even earlier than birth.

In a study at the University of Kansas, researchers used a magnetocardiogram, which is noninvasive and able to detect tiny magnetic fields that surround electric currents from the maternal and fetal bodies,[5] to determine if there was a sensitivity to language discrimination in utero. Fetuses were found to be responsive to the speech of their English-speaking mothers. However, researchers discovered there was a change in fetal heart rates after an unfamiliar, rhythmically distinct language, such as Japanese, was spoken. Previous studies showed that fetuses were sensitive to the change in speech sounds but not differences in language or speaker. The hope is that by understanding prenatal sensitivity to the rhythmic properties of language, we will be able to provide children with one of the very first building blocks in acquiring language.

Another research study by Jeanne Holland[6] focused on a six-month-old infant, Maggie, whose parents read aloud at least three books daily while she was in utero. After she was born, her parents continued reading aloud as well as singing rhythmic tunes such as "Five Little Monkeys" and reciting Mother Goose rhymes. Maggie's grandmother, who served as her caregiver, also read aloud and provided various literacy experiences like playing "Pat-a-Cake" and "Itsy Bitsy Spider." What Holland found is that Maggie demonstrated signs of comfort and pleasure by cooing and snuggling close to her parents when they were reading aloud. Beginning her second month, Maggie would "talk" along with her parents and grandmother as they read books aloud. She would babble and mimic the sounds of words in the story. Each month, Maggie became more engrossed in the read-aloud experience in wanting to hold the book, point to illustrations, and turn pages.

While board books are generally shared with infants, Maggie's parents also read picture books for her to learn vocabulary and to be introduced to a variety of stories. Part of Holland's research also included observing Maggie once she was placed in nonfamily childcare. Unfortunately, there were very few times when Maggie interacted with a book or when reading aloud occurred in this setting. Children in care outside the home are read aloud to an average of 1.5 minutes per day.[7] It appears we need to do a better job of informing child caregivers that reading aloud is essential, regardless of the setting.

Research has established a child becomes familiar with certain sounds while in utero and associates them with comfort and security. The baby is being conditioned—his first class in learning. Not only should this encourage us to read to the fetus, particularly during that last trimester, but imagine how much more will be accomplished once a newborn can see and touch the book, understand the words, and feel the reader.

Expectant parents shouldn't believe that research studies must confirm everything. They should also trust their own instinct that the soon-to-be addition to their family is responding to their voices as they create a bond that will continue once the child is born.

What Could You Expect If You Read to Your Child?

Clara Lackey began reading to her three sons from the moment they were born until they graduated from high school. "It was second nature. When I wanted to calm them down, that's what I'd do, and then I just continued. They enjoyed listening to stories, like all children. It was our special time. It was kind of cool."

Clara read to her sons every night. She generally read the same story to the three of them because they are relatively close in age. Sometimes she would select the book, other times it was one of the boys that would pick a story such as the Choose Your Own Adventure series. This tradition of reading aloud continued through high school. As the boys got older, the books often prompted discussion about different and sometimes awkward situations. "Even though we weren't personally experiencing that particular issue, reading a book was a good way to talk about a difficult subject." Clara didn't specifically select books that were controversial, but she didn't shy away from them. It sometimes made it easier to talk about things through the lens of a character. As the boys entered high school and their schedules became more hectic, Clara continued reading aloud in the evening. "It was the last thing before we brushed our teeth and went to bed. We had a routine."

The practice of reading aloud now applies to Clara's twelve-year-old grandson, Trevor, who lives with his grandparents whenever his father is working out of town. Trevor isn't a reader, but he loves to be read to every night. When Trevor reads independently, he sometimes has trouble concentrating. But when Clara reads to him, he has no difficulty comprehending what he hears. Trevor is like a lot of kids who are auditory rather than visual learners. Having adventure stories like *Hatchet* by Gary Paulsen or humorous poetry from Shel Silverstein read aloud to him makes books more accessible. Recently, Clara read aloud *Tuck Everlasting* by Natalie Babbitt, which tackles the question, "What if you could live forever?" Clara and Trevor had a great conversation around that topic, and both decided that it wouldn't be all that great to outlive everyone they know.

Clara's sons were all reading when they began school; they are all successful in their careers, and they are all readers. "Something about reading stuck with them, and I think reading aloud created a positive experience and atmosphere that continued throughout their schooling and now in their adult lives."

One of Clara's sons, Mark, now has two children of his own, and the tradition of reading aloud is prevalent in his home as well. Here is what Mark told me about his experience. "I think having my parents read aloud to me influenced me to do the same with my children. Reading aloud is about spending time with them and making connections. After reading the first couple chapters of *Ms. Bixby's Last Day* aloud to my fifth-grade son, the following dialogue took place:"

ME: I think this is going to be a really good book, but it might be sad.

MY SON: Why?

ME: I think the book is well written, and it's going to be fun to follow the characters on their journey. But, I think the book might be sad because Ms. Bixby may die at the end.

MY SON: Why is that sad?

ME: Well, it makes me think of Grandma (my mom). She has cancer like Ms. Bixby.

MY SON: I know Grandma has cancer, but she looks healthy.

ME: You're right. She does look healthy, but she still has to receive treatment. When you have cancer, things can change pretty fast. We need to appreciate that Grandma is doing well right now and take advantage of it.

MY SON: That doesn't make me sad, it makes me happy.

ME: Why?

MY SON: Because Grandma is doing well.

ME: That is a great perspective. Maybe what is going to make this book good is that we will be able to relate to it.

MY SON: It is also going to be funny.

ME: I hope so. A book can be both funny and sad.

MY SON: I know.

ME: The only way to find out is to read it.

Mark goes on to share: "My mother was diagnosed with cancer a few years back. I don't talk about her having cancer that often, especially with my children. However, this story gave me a brief chance to talk to my son about my mom and the disease. It also gave my son the opportunity to ask questions about why I feel a certain way. Reading aloud prompted a conversation that I wouldn't have otherwise had. Conversations like this one help my children better understand who I am as a person, which will help me create strong relationships with them as they grow into young adults."

As an auditory learner, Trevor benefits from stories being read aloud by his grandmother.

If you start and continue reading aloud, like Clara and Mark, can you be assured that your child will become a proficient and lifelong reader? There is no guarantee. What you will do is nurture the parent-child relationship, instill a love of books and reading, and send a clear message that spending uninterrupted quality time with your child is enormously important.

How Is My Child's Reading Going to Get Better If *I'm* Doing the Reading?

Listening comprehension feeds reading comprehension. Sounds complicated, right? So let's make it simple. We'll use the most frequently used word in the English language: *the*. In the previous edition of *The Read-Aloud Handbook*, Jim Trelease shared that he often asked his lecture audiences if there was anyone present who thought this little three-letter word was a difficult one to understand. Out of three hundred people he would get about five who raised their hands—amid snickers from the rest.

He then asked those who didn't raise their hand to "pretend I am a Russian exchange student living in your home. It's also important to know there is no equivalent word in Russian for *the*, as we use it." Indeed, many languages—Chinese, Japanese, Korean, Persian, Polish, Punjabi, Croatian, and Vietnamese—don't have such articles.

"Now, as the Russian exchange student, I've been living in your home and listening to you and your family for three weeks when one day I come to you and say, 'I don't understand this word you use over and over. What means word *the*'?"

How would you begin to explain the meaning of *the* to this person? Everyone in the audience would laugh in embarrassment. Defining this simple word is very difficult, yet most of us knew how to use it by the time we showed up for kindergarten.

How did you learn it? One morning when you were three years old, did your mother take you into the kitchen, sit you down at the table with a little workbook, and say, "*The* is a definite article. It comes before nouns. Now take your green crayon and underline all the definite articles on this page"? Of course not.

We learned the meaning of this tiny but complex word by hearing it. In fact, we heard it in three ways:

1. over and over and over (immersion),
2. from superheroes—Mom, Dad, brother, and sister (role models), and
3. in a meaningful context—the cookie, the crayons, the potty.

Whenever an adult reads to a child, three important things are happening simultaneously and painlessly: (1) a pleasure connection is being made between child and book, (2) both parent and child are learning something from the book they're sharing (double learning), and (3) the adult is pouring sounds and syllables called words into the child's ear.

The research on oral comprehension versus reading comprehension certifies this concept and offers a sobering note about children who enter school with small vocabularies. Where you might expect school to narrow the gap between children with small oral vocabularies and those with larger ones, the reverse is true: The disparity between these vocabularies widens instead of narrows.[8]

The reason is twofold: Since children in the early grades are reading only the words most of them already know (decodable text), neither the slow nor the advanced child is meeting many new words in class through the books they are reading; and the students' only exposure to new or advanced language would have to be from parents and peers.

At home, the child acquiring an expanded vocabulary is more likely to be read to from advanced books, to be exposed to educational television, and to be engaged in meaningful conversation for longer periods of time. The child with the smaller vocabulary ends up hearing the same routine words without having the added stimuli.

In Nell Duke's study of ten urban and ten suburban first-grade classes, seven out of the ten suburban classes were read chapter books, while only two of the ten urban classes experienced chapter books.[9] The children with the smallest vocabularies were exposed to the fewest words and the least complex sentences; thus the gap expands.

A noble objective of the government's No Child Left Behind, Race to the Top, and Every Student Succeeds Act was to reduce the divide between children's achievement levels. The success of these initiatives depended entirely on bridging the vocabulary gap. The most efficient way to do that is to tap into the 7,800 hours the child spends at home. Imagine the impact if even half the parents of children who are at risk were reading to them from library books beginning at infancy (or listening to recorded stories and audiobooks if family literacy is a problem). A second strategy would be for the classroom teacher to read aloud from high-quality literature that contains richer language than decodable texts.

Children's books, even picture books, are much richer than ordinary home or classroom conversation. A study found that although parents can build their children's vocabularies by talking to them, reading to them is more effective.[10] Reading aloud helps to develop word mastery and grammatical understanding, which is the basis for learning how to read. The study determined that picture books are two to three times as likely as parent-children conversations to include a word that isn't among the five thousand most common English words.

Consider for a moment the classic picture book *Where the Wild Things Are*. In telling the story, author Maurice Sendak used the words *mischief*, *gnashed*, and *rumpus*. These are not words commonly used in everyday conversations between parent and child or even in the classroom. Chapter books such as *Charlotte's Web*, which is often read aloud to younger children (and contains that awesome opening sentence shared at the beginning of this chapter), also provide extensive vocabulary. In chapter 6 of *Charlotte's Web*, you'll encounter the words *morals*, *scruples*, *decency*, *consideration*, *compunctions*, *ancient*, and *untenable*. Again, these are not words used on a daily basis in conversation with children. Reading books at a child's listening level rather than books at his reading level increases the probability that he will hear more profound vocabulary while also having the opportunity to engage in dialogue with you about both the words and the story.

What If My Child Prefers to Read on Her Own?

One of the goals of reading aloud is to inspire children to read on their own. But reading alone and reading aloud are not mutually exclusive. We can do both—and should. (See chapter 4 for more on read-aloud's partner, independent reading.)

To be honest, not all older children are responsive listeners, although the vast majority are once they are acclimated to it. Some, especially the more precocious readers, grow impatient with the read-aloud pace (which is slower than silent reading) and prefer to read on their own. Such was the case with Kathy Brozina, who told her father, Jim, a school librarian who incorporated read-aloud into every school day, that she'd take it from there now that she was in fourth grade. Abruptly his read-alouds were over—with Kathy. There was, however, a much younger sibling, Kristen, and their readings continued.

When the fateful fourth-grade year arrived, Jim, remembering his older daughter's earlier response, suggested to Kristen: "How about if we try to read for a hundred straight bedtimes?" When that goal was reached, Kristen requested they go for a streak of a thousand consecutive nights. On it stretched, through sickness and health, a divorce, and even an auto accident. From picture books to classics, nothing stood in the way of what they called "the Streak."

But nothing lasts forever, and the Streak finally came to an end when another streak intervened: four straight years of college. In a college dormitory's stairwell on Kristen's first day on campus, they read one last chapter—it was night number 3,218.

During his thirty-eight years in education, Jim Brozina once worked for an elementary school principal who told him he was wasting valuable instructional time reading to his students. Are you kidding? After 3,218 consecutive readings to Kristen, with no worksheets or vocabulary quizzes attached, what did she have to show for her father's efforts—beyond the affection, bonding, and shared experiences? You could start with a four-year college record that was all As and one B, as well as winning two national writing contests. And one more thing—a nationally published literary memoir called *The Reading Promise: My Father and the Books We Shared*,[11] written under her pen name, Alice Ozma, one year out of college. How's that for "wasting valuable instructional time"?

What About Reading Aloud to Children with Special Needs?

Some of the most heartwarming stories received over the past few years have been those from parents and teachers of children with special needs such as the letter from Marcia Thomas, then of Memphis, Tennessee:

> When our daughter Jennifer was born, one of the first gifts we received was a copy of *The Read-Aloud Handbook*. We decided to put our daughter on a "diet" of at least ten books a day after reading one of the stories in the introductory chapter. Jennifer had to stay in the hospital for seven weeks as a result of a heart defect and corrective surgery. However, we began reading to her while she was still in intensive care; and when we couldn't be there, we left story tapes and asked the nurses to play them for her.

For seven years we read to Jennifer at every opportunity. When she was in the first grade, she was one of the best readers in her class. She consistently made perfect scores on reading tests and had a very impressive vocabulary. She could usually be found in the reading loft at school during free time, and at home, she loved to sit with my husband or me and read a book.

What makes our story so remarkable is that Jennifer was born with Down syndrome. At two months of age, we were told Jennifer most likely was blind, deaf, and severely retarded. When she was tested at age four, her IQ was 111.

Jennifer Thomas graduated from her Concord, Massachusetts, high school, passed her state MCAS test, and was a member of the National Honor Society. A talented artist, Jennifer competed in the juried VSA competition in 2003 for artists between the ages of sixteen and twenty-five who live in the United States and have a disability. Her piece was one of the fifteen chosen to tour the United States. In 2005, she enrolled in the Threshold Program at Lesley University in Cambridge, Massachusetts, and graduated in 2008. Today she has her own condo in Cambridge, is still an avid reader, has two dictionaries on her desk that she consults frequently, and is an ardent fan of Wikipedia.

All children benefit from having books read aloud to them. There are times we might need to make accommodations to ensure the experience is pleasurable and supports language development, print awareness, story structure, and basic concepts. Children with special needs might have language and cognitive delays exhibited by losing attention quickly, having difficulty in following directions and answering questions, or being disruptive or reluctant to participate. It is critical to consider the books you select for reading aloud. Here are a few tips:[12]

- Pay attention to the illustrations, print size, book size, and even the texture of the cover or pages.
- Choose books with rhymes or repetition to support children with speech or language delays. A good book to share is *Rhyming Dust Bunnies* by Jan Thomas where all the dust bunnies love to rhyme except for Bob who can never get the rhyme correct. Another book, *Is Your Mama a Llama?* by Deborah Guarino, supplies repetitive questions with a rhyming response.

- Select shorter books or those that don't involve as much text for children who have brief attention spans but still want to be entertained. *Hi, Fly Guy!* is the first in a successful series of beginning chapter books by Tedd Arnold where boy and fly become friends. Karen Beaumont's *I Like Myself!* has a positive story line about just being yourself.

- Books with simple, uncluttered, and colorful illustrations work well for children with visual or hearing impairments. *A Kitten Tale* by Eric Rohmann delightfully depicts four kittens who have never experienced snow. The extensive use of white space on each page makes it easy to focus on the kittens. Brief text is coupled with engaging illustrations that feature the inquisitive kittens.

- Select stories that ask questions. *Have You Seen My Cat?* by Eric Carle asks that question on each page. The newer edition of the book contains a portion of the illustration that slides out to reveal each animal. Or select books that make statements such as *No, David!* by David Shannon, and talk about all the mischief this naughty boy gets into.

Sometimes children on the autism spectrum or with attention deficit disorders have difficulty sitting and listening when you are reading aloud a book. Let them move or roam around. Give them something to fidget with or materials for drawing as you are reading. The objective of reading aloud for any child is to engage in a pleasurable experience, and that doesn't always mean they have to sit quietly beside you.

How Can I Expand My Child's Attention Span?

The best tool for expanding attention span is one-on-one time with a child; it is by far the most valuable teaching/bonding arrangement ever invented. In studying methods to reverse language problems among disadvantaged children, Harvard psychologist Jerome Kagan found intensified one-on-one attention to be especially effective.[13] His studies reveal the advantages of reading to children and of listening attentively to their responses to the reading. He also points to the merit of reading to each of your children separately, if possible, to improve their focus and concentration.

Time spent reading to your children when they are young will help them understand the purpose of books while experiencing the pleasure of hearing a story read aloud.

This approach does pose an extra problem for working mothers and fathers who have more than one child. But somewhere in that seven-day week, there must be time for your child to discover the specialness of you, one-on-one, even if it's only once or twice.

One-on-one time between adult and child—be it reading, talking, or playing—is essential to teaching the concept of books or puppies or flowers or water. Once the idea of something has been learned, the foundation has been laid for the next accomplishment: attention span. Without a notion of what is happening and why, a child cannot pay attention to it for any considerable amount of time.

Let's begin with a simple concept. Books contain stories that give us pleasure if we listen and watch. When a child has little or no experience with books, it is impossible for him to have a concept of them and the pleasure they afford. No experience means no attention span.[14]

When children begin that restless stage and can sit still only for brief periods, you gauge your selection of books and length of time for reading aloud. Maybe start with one or two short picture books or read one and then choose another book to read later.

Books with animals or insects such as *The Very Hungry Caterpillar* or *The Very Busy Spider* by Eric Carle work well because they are interactive and engage children in some way either orally or physically. *The Very Hungry Caterpillar* invites children to interact with the story through the repetitive phrasing, ". . . but he was still hungry." In *The Very Busy Spider*, children soon begin chanting the phrase, "The spider didn't answer. She was very busy spinning her web." There is also a tactile element to the book as the spider's web grows from a simple line into a complex and beautiful creation that children can touch. *Press Here* by Hervé Tullet is also a fun book to grab kids' attention and have them participate in pressing the dots on each page.

Next, start reading aloud books with more text and an engaging story line. *Muncha! Muncha! Muncha!* by Candace Fleming is a story about Mr. McGreely trying to stop the rabbits from eating the vegetables in his garden. But they continue to *muncha, muncha, muncha!* *Officer Buckle and Gloria* by Peggy Rathmann grabs kids' attention because the illustrations show an animated Gloria, the dog, acting out the safety tips presented by the rather dull Officer Buckle. The text doesn't refer to Gloria's antics; only the illustrations show the hilarious canine.

While you can continue to increase the number of picture books you are reading at one sitting, also begin incorporating beginning and short chapter books such as the Elephant and Piggie series by Mo Willems or the *Ivy + Bean* chapter books by Annie Barrows.

The key to expanding a child's attention span is doing so over a period of time—it won't happen in a few days or a week. When you begin reading aloud to young children, you have the opportunity to lengthen the amount of time they can listen to a story before they go to preschool or kindergarten. Also, remember that the more engaging the story is, the longer a child will listen. Choose books wisely! There are numerous book suggestions in the Treasury that serve this purpose.

Is There Something I Could Buy That Would Help My Child Read Better?

Some parents often think there are quick fixes they can buy like a kit or phonics game to help a child do better at school. Think about what you had (or wish you had) that enabled you to become a reader. For me, it was the public library. There are also the Three Bs, which encompass an inexpensive "reading kit" that nearly all parents can afford.

The first B is books. Ownership of a book is treasured, with the child's name inscribed inside, a book that doesn't have to be returned to the library or even shared with siblings. Chapter 6 shows the clear connection between book ownership (or access) and reading achievement.

The second B is book basket (or magazine rack), placed where it can be used most often. There is probably more reading done in the bathrooms of America than in all the libraries and classrooms combined. Put a book basket in there, stocked with books, magazines, and newspapers.

Put another book basket on or near the kitchen table. With more and more children eating at least one daily meal alone, the kitchen is a prime spot for recreational reading. If there's a book on the table, they'll read it—unless, of course, you have a television in your kitchen, as do more than 60 percent of parents in America.[15]

Another spot for a basket is in the car. Turn off the video screens and provide books to keep kids occupied in the backseat. If your child gets carsick while reading, then have an audiobook you can all listen to and talk about.

Studies have shown that children with the most interest in reading came from homes where books and print were spread throughout the house, not just in one or two places.[16]

The third B is bed lamp. Does your child have a bed lamp or reading light? If not, and you wish to raise a reader, the first order of business is to go out and buy one. Install it, and say to your child: "We think you're old enough to stay up later at night and read in bed like Mom and Dad. So we bought this little lamp, and we're going to leave it on an extra fifteen minutes [or longer, depending on the age of the child] if you want to read in bed. On the other hand, if you don't want to read, that's okay, too. We'll just turn off the light at the same old time." Most children will do anything to stay up later—even read.

At What Age Should I Stop Reading to My Child?

Almost as big a mistake as not reading to children at all is stopping too soon. The previously mentioned 2016 national survey conducted by Scholastic found that only 17 percent of parents were still reading to their children after age nine.[17] Was this because children didn't want to be read to anymore? According to the report, 87 percent of children ages six through eleven said they liked being read to and wished their parents would continue. This incredible bonding experience between parent and child, teacher and student, should remain not only for enjoyment but also for all the reasons cited for why we read aloud. These include increasing vocabulary, introducing children to books beyond their listening level but above their reading level, and promoting reading enjoyment.

Consider the hugely successful marketing strategy of McDonald's. The fast-food chain has been in business for more than a half century and has never cut its advertising budget. Every year McDonald's spends more money on advertising than it did the previous year, which comes to more than $5.4 million per day. Its marketing people never think, "Everyone has heard our message. They should be coming to us on their own, instead of our spending all this money on advertising."

Every time we read aloud to a child, we're giving a commercial for the pleasures of reading. But, unlike McDonald's, we often cut our advertising each year instead of increasing it. The older the child, the less she is read to—in the home and in the classroom. The percentage of children who say they enjoy reading for pleasure continues to drop and is now just a little over 50 percent.[18] A six- to eleven-year-old child is more likely to read independently if she is being read aloud to at home.

Parents (and sometimes teachers) say, "He's in the top fourth-grade reading group—why should I read to him? Isn't that why we're sending him to school, so he'll learn how to read by himself?" There are many mistaken assumptions in that question.

Let's say the student is reading at a fourth-grade level. Wonderful. But what level is the child listening on? Most people have no idea that one is higher than the other until they stop and think about it. Here's an easy way to visualize it:

In 2013, Walt Disney Pictures released the movie *Frozen*, which was inspired by Hans Christian Andersen's fairy tale *The Snow Queen*. *Frozen* tells the story of a fearless princess, Anna, who embarks on a journey alongside a rugged iceman, his loyal reindeer, and a naive snowman to find her sister, Elsa, whose icy powers have trapped their kingdom in eternal winter. It soon became the top-grossing animated movie of all time. *Frozen*, recommended for children ages five and above, engaged young moviegoers with the plot and the music (it's amazing how many children can sing "Let It Go" in its entirety). Few, if any, of the five- to eight-year-olds watching the movie would be able to read its script. But most could understand it if it was read to them—that is, recited by the actors.

According to experts, it is a reasonable assertion that reading and listening skills begin to converge at about eighth grade.[19] Until then, kids usually listen on a higher level than they read. Therefore, children can hear and understand stories that are more complicated and more interesting than what they could read on their own—which has to be one of the greatest blessings for first graders. The last thing you want first graders thinking is what they're reading is as good as books are going to get! First graders can enjoy books written on a fourth-grade level, and fifth graders can enjoy books written on a seventh-grade reading level. (This is, of course, contingent upon the social level of the books' subject matter; some seventh-grade material is above the fifth grader's social experience and might be off-putting.)

Now that the idea has been established about the significant difference between listening level and reading level, it's easy to understand why one should continue to read aloud to children as they grow older. Beyond the emotional bond that is established between parent and child (or teacher and class), you're feeding those higher vocabulary words through the ear; eventually, they'll reach the brain and register in the child-reader's eyes.

That's the argument for continuing the reading to a higher level. Now let's divert to a lower level. If you have a beginning reader in your home or classroom—five-, six-, or seven-year-old—and you're reading to the child, wonderful! Keep it up. But if you're still reading aloud those Dr. Seuss controlled-vocabulary books like *The Cat in the Hat* or *Hop on Pop*, you're insulting the six-year-old's brain cells nightly! With either book, you have a volume of 225 words and a six-year-old with a six-thousand-word vocabulary. The child has understood and has been using all 225 of those words since she was four years old.

At age six, your child is a beginning reader. As such, she has a limited number of words she can decode by sight or sound. But she is not a beginning listener. She's been listening for six years; she's a veteran listener! Dr. Seuss deliberately wrote the controlled-vocabulary books to be read by children to themselves. And to make sure people understood this was a book to be read *by* the child and not *to* the child, the covers of the controlled-vocabulary books like *The Cat in the Hat* and *Hop on Pop* contain a logo with the words "I Can Read It All by Myself."[20] The *myself* refers to the child, not the parent!

If you are still doubting that kids need to be read to as they get older, here is what intermediate grade teacher Tiffany Nay shared with me about her experience:

> The year I moved from teaching second grade to fifth grade, I had a notion that "big kids" wouldn't want to hear a book read aloud. I couldn't have been more wrong! I was in a high-needs Title 1 school, and my students hadn't interacted enough with quality text. The teachers were so busy trying to catch the students up to grade level in reading and math that they inadvertently omitted the most important element of teaching—becoming lifelong learners and enjoying literacy! I began that year with a novel, *The BFG*, by Roald Dahl. I was intent on keeping the students engaged, so we used it as our teaching text. As the year progressed, picture books became an important factor. What I discovered that year changed my entire teaching perspective. My intermediate students needed me to read to them *more* than my primary students and to bring read-alouds into my classroom as much as possible.

You're Not Suggesting That I Read Aloud to My Teenager?

A child's literacy development doesn't stop in elementary grades. Author Kate DiCamillo, who served as the National Ambassador for Young People's Literature, said in an interview, "We forget how much we love to be read to. And as long as your kid is receptive to it, and almost all of them are, even the really gnarly ones when they get to be twelve and thirteen, that time to sit down and read together gives you as parents as much as it gives the kids. It deepens the relationship."[21]

In the Scholastic report, the percentage of parents reading aloud to their child after the age of five drops significantly. By the age of

Scott Riley believes it is important to spend quality time with his teenage daughter, and reading aloud fills that purpose.

eleven, very few children are hearing a book being read aloud, and the numbers continue to decline in high school.

In an op-ed published in the *New Yorker*, David Denby shared: "It's very likely that teenagers, attached to screens of one sort or another, read more words than they ever have in the past. But they often read scraps, excerpts, articles, parts of articles, messages, pieces of information from everywhere and from nowhere."[22] He goes on to relate that teens are busy with school, homework, jobs, sports, dating, etc., and that not reading "for pleasure" is perfectly acceptable to them. Of course, those of us who enjoy reading are horrified by this ongoing trend.

All the reasons we read to young children—the gift of uninterrupted time, the message that reading is valued, and the shared experience of responding to a book together—are the very same reasons why we should continue reading aloud to teenagers.

When I suggest parents read aloud to their teenagers, generally the response is, "Who has time?" That's where you need to be creative. Maintaining a nightly ritual of reading aloud may not happen. Grab other times in the day—at breakfast, after homework, on the weekends. It might take some time to complete a book, but the reward will be worth it. Here's how Marie LeJeune and her husband Nathan Meyer find time for reading aloud to their children, teenagers included:

> We have four children, and both of us work long hours at jobs that
> go far beyond a nine-to-five schedule. Still, we try to squeeze in

reading aloud a chapter a night with our children. Sometimes we do miss a night. One week when we were between books for a read-aloud, I noticed that my then eight-year-old was reading *The Tale of Despereaux* aloud to his five-year-old sister. I was so tickled by this that I quietly watched from outside her room and then encouraged them to keep up the practice as often as they could. This has resulted in the sibling read-aloud club at our house. My son and daughter have experienced multiple amazing titles together, many read by me, but others read by an older sibling. I often hear them discussing the books they are reading, and I love watching this literate community develop between the kids.

We also continue these read-aloud traditions on road trips. I'm lucky enough not to get carsick and will often read a favorite chapter book aloud in the car as we travel as a family. If it's a trip where I'm doing the driving, I always make sure we have a book on CD or downloaded onto my phone, so we can enjoy having someone else read aloud to us as well. I especially love to revisit favorites from my childhood like *From the Mixed-up Files of Mrs. Basil E. Frankweiler* and *Harriet the Spy.*

Just think of how much time we spend in the car with our children, particularly teenagers, and the missed opportunity if we aren't reading and talking about books.

Reading aloud to older children can also open a pathway for the discussion of difficult subject matter. Many books being published today such as *Wonder* by R. J. Palacio, which focuses on a boy with facial anomalies, or *Ghost Boys* by Jewell Parker Rhodes, a powerful story about a teenager being shot by police, open up topics and experiences that many children will never encounter. Reading and discussing issues in a book that you are sharing gives parents and kids a no-judgment, no-stress opportunity to talk about matters in the context of the characters and to make connections to real-world social issues.

Is It Ever Too Late to Start Reading to a Child?

They're never too old—but it's not as easy with older children as it is when they're two or six years old.

Because she has a captive audience, the classroom teacher holds a distinct advantage over the parent who suddenly wants to begin reading to a thirteen-year-old. Regardless of how well intentioned the parent may be, reading aloud to an adolescent at home can be difficult. During this period of social and emotional development, teenagers' out-of-school time is largely spent coping with body changes, sex drive, vocational anxieties, and the need to form an identity apart from that of their families. These kinds of concerns and their attendant schedules don't leave much time for Mom or Dad to read aloud, but the situation is not hopeless if you pick your spots. Don't suggest that your daughter listen to a story when she's sitting down to watch her favorite television show or fuming after a fight with her boyfriend. Along with timing, consider the length of what you read. Keep it short—unless you see an interest in more.

When the child is in early adolescence, from ages twelve to fourteen, try sharing a small part of a book, a page or two, when you see she is at loose ends—and downplay any motivational or educational aspects connected with the reading. Poetry is brief and can invoke myriad emotions that might capture an adolescent's attention and entice him to ask for more.

Chapter 3

The Stages of Read-Aloud

It has been a terrible, horrible, no good, very bad
day. My mom says some days are like that. Even
in Australia.

—*Alexander and the Terrible,*
Horrible, No Good, Very Bad Day
by Judith Viorst[1]

O VER the past decade, a heated debate has raged over the importance of the infant years in a person's brain development. Although psychologists and neuroscientists have argued in public
conferences, newsmagazines, and professional journals, the jury remains out on exactly how critical the first three years of life really
are. Do the doors of opportunity really slam shut after age three, or
are there second, third, or fourth chances later on?

I tend to compromise between the two extremes: Learning (and
life) is easier if the first three years are enriched, but later opportunities can be rewarding if there is an ideal learning environment
and if—a big *if*—the brain's architecture has not been damaged by
emotional or physical distress. Anyone wishing to pursue the debate
will find it fully explored in *The Scientist in the Crib: Minds, Brains,
and How Children Learn* by Alison Gopnik, Andrew Meltzoff, and
Patricia Kuhl and *The Myth of the First Three Years* by John T. Bruer.

A less time-consuming option available for those pursuing children's brain issues is the internet. There, you'll find the work of Dr.
Jack Shonkoff, director of the Center on the Developing Child at

Harvard University. Dr. Shonkoff is one of the nation's leading authorities on children's brain development and can make complicated ideas understandable to parents and teachers. Supported by extensive brain research, he is adamant that early childhood education should not be just about education but also about playing, exploring, and nurturing emotional development—in short, the whole child.

Under Dr. Shonkoff's direction, the Center on the Developing Child offers a half-dozen short videos online, ranging from two to seven minutes.[2] A crucial point made by the center is that childhood trauma, such as malnutrition or emotional deprivation (both of which go hand in hand with addicted or alcoholic parents), often causes structural damage to the young brain. This damage, especially if it occurs between birth and age three, cannot be repaired later in special education and remedial classes.[3] The center believes a good part of our present remediation could be prevented with proper care and heightened awareness of "toxic stress" in early childhood.[4]

Also firmly established by the research is that measurable long-term storage of sound and word patterns begins as early as eight months of age. Children hearing the most language will have the best chance of having the best language skills.[5] Speaking with children and exposing them to books, stories, and songs helps strengthen children's language and communication, which puts them on a path toward learning and succeeding in school.

None of this is intended to create a superbaby. The focus should be on nurturing whatever abilities are already there, creating an intimate bond between parent and child, and building a happy bridge between child and books that can be crossed whenever the child is developmentally ready as a reader.

Infants enjoy books containing familiar objects and bright colors.

Which Books Are Best for Infants?

Your book selections for the first year should be ones that stimulate your child's sight and hearing—colorful pictures and exciting sounds upon which the child can easily focus. One of the reasons for Mother Goose's success is that it echoes the first sound a child falls in love with—the rhythmic, rhyming *beat-beat-beat* of a mother's heart.

Mother Goose and Dr. Seuss not only rhyme in name and text, they also must have sensed what researchers would later prove. According to learning specialists at the National Institute of Child Health and Human Development in Bethesda, Maryland, the ability to find words that rhyme appears to be an important one in children.[6] Indeed, kindergartners who struggle in finding words that rhyme with *cat* are prime candidates for later reading problems. Moreover, considering the many rhyming chants found in children's games (such as jump rope rhymes) and popular children's books like Dr. Seuss's *The Foot Book* and Mem Fox's *Ten Little Fingers and Ten Little Toes*, it's obvious children find pleasure in words that rhyme. But why? Researchers say it is for the same reason adults subconsciously enjoy looking at stripes and plaids or listening to musical harmony—they help to arrange a chaotic world.

We don't turn to Mother Goose for the plot—most of the rhymes were politically based and generally don't make sense to children. We turn to these familiar rhymes because they encompass sounds, syllables, endings, and blends and mixes them with the rhythm and rhyme of language. This feeds to a child who already takes delight in rocking back and forth in his crib, repeating a single syllable over and over: "Ba, ba, ba, ba, ba . . ."

There are many collections of Mother Goose, but some of my favorites are *My Very First Mother Goose* by Iona Opie and Rosemary Wells, *Tomie dePaola's Mother Goose*, and *The Neighborhood Mother Goose* by Nina Crews. If you're musically inclined, Crews has a marvelous collection of favorite childhood songs (like "Wheels on the Bus") in *The Neighborhood Sing-Along*, including colorful photos of children playing. A new Mother Goose favorite is *La Madre Goose: Nursery Rhymes for los Niños* by Susan Middleton Elya that incorporates Spanish into the familiar rhymes. Fitting right in with these books is the aforementioned *Ten Little Fingers and Ten Little*

Toes, also available as a board book and in Spanish. You can download many of these rhymes from the iTunes Store or view them on YouTube.

Books for very young children don't stay in print long, and unless they're in board book format, they don't "live" long among the rambunctious toddler. One group of books that seems to defy that norm: the gosling series by Olivier Dunrea, which began with *Gossie*, back in 2002 and is still in print (hardcover, board book, and ebook). Small in size (six inches) and plot, it uses the little gosling's barnyard adventures to reflect the curiosity and life of babies and toddlers, including playing with favorite toys, sharing with others, and avoiding naps. The uncomplicated but luminous illustrations also make them appealing. Other books in the Gossie & Friends series include *Gossie and Gertie, Ollie, Ollie the Stomper, BooBoo, Peedie, Jasper & Joop, Gideon, Gideon and Otto, Gus,* and *Gemma and Gus.*

Board books have become increasingly popular given their size and durability. However, be watchful for picture books published in board book format. Taking a thirty-two-page picture book and altering it to fit into a board book format of twelve pages doesn't work well. Select board books originally designed for that size and a very young audience such as Nina Laden's *Peek-a Who?* and *Peek-a Moo!*

Keep in mind the physical bonding that occurs during the time you are holding your child and reading. To make sure you never convey the message the book is more important than the child, maintain skin-to-skin contact as often as possible, patting, touching, and hugging your child while you read.[7] Linked with the normal parent-infant dialogue, this reinforces a feeling of being loved.

What Is Normal Behavior of the Infant or Toddler During Readings?

Recent interest in early learning has spurred investigations into how infants and their parents react in read-aloud situations, though any reading parent can tell you a child's interest and response to books varies a great deal from child to child or day to day. But if you are a new parent, any seeming lack of interest can be discouraging. Here is a forecast so you will not be discouraged or think your child can't be engaged with a story.

♦ At four months of age, since he has limited mobility, a child has little or no choice but to listen and observe, thus making a passive and noncombative audience for the parent, who is probably thinking, *This is easy!*

♦ As you read aloud, your arms should encircle the child in such a way as to suggest support and bonding, but not imprisonment, while allowing the child to view the pages of a board book or picture book. Select books that contain limited text coupled with large, colorful illustrations.

♦ By six months, the child is more interested in touching and grabbing the book to suck or chew on while listening (which he's also doing). Board books are excellent to use at this age because they are small enough for little hands to hold. They are also durable and generally laminated, which makes them easy to wipe off. If the books aren't yours, you might want to provide your baby with a toy or teething ring to chew while listening. Cloth books are good because they can be thrown into the washing machine. Soft plastic books can be shared at bath time.

♦ At eight months, he may prefer turning pages to steady listening. Allow him ample opportunity to explore this activity, but don't give up the book entirely.

♦ At twelve months, the child's involvement grows to turning pages for you, pointing to objects you name on the page, and even making noises for animals on cue.

♦ By fifteen months and the onset of walking, his restlessness blossoms fully, and your reading times must be chosen so as not to frustrate his immediate interests. If your baby loses interest, then put the book away for another time.

Introduce read-aloud time incrementally. Start with a minute or two several times a day and then gradually increase it. The attention span during infant reading time averages around three minutes, though several daily readings may bring the total as high as thirty minutes a day. Some one-year-olds will listen to stories for that long, but they are more the exception than the rule.

As babies mature, good parent readers profit from earlier experiences. They don't force the reading times; they direct attention by pointing to something on the page, and they learn to vary their voices between whispers and excited tones. They also understand that attention spans are not made overnight—they are built minute by minute, page by page, day by day.

Once the child starts to respond to the sight of books and your voice, begin a book dialogue. Talk about the story and illustrations on each page, especially if it's a book that has been read aloud previously. This will offer your child an opportunity to retell the story and also give him the sense that he is reading the book. Reading aloud with a young child shouldn't be a solitary, passive experience. As much as possible, you want the child to interact with you and the book. You elicit the interaction by the questions or comments you interject in the reading. What you want while reading is the same thing you desire when you talk with a child—give-and-take, or, as one educator put it, "Play Ping-Pong, not darts." When you simply throw words or orders at a child, you're playing verbal darts.

Here is a sample dialogue between a mother and her twenty-month-old during a reading of *Blueberries for Sal* by Robert McCloskey. Note that the parent doesn't stay tied to the exact text, which is underlined here.

> PARENT: <u>Little Bear's mother turned around to see what on earth could make a noise like kerplunk!</u> And there, right in front of her, was—Sal!
>
> CHILD: Saa.
>
> PARENT: Right, Sal. And <u>mother bear</u> was very surprised to see Sal and not <u>Little Bear</u> behind her. Look at the surprised look on her face. Sal looks a little surprised too, don't you think?
>
> CHILD: Yeh.
>
> PARENT: Yes. <u>"Garumpf!" she cried. This is not my child!</u> Where is Little Bear? And mother bear ran off to find him. Where do you think Little Bear is?
>
> CHILD: D-no.
>
> PARENT: You don't know? Well, let's turn the page—you can turn it—and maybe we'll find him *there*.

In this simple exchange, a number of important things are being accomplished with language.

1. Parent and child are sharing the pleasures of a book together, a story that unfolds gradually at their pace (not a video's pace) on pages that have illustrations that are stationary for the child to scrutinize closely.
2. The mother uses both her own words and the words in the book. How closely you follow the exact text is determined by the age of the child and the attention span.
3. The dialogue is interactive—that is, the parent interjects simple questions that elicit responses.
4. When the child answers, the parent affirms the response ("Right") and/or corrects it (pronouncing "Sal," "yes," and "don't know" correctly).

What Comes After Mother Goose?

During the toddler stage, a critical parental role is to serve as a welcoming committee—welcoming the child into your world. Think of yourself as the host of a huge party, with your child as the guest of honor. Naturally, you want to introduce her to all the invited guests to make her feel at home. As the child grows older, a multitude of things become objects of fascination: holes, cars, snow, birds, bugs, stars, trucks, dogs, rain, planes, cats, storms, babies, mommies, and daddies. This stage is called "labeling the environment."

Picture books are perfect teaching vehicles at this stage. Point to the various items illustrated in the book, call them by name, ask the child to say the name with you, and praise any responses. A few books that are excellent for this purpose are *The Everything Book* by Denise Fleming and books by Roger Priddy, including *First 100 Words*, *First 100 Farm Animals*, and *Numbers Colors Shape*. The Priddy books contain a collection of photographs of one hundred everyday items and animals. *The Everything Book* includes images of animals, shapes, colors, rhymes, finger games, food, faces, letters, traffic, and toys depicted through Fleming's distinctive collage illustrations.

Wordless picture books, or those without text, are also great to use with toddlers, particularly titles with realistic, colorful, yet simple illustrations that do not contain too many images or objects. Some new and classic wordless books include *Uh-Oh!* by Shutta Crum, *Little Blue and Little Yellow* by Leo Lionni, or *Boom Boom* by

Sarvinder Naberhaus. These books encourage creativity, conversation, language development, and personalization of the story. You can compose as long or as short of a story as you want depending on your child's attention span.

The very best picture book for toddlers may be the one you make, using photographs taken in your home and of your family. Desktop printing has made this style of publishing easy for families. Take photos of your child's day and environment, add some captions, print them out, laminate the pages, punch a couple of holes, and you've got a homemade family book.

Between the ages of eighteen months to four years of age, toddlers and preschoolers experience tremendous intellectual, social, and emotional growth. In addition to wordless books, they enjoy books that are predictable because they are written in a way that makes it easy to predict what will happen. Predictable books often repeat words, phrases, or sentences throughout the text. Some contain a question-and-answer format while others have a circular story that essentially ends where it began. Other predictable books build on story lines or sequences familiar to children.

Some favorite predictable stories include *If You Give a Mouse a Cookie* (and other If You Give . . . books) by Laura Numeroff; *The Napping House* by Audrey Wood; *Do You Want to Be My Friend?* by Eric Carle; and *I Know an Old Lady Who Swallowed a Fly*, along with its numerous variations including *I Know an Old Lady Who Swallowed a Pie* by Alison Jackson. A list of other predictable books is located in the Treasury.

Why Do They Want the
Same Book Read Over and Over?

If you are like most parents, you have probably read *Goodnight Moon* by Margaret Wise Brown a dozen if not two dozen times—and that was just in one month! After a while, you might have noticed that your child knew exactly what was next in line for saying good night, whether it was the bears and the chairs or the clocks and the socks. And sometimes they added other items because they understood the repetitive language in the book. Young children learn through repetition, so asking for the same book over and over and over again is part of their developmental process in learning language as well as the structure of stories. This is called immersion. Hearing the same story again and again is a part of that immersion process. Repetition also changes the brain because when a child hears and practices a word, concept, or skill, the pathways between brain cells are strengthened and solidified.

Children also need repeated readings to facilitate learning. A study in 2011 found that when kids were read the same book multiple times, they remembered and retained the meaning of a new word more than children who heard different books that contained the same word.[8] So although reading a different book every day may keep the adult from being bored, it prevents the child from getting the reinforcement needed for learning. Prior to age two, repeated readings of fewer books are better than a vast collection read infrequently.

As adults, we need to remember that we also like to reread the same book or watch a movie multiple times. We realize how many subtleties escaped us the first time. This is the same for children and books. Because they are learning a complex language at the adult's speaking pace, there often are misunderstandings that can be sorted out only through repeated readings. Even though many parents have read Bill Martin Jr. and Eric Carle's *Brown Bear, Brown Bear, What Do You See?* more times than they can count, it does take a while for a young child to sort out the different animals. Once when I was reading this book to a preschooler, she thought that the bear had eaten all of the other animals because the bear had "seen" them. After we reread the book a few more times, she understood that each animal was safe and no harm had been inflicted by the bear.

For as long as possible, your read-aloud efforts should be balanced by outside experiences. The words in the book are just the beginning. What you as a parent or teacher do after the reading can turn a minilesson into a sizable learning experience. In Candace Fleming's *Bulldozer's Big Day*, a little bulldozer zips around the construction site while secretly hoping that the other machinery will acknowledge his birthday. As his blade droops lower and lower, a "Wooot! Feeef! Tooot!" at the end of the day signals a surprise birthday party. Of course, a natural springboard would be to talk about other trucks and earthmoving machinery as well as the child's birthday. And it works in reverse as well: When you find a caterpillar outside, read Eric Carle's *The Very Hungry Caterpillar* inside the house or classroom.

What's with All the Questions?

Children have a natural curiosity about the world around them. This curiosity helps them develop skills, learn vocabulary, build concepts, and generate an understanding of new information. Parents sometimes are irritated by a child's incessant questions, particularly during read-aloud: "My child interrupts the book so often for questions, it ruins the story." First, you need to define the kinds of questions. Are they silly? Are they the result of curiosity or extraneous to the story? Is the child sincerely trying to learn something or just postponing bedtime? You can solve the latter problem if you make a regular habit of talking about the story when you finish instead of merely closing the book, kissing the child good night, and turning off the light.

Next, in the case of intelligent questions, try to respond immediately if it involves background knowledge ("Why did Mr. McGregor put Peter's father in a pie, Mom? Why couldn't he just hop out?"), and thus help the child better understand the story of *Peter Rabbit*. Extraneous queries can be handled by saying, "Good question! Let's come back to that when we're done." And be sure to live up to that promise. Sometimes I place a sticky note on the page to remind me that we need to go back. This also signals that the page and the question are important. Ultimately, one must acknowledge that questions are a child's primary learning tool. Don't destroy natural curiosity by ignoring it.

One way to foster children's questioning abilities and to support their learning is to read aloud books that contain questions. The baby bird in the classic book *Are You My Mother?* by P. D. Eastman asks that same question of each animal it meets. Asking questions of a different type can be found in Robin Page's *A Chicken Followed Me Home!: Questions and Answers About a Familiar Fowl*. This nonfiction picture book asks questions about what a chicken eats and if it lays eggs. The book contains simple text that can be read aloud along with detailed information about chickens. Parents or teachers can either read the particular details or paraphrase it. Many books provide stories and information that are framed around asking questions and seeking answers.

If We Have Only a Small Amount of Time for Read-Aloud, How Do We Incorporate Discussion?

When I was in fifth grade, my teacher, Mr. Guymon, would read aloud to us after lunch. It's probably one of the most commonly used strategies for getting kids to calm down and refocus for the afternoon. I vividly remember him reading aloud *Where the Red Fern Grows* by Wilson Rawls. This classic book tells a heartwarming story of a boy and his two hunting dogs, Old Dan and Little Ann. After Mr. Guymon read a chapter or two, I so wanted to discuss the story, but, unfortunately, he would close the book and announce that it was time for math. I thought then, and I still believe today, that if a book is worth reading aloud, then time should be given to discuss it even if it means that math has to wait.

Discussion after reading aloud a story is of critical importance, but it doesn't have to last forever. Just a simple, "What do you think? How do you feel? What do you wonder?" question might prompt lots or little discussion. However, the point is to provide time to think and talk about what resonated with the listener.

Students from classrooms where there are book discussions tend to score higher in national reading assessments[9] and engage in reading outside school.[10] Look at the more than fifty books Oprah's Book Club put on the *New York Times* bestseller list. How many would have made the list if there had been only advertisements for the books on her show instead of discussions? For many people (though not all), reading needs to be a social experience, giving them the chance to share their feelings about the book and critique its characters. If there is a shortage of time, steal it from other subjects that are not as essential as reading, which includes pretty much everything else.

At home, the same importance for discussion applies. Sure, it might be a diversion from having to go to sleep, but if your child really wants to discuss the book with you, try to be receptive to it. Waiting until the next day takes away the wonderful opportunity to learn what aspects of the story your child is connecting with, and also maybe insights into what is happening in her life. Issues and concerns can be discussed through the perspective of the characters or plot. Some of the richest discussions I have had with kids about their lives occurred during or after reading aloud to them.

Is There a Natural Transition from Picture Book to Novel?

Thanks to our primal need to find out what happens next, read-aloud is a particularly useful tool in stretching children's attention spans. Just keep in mind that endurance in readers, like runners, is not overnight; start slowly and build gradually. Begin with short picture books, then move to longer ones that can be read over several days, then to short novels (already broken into convenient chapters), and finally to full-length novels (longer than one hundred pages).

The amount of text on a page is a decent way to gauge how much the child's attention span is being stretched. The transition from short to longer should be done gradually over many different books. While you don't want to drown the child in words, you do want to unconsciously entice him away from a complete dependence on illustrations for comprehension.

When I taught first grade, I couldn't assume that all children had been read to at home or even in preschool or kindergarten. I also wanted to lay the foundation that reading is fun and purposeful. So I selected books for reading aloud that would immediately engage my students and begin the formation of our classroom community through shared reading experiences.

One of the books I initially read aloud was *First Day Jitters* by Julie Dannenberg. It is apparent in the story that someone is getting ready for the first day of school, and the ending reveals it is the teacher. I would share with my students that I get excited and nervous for the first school day, just like they do. *School's First Day of School* by Adam Rex would be another choice; this book shows even a school gets anxious for the first day. The next book I would read was *No David!* by David Shannon because it is humorous, relatable, and easy to read. This book provided children with the enjoyment factor of reading aloud and was also a book they wanted to revisit independently.

Sometimes I read aloud a book such as *The Very Hungry Caterpillar* or *Where the Wild Things Are* because the kids might be familiar with them. This also facilitated the home-school connection of reading books. A short chapter book like *Dog and Bear: Three to Get Ready* by Laura Vaccaro Seeger would be shared. The three delightful stories about friends, Dog and Bear, would offer the opportunity to talk to my first graders about how they would be reading longer books during the school year.

Multiple books were read on the first day of school because I wanted kids to talk about them later with their parents. This would provide an answer to the question, "What did you do in school today?" I made sure those first read-alouds introduced and reinforced the magic and pleasure of reading.

Every day I continued to read aloud a variety of stories to hook my students on books. They borrowed the books to take home so their parents could read it aloud as well. I shared stories about friendship such as *A Sick Day for Amos McGee* by Philip C. Stead, which tells about a zookeeper who takes care of his animal friends until one day they have the opportunity to take care of him. Another favorite is *Should I Share My Ice Cream?*, which is an Elephant and Piggie book by Mo Willems. This prompted a discussion about sharing with others and whether it should be one of our classroom rules.

Some weeks we would explore a fairy tale like "The Three Pigs," focusing on different versions of those home-building swine. The first book would be a traditional telling of the story, *The Three Little Pigs* by James Marshall. Other versions were fun to read aloud including *The True Story of the Three Little Pigs!* by A. Wolf (or in reality, Jon Scieszka), which shares the Wolf's perspective just in case you want to know the *real* story; *The Three Little Javelinas* by Susan Lowell for a southwestern flavor; *The Three Little Pigs: An Architectural Tale* by Steven Guarnaccia with a nod to three famous architects including Frank Lloyd Wright; and *The Three Ninja Pigs*, by Corey Rosen Schwartz, who refuse not to be bullied anymore and enroll in aikido lessons.

At times, we would focus exclusively on one picture or chapter book author's work. A good author to start with is Kevin Henkes since he has a range of stories including picture books like *Lilly's Purple Plastic Purse*, *My Garden*, and the Caldecott Medal–winning *Kitten's First Full Moon* as well as the beginning chapter book *Penny and Her Marble*. I would also read aloud the Mercy Watson series of beginning chapter books by Kate DiCamillo and then later her longer chapter books, culminating in an author study near the end of the school year.

Poetry would be sprinkled in throughout the day. I looked for poetry books by Lee Bennett Hopkins, Joyce Sidman, Douglas

Florian, Alan Katz, Laura Purdie Salas, Rebecca Kai Dotlich, and J. Patrick Lewis. Of course, Shel Silverstein and Jack Prelutsky are always childhood favorites.

As we established lengthier attention and listening spans, it was an easy jump to longer picture books or short novels. These are books that don't have to end on Monday but can be stretched into Tuesday and Wednesday. Primary grades are a fine time to introduce short series books to students: Ivy + Bean, Junie B. Jones, Encyclopedia Brown, Cam Jansen, Magic Tree House, Here's Hank, and many others. Read one chapter from the first book in the series and see how quickly kids rush to finish that one and ask for more. This strategy works great for older kids too.

Can You Begin Chapter Books in Primary Grades?

Let me give you an idea of how widespread the misunderstanding is about the difference between listening to and reading levels, as well as the magic that can occur when they are understood. In the previous edition of *The Read-Aloud Handbook*, Jim Trelease shared a story about a young teacher he met about twenty years ago when he was speaking to a group about the importance of reading aloud chapter books to young children. Melissa Olans Antinoff introduced herself to Jim and told him, "You'd love my kindergarten class!" She explained that she read one hundred picture books a year to the class in addition to ten to twelve chapter books. The socioeconomic level of the class had 60 percent of the children on free lunch. Melissa was in her fourth year of teaching and understood that she was fostering longer attention spans and increasing the students' vocabulary by incorporating chapter books into the school year. In follow-up correspondence with Melissa, it was no surprise she was named Burlington County Teacher of the Year in New Jersey in 2017. This recognition illustrates that her exceptional teaching continues.

Megan Sloan, the teacher you were introduced to in chapter 1, has previously taught first and second grade. She believes we sell kids short by not including chapter books in the primary grades, including kindergarten. Megan starts the school year with picture books. By the second week, she is reading one of many short chapter book series she knows her students will enjoy: Henry and Mudge by Cynthia Rylant, a delightful series about a boy, Henry, and his

Melissa Antinoff currently teaches third grade and continues to read aloud multiple times during the day to her students.

lovable 180-pound dog, Mudge; Nate the Great by Marjorie Weinman Sharmat, about boy detective Nate on the case; or Horrible Harry by Suzy Kline, which humorously tells of the misadventures of a third grader, Harry.

Many series books provide the best introduction to chapter books for kindergarten and first graders. They are short, contain engaging characters, and often have humorous story lines. When emergent readers discover a character or plot through a series book they enjoy, it creates the desire to read independently. When they ask for another book like the one you just read, there are generally dozens more to select from, especially if the series is Junie B. Jones, The Boxcar Children, or other books mentioned above.

After Megan shares several of these series books, she moves on to longer chapter books. *Poppy* by Avi, about a young deer mouse, features an exciting plot and well-developed characters. *Charlotte's Web* by E. B. White is a perennial favorite about Wilbur the pig and his friendship with barn spider, Charlotte. Megan believes that chapter books can stretch her students' listening comprehension. "I do think kids yearn for that longer story and can handle it with the right guidance and enough time spent on reading each day."

What About Reading Chapter Books at the Preschool Level?

Over the years, I have spent a significant amount of time in early childhood classrooms, particularly at the preschool level. There have been preschools where hearing stories encompassed large portions of the day and others where little to no reading aloud occurred. Occasionally, I observed the reading aloud of chapter books by enthusiastic teachers.

What are the characteristics of a good chapter book to read aloud to preschoolers? Fortunately, there are a number of blogs by teachers and parents available on the internet that provide helpful suggestions, not only about reading aloud chapter books, but also recommendations for which books to read. Of course, not all books work well with all children, so here are a few things to consider:

- Pre-read a variety of chapter books before selecting one to read aloud. Consider if the plot will be interesting, relatable, humorous—whatever you think will appeal to your child and hold her attention. I have found the best books are ones with short chapters of five to seven pages with large font.

- Introduce the story. For example, when I read aloud *Mercy Watson to the Rescue* by Kate DiCamillo to a group of preschoolers, I start by showing the cover and telling them this is a story about a pig adopted by people. I also say how Mercy loves buttered toast and ask the children how many of them love buttered toast. They now have a little information about Mercy, and some of them already had a connection—they love buttered toast too!

- If the chapter book is illustrated, show the pictures as you read aloud. Often it is easier to transition from an illustrated chapter book to one with few or no pictures. Be sure your reading speed is at a pace where children can follow the action of the story.

- When you come to a word that might be unfamiliar, stop and explain the meaning. Chapter 2 of *Mercy Watson to the Rescue* contains the word *snuffled*. It was fun to hear what the kids thought snuffled meant.

- Pause frequently to make sure children are comprehending the story. That doesn't mean asking questions like, "What type of animal is Mercy?" but rather, "What do you think will happen next?" or "Why do you think Mercy did that?" Also, pause when you know a meaningful part of the story is coming up to ensure they are listening. This is one of the reasons for pre-reading the book.

+ Read as long as children are interested. It might be a chapter or two or possibly a few pages. There will be days when kids are glued to the story while other days they are easily distracted (changes in the weather always seems to contribute to their distraction).

+ The next time you pick up the book to continue the read-aloud— whether it's a few hours, a day, or several days—either review the story so far or ask a child what she remembers about it.

+ At any point, if it appears the book has lost its appeal, ask the children if they want to continue hearing it. One thing about preschoolers is that they are brutally honest in their response.

As with any book that is read aloud, it should be a pleasurable experience for all. The advantage of reading aloud chapter books to preschoolers is that it exposes them to other types of stories and increases their listening ability and attention span.

Are There Pitfalls to Avoid in Choosing Long Novels?

The difference between short and full-length novels is sometimes found in the amount of description: The shorter ones contain less detail, while the longer ones require more imagination on the part of the listener. I previously used one hundred pages as a guide in identifying a short novel, but many short chapter books are well beyond that number because they contain illustrations. Children whose imaginations have been atrophying in front of a television or tablet screen for years are not comfortable with long descriptive passages. But the more you read to them, the less trouble they have in constructing mental images.

In approaching longer books, remember that all books are not meant to be read aloud; indeed, some books aren't even worth reading to yourself, never mind boring a family or class with them. There are books written in a complicated or ambiguous style that can be read silently but not aloud.

The great Canadian novelist Robertson Davies defined one of the best rules on the difference between listening to text and reading text in the preface to a volume of his speeches. He asked readers to remember they were reading speeches, not essays: "What is meant to be heard is necessarily more direct in expression, and perhaps more boldly coloured, than what is meant for the reader."[11] This is a fact missed by many speakers, preachers, and professors who write their speeches as if the audience were going to read them instead of listen to them. Be sure to take Davies's advice into consideration when choosing your longer read-alouds.

Also be alert to the subject matter of the novels. The length of such books allows authors to treat subject matter that can be very sensitive, far more so than in a picture book. As the reader, you should familiarize yourself with the subject and the author's approach. Ask yourself as you preview it: "Can my child or class handle not only the vocabulary and the complexity of this story but its emotions as well? Is there anything here that will do more harm than good to my child or class? Anything that might embarrass someone?"

Reading a book ahead of time enables you to avoid those kinds of damaging situations. You will be reading it to the class or child with more confidence, accenting focal passages, and providing sound effects to dramatize the story line (I'm always ready to tap on a table or wall where the story calls for a knock at the door).

At What Age Do You Stop Reading Aloud Picture Books?

In a word—*never*. There is often a misunderstanding that picture books are only for young children. It's important to remember that a picture book is a format. It's not always indicative of listening or reading ability. Although I understand the impatience to get on with the business of growing up, I wince whenever I hear that question. A good story is a good story, whether it has pictures or not. The key is reading aloud picture books that engage the listener and continue to develop an appreciation of literature and the value of reading.

Judith Viorst's *Alexander and the Terrible, Horrible, No Good, Very Bad Day* is an excellent example of a picture book that transcends age and grade levels. Preschoolers enjoy this book as much as high schoolers. They also respond to it in different ways—a bad day for a four-year-old will certainly be different than that of a sixteen-year-old. On the other hand, *Ducks Away!* by Mem Fox doubles as a counting book as five ducklings, one by one, tumble off the bridge and into the water below. The number words are printed in orange, which is great for younger children but might not be as appreciated by a middle schooler.

Because of the content, a picture book may be appropriate for an adolescent audience. For example, Shaun Tan's *The Arrival* is a lengthy wordless picture book that uses strong visual metaphors to tell the story of an immigrant's experience in a new world. It requires background knowledge to understand the nuances of Tan's illustrations. *Will's Words: How William Shakespeare Changed the Way You Talk* by Jane Sutcliffe explains how many of the words and phrases we use today, such as "fashionable," "well-behaved," "all of a sudden," and "too much of a good thing," were ones he coined or popularized with his plays. Older students have an understanding of Shakespeare and will enjoy having another perspective as they read his work.

Picture books can teach higher-level thinking skills. They make stories accessible and offer an engaging experience for older kids who might not like to read or have stopped reading except for school assignments. Rarely have I experienced a middle or high school student who did not react favorably when I read aloud an appropriate picture book to them.

Some picture books also lend themselves to be paired with classic literature such as Mac Barnett's *Sam & Dave Dig a Hole*, a story of "starts and stops and missed opportunities" that can be combined with the reading of John Steinbeck's *Of Mice and Men*. You could also link Yangsook Choi's *The Name Jar* with Arthur Miller's *The Crucible* because both communicate the importance of a person's name.[12]

One benefit of selecting a picture book to read aloud in a secondary classroom is that many times the class periods are short. Trying to read a chapter from a novel or even a short story might take more time than what is available to teach the content for the day.

But what about reading picture books with your teen at home? Many of the reasons cited above are also applicable to the home environment. Teenagers are busy people, so reading aloud a picture book might be the solution when time is limited for interaction.

Returning to the picture books that your kids loved when they were younger is excellent for experiencing those special moments again. In the movie *The Blind Side*, about NFL player Michael Oher, adoptive parent Leigh Anne Tuohy reads aloud *The Story of Ferdinand* by Munro Leaf to her young son and Michael. Later, Michael captures the essence of the story as he talks about courage in a school essay. As a teenager, Michael had never heard the story before. It created a memorable scene in the movie and demonstrated the impact a simple story had on the football player. There was so much interest generated around *The Story of Ferdinand*, a couple of years later an animated film was created based on the story.

Here are a few recommendations to win over those who think older students won't respond to picture books:

- *We Troubled the Waters* by Ntozake Shange. This triumphant book captures the power of the human spirit and chronicles the events and people of the civil rights era through stirring poetry and striking illustrations.

- *After the Fall: How Humpty Dumpty Got Back Up Again* by Dan Santat. Don't let the title and illustrations fool you into thinking this is the same Mother Goose rhyme you heard growing up. *After the Fall* is about the importance of getting back up and confronting debilitating fear, even when it takes time to do so.

- *Ada's Violin: The Story of the Recycled Orchestra of Paraguay* by Susan Hood. Ada Ríos lives in a small town in Paraguay built on a landfill. She dreams of playing the violin, but there is no money for instruments, only the essentials. When music teacher Favio Chávez arrives, he devises a plan to make instruments out of materials found in the trash. This true story shares how one idea can change a community.

- *Game Changer: John McLendon and the Secret Game* by John Coy. In 1944, the members of the Duke University Medical School basketball team drove through Durham, North Carolina, to play a secret game against the players from the North Carolina College of Negroes (now North Carolina Central University). The true story of *Game Changer* occurred during a time of segregation and racism when it would have been illegal for the white Duke players to play the black team.

+ *The Man Who Walked Between the Towers* by Mordicai Gerstein. Winner of the 2004 Caldecott Medal, this is the true story of the young French aerialist Philippe Petit, who strung a tightrope between the two unfinished towers of the World Trade Center in 1974 and walked between them for two hours during morning rush hour. The story focuses on that event and not on the 9/11 tragedy twenty-seven years later, although there is a fleeting reference to the fact that the towers are no more.

+ *The Legend of Rock Paper Scissors* by Drew Daywalt. Everyone has played the game of rock, paper, scissors. This book will extend a little silliness to the game and have teenagers in stitches.

When It's Obvious You've Made a Poor Book Choice, Is It Okay to Abandon It, or Parts of It, and Move On?

There are so many books that are outstanding read-alouds. However, once in a while you start one where the text doesn't flow, or your listener has lost interest. I suggest you give the book a chance by reading several chapters before setting it aside.

It's always good to ask your child if she wants to abandon the book. Scott Riley was reading aloud *Restart* by Gordon Korman, a novel about a boy who falls off the roof and has amnesia. Scott thought his teenage daughter was losing interest and wanted to stop reading. But she insisted they continue because she wanted to know what happens to the main character. You never know if the book is working unless you ask.

Support for this approach comes from Nancy Pearl, former executive director of the Washington Center for the Book, who conceived the One City, One Book movement that swept through many American cities and towns. In *Book Lust: Recommended Reading for Every Mood, Moment, and Reason*, Pearl offers advice to adults that applies to reading to children and children's own reading. She calls it the "rule of fifty": If you're fifty or younger, give every book about fifty pages. If you're over fifty, then subtract your age from one hundred and give it that many pages.[13] Simply put, there's a limit to how many pages a child should have to endure if the story doesn't interest or resonate with her in any way.

Do Children Have to Follow Along in a Book as You Read Aloud?

While it's not always necessary, it can be extremely helpful for certain students to follow along as you read aloud. Here's how.

Karl "Skip" Johnson, the principal at El Crystal Elementary in San Bruno, California, can't take all the credit for his brainstorm. He pretty much stumbled on it. As we pick up his story, Johnson had been principal there for fourteen years, one of the many stops he'd made in a three-decade career in education. His first love had always been reading, so it figures that subject would be linked to his brainstorm.

So now it was 2004, his district was using a standard textbook approach to reading supplemented by one of the computerized reading incentive programs (theirs was Reading Counts), and No Child Left Behind was turning up the pressure to get everyone scoring at the same reading level. It wasn't going to be easy. (The computerized reading incentive programs usually offer prizes and grade points for the number of books read, according to their difficulty.)

San Bruno is a small community that runs blue-collar to affluent. It geographically bounds the west edge of the San Francisco airport. Johnson's 250-student body is 40 percent Caucasian, 40 percent Latino, and the remaining 20 percent is a diverse mix. What preoccupied Johnson and his faculty was the challenge of lifting the kids who came from homes where English was not the primary language—English Language Learners (ELL). They wanted to read what the other students were reading and pass the Reading Counts test. Unfortunately, they couldn't understand the text well enough to pass the test.

As Johnson and his teachers saw it, there was a language gap. These students hadn't heard enough of the words and expressions that make up everyday English conversation and its idioms: *gets on my nerves, hopping mad, cute as a button, hits the spot, sweating bullets, on the double, give me a break*, to name a few.

If only there was a way to enrich their English during home

hours. Johnson knew firsthand how significant the home environment was for nurturing early reading experiences. Back when he was in elementary school, he loved to read so much his mother would reward him with days off from school just to stay home and read all day. That, however, isn't going to happen today in a world where both parents are working outside the home.

Someone gave Johnson a fifty-dollar iTunes gift card and he thought, "I already have enough music on my iPod to last a lifetime, so what am I going to spend this on?" And that's when he saw the audiobook category in the iTunes Store, which included children's titles. Maybe he would download a few and discuss them with the kids in school after he listened to them. But before that happened, another idea intruded, one that would help bridge the gap between home and school, as well as the variance between proficient readers and the strugglers.

His brainstorm became known as eCAP (El Crystal Audiobook Project) and added up to sixty iPod kits (from grant money), along with six hundred audiobooks. When a teacher identifies a nonproficient reader, she sits down with the student, and they construct a fifteen-book playlist from the school's master list. The playlist is loaded onto an iPod with a kit accompanying it that includes the book's text, a charger, headphones, and any necessary instructions. Best of all, it stays with the student—in school and out—for the entire school year, with more books loaded as needed. The student listens to the audiobook while following along with the printed text. The reader's voice and inflection, in turn, serves as a vocabulary and reading coach, especially during critical hours away from the classroom.

El Crystal Elementary teachers use a textbook for instruction, continue to read aloud to their K–6 classes, and then adopt a facilitator role in literature circles, in which independent reading is shared among the children. How well is the program working? El Crystal's students are sixty points higher than the state's Academic Performance Index and annually read one million words more than their closest district rivals.

While we may not still be using iPods, devices can be obtained for a nominal cost where audiobooks can be uploaded. What's important is that children can increase their vocabulary and also improve their reading performance if they have access to books in audio and/or print format.

Shouldn't There Be a Test to See If the Class Is Truly Learning from Read-Aloud?

By all means, there should be a test—and there *is* one. Only you don't *give* it. It's the test of time, the real measure of anything we teach. What do they remember ten, twenty, thirty years from now? Of all the lessons taught, what lasted?

Kimberly Douglas, of Hillsboro, Ohio, had the satisfaction of learning the answer to that question. Back in 1989, she was in her second year of teaching when she picked up an early edition of this handbook and began reading to her classes. I'll let her share her story:

> I am now an administrator who works with first-year teachers. In planning for an upcoming meeting and presentation on building relationships with students, I Facebook-messaged seventy-one of my former students, asking them to share their memories of being a sixth grader in my classroom. I told them it didn't matter if they remembered how to divide fractions or knew the chemical symbol for copper, I wanted to know what they truly remembered. The response has been overwhelming. They've remembered some pretty incredible things, but the common theme among all their memories is the books we read together. We've discussed titles and authors and how they've read those same books to their own children. Keep in mind, these "kids" range in age from twenty-six to thirty-seven, and they've remembered *Gentle Ben, Bridge to Terabithia, From the Mixed-up Files of Mrs. Basil E. Frankweiler, Hatchet, Where the Red Fern Grows*, and many others. Several of them have also commented that they wish their children's teachers would read to them the way I did all those years ago.[14]

I would say both Kimberly and her students passed the test handsomely. As Kimberly's story attests, the read-aloud is planting seeds she hopes will bear fruit with the students' future children. It might even be motivating enough to get students to class on time or at least more regularly. Consider the experience of Nancy Foote, of Higley, Arizona, a former recipient of the Presidential Award for Excellence in Mathematics and Science Teaching, a National Board Certified teacher, and a devotee of reading aloud and its impact on reluctant teens. As she explains it:

I was a teacher for almost twenty years in traditional schools. For several years, I taught at an alternative high school. Many of my students were convicted felons who were on probation, some on house arrest, allowed to leave home only to go to school. Many had drug addictions they were fighting. They were wonderful kids who had bigger problems than I could ever imagine.

We had a relatively long passing between classes, amounting to five minutes. Our campus was rather small, so there was no reason for kids to come late to class. Yet day after day they arrived late—sometimes just a minute or two, other times much longer. I wanted to find a way to motivate them to get to class on time. I thought about the book *Frindle* by Andrew Clements, a book I had heard you talk about in your workshops. I wasn't sure if these kids would like the book—they were tough kids—but decided to give it a try.

Exactly three minutes before the tardy bell rang, I would begin reading aloud from the book. Once the tardy bell rang, I continued reading until I finished the chapter. At first, I felt sort of foolish. I was reading to a totally empty classroom! That was OK because I loved the story, and Nick is one of my favorite characters. Within a few days, the kids started getting to class early so they could hear about Nick. Within one week, I no longer had problems with tardy students. Once we finished *Frindle*, we moved on to *Loser* by Jerry Spinelli and then Clements's *Things Not Seen*.

Not only did reading aloud get my students to class on time, but attendance improved. Whenever students came back to school after being absent, they wanted to hear what they missed. Some would borrow the book and read it themselves, but most wanted to come in at lunch so I could read it to them. (These were not young children—they ranged in age from thirteen to nineteen.) They couldn't wait to hear what happened next.

Near the end of the year, one of my students, a tall, gangly young man, came in to see me. He was nineteen years old and fighting a crystal meth addiction. He was trying to raise his young son, since the baby's mother abandoned him in favor of drugs. He had an uphill battle, as did his infant son, yet in spite of his challenges, he made it to school most days and kept off drugs. He thanked me for being a great teacher and helping him. He told me that my reading to them was wonderful, and he really enjoyed it.

He also told me that no one had ever read aloud to him—I was the first. And he promised he would read aloud to his son.[15]

The seeds that are planted for the love of reading may not always bear immediate fruit, but if we are patient enough, there will be rewards.

Chapter 4

Sustained Silent Reading and Reading for Pleasure

So Matilda's strong young mind continued to
grow, nurtured by the voices of all those authors
who had sent their books out into the world like
ships on the sea. These books gave Matilda a
hopeful and comforting message: You are
not alone.

—*Matilda* by Roald Dahl[1]

AMONG the many purposes of reading aloud, a primary one is
to motivate a child to read independently. Take a book, a newspaper, a magazine, and enjoy it! No interruptions for questions, no
comprehension tests, and no book reports; just read for pleasure.
Because we adults have done this thing called reading for much of
our lives, we take many of its facets for granted. Children do not, as
evidenced by Lee Sullivan Hill, of Clarendon Hills, Illinois, who
shared this story:

One day, her young son Colin observed her silently reading to
herself and asked, "What are you doing?"

"Reading," she answered.

"Then why aren't you making any noise?"

She explained how people read to themselves as well as to others, like when she reads to him. Hearing that, the light dawned for

Colin. "So that's what Daddy does!" he exclaimed, recalling when he had seen his father reading silently to himself.

Colin's father was engaged in independent reading. Until it is explained, silent reading is sometimes a mystery to young children.

The concept of independent reading in school may operate under a variety of acronyms, including SSR (sustained silent reading), DEAR (drop everything and read), DIRT (daily individual reading time), SQUIRT (sustained quiet uninterrupted reading time), and FVR (free voluntary reading).

Sustained silent reading is a term used in schools referring to a specific time during the school day when students are selecting books they can read independently. Outside the school day, the term *independent reading* is common. The premise for both is to encourage and support children to read on their own. However, there are some differences such as how the time is structured, who is selecting the child's books, and what accountability measures are being implemented.

Didn't the National Reading Panel (NRP) Condemn SSR?

"Condemn" is a little harsh, but the panel didn't exactly give an unqualified endorsement of it, and that bumped the practice from some districts afraid of losing federal funds. In a nutshell, here's the scoop on the NRP versus sustained silent reading. (Don't confuse the National Reading Panel of 2000 with the 1985 Commission on Reading—they are two very different animals but probably had the same goals.) Even though the NRP report came out over a decade ago, the interpretation of it and its impact continues today.

The National Reading Panel's 2000 report noted that there wasn't sufficient scientific evidence to support SSR's use in school, especially if it is being used as the only method of instruction.[2] No one in their right mind would advocate SSR being the *only* way to teach reading. Certainly, there needs to be instruction, but you also need the opportunity to put it into practice. How can anyone imagine students' reading improving without reading *a lot*?

The NRP study subgroup deemed only fourteen short-term studies worthy of their disputed[3] "medical-scientific" standards and found insufficient evidence among them to support SSR, even though SSR students performed the same as ten of the control groups and surpassed the control groups in the four remaining studies. There was not one negative SSR performance in their fourteen "scientific" studies, but this was not convincing enough for the NRP.

Which brings us to Stephen Krashen, the leading proponent of the inclusion of SSR in the classroom schedule. If you are contemplating SSR for your school or class and haven't read his book *The Power of Reading*, do so immediately! This professor emeritus from the University of Southern California has thoroughly refuted the NRP's claims, as have a host of other qualified reading authorities.[4] Krashen examined not fourteen short-term SSR studies, as the NRP did, but a total of fifty-three studies, long ones and short ones. Overwhelmingly, the results favor SSR, especially in the yearlong studies. The only three negative results for SSR were in short-term studies, compared with twenty-five positive results. If that were a baseball or football score (25–3), could it be more decisive?

SSR is based upon a single simple principle: Reading is a skill—and the more you use it, the better you get at it. Conversely, the less you use it, the more difficult it is.[5]

In 2002, the Organisation for Economic Co-operation and Development (OECD), which for decades has helped its thirty-four member governments monitor school achievement worldwide, issued a report in which it examined the reading literacy of 250,000 fifteen-year-olds in thirty-two countries.[6] In every country, those who read the most read the best, regardless of income level. A decade earlier, a similar study by the International Association for the Evaluation of Educational Achievement (IEA) compared the reading skills of 210,000 students from thirty-two different countries. It found the highest scores (regardless of income level) among children who

♦ were read to by their teachers daily
♦ read the most pages for pleasure daily.[7]

Moreover, the frequency of SSR had a marked impact on scores: Children who had it daily scored much higher than those who had it only once a week. The National Assessment of Educational Progress (NAEP) assessment found an identical pattern for the nearly thirty-five years the NAEP has been testing hundreds of thousands of U.S. students.[8] Other studies have reported that middle school students in classrooms where time was provided for SSR showed reading gains of up to 3.9 grade levels after a year's participation.[9] Vocabulary scores also improved up to twenty-four points. The evidence for reading aloud to children and having time set aside for SSR is overwhelming; yet most children are neither read to nor experience opportunities to read on their own in the course of a school day.

When Does SSR Become Effective?

Time spent reading, including reading silently, has consistently correlated strongly with reading achievement.[10] According to Nancie Atwell, "Every measure that looks at pleasure reading and its effect on student performance on standardized tests of reading ability tells us that the major predictor of academic success is the amount of time that a student spends reading."[11]

In its simplest form, SSR allows a person to read long and far enough that the act of reading becomes automatic and builds reading stamina. If one must stop to concentrate on each word, sounding it out, then fluency is lost along with meaning. Reading this way is also fatiguing. Being able to do it automatically is the goal. The selection of books is also a key factor in the success of SSR.

Young readers show significant improvement in both attitude and skills with SSR. Richard Allington, leading researcher and former president of the International Reading Association (now the International Literacy Association), points out, "Poor readers, when given ten minutes a day to read, initially will achieve five hundred words and quickly increase that amount in the same period as proficiency grows."[12]

By the third grade, time spent reading independently can be the student's most important vocabulary builder, more so than basal textbooks or even daily oral language. The Commission on Reading noted: "Basal readers and textbooks do not offer the same richness of vocabulary, sentence structure, or literary form as do trade books. . . . A diet consisting only of basal stories probably will not prepare children well to deal with real literature."[13]

Research scientists in 2009 at Carnegie Mellon University demonstrated that struggling young readers receiving one hundred hours of reading remediation had significantly rewired their brain networks in the process. Earlier scans of the children indicated a low amount of white matter connecting different parts of the brain. After the additional intensive instruction focused on reading skills, the white matter increased to normal, giving the students increased reading ability,[14] not unlike going from hardwired internet connectivity to Wi-Fi.

How Can I Ensure That SSR Is Successful?

Recent research has indicated we need to examine the use of SSR in the classroom to ensure that students derive the maximum benefit from it. In 2010, well-known literacy researchers Hiebert and Reutzel[15] provided suggestions to improve SSR including:

- ◆ Student self-selection of books. Teachers and librarians should guide students to choose texts that are of interest to them, and they will be successful in reading independently.
- ◆ Student engagement and time on task during silent reading. This means practicing reading, not talking with peers, or participating in other classroom activities.
- ◆ Accountability of what has been read, which may help build reading stamina and proficiency. That doesn't mean the child should be given a list of questions. They should have an opportunity to turn and talk briefly to another student about their reading.

Hiebert and Reutzel's idea that teachers shouldn't be reading during SSR is something I disagree with. The teacher serves as a critical role model in SSR. Students will often imitate his independent reading habits. They might notice the teacher interrupting his reading to look up words in the dictionary and do the same. If the teacher spends the SSR period doing paperwork or policing the room, the role modeling effect is lost. It can also be distracting to other students if the teacher is talking to a child about what he is reading as Hiebert and Reutzel suggest.

There have been multiple published research studies that have questioned the effectiveness of SSR. Some studies have indicated "fake reading" was taking place during SSR where students were pretending to read by turning pages in an attempt to fool the teacher.[16] If it appears that children are not reading, then there might be something wrong in how SSR is being structured in the classroom.

What are some of the problems that might be occurring? It may be SSR is being rigidly enforced.[17] Krashen found that sometimes students were not allowed to leave their desks during SSR. Multiple disruptions, often by the teacher, disturbed the students during SSR and interrupted their reading. Some students were not aware they could select another book if the one they were reading was too difficult or not interesting.[18] Students also developed negative attitudes about SSR when they were required to respond to questions about their book. When this occurred, it was no longer considered pleasure reading because an accountability measure had been imposed.

How Can We Determine If Readers Have Actually Read the Book?

Stephen Krashen has described independent reading, or as he calls it, free voluntary reading (FVR), as "reading because you want to. For school-age children, FVR means no book report, no questions at the end of the chapter, and no looking up every vocabulary word."[19] We need to think about ourselves as readers and whether we would want to have to write a book report or take a quiz after each chapter or book that we read. Kids feel no differently in wanting the time to read for pleasure and not be held accountable in a manner that whips the wonder away from the enjoyment they have just experienced.

Our goal is to create lifelong readers. Give kids an opportunity to explore topics, authors, genres, and formats they deem as worthy of their time. If an administrator, teacher, or parent feels they need to rationalize the time spent on reading independently, all they have to do is observe kids. I've been in classrooms where kids are laying under tables, curled up in the corner propped up by a pillow, or sitting at their desks hunched over a book. Most are not even aware that anyone else is in the room. I've seen (and heard) kids laugh, frown, shake their heads, or even blurt out a comment or question—"I can't believe it!" I've also witnessed kids with tears running down their faces. When kids turn and talk to another person or within a group, you might hear, "Is your book sad? What made you laugh? Would you recommend the book you are reading?"

The assessment is the engagement with the book and also the opportunity to share it with others. Reading for pleasure is what makes us readers.

What Do I Say If My School Administrator Objects to Students Participating in SSR?

Unfortunately, in this day of testing, testing, and more testing, teachers are experiencing a lack of support for class time used for SSR. This was the case when a middle school principal evaluated an eighth-grade language arts teacher who had included a forty-minute period for independent reading in her students' weekly schedule (as prescribed by the school improvement plan). The principal remarked, "I see a great deal of free reading taking place in your classroom. I realize the students are working on assigned reading. However, I feel that much of the reading taking place in the classroom could take place out of the class. This would allow you more time to interact with the students. Decisions as to how class time is used must be sound if our students are going to be successful later on."

If I were the teacher, this is how I would respond to that principal:

1. It's almost impossible to interact with students about literature they haven't read, so I give them time to read it.
2. Students who are the least likely to read outside school are the ones who either hate reading and/or come from homes where there is the least space and quiet for solitary reading. My classroom is a clinic where such reading ills can be cured.
3. There is a natural falloff in recreational reading during adolescence due to the hormonal and social conflict in their twenty-four-hour day. This is most often reflected in how poorly they use their out-of-school time, so I'm providing structured time for reading.
4. My classroom may be the only place where some of them ever see other people reading silently to themselves, and it might be the only place they ever see an adult reading for pleasure and not just for work. My classroom is a laboratory for positive role modeling.

5. I want my students to know that I value reading for pleasure, and giving them time to do so demonstrates that.

Support your response with research showing the effectiveness of SSR and you should have a winning argument.

What About Summer Reading Programs?

Independent reading can reduce the impact of what has been referred to as the "summer slide," where students lose some of the achievement gains they made during the school year. Many parents, especially those whose children are having difficulty with school, see summertime as a vacation and take it literally: "Everyone needs a vacation, for goodness' sake. He needs to get away from school and relax. Next year will be a new start." That attitude can be extremely detrimental, especially to a poor reader, because the better readers don't take the summer off and thus the gap widens. Everyone—top students and poor students—learns more slowly in the summer. Some, though, do worse than slow down; they actually go into reverse.[20]

The Collaborative Summer Learning Program partnered with NPC Research to examine the data related to the need and effectiveness of summer reading programs.[21] Some key findings included convincing evidence for summer reading programs, particularly for children at lower socioeconomic levels. Lower SES children generally experienced a loss of reading achievement during the summer, while higher SES children either maintained or gained reading skills. The report also stated that summer reading programs provide "clear and consistent evidence in preventing summer learning loss and improving reading achievement." These programs can be school or home based, or offered by public libraries, youth organizations, or other community entities.

Top students' scores rise slightly between the end of one school year and the beginning of the next. Conversely, the bottom 25 percent (largely urban poor) lose most of what they gained the previous school year. Average students (the middle 50 percent) make no gains during the summer but lose nothing either—except in the widening gap between themselves and the top students. Projected across the first four years of school, the "rich-poor" reading gap that was present at the start of kindergarten has actually widened.

Many factors cause the loss.[22] The affluent child's summer includes a family of readers in a home that is digitally and print rich with books, magazines, and newspapers. Visits to the bookstore or library assist in locating new and interesting reading material. Children from higher socioeconomic families might embark on a family vacation or summer camp out of town in which people, places, and experiences extend background knowledge and offer new vocabulary. There is a high probability that educational and informational TV and radio are seen and heard.

Conversely, the lower SES child's summer includes a home without books, magazines, or newspapers, and lacking adults who read avidly. Transportation is limited to visit bookstores, a local library, or even to leave the neighborhood. Children seldom encounter new people, experiences, or vocabulary, which would provide growth in background knowledge. The likelihood that educational and informational TV or radio will be seen or heard is minimal.

How can you prevent the customary summer reading slide? Research gives little support to traditional summer school but a great deal to summer reading—reading *to* the child and reading *by* the child. Jimmy Kim's study of 1,600 sixth graders in eighteen schools showed that reading four to six books during the summer was enough to alleviate summer loss. The chances of a book being read during the summer were measurably increased if schools required a written report or essay, or if parents verified their child had read the book.[23]

Most libraries have summer reading incentive programs, so make sure your child is enrolled and participates. Reading Is Fundamental's (RIF) Read for Success program addresses the summer slide by motivating children to read by providing high-quality books. Access books online at sites such as Storyline Online, where actors read aloud stories; International Children's Digital Library, which contains stories from around the world; and BookSpring, which offers narrated books children can also read on their own. Finally, take your child on field trips to visit local places like a fire station, the museum, or the zoo—and talk and listen.

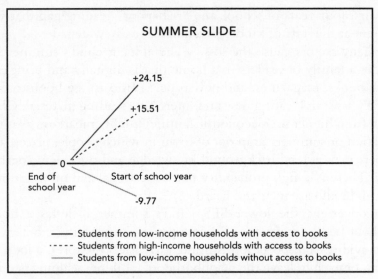

Studies show that having access to books during the summer prevents a drastic loss in reading skills, especially for children from low-income households.

Source: Slates, Stephanie L., Alexander, Karl L., Entwisle, Doris R., and Olson, Linda S. Counteracting Summer Slide: Social Capital Resources Within Socioeconomically Disadvantaged Families, *Journal of Education for Students Placed at Risk* (JESPAR), 17:3 (2012), 165–85.

How Can Independent Reading Be Encouraged at Home?

The same principles related to supporting children as independent readers at school apply at home, even more so. Indeed, consider that by the end of eighth grade a child has spent only nine thousand hours in school compared with ninety-five thousand outside school. For this reason, it behooves parents to involve themselves in reading independently at home before they challenge a teacher, "Why isn't Jesse doing better in reading this year?"

If the classroom teacher is pivotal, so is the parent. Don't tell your child to go read for fifteen minutes while you watch television. You can, of course, tailor time for pleasure reading to fit your family. Start by everyone reading for ten or fifteen minutes. Later, when they are used to reading in this manner and are more involved in books, the period can be extended—often at the child's request. As in the classroom, it is important to have a variety of available material such as magazines, newspapers, novels, picture books, and comic books. A weekly trip to the library can do much to fill this need. Three decades of NAEP research along with a thirty-two-nation study of teens showed that the more kinds of reading material in a home, the higher the child's reading scores in school.[24] Encourage children to read everything they see in the home including everyday items like shopping lists, mail, and food packaging. I should also note that the Three Bs (books, book baskets, and bed lamps) mentioned in chapter 2 are invaluable to the success of family engagement in independent reading.

The time selected for family independent reading is also significant. Involve everyone in the decision, if possible. Bedtime seems to be the most popular time, perhaps because the child does not have to give up any activity except sleeping—and most children gladly surrender that. But some children are too tired to read with engagement, so you need to take that into account as well.

When children are selecting a book to read independently, assist them by applying the "five finger rule." Using this strategy, a child opens a page in the middle of a book and begins to read, raising a finger each time she encounters an unknown word. If five fingers are raised before the end of the page, the book is probably too difficult for independent reading.[25] It might be a better choice as a read-aloud so she can still have the opportunity to hear the story.

Is Reading Independently on the Decline?

The Scholastic *Kids & Family Reading Report* surveyed 2,718 parents and children to determine attitudes and behavior regarding reading. While 86 percent of children ages six to seventeen indicated reading was very important for their future, fewer of them said they engaged in reading for fun. This was especially true with the twelve to fourteen age group.[26] A reason for not reading was the inability to find books they liked to read. The Scholastic survey also reported that Hispanic rather than African American children were more likely to be frequent readers and read books for fun.

There has also been a decline in reading among adults. The

percentages of American adults who read literature, whether it was a novel, short story, or poetry, fell to a three-decade low to 43 percent in 2016.[27]

Why do people read? They may enjoy reading anything that allows them to escape into a story. Others find satisfaction in gathering information. Some expect pleasure from the grades or diplomas they'll earn. They also might perceive that there will be more respect with peers, book club members, or a boss or teacher.

There exists oodles of challenges or difficulties confronting us while reading. Distractions are a major problem for some—TV, cell phone, video games, emails, social media, the computer, or just the chaos in the home or school. For others, there's a lack of print—no newspapers, magazines, or books to read. Perhaps people have a lack of time because they are working too many hours, raising kids, or attending school or social activities. For some, learning disabilities may impede their reading ability. A negative attitude about reading by family or peers may also influence the desire for pleasure reading.

All these factors are going to determine how often an individual reads. Remove distractions and allocate time in the day, and you will see a higher frequency of reading. And the higher that number is for students, the higher will be their chances of success in school. Those who read the most read the best.

Will Requiring Children to Read Eventually Turn Them Off?

Most parents make their child brush their teeth, clean their bedroom, or feed the family pet. Sometimes these tasks are done willingly, and other times it's not as easy. We can all concede that it's easier if the child can be *enticed* instead of forced into doing those things, but sometimes we haven't the time, choice, or patience. Why can't we apply this same logic to reading? The reason parents avoid forcing reading is fear the child will grow to hate reading and eventually stop. How true is that? Take ten-year-olds who are forced to brush their teeth or change their underwear—do they stop doing those things when they grow up? No. So why do we think forcing children to read will kill the love of reading?

Of course, the better word to use here is *require*, as opposed to *force.* Nearly all children are required to attend school, and all adults are required to observe the speed limit. The way to take the sting out of the "requirement" is to make it so appealing and delicious that it becomes a pleasure—and that's where reading aloud comes into play.

First, remember that pleasure is more often *caught than taught* (that means read aloud to them). Next:

- Make sure you, the adult role model, are seen reading daily. It works even better if you read at the same time as your child.

- Recognize that for young children, looking at the pictures in books and turning pages qualifies as "reading." Knowing how to hold a book, understanding that text goes from left to right, and learning to love stories are all early literacy skills.

- Allow children to choose the books they wish to read independently, even if they don't meet your high standards.

- Set some time parameters, short at first and then longer as children get older and read more.

- Accept newspapers, magazines, and comic books as materials that count toward reading time.

The self-selection, self-interest factor is important here. Let children read what interests *them.* Unfortunately, school summer reading lists mandate kids read what interests teachers. If that happens, read those required books at the same time as your child so you can engage in conversation about them.

If this idea of a reading obligation still puts you off, think about this: If you require a child to pick up her room or brush her teeth but don't require her to read, then it could be said that you think household and personal hygiene is more important than the child's brain cells. Doing your own independent reading also sends an obvious message that you value it for yourself as much as you do for your child.

Do Computerized "Reading Incentive" Programs Encourage Reading?

When I began teaching first grade, I was required to use a basal reader for reading instruction. Each story in the basal was usually divided up into multiple sections—one for each day of instruction—which lasted anywhere from three to six days. The stories all contained controlled and limited vocabulary. At the end of each section was a long list of questions that were intended to check children's comprehension. The stories were usually written specifically for inclusion in the basal series and were neither engaging nor exciting to read or discuss.

Children in the class were divided into reading groups based on their ability. At one point, the reading group with the most proficient readers had a "real" story, *Ira Sleeps Over* by Bernard Waber. It's a story most children can relate to about a boy who is invited to sleep over at his friend's house, but is afraid he will be made fun of if he brings his stuffed bear. The children enjoyed reading the story over two days instead of the six recommended (I finally wised up that reading a page or two a day did nothing for comprehension or fluency). On our visit to the school library the following week, one of the children located *Ira Sleeps Over* on the shelf and immediately checked it out. He couldn't wait to read it. Unfortunately, he struggled because the basal reader version had "dumbed" down the text, often eliminating some of the engaging language that makes Waber's book so enjoyable. Sadly, my student returned the book to the library the next day, filled with disappointment and frustration.

When computerized reading programs were introduced, I was excited that "real" books would be used. I wasn't thrilled that extrinsic rewards, prizes, or grades were the focus of these programs. I preferred intrinsic rewards such as reading a book for pleasure. Regardless, it seemed like a step in the right direction.

Renaissance Learning's Accelerated Reader and Scholastic's Reading Counts, the two industry leaders, work this way: The classroom or school library contains a core collection of popular and traditional children's books, each rated by difficulty (the harder and thicker the book, the more points it has). Accompanying the books is a computer program that poses questions after the student has read each book. Passing the computer quiz earns points for the reader, which can be redeemed for prizes like school T-shirts, pizza parties, or items donated by local businesses. Both programs strongly endorse independent reading as an integral part of their curriculum. The programs also require substantial library collections. Both Accelerated Reader and Reading Counts have expanded their scope to include considerable student management and assessment tools.

Over the past few years, I have grown progressively alarmed how the Accelerated Reader and Reading Counts programs are being used by school districts. An increasing number of dedicated educators and librarians also are concerned. The original design was a kind of carrot on a stick—using points and prizes to lure reluctant readers to read more. For a while, the big complaint from critics was about using points and incentives. What started as a way to encourage readers has gotten out of hand. After using this type of process, nobody reads without expecting some kind of reward.

Here is a scenario that has been painted by more than a few irate librarians (school and public) in affluent districts that are using the computerized programs:

> The parent comes into the library looking desperately for a "seven-point book."
>
> "What kind of book does your son like to read?" asks the librarian.
>
> The parent replies impatiently, "Doesn't matter. He needs seven more points to make his quota for the marking period, which ends this week. Give me anything worth seven points."

Recently, I read a post on social media from a grandmother who was concerned about her grandson in second grade. He had access to many books at home and selected those he was successful in reading independently. Unfortunately, he did not meet his Accelerated Reader yearly point goal at school. The class was going to have an all-day celebration for the kids who did reach their goal, and those who didn't would spend the day in another room, reading. In the grandmother's view, this was punishment and certainly wasn't going to motivate her grandson to read.

Another insight about the Accelerated Reader program comes from an award-winning children's book author. During a recent school visit, she was curious what the Accelerated Reader test questions were on her popular book. When she attempted to take the computerized test to determine how well she comprehended the story, she failed miserably. What does that say about the type of

READING REWARDS

Pleasures
- Escape
- Information
- Prestige
- Grades/Rewards

READING DIFFICULTIES
- Distractions
- Lack of print
- Lack of time
- Disabilities
- Negative peers

The reward for reading should be intrinsic rather than relying on a pencil, pizza, or party to be the reward.

questions being asked about the books? Structured questions also eliminate the possibility for kids to make personal connections to stories.

There are no long-term research studies with adequate control groups showing a statistically significant difference in children's reading scores using computerized reading programs. True, the students read more, but is that because the district has poured all that money into school libraries and added independent reading to the daily schedule? Where's the long-term research to compare twenty-five "computerized" classes with twenty-five classes that have rich school and classroom libraries and time for independent reading in the schedule? So far, it's not there.[28]

On the other hand, high reading scores have been achieved in communities with first-rate school and classroom libraries. In these environments, teachers motivate children by reading aloud to them, librarians give book talks, and independent reading time is an essential part of the daily curriculum. James K. Zaharis Elementary School in Mesa, Arizona, under principal Mike Oliver, is just such a place. And the money that would have gone to the computer programs went instead to building a larger library collection. Unfortunately, such schools are rare. Where the scores are low, often teachers' knowledge of children's literature is also low, the library collection is meager to dreadful, and drill-and-skill supplants time for kids to self-select books to read for pleasure.

Are There Any Other Issues Associated with These Computerized Programs?

Here are some serious negatives to guard against:[29]

- Some teachers and librarians stop reading children's and young adult books because the computer will ask the questions instead.

- Class discussion of books decreases because that would give away test answers, and all that matters is the electronic score.

- Students narrow their book selection to only those included in the program (points).

- In areas where the points are part of the grade or classroom competition, some students attempt books far beyond their level and end up frustrated.

Before committing precious dollars to such a program, a district should decide its purpose: Is the program there to motivate children to read or to create another grading platform?

All of this isn't to disparage computerized reading programs, but rather to step back and look at how they are being used. When we begin testing comprehension of real books that have been assigned a reading level, we are leveling or labeling children and their ability to read, which limits access to books they might enjoy. I'm not sure how this creates independent reading, much less lifelong readers.

What Is a Lexile and How Does It Impact Independent Reading?

Lexiles were developed in the 1980s by Malbert Smith and A. Jackson Stenner, the president and CEO of MetaMetrics. They thought education lacked what philosophers of science call unification of measurement or, in other words, a common scale that could be used for reading. What resulted was a proprietary algorithm that analyzes sentence length and vocabulary to assign a Lexile score from 0L to 2000L for the most complex texts. The Common Core State Standards adopted Lexiles to determine what books are appropriate for students at each grade level.[30]

It's not that we don't want children to find books they can read successfully. What is concerning is when Lexile measures become the sole factor in book selection and recommendation.[31] Books for a fourth grader, depending on his Lexile, could range between 470L to 950L. While *Diary of a Wimpy Kid* by Jeff Kinney would be an option for a child reading at a Lexile measure of 950L, so would Harper Lee's *To Kill a Mockingbird* at 870L, or John Steinbeck's *The Grapes of Wrath* at 680L. *Diary of a Wimpy Kid* would clearly be more appealing to most children in fourth grade, while the other two books would require a level of emotional maturity in order to grasp the critical issues dealt with in the stories.

Parents, teachers, and librarians need to be cautious in rigidly adhering to these types of measures. We want to promote reading, not restrict it. We also hope that children learn to self-select books, particularly for independent reading, without having to consult a list to see if it is within their Lexile numbers.

How Can I Make Sure They Are Reading "Quality" Literature If There Aren't Lists To Tell Me?

It's important to remember a major component of independent reading is choice. And often the choice is a series book. Many of us developed our "reading teeth" on series books such as Nancy Drew, Junie B. Jones, Goosebumps, or the Matt Christopher sports books. Authors recognize series books are part of our literary heritage, and they treat them as such.[32] During a presentation at the American Library Association Conference, author Avi stated, "Series books are 'children's literature' more than anything else because kids don't see adults reading them. Kids treat them as their *literary* family."

Why do kids love series books so much? One reason is the familiarity of getting to know the character. They laugh at their antics and understand their behavior because the author is consistent in the continued development of the character. When author Annie Barrows had determined that ten books in the Ivy + Bean series would be enough, readers thought otherwise. They started sending Barrows letters to try to convince her to continue the series, and it worked! The eleventh book, *Ivy + Bean: One Big Happy Family*, was published in 2018. Readers had come to know and love the two central characters in her books.

Children also select series books because the plot is often predictable with a simple sentence structure. Amateur detectives who enjoy Nate the Great by Marjorie Weinman Sharmat are generally able to solve the mystery before the boy sleuth. This is because readers have come to understand the formula Sharmat uses in crafting this popular series.

And finally, kids experience a sense of accomplishment when

they finish reading a book and eagerly anticipate the next one. Feeling like a successful reader is empowering for children.

Comic books are another frequent childhood choice of people who grow up to become fluent readers.[33] The reasons for their popularity and success are the same as for series books. Comic books have evolved into what is termed a "graphic" format. Young children may need to be shown how a comic "works": the sequence of the panels, how to tell when a character is thinking and when he is speaking, and the meaning of stars, question marks, and exclamation points. For many children who are struggling with reading, connect him or her with comics. More information about graphic novels is provided in chapter 8 along with recommended titles in the Treasury.

How Did Oprah So Successfully Get People Reading?

Oprah and her producers were smart enough at the very beginning not to use the word *class*. They knew very well the connotations carried by that word with many in their audience: requirements, demands, and tests. So they used the word *club*, which suggests belonging, membership, and invitation.

Having selected a book, Oprah walked out to her audience of twenty-two million people and talked about the book she'd chosen. She talked animatedly, passionately, and sincerely. No writing, no tests, no dumb dioramas to make, just good old-fashioned enthusiasm. Although she went off the air in 2011, she continues making book recommendations through her website and magazine.

Above everything else, that is the key to Oprah's Book Club success—she recognized what too many educators have forgotten: We're an oral species. We define ourselves first and foremost orally. When we see a suspenseful movie, an exhilarating ball game, a stimulating concert—the first thing we want to do afterward is talk about it. After my husband and I see an awesome movie, do you think we rush out to the car, pull napkins out of the glove compartment, and write down the main idea? "Honey, what do you think was the theme?"

When Oprah began her book club, there were 250,000 discussion groups nationally. Today, there are more than 500,000 such groups[34] (and I regret to say nearly all of them are female). Other celebrities have created book clubs such as Jimmy Fallon, who offers five options and then asks his viewers to go online and vote for their favorite book. There's also Reese Witherspoon, who has made such a success of her literary picks that publishers are now putting "Reese's Book Club" stickers on her selections. And then there's Sarah Jessica Parker, who partnered with the American Library Association to share her book suggestions. What this says is that reading is valued. It also shows what can happen when a celebrity suggests a book, and even though they aren't literary experts, they show they are readers.

If you're contemplating a book discussion club for a family or class, my favorite guide is *Deconstructing Penguins: Parents, Kids, and the Bond of Reading* by Lawrence and Nancy Goldstone, a manual on how to "dig a tunnel" into the heart and soul of a book. As the authors note, "You don't need an advanced degree in English literature or forty hours a week of free time to effectively discuss a book with your child. This isn't *Crime and Punishment*, it's *Charlotte's Web*."[35]

While Oprah, Reese, Sarah, and Jimmy aren't technically reading teachers, they are inspiring others to read. That is the type of person who we hope a child meets when he enters a school or library. If children encounter a teacher or librarian who is essentially a celebrity book club clone, they're far more likely to be inspired to start reading the particular author or book she recommends. Now the kid is reading, and reading a lot—outside of school, where he has the most time: on the bus, in bed, on the toilet, in the car, and at the breakfast table. And through all those pages, he's accumulating the vocabulary words he might not be hearing at home or from family. That is a gigantic gift for any child.

Chapter 5

The Importance of Dads

> With Dad by my side, there's nothing we
> can't do.
>
> —*Dad by My Side* by Soosh[1]

IN author and illustrator Soosh's debut picture book, *Dad by My Side*, a father engages in a variety of memorable activities with his child such as playing make-believe, trying new things, and even warding off monsters that lurk under the bed. These activities promote a positive and lasting parent-child bond—as does a father reading aloud a story to his child.

A colleague, Sean Dudley, is a single father of two boys and serves as the executive director of research technology at Arizona State University. Sean is someone who is always pushing himself both personally and professionally, especially in the area of technology. He traces his inquisitiveness back to his parents—particularly his father. Both his parents read aloud to him and his siblings, but it was predominantly his father. Sean recalls a Reader's Digest book series that contained stories such as *Rikki-Tikki-Tavi* by Rudyard Kipling. "It was always something a little bit beyond our level. I realize now that he didn't hold us back, and by the time I was seven, we were reading *The Lord of the Rings* by J. R. R. Tolkien. He would ask us questions like, 'What do you think about that? What do you think that means?'" Sean treasures the time he spent listening to stories. Today, he is creating that sense of bonding, through read-aloud, with his sons.

Sean's sons are fortunate their father reads to them and contributes markedly to their literacy development. Unfortunately, this isn't the case in all households. Research studies indicate there are problems with boys and schooling. Here are some recent statistics:

♦ The Brown Center Report on American Education stated that boys continue to lag behind girls in the area of reading.[2] This isn't something that is occurring only in the United States but is prevalent around the world. The Progress in International Reading Literacy Study (PIRLS)[3] and the Programme for International Student Assessment (PISA)[4] both found evidence of this gender gap that has continued for more than a decade. The disparity exists between scores with younger children as well as for those in high school.

♦ On Scholastic's 2016 survey of over two thousand U.S. children ages six to seventeen, the percentage of boys who read books frequently had decreased from 32 percent in 2010 to 24 percent in 2014.[5] The report shared that girls are more likely than boys to say reading books for fun is extremely or very important. Positive views of independent reading at school were voiced by 61 percent of girls compared to 44 percent of boys. For years, librarians, teachers, and parents have witnessed the decline of boys reading independently, and research continues to examine the reasons why this is occurring.

♦ Unlike four decades ago, it is now common for girls to dominate a high school's highest academic positions with 70 percent of them serving as valedictorian.[6] Girls are being elected to class leadership positions, occupying advanced placement spaces, and participating in multiple school activities.[7]

♦ Between 2005 and 2015, the number of female students enrolling in colleges and universities rose 12 percent, while the number of male students rose 17 percent. However, 56 percent of college students in 2015 were female,[8] and this trend continues.

Tom Chiarella is one of the best long-form writers in the country today, covering everything from food to cinema, from sports to architecture. He's also a visiting professor at DePauw University, and it was the male culture he witnessed on college campuses that provoked him to write an article for *Esquire* titled "The Problem with Boys . . . Is Actually a Problem with Men." It's a piece so powerful, pediatricians should print out copies and hand it to every new father they encounter. Chiarella summarizes his concerns for boys in this country today:

> You're twice as likely as a girl to be diagnosed with an attention-deficit or learning disorder. You're more likely to score worse on standardized reading and writing tests. You're more likely to be held back in school. You're more likely to drop out of school. If you do graduate, you're less likely to go to college. If you do go to college, you will get lower grades and, once again, you will be less likely to graduate. You'll be twice as likely to abuse alcohol, and until you are twenty-four, you are five times as likely to kill yourself. You are more than sixteen times as likely to go to prison.[9]

Naturally, there is a vocal group of male defenders who say it's all a mirage. They blame Hispanic and African American boys, claiming their scores lower the overall male average.[10] While it's true that African American boys have the lower reading scores, that can't account for the lack of white male participation in school activities, leadership positions, and graduation rates. The public schools in Maine are 96 percent white, yet the male-female achievement gap is among the five widest in the United States at both the high school and college levels.[11]

What Do We Know About Boys as Readers?

One reason boys are lagging behind in reading is because they have fewer male role models who encourage them to read.[12] Boys also claim they don't view reading as enjoyable because the material they like to read is often not allowed in school or doesn't count as "real reading."[13] There is also a prevailing belief that boys don't like to read. That common misperception inadvertently reinforces the idea boys have a lower aptitude for reading. In an article printed in the *Telegraph*, Frank Furedi affirmed, "If we want to cultivate a love of reading among boys, we need to raise our expectations of them. This requires a drastic rethink by those educators who have internalized the doctrine of male-reading deficit."[14]

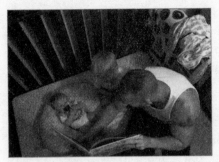

Fathers reading aloud to their children have a profound and lasting impact on both sons and daughters.

Boys do read! However, it might not be the books that parents, teachers, and librarians are putting in their hands. When Matt de la Peña received the Newbery Medal in 2016 for his lyrical picture book *Last Stop on Market Street*, he shared in his acceptance speech about reading when he was younger:[15]

I didn't read past page twenty-seven of *The Catcher in the Rye*, but I read *Basketball Digest* cover to cover. Every single month. I'd show up at my junior high library an hour before school, find an empty table in back, and tuck the latest issue inside the covers of the most highbrow book I could find—usually some Russian novel with a grip of names I couldn't pronounce. Mrs. Frank, the warm-smiling librarian, would occasionally stroll past my table and say, "*War and Peace*, huh? How are you liking that one so far?"

"Oh, it's great, miss," I'd tell her. "I really like all the wars and stuff. And how it eventually turns peaceful." She'd grin and nod and move on to the next table. I'd grin, too, marveling at my own slick ways. But then a few days later she'd confuse me by sliding the newest *Basketball Digest* across the table to me with a wink.

Back then I never would've described myself as a reader, but Mrs. Frank knew better. And the truth is, I wasn't reading those magazines for stats or standings, I was reading to find out what certain players had to overcome to get where they were. I was in it for the narrative. And what I found in some of the better articles wasn't that inferior to what I would later discover when I read *War and Peace* for real.

Matt didn't see himself as a reader, which unfortunately is fairly common with boys. But he was reading. Maybe not *War and Peace* but rather something he was interested in and later gave him the basis for what would become his first novel, *Ball Don't Lie*. We need to value what boys want to read. Otherwise, they'll never navigate through the difficult text encountered as they progress through school.

What are the characteristics of books boys gravitate toward? They are generally humorous stories rather than ones filled with drama and emotions.[16] Boys also prefer books that are visually appealing such as graphic novels or magazines, contain main characters they can relate to, and focus on nonfiction topics that interest them. Chapter books under a hundred pages, short stories, poetry, and novels in verse are also desirable reading material.

For boys, it comes down to choice. Home, school, and classroom libraries should contain a variety of magazines, newspapers, comics, graphic novels, nonfiction, and picture books. Let's support boys in their reading journeys and stop perceiving them as nonreaders.

What Role Do Fathers Play in Reading Aloud?

In the National Literacy Trust's white paper *Why Fathers Matter to Their Children's Literacy*, several studies are cited indicating men may be "discouraged from becoming involved in literacy activities because of preconceived gender roles, feelings of inadequacy in their own literacy, and prioritizing their needs, abilities, and interests."[17] Other studies have documented that fathers' involvement with their children can be linked to higher educational achievement.[18] A father's interest in his children's education has been found to have more influence on education success than family background, the child's personality, or poverty.[19]

Often dads select humorous books to read aloud.

Linda Jacobson's article "Why Boys Don't Read" suggests it may be more cultural,[20] concluding that many boys do not have a male role model who reads. She suggests this lack of influence and motivation discourages boys from picking up books for enjoyment. Sometimes fathers are uncertain about their role in their children's learning and often defer to their wives for reading to the kids.[21]

Why is it so important fathers read aloud to their children?

- The time a father spends with his child is one of the most consistent links to the development of literacy skills throughout the child's schooling.[22] Fathers have a profound impact on their child's desire for reading and their success in doing so.

- Children are motivated when they see their most important male role model, their father, reading, and that includes picking up a book and reading it aloud.

- Fathers tend to take a book to another level as they try to connect what is in the story to something in the child's life. Mothers focus more on a character's feelings, but dads push kids in their thinking.[23] For example, if the book is about dinosaurs, dad might say, "Do you remember how big the stegosaurus was we saw at the museum?"

- Bedtime read-alouds create one of the strongest bonding times, especially between fathers and sons. This positive influence is also experienced by their daughters.[24]

- Reading aloud is a time to relax. Who can't help but laugh when reading *The 13-Storey Treehouse* by Andy Griffiths? Hearing a story relaxes not only a child, it does the same for dad.

- Dads read different books and read books differently than moms. *Walter the Farting Dog* by William Kotzwinkle sounds sillier when dad reads it. The rollicking Elephant and Piggie series by Mo Willems contains speech bubbles and invites mom and dad to find their inner theatrical self. Both can do a great job reading these books aloud, but they sound different because the readers are different. *Diary of a Wimpy Kid* by Jeff Kinney is also a superb book for dads to read aloud. He can tell about his own experiences in middle school.

In chapter 2, I shared the story that inspired *The Reading Promise: My Father and the Books We Shared* by Alice Ozma. This engaging book conveys the literary and personal journey between a father and daughter who began by trying to read for a streak of 100 days that stretched to 3,218 days. In the introduction, Alice writes, "This is a book about how books can bring people together and how that bond can last a lifetime." The books they read were secondary to the experiences they created and the discussions about their lives that ensued. Alice's father, Jim Brozina, sums it up: "The greatest gift you can bestow upon your children is your time and undivided attention."

How Can Fathers Read Aloud If They Aren't Always Home?

Sometimes a dad's quality time spent with his children can be limited. That might be caused by the family situation when parents don't live together, economic pressures that require working long hours or multiple jobs, or participating in outside interests such as sports. Even without a consistent physical presence in the home, dads can still fulfill the promise of reading aloud.

While I was patiently waiting at the Department of Motor Vehicles to obtain new license plates for my car after moving to Arizona, I struck up a conversation with the gentleman sitting next to me. He noticed I had *The Read-Aloud Handbook* in my hands (as I carried it with me everywhere while working on the revisions). He said that he enjoyed reading aloud to his young children, but he's now divorced and doesn't have that opportunity. I asked if he spent time with them during the week or on weekends. He replied yes, but that time was usually filled with doing homework or spending quality time together in activities like going to movies, out to the local fast-food restaurant, or to the kids' soccer games. Besides, the kids' books were not at his home. Naturally, I shared with him that I thought quality time *was* reading aloud to children and that they should have a library at his home as well.

He also told me he video chatted with the kids each night when they weren't with him. I suggested he spend part of that time reading aloud a picture book or a chapter in a longer book that would set up the excitement and anticipation of continuing the story the next time they saw him.

When my number was finally called to get my license plates, I told him if he needed suggestions for books or other ideas for reading aloud, please contact me. He sent me an email a few weeks later and shared he was enjoying reading aloud again with his children and it was strengthening the bond that was somewhat fractured after his divorce. Hooray! Another success story.

A worthy suggestion author Mem Fox provided in her book

Reading Magic was for fathers to take a book with them to work or when they travel so if they have to stay late at the office or are out of town for several days, they can still read aloud to their children. This goes for dads who live with their children and for those who don't. One of the advantages of technology is that it offers us the opportunity to have these interactions. While it's always better sitting side by side during a read-aloud, video chat presents a viable alternative.

There are many fathers (and mothers) who serve in the military. One organization, United Through Reading, states on its website, "Every year, more than 100,000 military parents deploy leaving nearly 250,000 children at home. A conservative separation is about six months—that means these military children have 180 nights without their parent home for a bedtime story. That's forty million bedtimes stories missed each year by military children."[25] This organization serves all branches of the armed services and has set up over two hundred locations for personnel to record the stories they read aloud. The recording and the book are then made available to their children. Because time zones and military schedules aren't conducive to always being able to call or video chat, the recorded read-aloud gives children the opportunity to create that virtual bond with dad or mom and also to revisit the read-aloud over and over.

There are other parent-child separations that occur. Unfortunately, too many men are incarcerated and separated from their children. In the Baltimore County Detention Center, fathers receive instruction on how to read aloud effectively. When children visit their dads or connect with them via video, the father reads aloud a story. Inmates have said they didn't realize how much fun reading could be. Others reported they initially were embarrassed by their lack of reading skills but now feel confident reading with their children.[26]

In the United Kingdom, over 200,000 children experience the trauma of parental imprisonment. Storybook Dads is a program where fathers can make bedtime story CDs, DVDs, and other educational gifts for their children from jail. It is reported that 50 percent of prisoners lose contact with their families, and those who maintain contact are up to six times less likely to reoffend.[27] Both of these unique programs help reunify and bond families while increasing the literacy skills of parent and child.

What if there isn't a father present at all in a child's life? Try to connect boys with men who read. Uncles and grandparents can help to fill that void. Look to male principals or teachers who will read aloud books before school, during lunch, or after school. Fathers, or their male counterpart, can form book clubs for boys. Or set one up with local community organizations such as the Boy Scouts or Boys & Girls Clubs of America. Are there male members of your church who might spend time reading aloud to your son or even talk about a book he is reading? If a local bookstore brings in male authors to speak about the books they write for children and young adults, make sure you take the time to attend. Grab the youth league soccer coach and ask him to spend a few minutes at the end of practice to read aloud a story about a soccer player or athlete to inspire the kids. There are a lot of male role models available in the neighborhood and community. Sometimes it just takes asking them to read a story to your child.

How Do We Get Dads Involved?

In the previous edition of *The Read-Aloud Handbook*, Jim Trelease talked about conducting parent programs in schools, public libraries, and local bookstores. Regardless of the community, there was always a shortage of fathers attending, usually by a ten to one ratio of mothers to fathers. I have discovered a similar ratio during programs I have presented about reading aloud.

The strange thing about "reluctant reading daddies" is they're found at all education levels. When poverty-level families and university-educated families were compared, fathers in both groups read to their children only 15 percent of the time, mothers 76 percent, and others 9 percent.[28] That could change if we publicized studies like the one conducted in Modesto, California, which showed that (1) boys who were read to by their fathers scored significantly higher in reading achievement, and (2) when fathers read recreationally, their sons read more and scored higher than did boys whose fathers did little or no recreational reading. When the dads were surveyed, only 10 percent reported having fathers who read to them when they were children.[29]

So how do we get fathers more involved with reading and school? How about having them read this chapter? Not the whole book (unless they want to)—just this chapter. If dad is lost as to what to read (since he might not have been a reader as a child), the list of books sprinkled throughout this chapter or located in the Treasury of Recommended Read-Alouds will help. If you're a father who has never been much of a reader, change that pattern for the next generation in your family. Start with picture books and work your way up to novels, side by side, with your kids.

Having an older sibling read to younger ones can provide another reading role model.

Sometimes the best picture books to create a bonding experience, as well as prompt discussion, are those that highlight the father-son relationship. *Made for Me* by Zack Bush begins with the birth of a child, to the first utterance of "Dada," to the unsteady steps of a toddler. "Of all the children that could ever be, you are the one made just for me."

A similar theme is in *If I Didn't Have You* by Alan Katz. Mike and his father think about all the different things they could be doing if they didn't have each other—father owning a two-seater sports car and pursuing his dream of being a rock star and Mike's thoughts about watching TV all the time and eating candy nonstop. But both decide, "I'd rather have you."

Every Friday by Dan Yaccarino celebrates that special time spent with dad. All week long, a boy and his father look forward to their Friday ritual of eating breakfast at the local diner. The time spent walking through the neighborhood is just as good as the pancakes they eat together.

If you're a dad who thinks he's amusing, then *My Dad Thinks He's Funny* by Katrina Germein is the perfect read-aloud. "When people say, 'How are you feeling?' Dad says, 'With my hands.'" Or what about a father who seems to know it all? Jane Yolen's *My Father Knows the Names of Things* would be the ideal read-aloud.

There are plenty of picture books that provide limitless fun and invite interaction. *The Legend of Rock Paper Scissors* by Drew Daywalt tells how those three famous and unbeatable warriors—rock, paper, scissors—became fighting foes that are still battling today. Expressive fonts and hilarious illustrations by Adam Rex make this a laugh-out-loud winner. Other books by Daywalt are just as side-splitting.

In *Snip Snap! What's That?* by Mara Bergman, an alligator comes calling at the children's door and moves through the house with a repetitive question being asked, "Were they scared?" eliciting the response (louder and louder each time), "You bet they were!" Kids (and dad) can't help but join in when they see that question on the page.

Papa tells his little red chicken to not interrupt during the bedtime story, but she can't help herself in *Interrupting Chicken* by David Ezra Stein. Whatever Papa reads, the chicken jumps into the story to save the hapless characters from their imminent demise. Can Papa make it to the end of the story without his own kind of interrupting?

How about reading poetry? *My Daddy Rules the World: Poems About Dads* by Hope Anita Smith is told through a child's voice and celebrates everyday displays of fatherly love from wrestling matches to bedtime stories. You can't go wrong reading aloud poems from *Where the Sidewalk Ends* or *A Light in the Attic* by Shel Silverstein. Another poet, Douglas Florian, pens hugely enjoyable poetry including *Poem Depot: Aisles of Smiles*.

Need to slip in some sports? The picture book *Becoming Babe Ruth*, written and illustrated by Matt Tavares, chronicles the legendary baseball player's life. For older kids, Kwame Alexander's Newbery Medal–winning *The Crossover* is a novel written in verse about twin brothers who play junior high basketball and their father, a former professional player. The short chapter book series *Who Was?* focuses on athletes from a variety of sports including *Who Is Wayne Gretzky?* or *Who Was Muhammad Ali?*

If you are looking for a great read-aloud for older children, try the brief novel *Stone Fox*, by John Reynolds Gardiner, about running the Iditarod or *Hatchet*, by Gary Paulsen, about surviving alone in the wilderness. Dip anyplace into the pages of *Uncle John's Bathroom Reader for Kids Only!* for a brain-boggling easy-to-read collection of facts, fads, quotes, history, science, origins, pop culture, mythology, humor, and more.

In case you missed David Lubar's short story "Kid Appeal" in *Guys Read: Funny Business*, a humor collection for boys, here's one paragraph:

There are lots of other things that make someone a great best friend, like loyalty and courage. Dwight's totally loyal. He'd never tell on me, no matter what I did. Even though he got six weeks of detention, Dwight never admitted he had help when he dumped twenty packs of cherry Kool-Aid into the school's new fishpond. I swear we thought there weren't any fish in it yet. I guess it's a good thing only two of them were hiding in there at the time. They looked real pretty right before they turned belly up. It was sort of like a Dr. Seuss story. One fish, two fish. Red Fish, dead fish.[30]

Dad—when you read to a child you get a second chance in life: to meet and enjoy the books you missed out on as a kid. Who knows, you might even meet some of your childhood buddies along the way, like Dwight.

Chapter 6

The Print Climate in the Home, School, and Library

> The library lady looked at Tomás for a long time.
> She said, "Tomás, would you like to borrow two
> library books? I will check them out in
> my name."
>   Tomás walked out of the library carrying his
> books. He ran home, eager to show the new sto-
> ries to his family.
>
> —*Tomás and the Library Lady* by Pat Mora[1]

TOMÁS Rivera, who was born to migrant parents and went on to become the first Mexican American to serve as chancellor at the University of California, Riverside, understood the importance of books early in his life. What if all children had access to high-quality literature? How would their reading lives be enhanced through book ownership? Unfortunately, there are homes, schools, and communities that contain few or no books and possibly have not seen a new book in decades.

It's difficult to get good at reading if you're short of print. Mandated government programs like No Child Left Behind and Race to the Top tried to ensure children who were behind in reading were entitled to after-school tutoring and extra help with phonics. However, giving phonics lessons to kids who don't have any print in their lives is like giving oars to people who don't have a boat—you don't get very far. In December 2015, President Obama signed the Every Student Succeeds Act (ESSA), which reauthorized the Elementary and Secondary Education Act from fifty years ago and focused on equal opportunity for all students.[2] A few years later, under a new administration, states were able to provide their own plan for meeting the provisions of ESSA and improving student outcomes, particularly in the area of reading. The results of implementing ESSA are yet to be determined.

This point bears repeating: *For students to progress and succeed in reading, they need to have access to print.* However, not all children have the same access to books and libraries. It would seem the gap in the American print climate—home or school—is entirely fixable. Price is not a problem. If we can rebuild Afghanistan and Iraq at the cost of $800-plus billion,[3] we can easily fix all the urban schools and public libraries in America. All we have to do is believe it's worth it. If we had to, we could build a strong case that it would fall under the purview of Homeland Security: Today's desperate fifteen-year-old semiliterate in urban America could be tomorrow's unemployed homegrown terrorist.

The past two decades of studies conducted by respected researchers like Susan B. Neuman,[4] Nell Duke,[5] Stephen Krashen,[6] Richard Allington,[7] and Keith Curry Lance[8] powerfully connect access to print with higher reading scores and, conversely, lack of access with lower scores. It's a shame the education experts haven't figured this out, even when one of the researchers (Neuman) was an assistant secretary of education in Washington.

The National Assessment of Educational Progress (NAEP) has measured student performance in most major subjects since 1972. It has also been surveying students on the number of books in their homes, then drawing correlations to their scores in reading, math, science, civics, history, and writing. In every test subject, the more books in the home, the higher the score, often by as much as forty points. In fact, the prevalence of books often compensates for differences in parental education.[9] International studies have drawn the same conclusion[10]—the larger the school and classroom libraries, the higher the students' reading scores.[11]

More than thirteen states have produced research connecting a stronger library program to increases in student scores. That includes James Baughman's research on the Massachusetts Comprehensive Assessment System (MCAS) exam. This research revealed a greater number of books per pupil along with a full-time librarian meant an eleven-point advantage. Also, a higher percentage of the student body visiting the library per week accounted for a twelve-point advantage.[12]

Aware of the negative impact of the summer slide,[13] the low scores of impoverished children, and how little access they have to print outside of school, researchers identified 852 early-primary student participants at seventeen high-poverty schools. That group would be compared with 478 similar students in a control group for study conducted over three consecutive summers.[14]

During the spring semester, the experimental students were allowed to select twelve paperback books at a school book fair. These books would not be given to the students until the beginning of each summer vacation but would be theirs to keep. The control group had no book fair and received no free books for the summer. The books placed in the fair were selected in advance and at early-primary reading levels. The selections were aimed at meeting students' interests in pop culture (movie, sports stars), series books, minority characters, science, and social studies.

The result after three years: The experimental group had significantly higher reading achievement, compared with the control group, directly attributed to more frequent reading over three straight summers. Personal ownership of the books and students' ability to make selections were key to their improvement in reading. Interestingly, the most disadvantaged students had the highest gains of all participants in the study.

Does the Disappearance of Newspapers in the Home Have an Impact?

Newspapers and magazines are the home's "soft" library. For a century they were commonplace enough to be taken for granted. But behind the scenes, they were conditioning children to print materials. Being so commonplace in the home, newspapers and magazines were literacy torches passed from parent to child.

The daily newspaper and weekly magazines are presently on life support and the slowest-growing industry in the United States from the largest cities to the smallest hamlet. The estimated total U.S. daily print and digital newspaper circulation in 2017 was thirty-one million for weekday and thirty-four million for Sunday, down 11 percent and 10 percent, respectively, from the previous year.[15]

Weekly and monthly magazine circulations are dropping as well. The print version of *Reader's Digest*, once the world's most popular American magazine, has sunk from 23 million to 2.6 million. However, the online version soared in 2018 with 11.7 million visitors, which was a 179 percent increase from the previous year.[16] Staffers at print magazines like *Time* permanently have their bags packed. Even the 110-year-old classroom staple *Weekly Reader* saw its demise in 2012.[17]

These are the publications by which whole generations in America were assimilated into the world of reading, and now the print versions have all but evaporated. David Carr of the *New York Times* painted a vivid portrait of the print chasm in today's family, recalling how he grew up in a home where his father and brother jousted for the newspaper (the Minneapolis *Star Tribune*) over breakfast. Watching them imbibing the scores and headlines over breakfast, Carr thought:

> This . . . is what it means to be a grown-up. You eat your food standing up, and you read the newspaper. So I did the same thing when I turned 13. I still do.
>
> Last Wednesday morning at my house, one of my daughters back from college was staying at a friend's house in the city, no doubt getting alerts on her cellphone for new postings to her Facebook page. Her sister got up, skipped breakfast and checked the mail for her Netflix movies. My wife left early before the papers even arrived to commute to her job in the city while listening to the iPod she got for Christmas.
>
> True enough, my 10-year-old gave me five minutes over a bowl of Cheerios, but then she went into the dining room and opened the laptop to surf the Disney Channel on broadband, leaving me standing in the kitchen with my four newspapers. A few of those included news about the sale of *The Star Tribune*, a newspaper that found itself . . . being sold at a reduced price to a private equity group.
>
> I looked around me and realized I didn't really need to read the papers to know why.[18]

Many newspapers are available for reading online, but that's done out of children's sight line, not with a paper waving in their faces. Furthermore, most young parents can't be bothered anymore. Reading a newspaper is becoming more out of fashion. A Pew Research Center study revealed only 18 percent of the population in 2017 got their news from printed newspapers.[19] We get the news from RSS feeds, blogs, notification alerts, Google, and, of course, from our 729 friends on social media sites such as Twitter, Facebook, and Instagram.

What does this say about access? Some online newspapers are free or you can read a limited number of articles. You never find someone's tablet laying around where you can read today's paper. We're discovering that the news appearing on Facebook and other social media sites can't always be trusted. It becomes an issue not only of having access but also having the knowledge and skills to identify fake news when you read it.

How Many Books Should Be in the Home Library?

The mere presence of books can often be enough. Not two hundred of them or even fifty, but a dozen to call your own, with enough pages to occupy a child's imagination on winter nights or rainy days.

Think of the impact a handful of books made on one boy and the impact he made on so many afterward. He was ten at the time, and he and his sister were considered a bit uncivilized, though he'd had a year's worth of schooling and had learned to read. His school didn't have enough books for each child, and his family owned no books until his stepmother arrived with a small collection. Although illiterate herself, she knew the power contained in print and impressed that immediately, but kindly, on the boy. She became his best friend, and eventually he became president of the United States.

The stack of books—what one writer later described as the equivalent of today's iPad—included *Aesop's Fables*, *Robinson Crusoe*, *The Pilgrim's Progress*, and *Sinbad the Sailor*. These weren't Little Golden Book versions; these were the real thing, and included text like this:

> My father left me a considerable estate, the best part of which I
> spent in riotous living during my youth; but I perceived my error,
> and reflected that riches were perishable, and quickly consumed by

such ill managers as myself. I further considered that by my irregular way of living I had wretchedly misspent my time which is the most valuable thing in the world. —from *Sinbad the Sailor*

What the little stack of books and Sarah Bush Lincoln did for a boy named Abraham was ignite the love of reading in him and open a world beyond the forty-family hamlet of Little Pigeon Creek, Indiana. As he "read everything he could get his hands on," it dawned on him there could be more to life than tilling and harvesting a field.[20] And that changed America forever.

Print in the home is a proven life changer worldwide. Using data from seventy thousand families in twenty-seven nations, accumulated over multiple decades, researchers showed more books in the home led to a higher grade-level completion rate.[21] The higher the number of books in the home library (0, 25, 75, 500), the greater were the chances of the student completing ninth grade, high school, or university, even after adjusting for parents' income, education, and occupation.

If book ownership and home libraries have a positive influence on reading, what about children who grow up in homes and go to schools where there are no books or very limited numbers of books? According to Reading Is Fundamental (RIF), a nonprofit literacy organization in the United States, there is only one book for every three hundred kids in underserved communities in this country.[22] And if there are no books in the home, there probably isn't much going on in relation to reading aloud to children.

The great thing about home libraries is they don't have to take up a lot of space. What's most important is your child has ownership of the collection (big or small) and that she feels it belongs to her. A corner of her bedroom is often the perfect spot where books are always readily available. Use a bookcase, crates, or anything that will hold books. Just make sure that the shelves are low enough for your child to reach. If there isn't space, then put shelves on the walls. Rain gutters make inexpensive and effective holders for books because the covers can be faced out (these are also great to use in a classroom). A book cover is more enticing than the spine of a book and will catch the eye and interest of your child.

Try to rotate books that are on display or in the collection. If your child received books as gifts or even from the school book order, put one or two out at a time. If the book isn't an all-time favorite, you can exchange a few books with other parents. Of course, one of the best ways to have a new selection of books is to go to the public library on a frequent basis. Kids can also make their own books to include in the home library.

Little Free Libraries are available in many neighborhoods and near schools, providing book access to children. Once finished, they can trade for another book.

It stands to reason that if children are going to become competent readers and we're not giving them time to read recreationally in school (because they're too busy doing test prep), then the reading must be done at home. The obstacles to home reading are (1) at-risk homes contain the least amount of print, and (2) libraries in at-risk neighborhoods are open the fewest hours and are the first ones cut or closed if there's a budget shortfall. This makes it imperative for communities to do everything in their power to cultivate a rich print environment for *all* families.

If Public and School Libraries Are So Important, Why Are They the First to Get Cut in Hard Times?

It has become the norm to cut library services whenever a community or state runs low on funds. The fact that the library has been there for so long, taken for granted, and is free leads some people to see it as worthless, a faceless victim. It even happens with school libraries.

Public libraries play such a pivotal role in communities. They offer free resources to everyone regardless of socioeconomic status. These resources extend beyond books to computers, résumé writing, filling out government forms, and providing information on numerous topics.[23] Libraries assist English-language learners with the opportunity to access magazines, newspapers, books, audiobooks, and the internet. Libraries often provide a refuge for the homeless and underserved populations. They also deliver programming for young children and teenagers throughout the year, particularly during the summer to keep kids reading.

Children's book author Gary Paulsen has shared that when he was thirteen, a public librarian "got me to read, and somehow the reading triggered something in me that made me want to be a writer. . . . The librarian was a wonderful lady and just steered me into books. I was a street kid, probably on my way to jail. My folks were drunks. And she saved me, she really did."[24] If Paulsen hadn't been motivated to read and write, we wouldn't have gripping survival stories such as *Hatchet* or *Woodsong* or experienced Paulsen's humor in *Harris and Me*. There are hundreds of stories like Paulsen's that illustrate the importance and impact on communities of public libraries and librarians.

In the previous edition of *The Read-Aloud Handbook*, Jim Trelease shared the story of an extraordinary public library rescue effort in 2012 in Troy, Michigan, that warranted being included in this edition.

With a median household income of $85,000 (nearly double the state average), Troy met the Great Recession with a resolve that it wasn't going to go the way of Detroit. When state support declined by 20 percent, the city told the Troy Public Library (243,000 books) that it didn't have the funds to keep it alive any longer. The library sought support through a tax increase of 0.7 percent, but voters turned it down twice, led by strong support from local political forces. Finally a last-gasp third vote was planned for August 2—just when many families would be away on vacation. If they lost on this vote, the library would be closed and its contents sold.

What to do? In mid-June, library supporters, with $3,500 in hand, sought help from the famous Leo Burnett advertising agency, which had a regional headquarters right there in Troy. The agency reasoned that if the same 19 percent of voters turned out for the next election, the results would be the same. How to convince the rest of Troy to turn out, the ones who took the library for granted?

Previous votes had focused on the tax increase, but the real issue was the life of the library. A vote to close the library would really be a vote to betray—*burn*, if you will—the books. Now *that* would start a different kind of conversation, wouldn't it?

The agency and library supporters formed a fake community action group called Safeguarding American Families (SAFe) and, posing as opponents of the tax increase, flooded Troy with announcements in social media, along with lawn signs, with the message: "Vote to close Troy library Aug. 2nd, book burning party Aug. 5th." They even placed an ad for clowns and ice-cream vendors for the burning party.[25]

Suddenly, the debate was no longer just about money but about the very life of the library. Library users of all ages were awakened, even secretly taking down SAFe's signs at night. (SAFe replaced them with more signs.) The debate and resulting furor made state, national, and international news, and finally, two weeks before the election, SAFe revealed itself as a faux opponent. By then, the patrons and voters were awake enough to double previous voter turnout (38 percent) and give the library a landslide victory. The advertising agency, in turn, won both national and international awards for the campaign.

California is one state that has been watched over the years as the number of school librarians has dwindled. This state has the largest child-poverty population and the lowest support for school and public libraries. Last in the nation for funding in 1996, support increased from 1998 to 2001 to $158.5 million, due to the California Public School Library Act.[26] In 2002, the funds were reduced by

87 percent, which equated to $3.46 per pupil spending; in 2003, it was further reduced by 5 percent or $1.51 per pupil and falling to $0.71 per pupil in 2004.[27]

A new funding model, the School Library Improvement Block Grant, allocated increased funding from 2005 to 2009. Since the demise of the block grant, the primary source of library funding for 51 percent of California schools comes from fund-raising activities. No surprise that wealthier schools are reaching out to parents to ask families to help fund school libraries while poorer communities aren't able to do so.

By the reckoning of its own Department of Education, the ratio of school librarian to student in California ranked dead last in the nation in 2014-15. This equates to one librarian for every 7,187 students, more than five times the national average.[28] Even the state's adult prison system does better, with one librarian to 4,283 inmates.[29]

Additionally, the Los Angeles Unified School District (LAUSD) utilizes a Local Control Funding Formula that allows autonomy in spending by district schools. Library staffing is one of the discretionary items[30] that could be reduced or eliminated.

Saving money by cutting school librarians has been a favorite tool in California whenever it hits a budget crisis, but the Great Recession added new dimensions to the state's daffiness. Before their positions were eliminated, librarians were interrogated in a Kafkaesque basement courtroom in hopes of tripping them into proving their incompetence. I cannot think of a more demeaning and egregious effort to drive good people out of their profession.

Veteran reporter Héctor Tobar of the *Los Angeles Times* published an article that described this bizarre interrogation process. For more than eighty librarians, their only chance of keeping a paycheck was to prove they were qualified to be classroom teachers. LAUSD attorneys spent days grilling each one, questioning their ability not only to teach but also to take attendance and issue grades. What was interesting about this entire scenario is that California, much like the majority of states, requires librarians to be licensed teachers in addition to earning their credentials to be hired as school librarians. They were more than qualified to return to the classroom.[31]

This is not an intent to beat up LAUSD as school librarians are being eliminated in other areas. California just seems to be leading in this regard. Many districts that have implemented site-based management programs allow the school principal to determine the fate of the school library. This occurred in the state's Oakland Unified School District (OUSD), which cut funding for library programs and staffing that essentially decimated the school library.[32] A few years later, new school district administration realized these cuts had caused huge inequities for students, particularly because OUSD is a large, diverse district with almost three-quarters of their students living in poverty. Funding was immediately restored to principals who developed and submitted a plan to restart their library programs.

Severe cuts to school libraries are also happening in Oregon, Pennsylvania, Vermont, and across the nation. A few districts have recognized the error of their ways and restored some if not all funding, while others are struggling to regain what has been lost.

It's imperative to realize school librarians do increase student achievement. Over thirty-four statewide studies suggest students earn better standardized test scores in schools with strong library programs staffed by certified librarians. The most substantial and consistent finding from these studies is the significant impact school librarians have on reading and writing tests, regardless of student demographics.[33] There are additional indicators of student success related to school libraries such as graduation rates. At-risk learners, low-income students, and students with disabilities also benefit. The National Center for Education Statistics (NCES) and the National Assessment of Educational Progress (NAEP) reported data that the decline or inferior gains in reading scores can be documented by the loss of librarians.[34] Unfortunately, since 2000, NCES reports a loss of over ten thousand full-time librarian positions nationwide, more than a 19 percent decline.

If There's a School Library, Why Do Teachers Need a Classroom Library?

The presence of a classroom library is all about access. The National Council of Teachers of English generated a position statement in 2017: "Classroom libraries—physical or virtual—play a key role in providing access to books and promoting literacy; they have the potential to increase student motivation, engagement, and achievement, and help students become critical thinkers, analytical readers, and informed citizens."[35] The educational benefits cited for classroom libraries included:

- motivating students by encouraging voluntary and recreational reading,
- helping young people develop an extensive array of literacy strategies and skills,
- offering access to a wide range of reading materials that reflect abilities and interests,
- enhancing opportunities for both assigned and independent reading,
- allowing students' choice in self-selecting reading materials for self-engagement, and
- facilitating opportunities to validate and promote the acceptance and inclusion of diverse students' identities and experiences.

When Christine Draper was a fifth-grade teacher, she knew it was beneficial to have books available in her classroom. Like most teachers, Christine had accumulated books for the library by purchasing them herself or by using points from the book club where her students ordered and bought their own books. Initially, Christine tightly controlled access to her books by making students check them out, issuing fines when they returned them late, and charging students for missing books. Soon, fewer students were visiting the classroom

Megan Sloan's students assist her in organizing their classroom library.

library, and Christine realized the reason why. "My second year of teaching, I let the kids just go for it. Did books walk away? Yes. Did they get grimy and slimy? Yes. Did they get read? *Yes!*"

Too often, teachers such as Christine have to use their own money to buy books to equip their classroom library. Jim Bailey, a principal at Hemmeter Elementary School in Saginaw, Michigan, advocated for classroom libraries in a post on the Nerdy Book Club website. Jim explained that after providing professional development to his teachers about the value of classroom libraries, he did something completely unexpected. He gave each teacher a hundred-dollar gift card to a bookstore so they could purchase books for their classroom libraries. Other principals asked how he could afford to do such a thing. His response, "I went through every line of my budget, asking myself, 'Is this program or resource better at raising student achievement than putting a book in a student's hand?' If the answer was no, then I had just found money to support classroom libraries. It turned out I was able to find thousands of dollars in my budget." Jim also eliminated Accelerated Reader and the workbooks purchased with the basal reading series. He made it clear in his blog post that he did not take money from the school library budget to build classroom libraries since he believes both are important and necessary.

There is some disagreement among educators about how the classroom library should be organized and who it's really for. Some teachers group books by reading levels assigned to them according to their Lexile designation. This contradicts the American Association of School Librarians position statement saying labeling books with a reading level should be avoided.[36]

I was quite clear in chapter 4 in expressing my opinion regarding leveling *real* books so I would never advocate adopting that practice for a classroom library. When teachers do so, they limit access to books, and children are restricted to reading books only at their level.

Since I firmly believe that a classroom library belongs to the students, I put my first graders in charge of it. It was always fascinating to watch how my students would organize our classroom library—and they did so frequently throughout the school year. Sometimes it was by the size or color of the book. Other times it was by the illustration on the front cover. As the students' reading skills progressed during the year, they would categorize books by topic, theme, genre, author, or illustrator.

The process of negotiating with each other in arranging the library signaled they cared about the books and felt ownership. At times, when I couldn't locate a book, I would ask one of the children, who always knew exactly where it had been placed.

Even though most of the same books were in our classroom library throughout the school year, as the students participated in the book reorganization, they always found something new. This recently discovered book might be our next read-aloud or a child's choice for independent reading. Having a feeling of ownership, and access to books, is important for both classroom and home libraries.

With the Internet and Ebooks, Who Needs a Library?

What a contrast between today's library worries and those of twenty years ago! Back then, the controversy was whether or not to allow beverages and snacks in the library, the way those dreadful mega bookstores were doing. Today, when there are more books available on a smartphone than from the New York Public Library,[37] the question is whether libraries will be replaced by the internet and ebooks.

While no one can predict the digital future with much certainty, there are things I would bet the mortgage on. Libraries are going to change. They will be smaller in size, scope, and budget. Simultaneously, the librarian's role will change by necessity into "data hound, guide, Sherpa, and teacher."[38]

And finally, the book will change, as it has for thousands of years. In the first quarter of 2012, more ebooks were sold in the United States than hardcover books.[39] The writing may not be on the wall, but it is on the receipts. Just as it took a decade for television sets to reach every American home, it will take at least that long for the ebook to pervade libraries. After all, there was no previous version of TV to supplant. It'll be a while before we can replace five hundred years of print—unless you want to declare the world started with Google.

In 2018, print books claimed 54 percent of public libraries' budget for materials while the budget for electronic books stands around 9 percent.[40] As of 2012, less than 3 percent of the average public library's collection consisted of ebooks. However, people still seem to prefer print. According to the Pew Research Center, 65 percent of survey respondents said they had read a printed book while only 28 percent reported that they had read an electronic book.[41]

What Is the Role of the Librarian in the Coming Digital World?

Over the past several years, we have begun to see examples of what future libraries will contain. Let's look at Cushing Academy in Ashburnham, Massachusetts (population 6,000). With an annual tuition of nearly $60,000, the 148-year-old ivy-covered boarding academy isn't your average school, but its library was facing usage problems similar to the average town or school library. So in 2009, Cushing converted its Fisher-Watkins Library to a digital collection.

The 450-student population (ninth grade to postgrad) had been using the "old" library as a study hall more than as a reference or reading room. Its twenty-five thousand books sat idly on the shelves, mostly untouched for years. Realizing the faculty had moved on to the internet's information services and that students were following suit, Cushing's library decided to join the crowd—or at least change its face enough to draw a crowd. Out went twenty thousand books (donated to faculty and area libraries), while five thousand reference volumes were retained. The library purchased ebooks and downloaded them to Kindles loaned to the student (minus any email or internet capabilities). The book processing room was converted into the Cushing Cyber Café, open 7:30 a.m. to 3:30 p.m., and became one of the most popular sites on campus. To draw the faculty back, their lounge and mailboxes were moved to a renovated space in the library. The area previously occupied by bookshelves was now filled with tables, chairs, and collaborative space for students wired to the internet. Noisier and busier than ever, the library now was an information resource instead of a book depository.

Five years later, Cushing began to reinstate printed books.[42] What happened? Apparently, the former headmaster had made the decision to go digital without consulting the faculty. It was determined that not all books faculty were using are available digitally. Some students, especially those who struggled with reading, had difficulty using the Kindle. The library's social and outreach programs, such as book clubs, poetry nights, and Banned Book Week, weren't quite as successful without physical books. In 2014, a new librarian was hired and charged with the daunting task of reviving a print collection while balancing it with ebooks.[43] Surprisingly, eight of every ten requests were for printed materials. Even though the print collection is returning, it will take time to restore the social aspect of the library that has been lost.

Public libraries have also explored the idea of being bookless. Pima County Library in Tucson, Arizona, opened a branch in a neighborhood where most residents did not have computer access.[44] After six years, the nearby community asked for a full-service library, complete with books. Newport Beach, California, also considered going this same route of being bookless, but the public outcry forced them to abandon the plan.

Libraries will change as we continue to navigate our digital society. The future library will shrink in size, but judging from present needs and behavior, there will remain a critical need for skilled librarians. Today's student is confronted with a mess of unorganized and sometimes unauthenticated information on the internet. School and academic librarians have always played a critical role in assisting students with their research skills, which includes accessing accurate sources. Community members rely on public librarians to assist them in locating information, both online and in print. Regardless of whether libraries are filled with print, ebooks, or computers, librarians will continue to be a valuable and necessary presence.

What Should We Consider Regarding Online Resources?

Wikipedia has become one of the most widely used websites in searching for information about a variety of people and topics. Founded in 2001, it is now the seventh most visited website (Google, Facebook, and YouTube rank as the top three). The free encyclopedia contains more than forty million articles in almost three hundred languages versus *Encyclopaedia Britannica Online*, with half a million articles in English. Wikipedia is entirely free online, while Britannica offers a limited amount of information free online and requires a subscription for more details. (The latter's print edition retired in

March 2012, much like an aging boxing champ no longer able to stay on his feet—weight: 129 pounds, age: 244 years, price: $1,395.)[45]

The bigger contrast, however, is in the respective "authors." Britannica has approximately four thousand authorities who contribute information to more than one hundred editors. Wikipedia is entirely "volunteer" in its composition and editing. Anyone, with or without credentials, may contribute, add to, or edit articles. Although there were serious liabilities with this approach through 2005, a series of "checks and balances" have since been added to curb the abuse. Anyone who has tried recently to edit or contribute to a Wikipedia article will tell you it is not easy. Want to contribute a snide remark to a movie star's Wiki page? Don't bother. You'll need some serious coding skills and be able to get by even more serious editors. Furthermore, the entire history of the page's editing process can be found by clicking on "View history," eliminating "stealth" contributors.

Since many of the Wiki contributors are not credentialed, how many errors can one expect to find? Back in 2005, the journal *Nature* had a panel of experts examine forty-two online scientific articles from both Wikipedia and *Encyclopaedia Britannica*. Wikipedia averaged four errors and *Britannica* averaged three. The experts discovered a total of eight "serious" errors among the forty-two entries, four in Wikipedia and four in *Britannica*.[46]

Other than the authorship issue, the biggest online difference between Wikipedia and *Encyclopaedia Britannica* is in their scope. Take the name of the community in which you were born and enter it into each site. *Britannica* had no entry for my birth city (Rock Springs, Wyoming), while Wikipedia had information about the local school district along with photographs of historic buildings and sites.

The Pew Research Center surveyed 2,500 high school students and discovered that only 12 percent used print sources for research. Google came in as the top choice while Wikipedia was second.[47] No less an authority than Bill Keller, former executive editor of the *New York Times*, is on record citing Wikipedia as his favorite web tool after search engines.[48]

Is Wikipedia perfect? No, but considering its size and scope as well as audience size, a free Wikipedia is one of the wonders of the digital age. It makes the entire world a better, smarter place because of the ability to have access to this online resource. For most of history, expensive encyclopedias were tethered to the hard maple tables of libraries, unavailable for public circulation. With the arrival of Wikipedia, instant information sits in our very pockets. "Let's look it up right now" has replaced "We'll go to the library tomorrow" in parent-child conversation.

Chapter 7

The Impact of Electronic Media on Reading

> I don't understand it any more than you do, but
> one thing I've learned is that you don't have to
> understand things for them to be.
> —*A Wrinkle in Time* by Madeleine L'Engle[1]

W HEN we examine the current reality of electronic media being the dominant force in a child's life outside family (and for some, even larger than the family), it must be included in any book or discussion about literacy. The consensus is electronic devices are here to stay. They do, and should, serve a purpose in children's lives. Electronic media can play a role in the complexities of today's family where considerable stress and time constraints are ever present. We need to observe what children are doing while engaged with television, tablets, and smartphones, and consider the experiences they are not having as a result.

Today's children and adolescents are immersed in various electronic platforms that allow them to consume and create content, including broadcast and streamed television and movies, sedentary and active video games, and captivating virtual reality. Social and interactive media can be innovative and engaging for individuals and groups.[2] The Kaiser Family Foundation report stated the amount of time kids spend with entertainment media has risen dramatically, especially among minority youth.[3] Here is what we know about the media landscape over time:

♦ In 1970, children began watching TV regularly at about four years of age, whereas today, children start interacting with digital media as young as four months.

♦ In 2015, the vast majority of one-year-olds had already used a mobile device, and most two-year-olds use them on a daily basis.[4] Preschoolers were already starting to use two or more forms of digital media simultaneously, such as watching TV while using an iPad.

♦ Preteens and adolescents use numerous digital media sources an average of eight to ten hours per day, often in the form of media multitasking, which has been associated with attention problems. Adolescents who frequently use digital media are more likely to develop attention deficit disorder (ADD).[5] Other studies have shown there is statistical significance, but modest association, between a higher frequency of digital media use and subsequent symptoms of attention deficit hyperactivity disorder (ADHD).[6] Additional research is needed, but this is something that parents, teachers, doctors, and tech companies should be aware of and continually monitor.

♦ Three-quarters of teenagers own a smartphone, 24 percent of adolescents describe themselves as "constantly connected" to the internet, and 50 percent report feeling "addicted" to their phones.[7] Teens who report feeling "addicted," primarily related to extreme text messaging, may exhibit antisocial behavior and eroding self-confidence.[8]

♦ Excessive use of digital media, especially too close to bedtime or viewing violent content, has been associated with restless sleep, higher obesity risk, and worse developmental and academic outcomes.[9]

♦ Electronic devices are also dramatically altering the reading environment of children. Our prior notion of reading involved sitting down with a book and turning the pages. Today, it could mean holding a screen and touching words to have them read aloud.[10]

How Much Screen Time Is Recommended?

As the popularity of electronic devices has increased, so has the perspective regarding how much time children should be connected to them. In 1999, the American Academy of Pediatrics (AAP) advised no screen time for children under the age of two. Recently, the AAP changed their stance to include video chatting for babies younger than eighteen months.[11] Virtual visits with family members may engage infants as young as six months, but there isn't much evidence to support any benefit in exposing very young children to laptops, tablets, or smartphones.

For toddlers, the AAP recommends limited screen time. The digital media they are viewing should be done with a parent or caregiver. The intent is to watch and talk with an adult rather than it being alone time for the child. A few studies have indicated some degree of language development if a toddler is watching educational media, but this is *only* if parents are watching and interacting alongside them.[12]

Other research details the harmful effects of very young children viewing television for over two hours daily. The toddlers in this study were approximately six times more likely to develop delays in language development.[13] A 2014 study of fifteen- to thirty-five-month-old children discovered those with language developmental delays spent more than double the amount of time viewing screens each day: 117.3 minutes versus 53.2 for children without language delay.[14] What these studies reveal is that digital media viewing should not replace interaction with parents. Parents continue to be a child's first teacher, and this is particularly true regarding language development.

Preschoolers age two to five should engage in no more than one hour a day of educational programming. Once again, this should be with a parent or other caregiver who can help a preschooler understand what he is viewing. The AAP has named Sesame Workshop and the Public Broadcasting Service (PBS) as "two trusted makers of evidence-based children's educational media."[15]

Parents should place consistent limits on screen time for children ages six to eighteen. This includes TV, social media, and video games. Electronic media should not take the place of getting enough sleep and being physically active.

The World Health Organization is reporting that the United

States has the highest obesity rates for boys and girls.[16] While we cannot blame children's weight gain solely on electronic media, the fact children are generally sitting in front of their devices for hours each day is probably having a negative effect.

Are Kids Still Watching Television?

For the first time in decades, the Kaiser Family Foundation study found that the amount of time spent watching regularly scheduled television declined by twenty-five minutes a day (2004 to 2009).[17] However, with so many other ways to watch television on the internet, smartphones, and tablets, there was an increase in TV consumption from three hours and fifty-two minutes a day to four hours and twenty-nine minutes. Today's technology now offers 24-7 access to media such as broadcast television as well as streaming and on-demand video.

Until recently, most critics could only point to "overdosing" as the problem, with television merely serving as an innocent bystander. However, new research is getting closer to identifying TV as more of an accomplice. But even if the studies fail to indict television completely, everything suggests the dangers of over-viewing among all age groups, with the youngest being the most prone to vulnerability. Recent findings from media research don't bode well for the future classroom as evidenced by the Kaiser Family Foundation Generation M2 report.

Let's start with the youngest "viewers" and work upward.

- While television is sometimes portrayed as a "family event," it is often experienced in isolation. When six-month-old infants living at or below the poverty level were monitored during more than four hundred television exposures, their mothers interacted with them only 24 percent of the time, most often during educational programs. Many programs they were exposed to were not intended for infants. Overall, children from lower income levels watch more television and achieve at lower levels in school.[18]

- When the television viewing habits of 2,500 children were tracked and examined by researchers at Seattle Children's Hospital, the doctors concluded that for each hour of daily TV viewed by the child before age three, the risk of attention deficit hyperactivity disorder by age seven increased by 10 percent.[19] (ADHD is now the most common childhood behavioral disorder.)

• Once children are in school, the impact of heavy television viewing is reflected in student achievements in both reading and math. In a study of 348 ethnically diverse third graders from six California schools, the presence of a television in the child's bedroom was significantly associated with lower math, reading, and language arts scores.[20] Kaiser media studies show bedroom TVs always correlate to more viewing hours.[21]

Even when televisions are not in kids' bedrooms, they still watch TV shows and movies on their digital devices.

By age eight, 71 percent of children lived in a home with three televisions and also had one in their bedroom, resulting in an additional hour of TV viewing daily.[22] If a video game is in the bedroom, the child plays thirty-two more minutes daily, and the availability of a bedroom computer doubles the usage when compared with no computer in the bedroom.

Several recent studies including the Kaiser survey conveyed that bilingual Hispanic children watch both Spanish- and English-language television approximately five hours and twenty-one minutes daily versus three hours and thirty-six minutes for white children.[23] However, socioeconomic status is more of a factor than ethnicity. Children from low-income and low-education families tended to watch 272.7 more minutes per week than their baseline peers.[24] Sometimes the parents' belief that there is educational and social value in television was the predominant factor for too much

TV time. The hope was that it would provide a jump-start in learning pre-academic skills.

Educational television does help in developing vocabulary, beginning around the age of three. But by ten years of age, little of what the average child hears on TV overall is adding to his everyday vocabulary. Each decade has seen a decline in television vocabulary level. In a 2009 study of eighty-eight television programs, researchers found that 98 percent of the shows' vocabulary consisted of the Common Lexicon, the words we use all the time. For native English speakers over ten years of age, TV offers few opportunities for learning new vocabulary.[25]

When children are watching television, they aren't doing things such as engaging in play that fuels their imagination and supports brain development. Since television viewing is passive, the child is not socializing with others, and not receiving feedback on their actions or behavior.[26] Also, excessive television viewing can lead to a diminished EQ, or emotional quotient, which is critical to the development of social skills and understanding that actions have consequences. Children will develop weaker language and vocabulary skills because they aren't interacting and can't ask questions, which assists them in developing the ability to problem solve.

Can Television Support Reading Improvement?

There are educational television programs that help support literacy development. However, there is one feature of your television that you might not have realized helps promote vocabulary development, fluency, and comprehension—closed-captioning. The Television Decoder Circuitry Act of 1990 went into effect on July 1, 1993, and mandated that all new television sets for sale in the United States must include caption-decoding technology if thirteen inches or larger. Previously, closed-captioning originated from an external decoder box that was expensive ($250), but the creation of an internal computer chip only added $3–10 to the cost of a TV. Today, closed-captioning is built into every TV sold in America, and you can access it through the TV remote.

It's not just the evening news that is closed-captioned. The first live sporting event that used closed-captioning was the Sugar Bowl on January 1, 1981. Real-time captioning of commentary of the

Super Bowl aired in January 1985. In 1980, *Sesame Street* became the second children's program to be captioned (*3-2-1 Contact* was the first!) and is now the longest-running captioned children's program.

National Captioning Institute (NCI) research indicates that there are benefits of captioned television for children who are deaf or hard of hearing, individuals learning English, and young children who are learning to read. Even those readers who want to improve their language and vocabulary skills can be aided by using closed-captioning.[27] An NCI study showed that when captions are used, hearing children were able to significantly improve their vocabulary and oral reading fluency. Researchers suggest that while children are watching cartoons and other television programs, they can also benefit from reading captions.

For individuals learning English as a Second Language, captioned TV improves reading and listening comprehension, vocabulary, word recognition, and overall motivation to read. Children and adults with learning disabilities obtain the same benefits as well as increasing self-confidence.

It stands to reason that moderate doses of captioned television can do no harm to students, and most likely it will help measurably

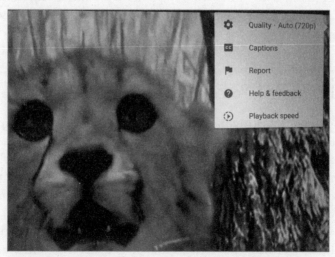

Closed-captions are available for programs and videos such as those on YouTube by clicking CAPTIONS in the right-hand corner.

with reading. There is enough research showing significant gains in comprehension and vocabulary development (especially among bilingual students) when receiving instruction with educational television that is captioned.[28]

Here is a story a first-grade teacher shared about a young girl entering her class in September:

> On the first day of school, she was already reading at a third-grade level. That's always unusual, but what made it more so was that her parents were both deaf. Usually, the hearing child of deaf parents is language deficient and therefore behind—but this child was three years ahead. I could hardly wait to conference with her parents. They beamed when I told them of their daughter's achievement, and they explained that she'd had closed-captioning all her life.

Many factors make closed-captioning so useful as a reading tutor. There is a thirty-to-one ratio of visual receptors over auditory receptors in the brain. The chances of a word (or sentence) being retained in our memory bank are thirty times greater if we see it instead of only hearing it.

Although a child may be too young to read yet, all the books, magazines, and newspapers in the home are acclimating him to the world of print. The same thing happens with closed-captioning. In fact, you could argue that the characters on the television show are reading aloud the closed-captioning to the child.

Why Should You Develop a Family Media Plan?

When parents enact media-related rules, children will spend substantially less time watching television or using their electronic media devices. It becomes key for parents to use media with their children in ways that will promote togetherness and learning. Just as parents have taught their children how to ride a bike and swim, they also need to show them how to use electronic devices. Digital media should be viewed as a tool to help meet parenting needs and introduce kids to learning experiences they may otherwise not encounter.

Throughout *The Read-Aloud Handbook*, I've expressed that parents serve as role models for their children. It's critical parents unplug during family times, have good social media manners, and talk about why they're using the media they consume.[29] Also, they should take time to help develop their children's language and social skills, whether it's during a trip to the grocery store or in the course of the ride to and from school. A missed opportunity happens when a mother is chatting on her cell phone instead of asking her children to read signs or labels out loud or discuss the school day.

It's crucial for parents to know what their child is viewing online. Electronic devices offer ways to screen or even limit what a child can see. Make sure your child understands online citizenship and safety, which includes treating others with respect, avoiding cyberbullying, and being wary of online solicitation. Know who your child is connecting with on social media and help her understand the type of information she can share on websites and with others.

What About Other Forms of Media Like Audiobooks?

As Americans spend more and more time in their cars, audiobooks have become a major player in the publishing industry, especially with the average round-trip commute lasting fifty minutes. The recorded book is a perfect example of how technology can be used to make this a more literate nation.

While audiobooks lack the immediacy of a live person who can hug a child and answer questions, they fill an important gap when the adult is not available or busy. Even when used as background noise while a child is playing, their verbal contents are enriching his language development and vocabulary more than television would with its abbreviated sentences. So, by all means, begin building your audio library with songs, rhymes, and stories. Community libraries, bookstores, and online sources for digital downloads have a growing assortment for all ages. You should record stories yourself and encourage relatives to do the same. Likewise, there are programs that support deployed military parents recording stories read aloud for their children. Other programs are available that do the same for parents who are incarcerated. Information about those initiatives can be found in chapter 5.

There is a distinct difference between an audiobook playing and a movie streaming on an electronic device. I can't tell you how many times I am behind an SUV and see kids strapped in the backseat, held captive by a video they are watching on small screens above their heads. Video streaming is the most recent addition to family transportation and does nothing but deprive the child of yet another classroom: conversation with parents or the shared intellectual experience of listening to an audiobook communally.

Consider audio recordings that can be experienced by those in both the front and back of the car. This allows the parent to pause the audiobook and ask, "Why do you think he did that? What do you think he meant by that?" Not only do audiobooks prompt conversation, they also increase listening skills of those in the vehicle—both parent and child.

Unfortunately, not all audiobooks are created equal. I often prefer those that are read by the author such as Jacqueline Woodson's powerful memoir, *Brown Girl Dreaming*, or Jason Reynolds's novel in verse, *Long Way Down* (both reviewed in the Treasury). The exception to this would be the popular A Series of Unfortunate Events novels. Actor Tim Curry narrated the first two books in the series (*A Bad Beginning* and *The Reptile Room*), but for books three through five (*The Wide Window*, *The Miserable Mill*, and *The Austere Academy*), the author, Lemony Snicket, did the narration. I positively prefer Curry! If possible, listen to a sample of a book's narration on www.audible.com or similar websites to see if the story and the reader appeal to you and your child.

In addition to daily commutes, incorporate audiobooks into family vacations. When Marie LeJeune and her family drove to San Francisco to visit Alcatraz Island, they listened to Gennifer Choldenko's *Al Capone Does My Shirts* from her Tales from Alcatraz series. This historical fiction chapter book is set on Alcatraz and is told by Moose, a boy whose father works as an electrician on the island. *Bull Run* by Paul Fleischman is a good choice if you are in the area where the first great battle of the Civil War took place. Or Kadir Nelson's *We Are the Ship: The Story of Negro League Baseball* is excellent if you are in the Kansas City, Missouri, area and want to visit the Negro Leagues Baseball Museum (be sure to get a copy of the book because Nelson's paintings are stunning).

There are also enjoyable audiobooks that don't have a geographic tie-in. Any book by Roald Dahl with an audio version such as *James and the Giant Peach* is sure to be a hit. You can't go wrong with the Percy Jackson series by Rick Riordan or the Harry Potter novels by J. K. Rowling. Many blogs and websites offer great suggestions for road-trip audiobooks. You have a captive audience in the car listening together. This is sure to eliminate the question, "Are we there yet?"

Are Ebooks Gaining in Popularity?

The vast majority of arguments I hear against ebooks involve traditional readers declaring how much they'll miss the feel of the pages and the smell of the book. Smell or no smell, the ebook is part of our reading options, for very legitimate reasons. It is a win–win situation: a moneymaker for the publisher and a money saver for the buyer. It also saves time, space, trees, and students' spines, to say nothing of what it does for the visually impaired.

For decades, schoolchildren have been straining under the increasing weight of textbooks. A fully loaded student backpack tips the scales at twenty to thirty pounds. As states raised academic standards, more pages were added to cover testing material.[30] No wonder school districts and colleges are moving to tablets that will hold all of a student's textbooks and weigh less than two pounds. Moreover, a science or math e-textbook can be quickly updated, unlike print textbooks, without buying new editions. This could result in huge cost savings for school districts (and taxpayers) as the cost of print textbooks increased by 812 percent from 1978 to 2013.[31] Good news for using e-textbooks is that the average cost of tablets in 2011 was $489, but the projected cost in 2018 is $247.[32]

And then there is the added life expectancy. When tax laws changed, and publishing houses had to pay taxes on the books in their warehouse, titles that were not consistent sellers went out of print faster. An ebook has no physical presence (no more warehousing costs) and isn't taxed as inventory. Therefore, it can stay in print for as long as the publisher and author have a contract. This dramatically extends the life of the book and allows publishers to instantaneously bring out-of-print titles back to life (as is happening now).

While the ebook version adds years to the book's life, the tablet adds multimedia to the reading experience. Suppose the class is studying the civil rights movement and reading books such as *Voice of Freedom: Fannie Lou Hamer, Spirit of the Civil Rights Movement* by Carole Boston Weatherford or *Freedom Walkers: The Story of the Montgomery Bus Boycott* by Russell Freedman. A hyperlink in the text on an iPad could bring up *Freedom Riders*, a PBS *American Experience* program that follows the trail of the four hundred black and white "riders" who set out to violate Jim Crow bus laws and make the struggle into a focal point for the entire nation.[33] Or they can watch and listen to Dr. Martin Luther King Jr.'s "I Have a Dream" speech.

Hyperlinks in ebooks will bring thousands of free tutoring lessons from the nonprofit Khan Academy, in any subject, to any student, anywhere in the world.[34] A child in rural Georgia can have the same online tutoring lessons as a child in urban Chicago.

Or think about audio information available through ebook links—the voluminous archives from public radio. For example, almost as famous as *The Catcher in the Rye* is its author, J. D. Salinger, and his reclusive lifestyle. Everyone told teenager Jim Sadwith not to bother reaching out to Salinger, that he didn't welcome visitors—stay away! Besides, they declared, you'll never find him. But the boy wanted to make a high school play based on the book and was sure Salinger would love the idea, so off he went in search of the recluse. More than forty years later, Sadwith told American Public Media's *The Story* about finding Salinger and the author's reaction. And as the adventure progressed, the boy dictated his exploits into a recorder and later submitted the tape to Harvard instead of the traditional college essay. (He got in.) Wouldn't that interview add dimensions for anyone studying the book? It's free online, accessed via a hyperlink.[35] In 2015, Sadwith wrote and directed the movie *Coming Through the Rye*, based on his Salinger encounter.

Worried about the venerable tradition of autographed books? They've even found a way for authors to personalize and sign ebooks.[36] The resources are unlimited, and none of them would add either a dime to the cost or a pound to the weight of the e-textbook.

What Are the Pros and Cons of Ebooks for Kids?

Even though ebooks have been available for over a decade, research regarding the advantages and disadvantages of them for children isn't as abundant. I have observed children learning early literacy skills by engaging with an ebook, especially those that are interactive. Some ebooks contain words that are highlighted when the narrator reads them. This helps a child associate the written word with its sound.[37] This feature also supports children with developmental delays in learning vocabulary.

Another advantage of ebooks is that a child can read a book over and over again. Just as with the print version, repeated reading of the same story increases the likelihood a child's literacy skills will be enhanced. Children can access the ebook independently and not have to wait for an adult to read the story. Since ebooks can be downloaded to a handheld device, they are readily available whether you are waiting at a doctor's office or sitting outside in a park. When an adult engages in the sharing of an ebook, a child is more apt to participate.[38]

One of the disadvantages of ebooks is that parents don't talk as much about the story and how it relates to their child's life.[39] When the ebook is highly interactive, there is more discussion about what it does in relation to the buttons and sounds, rather than about the story itself. One study found children who read a book in print rather than as an ebook comprehended the story much better.[40] This may have been the result of too many features distracting the child. When the ebook resembles a game or toy rather than a book, then the purpose of reading a story is defeated. In selecting ebooks, choose those that don't have an overabundance of animation, music, or features that are distracting.

Ebooks can promote children's language and literacy skills. They may also be motivating for children who need more visual stimulation to encourage reading. Parental involvement is still the main factor when reading electronic books or those in print.

Will Printed Books Become Obsolete?

A Pew Research Center study in 2016 found there is a growing number of Americans who are reading ebooks on their tablets or smartphones. However, print books remain much more popular for reading than their electronic counterparts.[41] Children prefer to read books on paper rather than on a device such as an iPad or Kindle. They use their electronic devices for just about everything except reading books. Research has found that the more devices a child has access to, the less they read in general.[42] This is true for young children as well as teenagers. School and public libraries that are removing paper books in favor of audiobooks and ebooks are limiting access to kids' preferred reading mode. Children also read more slowly (6 to 11 percent) from a screen than from paper.[43] As with automobile driving, humans may get better and faster at e-reading over the years, but that could take generations.

However, in all fairness, audiobooks and ebooks are more accessible as long as there is a device to use. Websites such as Overdrive and Hoopla have books for both adults and children. All you need is a participating library and a library card. Project Gutenberg provides free access to thousands of classic books.[44] The International Children's Digital Library contains thousands of free ebooks for children of all ages, written in over fifty languages. There are also websites such as Epic! that provide access to ebooks for children at a nominal cost.

Stories being read aloud on the internet are also available. Storyline Online[45] has favorite books read by members of the Screen Actors Guild. Since these are actors, the books are generally read with expression and are entertaining. And the stories are either closed-captioned or signed for the hearing impaired. Story Time from Space[46] is a project spearheaded by the Global Space Education Foundation in partnership with NASA and the Center for the Advancement of Science in Space. The intent is to encourage a love of STEM education. It's riveting watching astronaut Kate Rubins read aloud *Rosie Revere, Engineer* while floating around the International Space Station.

There are a number of books being read aloud and available on YouTube, but be selective in what you and your child take time to listen to. The advantage of having all these outlets is not only that you can listen to a story read aloud, but it may be a book you might not have access to otherwise.

What About Educational Apps?

Children have learned at an early age how to turn a tablet on and off as well as developing the dexterity to tap, swipe, and drag. There are numerous educational apps available for young children. These are multiplying at a rapid pace, and many are focused on early literacy skills.

In an analysis of the top free and paid educational apps for preschoolers, researchers explored whether these tools were successful in teaching children what was asserted would be learned.[47] They found that 50 percent of the apps did not furnish instructions, with 33 percent of them providing only moderate instructions. Less than 15 percent of the apps repeated instructions. This is problematic given toddlers' short attention spans. More than two-thirds of the apps reviewed did not reduce the level of difficulty even when children struggled to answer the questions.

Young children can use tablets and apps independently and competently in literacy learning,[48] which may be perceived as an advantage. However, children can be distracted by the sounds, animation, and illuminated text many apps contain. Of course, these features are what engage and motivate children to use the apps. What could be more fun than singing a silly song or seeing objects appear or disappear while learning the alphabet? Knowledge is fostered through visual, auditory, tactile, and physical or kinesthetic experiences.[49]

There is a place for educational apps in developing literacy skills. As with any product you use or purchase, you need to know the quality of it and how well it fits the learning needs of your child. Keep in mind, tablets and smartphones should never replace interaction between parent and child.

When Is It Time to Disconnect?

It's possible that fans of electronics are overestimating both the gadgets and the kids. If the challenge is juggling, then a digital device is like a rubber ball that you're juggling between your hands. Add another ball to the mix, and the process becomes more challenging. Add a third or fourth and you've got your hands full. It gets harder and harder to add more.

From 2,272 text messages a month in 2008, American teenagers' (ages thirteen to seventeen) texting ballooned to 3,339 messages a month in 2010. Approximately 15 percent of teens send more than 200 texts a day in 2018 or an average of one text every few minutes. Simply put, children in one of the most formative periods of their intellectual and emotional lives are interrupted over a hundred times a day for messages. High schoolers are now texting, scrolling, and using social media instead of reading books. A study revealed one in three high school seniors in the United States did not read a book for pleasure in 2016.[50]

Today, teenagers are spending more than one-third of their day, or an average of nine hours, using media.[51] For children ages eight to twelve, that average is around six hours. Kids are devoting their time to watching online videos or listening to music. And they are often multitasking with media in the background.

Because so many teens and adults are connected 24-7, there is minimal downtime or disconnect. What's wrong with that? The more you work, the more you accomplish, right? Not necessarily, say the experts.

Most creative artists and thinkers admit there comes a point when they must stop, put their tools aside, and think about something else (like biking or vacuuming) while the work "percolates." This allows the creative muse to speak to them. And since muses seldom shout, solitude is needed to hear them.[52] There are countless examples in history of significant discoveries or insights arriving during idle time, away from the workbench.[53] Einstein frequently abandoned a math problem and retreated to music to unwind the problem.

So what happens to the creative process when there is no disconnect time, when our children are constantly downloading, uploading, texting, YouTubing, Googling, or tweeting their 742 "online friends"? Less "deep thinking" takes place, less creativity.[54] Where will the next Steve Jobs come from, or the next Edison, Salk, Spielberg, Ellington, or Steinbeck? It's unlikely he or she will come from noisy multitasking, that's for sure.

While we're all connected, we're also running down both batteries—the device's and our own. From recent scientific observations of both humans[55] and rats,[56] the research is compelling that constant stimulation of the brain from multitasking debilitates brain function. In other words, it's a lot harder to have those "aha" moments if you don't have enough "ah" moments.

Chapter 8

Visual Literacy and Reading Aloud

"And what is the use of a book," thought Alice,
"without pictures or conversation?"
—*Alice's Adventures in Wonderland* by Lewis Carroll[1]

W HENEVER I read aloud a picture book, whether it's to a toddler or a class of fourth graders, they all want to talk about the illustrations and point out something appealing, unique, or funny that they see (adolescents and adults want to do this as well but often refrain from doing so). We do judge a picture book by its cover and also the images inside. Author and illustrator Kevin Henkes, the Caldecott Medal winner for *Kitten's First Full Moon*, said, "The great thing about a successful picture book is that you can't have great illustrations without a great text, and you can't have a great text without great illustrations. . . . The art form of the picture book is, in fact, all thirty-two pages—pictures and words—working together."[2]

Picture books appeal to readers of all ages, but children are generally the ones who examine the images more closely and point out details adults often miss. Illustrations make us slow down and relish the story that is unfolding.

Every aspect of a picture book, illustrated chapter book, or graphic novel is carefully considered from the book jacket to the font size, from the endpapers to the use of space. Can you read aloud a story without exploring the complete book literally from cover to cover? Of course, you can, but possibly that read-aloud experience will be enhanced when you find a "hidden treasure" under the book jacket or make your voice louder because the text size increases. I don't advise noticing every single artistic or design element of a picture book, as that will bring the story to a grinding halt. However, it is possible to develop a deeper understanding and appreciation of a book and boost the level of enjoyment a little higher by savoring the illustrations.

Why Is Visual Literacy Important?

We live in a world where we are constantly bombarded with visual images. Think about the images we encounter daily on television, through social media, at the grocery store, and on the internet. We express our feelings through emojis and use images in place of words when we send text messages. We are a visual society. But how did we learn to interpret these images and their meaning, and why is it important for kids to do so today?

The term *visual literacy* has been around for quite some time. Visual literacy is broadly defined as the ability to "interpret and construct meaning from visual images."[3] At home and school, our focus is usually on verbal literacy skills as we expand children's vocabulary and enhance their ability to communicate. As adults, we have spent years accumulating vocabulary to express ourselves. We may avoid slowing down to talk about illustrations in picture books because we don't possess the same level of confidence in our vocabulary to talk about art. When encountering a graphic novel, a book not as familiar to adults as adolescents, we may grapple with navigating reading this visual format.

The Common Core State Standards (CCSS), introduced in 2010 and since adopted by over forty states, contain measures that support visual literacy standards and emphasize students being visually literate.[4] The CCSS deemed that students in K–12 need to "demonstrate the ability to interpret, recognize, appreciate, and understand information presented through visible actions, objects, and symbols"[5] There is one specific standard in the CCSS K–5 for reading literature that is specifically related to illustrations. At the kindergarten level the standard states: "With prompting and support, describe the relationship between illustrations and the story in which they appear."[6] And at the fifth-grade level the standard is: "Analyze how visual and multimedia elements contribute to the meaning, tone, or beauty of a text (e.g., graphic novel, multimedia presentation of fiction, folktale, myth, poem)."[7]

The initial intent of the CCSS was to standardize skills at each grade level to ensure students were college or career ready. By 2014, the Common Core was facing criticism, in part because the assessment didn't align well with the standards. States' rights to control local education was being questioned.[8] Couple this with the belief that the federal government was overreaching in its attempt to standardize education. Subsequently, parents and even one state governor filed lawsuits arguing the standards threatened states' sovereignty.[9] However, these lawsuits were not successful. Today, many states have retained the standards, tweaked them to serve as state guidelines, and eliminated assessment of them.

Many websites offer approaches to assist students in their acquisition of visual literacy.[10] One example is Abigail Housen and Philip Yenawine's Visual Thinking Strategies (VTS).[11] VTS is a specific method of viewing and talking about art using the following questions: "What do you notice? What do you see that makes you say that? What more can we find?"[12] The *New York Times* provides weekly VTS lessons online that feature a photograph or drawing.[13] An online VTS discussion is held each Monday, for students thirteen and older, focused on that week's image.

Today, with the number of symbols, infographics, maps, charts, and other visual communication kids experience, it is vital for them to be able to interpret, negotiate, and make meaning from what they are seeing. This also includes illustrations they encounter in books. What better way to acquire and strengthen visual literacy skills than through pictures and conversation!

What Are Design Elements of Picture Books?

Have you ever noticed that the white space grows smaller in *Where the Wild Things Are* as Max's imaginary adventure becomes bigger? I didn't until a six-year-old student showed it to me. I realized I needed to learn about illustration and design so that I could be part of discovering, along with my students, fascinating facets of picture books.

While at the public library one day, I stumbled upon a book by John Warren Stewig, *Looking at Picture Books*, that completely changed my perspective and understanding of picture books (unfortunately, this book is now out of print but still available from a few online bookstores). I had no idea line, color, proportion, and shape played such a primary role in telling a story. Stewig "walked" me through a variety of books and helped me "see" what I was missing. I needed to slow down and appreciate the whole book rather than focus only on the text.

I'm not advocating that you stop and talk about every little detail or deconstruct a book to the point that the enjoyment is gone and the written story becomes secondary. Instead, I'm hoping to increase your visual literacy skills and vocabulary by pausing and pondering with your child or students as you read aloud picture books. In turn, you'll recognize the layout and design of a book are conscious decisions. These features become an integral part of the total reading experience.[14]

Here are a few design elements to explore:

♦ **Size and orientation.** Board books are usually square and smaller in size so toddlers, the intended audience, can hold them comfortably. Most picture books are rectangles that are horizontal (landscape) or vertical (portrait). *Madeline* by Ludwig Bemelmans is vertical and larger than most picture books, possibly to accommodate "twelve little girls in two straight lines" who live in an old house in Paris covered with vines. Or, perhaps it is to create a sense of the Eiffel Tower's height that looms in the background.

Mo Willems's humorous story *Nanette's Baguette* has a landscape orientation that perfectly accommodates the journey Nanette makes to get the baguette. The size of the picture book visually displays the elongated warm toasty bread and the loud *KRACK!* when the baguette is broken in two because Nanette cannot resist taking a bite, or two, or three.

Martha V. Parravano, in *A Family of Readers*, says that the size of a picture book opens wide enough so that a circle is formed whether it's when a child is sitting on a parent's lap or the two are side by side.[15] The image of book, reader, and listener being connected in one continuous circle is a powerful one.

♦ **Jacket and cover.** While perusing the shelves of a library or bookstore, you'll probably pick up a book because the cover catches your eye. The cover illustration serves as an invitation to the reader, so it needs to be attention-getting.

Boo! by Ben Newman is an engaging cumulative story about a little mouse who is brave until he meets an owl. The cover features the wide-eyed mouse along with the two *o*'s in *boo*, cut out. Once we open the cover, we are surprised to see that the two *o*'s are now the eyes of the crocodile on the endpapers.

All the World by Liz Garton Scanlon is a celebration of the world and humankind that is depicted on the cover by Marla Frazee's illustration of two main characters standing on a path with the beautiful cloud-filled sky as a backdrop. Definitely a work of art that is pleasing to the eye because of its pastel colors, but also intriguing because we want to know more about these characters and this setting.

Covers don't need to be full color to be noticed and appreciated. Mac Barnett and Jon Klassen's shape trilogy— *Triangle*, *Square*, and *Circle*—features a single shape illustrated in black on a white background. These three books nudge readers to look at things a little differently. The same holds true for several books by Chris Van Allsburg including *Jumanji*, a story about a surreal board game, and *The Z Was Zapped: A Play in Twenty-Six Acts*, which is not an alphabet book but rather an alphabet theater where the letters undergo a physical transformation.

Sometimes when a book jacket is removed, the identical illustration is on the hardcover (or casing). Or there may be what I term a "treasure," which might be a different picture, an embossed image, or a single color.

The hardcover under the book jacket of the hilarious *We Don't Eat Our Classmates* by Ryan T. Higgins shows a fish drinking apple juice from a straw. Only until you read the story of dinosaur Penelope Rex's desire to eat fellow classmates (who happen to be children) will you understand the cover.

Brian Floca's Caldecott Medal–winning *Locomotive* is oversize and shows the engine of a train on the front jacket and a side view of the locomotive on the back. However, when you remove the book jacket, an illustration covering both back and front covers shows buffalo grazing. This provides an opportunity to talk about the Wild West and early locomotives.

All the Animals Where I Live by Philip C. Stead depicts a forlorn city dog on the book jacket in front of a red house, looking at the world around him. Now that he lives in the country, there are a lot more animals to share his space. Under the jacket is a red book cover embossed with the image of a rooster. What significance does that rooster have in the story?

Next time you pick up a picture book, take a peek under the book jacket and see what treasure you might discover.

+ **Endpapers.** When a hardcover book is opened, the endpapers are the first and last pages you see. Think of them as curtains that open and close on a performance or play. Often when we pick up a picture book, we immediately go to the title page and overlook the endpapers entirely. Sometimes these pasted pages provide the beginning and end of a story.

The front endpapers of the story *Wolf!* by Becky Bloom and illustrated by Pascal Biet shows the wolf entering a town. The story narrative tells about all the animals completely ignoring the predatory animal because they are engrossed in reading. The wolf is befuddled by their actions and decides to discover what he's missing. The back endpapers show the wolf sitting with his new friends, book in hand.

The endpapers of Giles Andreae's *Giraffes Can't Dance* contain three horizontal rows of the gangly giraffe, Gerald, in a variety of poses. If you move your eyes quickly across the row, you might see Gerald dancing.

Brown Bear, Brown Bear, What Do You See? by Bill Martin Jr. and illustrated by Eric Carle shows bands of color that represent the colors of the animals in the story in the order they appear.

+ **Front matter.** In a rush to start reading, we may overlook the front matter—the first illustration after the endpapers that sometimes comes before the title page.

If you skip the initial illustration of *Bully* by Laura Vaccaro Seeger, then you miss a vital part of the story. This picture shows a big gray bull yelling, "GO AWAY!" to the little brown bull. You can see how rejected the smaller bull feels, which leads him to become a bully as well.

The first page of *The Only Fish in the Sea* by Philip C. Stead shows a boy on a bicycle pedaling furiously. When you turn the page, he has stopped and is yelling at Sadie. Apparently, Little Amy Scott received a goldfish for her birthday and immediately proclaimed, "GOLDFISH ARE BORING!" She subsequently tossed the newly acquired gift into the ocean. The seventh page of the book is the title page. Just think how much you would have missed if you didn't start reading on that very first page. Of course, you need to continue reading and find out what happens to the hapless goldfish.

♦ **Typography.** We've all thought about the style and size of font to use in writing an email, a text, or a paper. Book designers need to make similar decisions. The font suggests visual clues for how the word or phrase should be said based on its size, shape, or color.

Bear just wants to find his hat in *I Want My Hat Back* by Jon Klassen. Font color and size play a significant role as bear questions a variety of animals until he realizes his hat is perched on rabbit's head. The bear's question, "Have you seen my hat?" is in black with the animal's response shown in red.

B. J. Novak's *The Book with No Pictures* has to rely on various sizes of black typeface, lots of white space, and color that highlights some of the text. A picture book with no pictures? You'll hardly notice because of the utterly ridiculous words and phrases that you are forced to read aloud, "no matter what."

♦ **Speech Bubbles/Speech Balloons.** You'll find speech bubbles in graphic novels, but they are also widely used in picture books. Speech bubbles are a graphic convention as well as a design element to represent the speech or thoughts of a specific character.[16]

The grandmother cries, "LEAVE ME ALONE!" repeatedly because her thirty grandchildren are driving her crazy. All she wants to do is to knit. In Vera Brosgol's humorous story, there is no doubt how to say the phrase (also the name of the book), and kids immediately join in whenever it appears on a page.

Sometimes when a character is shouting, there is a jagged or thicker outline for the speech bubble. The font may also be larger than the rest of the text. Probably the master of speech bubbles is author and illustrator Mo Willems and his Elephant and Piggie series of books for young readers. Willems conveys a range of emotions in *Waiting Is Not Easy!* through the characters' speech balloons that are color coordinated, so it's clear which animal is talking. Willems also uses speech balloons effectively in his Pigeon series books such as *Don't Let the Pigeon Drive the Bus!* or *The Pigeon Wants a Puppy!*

♦ **Borders and Frames.** A border surrounds the entire illustration on a page, while frames contain a sequence of actions or movements or the passage of time. When you look at *Bulldozer's Big Day* by Candace Fleming and illustrated by Eric Rohmann, you'll notice the black borders surrounding the cover and interior illustrations. The borders complement the thick black lines outlining the bulldozer and speech balloons. Sometimes the other machinery in the story cannot be contained by the borders, and only portions of them can be seen, indicating their massive size.

Author-illustrator Jan Brett effectively uses borders to provide additional information and story elements. In her classic retelling of *The Mitten*, multiple animals attempt to climb into a found mitten to get out of the cold winter weather. Mitten-shaped cutouts appear in the left-hand border to show the previous inhabitants of the mitten, and the approaching arrivals are shown in the right-side border. Also by Brett is *Mossy*, a story about an amazing turtle with a gorgeous garden growing on her shell. But when Dr. Carolina, a biologist, takes Mossy to live in her Edwardian museum, the turtle soon misses her freedom and the outdoors. Brett's lush borders display wildflowers, ferns, butterflies, and birds in contrast to elegant spreads of the museum filled with visitors in stylish Edwardian dress.

Children enjoy slowing down to appreciate the illustrations in picture books.

All these design elements provide another layer of enjoyment and meaning to the story. One of the many reasons why it's pleasurable to reread stories is that we might see something we missed during the initial reading. An excellent resource to further expand your understanding of these elements is Megan Dowd Lambert's *Reading Picture Books with Children: How to Shake Up Storytime and Get Kids Talking About What They See.* Lambert developed her Whole Book Approach while working as a museum educator at the Eric Carle Museum of Picture Book Art in Amherst, Massachusetts. If you are ever in the area, this museum is worth visiting, especially with children.

How Do Illustrators Use Artistic Elements?

While design elements are how books are constructed, artistic elements reveal how illustrators convey meaning through their art. Whenever I visit an art museum, I am in awe of what artists have created. I feel the same about picture books and graphic novels that are like a mini art museum in your hands. If the paintings were hanging on a wall instead of on pages inside a book, few would even question the image they are viewing is a work of art.

One of my many favorite books to read aloud is *A Sick Day for Amos McGee* written by Philip C. Stead and illustrated by Erin E. Stead. There's something comforting about the woodblock illustrations that tell the story of the zookeeper who takes terrific care of the animals. When he is sick one day, the animals decide upon themselves to care for him in their unique way. From the striped yellow wallpaper to Amos's green pajamas, to the red balloon that continually reappears on the pages, there is a desire to pause and take in the stylistic nuances of Erin Stead's art. These aren't cute pictures but rather paintings that portray the emotional bond between man and animals as well as the personalities and characteristics of each.

There are numerous other illustrators that draw me in with their art—Brian Selznick, Melissa Sweet, James Ransome, Duncan Tonatiuh, Eric Carle, Bryan Collier, Yuyi Morales, Dan Santat, Molly Idle, and on and on. Each has a unique artistic style, each uses a different medium to create his or her art and each uses design and artistic elements in innovative and spectacular ways. You don't have to be an art expert to appreciate picture books. The creative process can be seen, felt, and explored by everyone. Here are a few elements that capture kids' attention:

- **Lines** can be thick, thin, curvy, straight, jagged, zigzagged, or diagonal. Lines help move your eyes as the skater glides across the page in Suzy Lee's *Lines* or draws attention to a specific part of the illustration like the little mouse on the cover of *Boo!*

- **Color** portrays mood, emotions, characters, and concepts. Color can range from a full spectrum to black and white. In *Green*, Laura Vaccaro Seeger explores various hues and textures of green through lush green forests, the juicy green of a freshly cut lime, and the vivid aquamarine of a tropical sea. In her follow-up book, *Blue*, she depicts the bond between a child and a dog through shades of blue whether it's the blue pastel baby's blanket, stormy blue weather, or feeling chilly blue in the winter.

- **Perspective** provides another layer of meaning or interpretation of the story. You might be given a bird's-eye view by looking down on a scene or a worm's-eye view gazing upward. The best example of this is Chris Van Allsburg's *Two Bad Ants* when the two adventurous insects explore the bizarre world of a kitchen where everything looks enormous.

Illustrators use the placement of objects or characters on a page for a purpose. If located in the foreground, it draws more attention; in the center, it prompts the eye to move up or down; in the background, we're given the perspective that items are farther away.[17]

- **Texture** conveys the illusion that an object feels hard or soft, smooth or rough. Kids will reach out and touch images, thinking there will be a texture to feel. The textured spiderweb in the hardcover version of Eric Carle's *The Very Busy Spider* provides a multisensory experience. The raised lettering on the cover of *Bulldozer's Big Day* by Candace Fleming will prompt kids to feel each letter in the title.

- **Space** is an element that you might notice but may not realize the importance of when reading a book aloud. As mentioned earlier, Maurice Sendak used space as a storytelling element in *Where the Wild Things Are*. The white space around the illustrations becomes smaller and smaller until you reach the double-page spreads featuring the wild rumpus.

If a Book Doesn't Have Words, How Can I Read It Aloud?

Some of the most visually appealing books published today are wordless. Wordless picture books are just that—they contain no words because the story is told entirely through images. These highly interactive books can be used to develop language, thinking skills, story creation, and retelling. They also enhance the ability to detect sequence, identify details, note cause-and-effect relationships, make judgments, determine main ideas, and make predictions. Wordless books can be "read" by pre-readers and beginning readers, speakers of all languages, and adults (even illiterate or semi-literate) who want to read to children.

When you pick up a book without text, you might wonder how you are going to read it aloud. At first glance, it might appear there is no story. Reading aloud a wordless book to a child offers an opportunity to slow down and appreciate the unfolding of a story—a narrative that you and your child create.

Begin by exploring the illustrations on each page. Discuss what the characters are doing. Predict what might happen next. Ask questions about the pictures. I'm always amazed at how children are much more observant than adults. What I probably enjoy most about reading aloud a wordless book to a child is that shared experience of using our imagination to generate a terrific story—one that might change the next time we pick up the book.

All the information about design and artistic elements shared above will come into play as you read aloud a wordless picture book. While looking at the book jacket and endpapers, ponder the use of line or color. Just as with books containing text, a wordless book has a beginning, middle, and end. Helping to create that visual narrative of the story sequence is imperative.

As you turn the pages, interpret what the characters' thoughts, feelings, and emotions might be.[18] It's important to remember that even though there is a story being told through illustrations, not everything may be understood. And since the illustrator isn't participating in the read-aloud, you and your child can interpret those illustrations in a way that makes sense to you. Look at the facial expressions, settings, the sequence of action—there's honestly no right or wrong answer.

A delightful wordless picture book is 2012 Caldecott winner *A Ball for Daisy* by Chris Raschka. The spot illustrations and horizontal panels show the progression of movement and action as Daisy plays with her favorite ball. When the ball is destroyed by another dog, kids easily recognize what has happened and how Daisy is feeling.

My Friend Rabbit by Eric Rohmann is a Caldecott Medal–winning story of well-intentioned Rabbit who accidentally tosses Mouse's new airplane high into a tree. The two must devise a way to retrieve it. Rohmann creatively uses space and borders as the stack of very annoyed animals sitting on each other's backs grows taller and taller, eventually extending beyond the frame of the page.

Barbara Lehman's wordless picture books generate a story that might change each time her books are read. *The Red Book* by Lehman is about a child who finds a red book in the snow. Inside the book is a series of square illustrations showing a map, an island, and a boy. The boy finds a red book in the sand and sees a different series of pictures. There are multiple possibilities about where the children are and how they are connected. This book is included in the Treasury along with a list of Lehman's other titles.

Wordless picture books are not just for the very young. Shaun Tan's *The Arrival* is a wordless book for older readers that tells a story of the immigrant experience. *Unspoken: A Story from the Underground Railroad* by Henry Cole is a superb wordless book to share with an older child particularly because background knowledge is needed to comprehend the visual narrative.

Aren't Graphic Novels Really Just Comic Books?

As adults, we probably have some sort of comic-book reading in our past. Growing up, I couldn't wait to go to the local drugstore to buy the newest copy of comic books that featured Archie, Jughead, Veronica, and Betty or Richie Rich as well as Superman and Batman. Today's comic books are often viewed as being read primarily by adolescent males. Comics are now mainstream with annual conventions devoted entirely to this format.

Publishers have noticed the popularity and have been offering comics and graphic novels that will attract both male and female readers. Some publishers have even created an imprint such as

Candlewick Press's TOON Books for young children or Roaring Brook Press's First Second Books that attract a range of readers. Graphic novels have great appeal to children who may have lost interest in the traditional narrative format of chapter books and novels.

Graphic novels have similar design features as picture books, but they are used or defined differently.[19]

- **Panels** are a combination of image and text to create a narrative sequence.
- **Frame** consists of the lines and borders that contain the panels.
- **Captions** are boxes with a variety of text elements including scene setting and descriptions.
- **Gutter** in a graphic novel is the white space between panels that transition between scenes, narrators, time, and perspective.
- **Bleed** is an image that extends to or beyond the edge of the page.
- **Font** can be used to create mood or tone, suggest phrasing and intonation, or add to the visual design.
- **Narrative boxes** describe the scene, provide insight into the characters, or contain additional information to enhance readers' understanding of the story.
- **Shading and coloring** convey feelings, moods, and emotions. Shading is done more in graphic novels than with other types of literature.
- **Graphic weight** is a term that describes the way some images draw the eye more than others.
- **Speech balloons** in graphic novels vary in size, shape, and layout and reveal either external dialogue between two characters or internal thoughts, which is generally designated by a balloon with a series of dots or bubbles going up to it.

Comics and graphic novels involve different reading skills that require readers to move across panels while paying attention to both illustrations and text.[20] According to Jacquelyn McTaggart, the term *comic book* describes "any format that uses a combination of frames, words, and pictures to convey meaning and to tell a story. While all graphic novels are comics, not all comic books are graphic novels."[21] Generally, a comic book is twenty-eight pages in length and looks similar to a magazine, while a graphic novel is longer and has either a soft or hard cover.

How Do You Read Aloud Stories in Graphic Format?

Young readers, as well as adolescents, are drawn to the graphic format because it contains less text and is more dependent on visual aspects for the story line. The style is also accessible to struggling readers as well as those for whom English is not their first language.

Boys and girls enjoy reading books with a graphic format. These books also work well for reading aloud, particularly one-to-one or with small groups of children.

Graphic books for young readers such as Geoffrey Hayes's *Benny and Penny in the Big No-No!* present relatable stories in an easy-to-read format. Benny and Penny are two siblings who sneak into their mysterious neighbor's backyard knowing that it's wrong and there might be consequences. As you read aloud books like *Benny and Penny*, you can show young children how a graphic format works in the sequencing of panels, when a character is thinking or speaking, or the meaning of stars, question marks, and exclamation points in the text.

When reading a book in graphic format, children also learn how to read between the lines and fill in what is missing from panel to panel in order to comprehend the story. If there are portions of panels without text or dialogue, you can use your finger to guide children from panel to panel[22] and make it exciting by moving quickly when the action is fast. You and your child can even add your own narration. Try to stop briefly and ask questions such as, "What's happening?" or "What do you think she's doing?"

When selecting graphic formats to read aloud for young children in preschool through first grade, choose ones that have only a few characters such as *Benny and Penny*. Two or three voices of characters will be enough of a challenge when reading aloud. Also, find books like *My Kite Is Stuck! And Other Stories* by Salina Yoon that have fewer panels on a page to make it easier for a child to follow the flow and for you both to stay on the same panel. Keep in mind that larger graphics are easier for sharing than smaller ones.[23] Since stories in graphic formats contain more dialogue than is normally in a picture book, the read-aloud might become a reading performance. So have fun!

Graphic novels help children learn about reading and narrative. Instead of one large illustration that goes with the text on a page, graphic formats show every step of a story. Bright colors and animal-oriented stories like Jennifer Holm's Babymouse series or Nick Bruel's Bad Kitty series have tremendous appeal. They keep children engaged and interacting with you by pointing at words they know and describing the sequence of actions as they occur.[24]

If you're looking to challenge a child's mind and vocabulary with comics, then *The Adventures of Tintin* is a recommended choice. When you've been in print for nearly ninety years, translated into eighty languages, sold three hundred million copies, and been made into movies by Peter Jackson and Steven Spielberg, you must be special. When the Pulitzer-winning historian Arthur Schlesinger Jr. listed his favorite read-aloud choices for his family, Hergé's *Tintin* ranked between Twain's *The Adventures of Huckleberry Finn* and the Greek myths.[25] Nice company.

Two years were spent researching and drawing the seven hundred detailed illustrations in each issue. *Tintin* must be read to be understood—and that is the key for parents and teachers. Each issue contains eight thousand words. The beautiful part of it is that children are unaware they are reading eight thousand words. (See *Tintin in Tibet*, in the chapter book section of the Treasury.)

One of the most popular books for kids over the past few years has been Jeff Kinney's Diary of a Wimpy Kid series about Greg

Heffley, an unforgettable boy encountering middle school. While some reviewers have classified it as a graphic novel, others have named the format as an illustrated novel. Either one seems to be an acceptable classification.

Other books in this style for middle schoolers include the Dork Diaries series by Rachel Renée Russell, about Nikki Maxwell, the female equivalent of Kinney's character. Sara Varon has created numerous graphic novels including *New Shoes*, a story about a donkey on a quest to make the perfect pair of shoes. Humorous graphic novels such as Cece Bell's autobiographical *El Deafo* or *Real Friends* by Shannon Hale and LeUyen Pham present a story with issues and situations that tweens and teens recognize or can empathize.

What Is an Interactive Book?

Interactive books have been around for decades, but they are becoming even more sophisticated, not to mention engineering marvels. We are probably all familiar with the classic gift given at baby showers, *Pat the Bunny* by Dorothy Kunhardt, that invites young children to touch and feel various textures. Today's interactive books incorporate flaps or pop-ups for children to lift, pull, unfold, jiggle, and press. Some books work well with a young child, while others are best for kids who know their own strength in pulling a tab.

Lift-the-flap books can be somewhat durable or downright fragile. Board book formats are best for young hands such as Salina Yoon's *Do Crocs Kiss?* that has children lifting the flap of each animal's mouth for the sound it makes. Rod Campbell's *Dear Zoo* has been around since 1982 but still enthralls kids as the book's character searches for the perfect pet. For a little older reader, *Flora and the Flamingo* and other Flora books by Molly Idle are an excellent choice.

If you have ever experienced a pop-up book by Robert Sabuda, Matthew Reinhart, or David A. Carter, then you know what a feat of paper engineering they have created. Sabuda's adaptations of *The Wonderful Wizard of Oz*, *Alice's Adventures in Wonderland*, *Beauty & the Beast*, or *The Little Mermaid* are masterpieces. Reinhart has worked with Sabuda on several pop-up books and has exhibited his own works of art with *Frozen* and *Harry Potter: A Pop-Up Guide to Hogwarts*. Many of David A. Carter's pop-up books are intended for children and adults. He has created the immensely popular Bugs series of pop-ups, selling over six million copies, including *How Many Bugs in a Box?: A Pop-Up Counting Book*, *Feely Bugs: To Touch and Feel*, *Birthday Bugs: A Pop-Up Party*, and *Builder Bugs: A Busy Pop-Up Book*. He also has ones for an older audience: *White Noise: A Pop-Up Book for Children of All Ages* and *Blue 2*.

Pop-up books are generally more expensive than picture or chapter books because they need to be hand-assembled. These are highly interactive books and aren't for everyday read-alouds. However, they bring a fun element to sharing a book together in a manner that is pleasurable and entertaining.

Chapter 9

The Significance of the Read-Aloud Experience

My name is India Opal Buloni, and last summer
my daddy, the preacher, sent me to the store for a
box of macaroni-and-cheese, some white rice,
and two tomatoes and I came back with a dog.

—*Because of Winn-Dixie* by Kate DiCamillo[1]

EACH chapter in this edition of *The Read-Aloud Handbook* opens with a powerful first sentence or quote from a children's book. Whether it's the text or the illustrations of a novel, chapter book, or picture book, quality literature grabs us and propels us forward to the end of the story.

Children from around the world understand the value of having someone read aloud to them. Unfortunately, not every child has someone who can or wants to serve in that role. Pam Allyn tells a story about a young boy whose childhood was troubled by poverty and loneliness.[2] When he experienced the joy of the read-aloud, he actually inspired Allyn and her organization, LitWorld, to create World Read Aloud Day.[3] It's basically a holiday for reading aloud that everyone can, and should, participate in.

When I asked middle school teacher Scott Riley what should be included in this new edition, he told me that sometimes parents don't know how to start reading aloud to their child nor exactly what they should do. His statement surprised me because in my mind I envision a child snuggled next to a parent on the sofa or tucked into bed, listening to a story. Of course, I'm assuming the parent had experienced being read aloud to when they were a child. This isn't always the case.

I'm often asked by parents and teachers how to choose a book to read aloud. My response is that it should be a book *they* enjoy. Maybe it's a childhood favorite such as *Make Way for Ducklings* by Robert McCloskey or *Harry Potter and the Sorcerer's Stone* by J. K. Rowling. Selecting a book might require a visit to the library or local bookstore to ask for suggestions. One of the advantages of the internet is that there are dozens of blogs and websites containing lists of books to read aloud. I've also provided my own recommendations in the Treasury.

Once the book is selected, the only other thing you need is an expressive voice. Remember, you are not only sharing a wonderful story but also serving as a model for how to read. The more you read aloud, the more comfortable you'll feel, and the better you'll become. After you have read aloud a book multiple times, you might observe your child picking it up and "reading" the story himself, using the same expression and inflection that you exhibited. Our voices are amazing devices that convey sadness, joy, anger, and humor. Your voice can be soft or loud depending on the story. And you might pause and let your voice be silent before a dramatic moment or to signal a change in the mood of the story.

The first line of a book should capture the interest of the reader and listener. Authors and illustrators then use what are called "page turns" to encourage you to continue reading. Brian Selznick's Caldecott Medal–winning *The Invention of Hugo Cabret* (525 pages) seizes your attention immediately with black-and-white illustrations that are peppered with narrative inserted along the way. *Where the Wild Things Are* by Maurice Sendak essentially uses one long sentence to read as you turn the pages and explore the imaginary world of Max alongside him. You'll know when you have an engaging book because your child will beg you to keep reading. She wants to know what's going to happen on that next page!

The ending of a book is equally important as the first sentence. It doesn't have to be an "and they lived happily ever after" type of conclusion, but it does need to provide closure to the story and maybe a hint of the next book if it's a series. Being left with a sense of hope for the characters is more satisfying than offering an unrealistic ending. Probably the best kind of book is one you wished hadn't ended.

The bottom line is, there isn't a right or wrong way of reading aloud, except if you just don't do it. So get a book and a child and start reading!

Will Reading Aloud Help Children with Grammar?

Grammar is more caught than taught, and the way you catch it is the same way you catch the flu: You're exposed to it. By hearing the language spoken correctly, you begin to imitate the pattern—both in what you say and in what you write. The easiest test of whether something is grammatically correct or not is to say it out loud. If, in response, you find yourself saying, "That doesn't sound right," there's a good chance it's not correct. The only way of determining if it sounds right or wrong is if you've read it or heard it said correctly.

In a nation that is becoming a more service-oriented economy, oral communication is an essential skill in the workplace. The richer the words you hear, the richer will be the words you give back—in speech and writing. Reading aloud as early in their lives as possible to all students and continuing through the grades will expose them to a rich, organized, and interesting language model as an alternative to the tongue-tied one of their peers.

Discounting both sign language and body language, there are two main forms of language: spoken and written. While they are intimately related to each other, they are not twins. Written words are far more structured than spoken words. Conversation is imprecise, often ungrammatical, and less organized than print. Therefore, children who enjoy speaking with adults and listening to stories are exposed to more extensive language than is the child who experiences only conversation (or emails and texts) with peers.

In chapter 2, research studies were cited indicating reading aloud to children has been found to increase vocabulary more than talking to them.[4] During the course of a day, children rarely hear words such as *oodles, coddled,* or *tantalizing,* much less see them in print. However, they would if they were listening to the picture book *Sarabella's Thinking Cap* by Judy Schachner, about a girl who is not only a thinker but is always conjuring, daydreaming, and creating special new worlds in her imagination. When was the last time your child heard the words *elemental, adoringly, perfidy,* or *renounce.* They are all woven into *The Tale of Despereaux* by Kate DiCamillo about a mouse in love, a rat who lives in darkness, and a slow-witted serving girl with a simple, impossible wish.

A benefit of reading aloud is for children to hear rich language and then discuss the meaning of those words with parents and teachers. Reading aloud becomes one of the best ways for children to develop word mastery and grammatical understanding, which is the basis for learning how to read.[5] There also becomes a leveling effect for families with less education and a limited vocabulary because when young children experience a range of picture books, they are also exposed to an abundance of new words.

How Does Reading Aloud Improve the Basics Like Writing and Spelling?

By *reading, reading,* and *reading.* The best way to learn vocabulary and spelling is not by looking up words in the dictionary. You learn the meanings and spellings in the same way teachers learn the names of students and parents learn the names of their neighbors: by seeing them again and again, and making the connection between the face and the name.

Nearly everyone spells by visual memory, not by rules. There is ample research to indicate that people who have the best recall of graphic or geometric symbols are also the best spellers. This, say the scientists, may have more to do with your memory genetics than with anything else.[6] Most people, when they doubt the correctness of what they have just spelled, write the word out several different ways and choose the one that looks correct. (That city in Pennsylvania—is it spelled *Pittsberg* or *Pittsburgh*? How about *humor, humer,* or *hughmer*? Does that celebrity have a large *eigo, eago,* or *ego*? Which ones look right?)

The more a child looks at published words, the greater the chances are he will recognize when the word is spelled correctly or incorrectly. Conversely, the less a child reads, the fewer words he meets and the less certain he is of both meaning and spelling.[7]

I've never met a strong writer who wasn't also an avid reader. Good writers are like baseball players. Baseball players have to play regularly, but they spend most of their time in the dugout, watching others run, hit, catch, and throw. Good writers do the same—they write, but they read even more, watching how other people throw words around to catch meaning. The more you read, the better you write—and the NAEP's Writing Report Card proves it.[8] The highest-scoring student writers were not those who wrote the most each day but rather the students who read the most recreationally, had the most printed materials in their homes, and did regular essay writing in class. As Lois Bridges, the editor of *Open a World of Possible*, states, "Every time we enter a text as a reader, we receive a writing lesson: how to spell, punctuate, use proper grammar, structure a sentence or paragraph, and organize a text. We also learn the many purposes writing serves and the different genres and formats it assumes to serve these varied purposes."[9]

Books children hear read aloud as well as those they read independently contain rich language and offer a structure for how stories are told.

What is flawed in our current writing curriculum is our failure to grasp the simple observation Jacques Barzun once made—writing and speaking are "copycat" experiences: "Wordings get in through the ear or the eye and come out at the tongue or the end of a pencil."[10] It's tough to write compound, complex, or good old simple sentences if you haven't seen them often. And when do you see them most often? When you read—you see them over and over and over.

Teachers lean on literature to serve as mentor texts in their classrooms. When Megan Sloan introduces books to her students, she invites them to "stand on the shoulders of the author" to learn about ideas, mimic the writer's style, and borrow their technique. There are picture and chapter books written as diaries, letters, travel logs, notebooks, or in verse. Sometimes children become so inspired by the way a book is written that they want to emulate that style in their own writing.

Here is a crucial fact to consider in the reading and writing connection: Visual receptors in the brain outnumber auditory receptors thirty to one.[11] The chances of a word (or sentence) being retained in our memory bank are thirty times greater if we see it instead of hear it. If our experience with language consists mainly of television dialogue and conversation, we will never be able to write coherent sentences until we see a lot more of them. If we wait until we're in middle management and worrying about our writing skills, it might even be too late. Learning to write well at age thirty-five is a lot like learning to skateboard or speak a foreign language at age thirty-five: It's not as easy as it would have been at age seven. Vocabulary and coherent sentences can't be downloaded onto paper unless they've first been uploaded to the head—by reading.

Can You Recommend Something That Will Teach My Child to Read Before Kindergarten?

Early reading isn't intrinsically bad, but some experts believe that children should arrive at the skill naturally, on her own, without a structured time each day when a parent sits down with her and teaches letters, sounds, and syllables. The "natural way" is how Scout learned in Harper Lee's *To Kill a Mockingbird*—by sitting on the lap of her dad and listening as his finger moved over the pages. Gradually, a connection is made between the sound of a word and the appearance of certain letters on the page.

There are children who come to reading prematurely, who arrive at the kindergarten door already knowing how to read without having been formally taught. These children are called early fluent readers, and they're worth our attention. During the past fifty years, intensive studies have been done of such children.[12] The majority of them were never formally taught to read at home, nor did they use any commercial reading programs.

Additionally, students who respond to initial classroom instruction without difficulty indicate factors in the home environment that influence young children:

1.   Early fluent readers had parents who engaged with their children in literacy activities such as reading, talking, or singing.[13] These children had higher reading achievement than children whose parents engaged them less frequently in early literacy activities.

2.   Parents taught letters, words, or numbers at least once a week and visited the library at least once a month.[14] Unfortunately, the NCES also reported in 2016 that there was a higher percentage of three- to five-year-olds who were not being read to three or more times a week than was previously reported in 2001.

3.   The 2016 PIRLS report of thirty-three countries specified that home resources, including books, could be attributed to higher reading achievement. Other factors were the presence of digital devices and parents who liked to read.[15] However, there was some concern regarding a decrease in parents' positive attitudes toward reading. Only 32 percent stated they liked to read a lot, while 17 percent indicated they did not.

4.   Family members stimulate a child's interest in reading and writing by answering endless questions, praising the child's efforts at reading and writing, taking the child to the library frequently, buying books, writing stories the child dictates, and displaying his paperwork in a prominent place in the home. None of the factors determined in these studies was expensive or involved much more than interest on the part of the parent.

Isn't There Something Parents Can Do to Promote Early Literacy Skills?

Reading aloud to a child is not a passive activity. As you read aloud, you are doing more than telling a great story. You are probably fielding as well as lobbing questions. That's part of the fun of reading aloud—to discover what is piquing your child's interest enough to ask questions. So what can you do to generate an interactive read-aloud and prompt those connections and questions? Here are a few possibilities and how they promote reading skills:

+ Show the cover illustration as well as stopping at various points in the story to ask, "What do you think this book is about?" or "What do you think will happen next?" (predicting)

+ Ask at certain points in the story, "What just happened?" or "Tell me what you think about . . . ?" (reading comprehension)

+ Extend thinking by saying, "Why do you think she did that?" (critical thinking skills)

+ Encourage thoughts beyond the story. "This reminds me of the time when we . . ." (connections)

+ Provide time to consider other possibilities. "What would you do if that happened to you?" (problem solving)

The paramount thing to remember is not to turn an enjoyable story into a textbook or something that feels like a test. Instead, focus on open-ended questions and give your child time to think about a response. The three questions I generally ask are pretty simple:

What do you think . . . ?

How do you feel (about the story, character, events)?

What do you wonder?

Probably the question that elicits the most thoughtful response, especially from older kids is, "So . . . ?" Open-ended questions don't have a right or wrong answer, nor can they be answered with a yes or a no. What they do is encourage children to

+ Think beyond the obvious.

+ Consider many possibilities.

+ Increase understanding and comprehension.

+ Offer time to share information, feelings, and attitudes.

+ Provide opportunities to explain or describe something, which will expand and develop speech, language, and vocabulary.

+ Encourage retelling of parts or all of the story.[16]

How Does This Fit with the Call for Higher National Standards?

As a nation, we want to be sure to raise educational achievement standards. Since 1983's *A Nation at Risk* report, CEOs and politicians have emphasized only one standard: IQ. And as the demands for higher scores are pressed on superintendents, principals, and teachers, the curriculum narrows to only what will be on the standardized test.[17] Since the tests include subjects that measure IQ, there remains little or no time for HQ subjects—the heart quotient. Who has time for the teachable moment when the class hamster dies and you've got test prep to cover? Who bothers to discuss the ethical thing to do if there are no ethics questions on the state standards exam?

As Clifton Fadiman once observed, "There is no shortage of smart people. We've got lots of those. The real shortage is in better people." And you make better people by educating children's brains and hearts. Daniel Goleman's enormously successful book *Emotional Intelligence: Why It Can Matter More Than IQ* is perhaps the most eloquent argument in support of that.[18]

So how do we educate the heart? There are only two ways: life experience and stories about life experiences, which is called literature. Great preachers and teachers—Aesop, Socrates, Confucius, Moses, and Jesus—have traditionally used stories to get their lesson plans across, educating both the mind and the heart.

In today's world, when school scores either dropped or failed to rise, administrators and politicians seized on nonfiction as a salvation tool. Since most standardized test questions didn't involve subjective thinking or personal values, they reasoned, let's narrow the reading curriculum to nonfiction.

That thinking is flawed on several counts: Neither education research nor brain science supports it. Literature is considered an essential medium because it brings us closest to the human heart. And of the two forms of literature (fiction and nonfiction), the one that brings us closest to the meaning of life is fiction. That's one reason most of the recommendations for read-alouds at the back of this book are fiction. It's also worth noting that in the Organisation for Economic Co-operation and Development (OECD) study of 250,000 teens in thirty-two nations, students who read the most fiction had the highest literacy scores.[19]

Stories can transport readers to another place or time or give insight into cultures other than their own.

Additionally, recent brain science tells us fiction engages a larger portion of the brain.[20] Fiction forces us to concentrate to find meaning and therefore deepens our engagement and helps comprehension. Furthermore, good fiction is often built on a carefully researched infrastructure of fact. For instance, *A Long Walk to Water* by Linda Sue Park relates the story of two eleven-year-olds in Sudan. Or read the Newbery Medal–winning *Number the Stars* by Lois Lowry, which is a compelling story about the Danish Resistance. *Esperanza Rising* by Pam Muñoz Ryan, set during the 1930s, tells of a Mexican girl's fall from riches and her immigration to California. And the historical fiction novel *The Watsons Go to Birmingham—1963* by Christopher Paul Curtis is both humorous and poignant as an African American family journeys to Alabama during the time of the church bombing that killed four young girls. None of these books can be read without the reader coming away with a wider understanding of another time and place (background knowledge).

Are You Saying That Nonfiction Shouldn't Be Read Aloud?

Nonfiction has changed tremendously over the past few decades. Gone is the stilted language and boring blue illustrations. Today, there are fascinating biographies and autobiographies about individuals from numerous professions, cultures, and countries; riveting observations in the area of science and engineering; and captivating details about historical events around the world. For six years, I was fortunate to serve on the Orbis Pictus Award Committee for Outstanding Nonfiction for Children; three as the committee chair. During that time I indulged in reading books that informed, intrigued, and inspired me and also quite a few that touched my heart: *Drowned City: Hurricane Katrina and New Orleans*, told in a graphic format by Don Brown; *The Girl from the Tar Paper School: Barbara Rose Johns and the Advent of the Civil Rights Movement* by Teri Kanefield; and *A Splash of Red: The Life and Art of Horace Pippin* by Jen Bryant.

Teachers almost exclusively select fictional picture or chapter books for reading aloud. Nonfiction in the classroom is generally relegated to support an area in the curriculum that is being studied such as insects or civil rights—the books are gathered from the library and are available for student use but not read aloud by the teacher. As a former school librarian, I know when children visited the library, they immediately rushed to the nonfiction section. This doesn't mean all nonfiction books serve as great read-alouds no more than all fiction books should be read aloud. However, there are quite a few you'll locate in the Treasury that will capture kids' and probably adults' attention not to mention the possibility of also touching their hearts.

Some of the suggestions for read-aloud fiction also apply to non-fiction, especially narrative nonfiction. Melissa Sweet's *Balloons over Broadway: The True Story of the Puppeteer of Macy's Parade* tells how Tony Sarg created the helium balloons for the Thanksgiving Day parade. Sweet's book not only shares a great story about Tony but also prompts conversation about this annual event.

It's difficult to read any picture-book biography about Malala Yousafzai, who was shot by the Taliban, without being inspired by this young girl's conviction to make the world a better place. For older children, books by Russell Freedman such as *Children of the Great Depression* or his biographies of Abraham Lincoln or Eleanor Roosevelt are excellent read-alouds. *We Are the Ship: The Story of Negro League Baseball* by Kadir Nelson is an impressive historical account with exceptional artwork.

Some nonfiction doesn't have to be read from cover to cover. You can read one page or the entirety of Steve Jenkins's book *Eye to Eye: How Animals See the World*. There are books of biographical poems that lend themselves to short readings like *Bravo!: Poems About Amazing Hispanics* by Margarita Engle or *Shaking Things Up* by Susan Hood, which focuses on fourteen young women who changed the world.

There are chapter books that weave together both fiction and nonfiction. The widely popular Magic Tree House series by Mary

Pope Osborne features siblings Jack and Annie who embark on numerous adventures via their magic tree house. At the conclusion of each fictional story, Osborne provides factual information about the time period or individuals that Jack and Annie encountered. The American Girl series of books has a tie-in with a particular doll along with information about the historical era in which the girl lived.

Consider Maria Rue's thoughts about nonfiction she read as a child and the books her daughter is reading today:

I remember nonfiction books being dull and uninspiring, almost like an afterthought. However, my daughter consumes books voraciously and does not discriminate between fiction and nonfiction. In fact, she seeks out nonfiction on a regular basis. Nowadays, we have these inspiring, honest, and beautifully portrayed stories intended to ignite a child's inquiry. I feel there is growing momentum toward confronting complex, difficult truths in a way that encourages a younger audience to engage, question, and hopefully understand topics historically not considered for children. Today's kids are exposed to very grown-up realities, and I think it's important to shed light on them versus pretending we can protect their innocence by avoidance. My daughter told me she enjoys learning the truth about things. She said, "I like real things like Malala. She is a real person, in a real experience, right now. Since I live in America, it's hard for me to understand what it might be like if I was growing up in another country. So I read about other people and places so I can understand better."

We should remember that not all children find their way into books through fiction. It's advisable to extend their reading palate to other offerings, including nonfiction.

What About Poetry?

Poetry is a rich source for reading aloud. It aids in language development, creativity, writing, and self-expression. Young children absolutely love hearing poetry. Nursery rhymes don't make sense, but they rhyme and have a lyrical quality that is soothing to the ear of an infant or toddler. Picture books for young children contain rhyming text and enjoyable plots as in *Llama Llama Red Pajama* by

Anna Dewdney; *Goodnight, Goodnight, Construction Site* by Sherri Duskey Rinker; and *How Do Dinosaurs Say Good Night?* by Jane Yolen. There are also silly rhyming books such as *I Ain't Gonna Paint No More!* by Karen Beaumont, a takeoff of a well-known song, and *Pete the Cat: Rocking in My School Shoes*, which is an original song by James Dean and can be accessed on the internet. And of course, there's Dr. Seuss, whose cartoon-style illustrated books contain fantastical language and unique story lines.

Unfortunately, something happens around fourth grade that turns the tide for enjoying poetry. The poems kids encounter no longer rhyme except for the occasional Shel Silverstein or Edward Lear. As students progress to the upper grades, they are also met with the requirement to memorize a poem and recite it or, worse yet, to analyze it and discover the meaning the poet is trying to convey. And then there is the writing of different forms of poetry— haiku, free verse, concrete, ode. Every year in school, poetry becomes a little less fun for many children, and the dislike for poetry grows to the point that adults won't even consider reading it aloud because of their own history with this literary form.

For kids who aren't sold on listening to poetry, try reading aloud a novel written in verse, which has a narrative told through the medium of poetry rather than prose. *Out of the Dust* by Karen Hesse received the Newbery Medal in 1998. This compelling story is set during the dust bowl years and is one of the most powerful read-alouds I think I have ever shared with middle-grade children. *Love That Dog* by Sharon Creech is a series of free verse poems about a boy who hates poetry but finds it can be a powerful way to express himself through writing. Kwame Alexander's *The Crossover* also received the Newbery Medal for its portrayal of family issues interwoven with playing basketball. This book is an excellent way for boys and girls to receive poetry through a gripping story. *Long Way Down* by Jason Reynolds is equally riveting for an adolescent audience and addresses gun violence.

Reading aloud poetry for children and teenagers is also great when there's limited time. Or, you can include a few poems during daily read-alouds at home or in school. If you don't feel confident in your reading of poetry, practice a few times so the poem flows easily. Seek out poets who write for children and young adults such as Lee Bennett Hopkins, J. Patrick Lewis, Jane Yolen, Rebecca Kai Dotlich, Alan Katz, Jack Prelutsky, Douglas Florian, and Naomi

Shihab Nye. There are some excellent poetry books included in the Treasury.

A Final Word on Why We Read Aloud!

There may come a time when you experience a full-circle moment as you step back to examine and consider what you believe in and why it is important. Reading aloud to children is something I never question and always advocate. I'm glad there are individuals like Jim Trelease, Rosemary Wells, Kate DiCamillo, and me, as well as others you have met throughout this book, who continually extol the many, many benefits of reading aloud.

In *Unwrapping the Read Aloud: Making Every Read Aloud Intentional and Instructional*, Lester Laminack offers a convincing statement for why we read aloud:

> Let me remind you that literature in all its many forms has such potential to expand the horizons of every child—regardless of background or baggage, privilege or poverty. When we read aloud to them, we offer them new vistas and new visions. We offer them new ways of coping with life's issues and pleasures. We offer them new opportunities to grow their language and their understandings. We help them realize how much there is to learn. When we read aloud, we show them how we gain a little knowledge to ask better questions, and that asking better questions drives us to read even more. When we read aloud, we introduce them to people just like them and like no one they have ever imagined. . . . We help them realize their families are one of the many ways families can be formed. . . . But perhaps the most important message that comes from our reading aloud to them is one that says you are worth the time this will take.[21]

Chapter 10

The Dos and Don'ts
of Reading Aloud

But it was her mother who loved her most of all.
A hundred times a day she would laugh and shake
her head and say, "Koala Lou, I DO love you!"

—*Koala Lou* by Mem Fox[1]

AUSTRALIAN author Mem Fox has written dozens of books
that have become favorites of children all over the world. Her lyrical language makes her books perfect for reading aloud. Fox not
only writes with an ear for reading aloud but also has long been a
strong proponent of it. In her book for adults, *Reading Magic: Why
Reading Aloud to Our Children Will Change Their Lives Forever*, she
states:

As we share the words and pictures, the ideas and viewpoints, the
rhythms and rhymes, the pain and comfort, and the hopes and
fears and big issues of life that we encounter together in the pages
of a book, we connect through minds and hearts with our children
and bond closely in a secret society associated with the books we
have shared. The fire of literacy is created by the emotional sparks
between a child, a book, and the person reading. It isn't achieved
by the book alone, nor by the child, nor by the adult who's reading
aloud—it's the relationship winding between all three, bringing
them together in easy harmony.[2]

There isn't a right or wrong way to read aloud. Some people are better at it than others, but often that is because of the books they select, the pre-reading they engage in, and the willingness to be expressive when reading. On the next few pages are a few dos and don'ts to consider when choosing books and engaging in the read-aloud process. And remember, the more *you* read aloud, the better you will become. And the more stories children hear will be one more step on their road to literacy.

Dos

As you begin . . .

+ Read to children as soon as possible, even before they are born. The younger you start, the easier and better it is.

+ Use Mother Goose rhymes and songs to stimulate an infant's language and listening.

+ Include predictable and rhyming books containing repetition especially when reading aloud to infants and toddlers.

+ Start with picture books that have only a few sentences on the page, then gradually move to books with more and more text and fewer pictures. Then build to chapter books and novels.

As you select books . . .

+ Vary the length and subject matter of your readings by selecting fiction, nonfiction, and poetry.

+ Occasionally choose books above children's intellectual levels to challenge their minds.

+ Avoid books with long descriptive passages until the child's imagination and attention span are capable of handling them.

+ Know your listeners. As a parent, tap into the interests of your children, which may vary widely. As a teacher, keep reading to discover new books to read aloud. Just because last year's third graders enjoyed a book doesn't mean the same will hold true this year. Try conducting an interest inventory to find out what types of books would interest them.

♦ Honor kids' choices of books. While you may not initially be enthralled with the Captain Underpants illustrated novel series, pay attention and you might discover from the child what draws him into the story.

♦ Try books with different writing styles or formats. For example, chapter books and novels written in verse can be very powerful.

♦ Picture books can be read easily to a family of children widely separated in age. Novels, however, pose a challenge. If there are more than two years (and thus social and emotional differences) between your children, each child will greatly benefit if you read to him or her individually. This requires more effort on the part of the parents, but it will reap rewards in direct proportion to the effort expended. You will reinforce the specialness of each child.

♦ Remember, everyone enjoys a good picture book, even a teenager.

♦ If you start a book, it is your responsibility to continue it, unless it turns out to be a bad choice. Don't leave the child or students hanging for three or four days between chapters and expect interest to be sustained.

As you prepare . . .

♦ Preview the book by reading it ahead of time. Such advance reading allows you to spot material you may wish to shorten, eliminate, or elaborate on.

♦ Bring the author to life, as well as the book. Google the author's name to find a personal webpage, and always read the information on your book's dust jacket. Either before or during the reading, tell your audience something about the author. This lets them know books are written by people, not by machines.

♦ Allow your listeners a few minutes to settle down and adjust their bodies and minds to the story. If it's a novel, begin by asking what happened when you left off yesterday. Mood is a significant factor in listening. An authoritative "Now stop that and settle down! Sit up straight! Pay attention!" doesn't create a receptive atmosphere.

♦ Provide unusually active children paper, crayons, and pencils to allow them to keep their hands busy while listening. (You doodle while talking on the telephone, don't you?)

As you read aloud . . .

♦ Say the name of the book, the author, and the illustrator—no matter how many times you have read the book.

♦ Discuss the illustration on the cover. Ask, "What do you think this is going to be about?"

♦ Stop at key words or phrases during repeat readings of a predictable book and allow the listener to provide the word or phrase.

♦ Invite the child to turn pages for you when it is time to encourage involvement.

♦ Keep listeners involved by occasionally asking, "What do you think is going to happen next?" or "What do you like about the story so far?"

♦ Use plenty of expression when reading, and don't hesitate to be animated. If possible, change your tone of voice to fit the dialogue. Is the character happy or sad? Yelling or whispering?

♦ Adjust your pace to fit the story. During a suspenseful part, slow down and lower your voice. A lowered voice in the right place moves listeners to the edge of their chairs.

♦ Read slowly enough for children to build mental pictures of what they just heard you read. Slow down enough for the children to see the pictures in the book without feeling hurried. Reading quickly allows no time for the reader to use vocal expression.

♦ Be a good "coach." When you come to a part of the story the audience might not sense is important, pause and then whisper, "Mmmmmm. This could be important."

♦ When reading a picture book, make sure the children can see the pictures easily as you read. Don't read the text and then show the illustrations, because the two work together in telling the story.

+ In reading a novel, position yourself where both you and the children are comfortable. In the classroom, whether you are sitting on the edge of your desk or standing, your head should be above the heads of your listeners for your voice to carry to the far side of the room. Do not read or stand in front of brightly lit windows. Backlighting strains the eyes of your audience.

+ If the chapters are long or if you don't have enough time each day to finish an entire chapter, find a suspenseful spot at which to stop. Leave the audience hanging; they'll be counting the minutes until the next reading.

+ Allow time for class and home discussion after reading a story. Thoughts, hopes, fears, and discoveries are aroused by a book. Allow them to surface, and help children to deal with them through verbal, written, or artistic expression if they are so inclined. Do not turn discussions into quizzes or insist upon prying story interpretations from children.

As family members read aloud . . .

+ Fathers should make an extra effort to read to their children. Because the vast majority of primary school teachers are women, young boys often associate reading with women and schoolwork. A father's early involvement with books and reading can do much to elevate books to at least the same status as sports in a boy's estimation. Also, select books of interest to your son.

+ Encourage older children to read to younger ones, but make this a part-time, not a full-time, substitution for you. Remember, the adult is the ultimate role model.

+ Encourage relatives living far away to record themselves reading a story, or better yet they can FaceTime with a child to share a story read aloud.

+ When children wish to read to you, it is better for the book to be too easy than too hard, just as a beginner's bicycle is better too small rather than too big.

+ Arrange for time each day for children to read by themselves (even if "read" means only turning pages and looking at the

pictures). All your read–aloud motivation goes for naught if time is not available to put that motivation into practice.

And remember . . .

- Reading aloud comes naturally to very few people. To do it successfully and with ease, you must practice.

- In addition to the time you have set aside for reading aloud each day, find additional opportunities such as during bath time, at meals, or in the car.

- Set aside at least one consistent time each day for a story.

- The art of listening is an acquired one. It must be taught and cultivated gradually—it doesn't happen overnight.

- Take books with you everywhere you go just in case you have a few minutes to read a picture book or squeeze in a few chapters if you are waiting in a traffic jam (and you're not driving) or long waits at the doctor's office.

- Lead (or is it *Read*?) by example. Make sure your children see you reading for pleasure other than at read-aloud time. Share with them your enthusiasm for whatever you are reading. If you're reading an ebook, it's important to let the child know you're reading a book, not checking your email or Facebook.

Don'ts

As you select books . . .

♦ Don't read stories that you don't enjoy yourself. Your dislike will show in the reading, and that defeats your purpose.

♦ Don't continue reading a book once it is obvious it was a poor choice. Admit the mistake and choose another. Make sure you've given the book a fair chance to get rolling; some, like *Tuck Everlasting*, start slower than others. (You can avoid the problem by pre-reading at least part of the book yourself.)

♦ Don't feel you have to tie every book to classwork if you are a teacher. Don't confine the broad spectrum of literature to the narrow limits of the curriculum.

♦ Don't overwhelm your listener. Consider the intellectual, social, and emotional level of your audience in making a read-aloud selection. Never read above a child's emotional level.

♦ Don't select a book that many of the children already have heard or seen on television or in the theater. Once a novel's plot is known, much of their interest is lost.

♦ You can read a book and view the video afterward. This way children will see how much more can be portrayed in print than on film.

♦ Don't choose novels for reading aloud that are heavy with dialogue; they are difficult for reading aloud and listening. All those indented paragraphs and quotations make for easy silent reading—the reader sees the quotations marks and knows it is a new voice, a different person speaking, but the listener doesn't. And if the writer fails to include a notation at the end of the dialogue, such as "said Mrs. Murphy," the audience has no idea who said what.

♦ Don't be fooled by awards. Just because a book won an award doesn't guarantee it will be a worthwhile read-aloud. In most cases, a book award is given for the quality of the writing, not for its read-aloud qualities.

As you read aloud . . .

• Don't start reading if you are not going to have enough time to do it justice. Having to stop after one or two pages only serves to frustrate, rather than stimulate, the child's interest in reading.

• Don't get too comfortable while reading. A reclining or slouching position is most apt to bring on drowsiness.

• Don't be unnerved by questions during the reading, mainly from very young children in your own family. If the question is not to distract or postpone bedtime, answer it patiently. There is no time limit for reading a book, but there is a time limit on a child's inquisitiveness. Foster that curiosity with patient responses, and then resume your reading. Classroom questions may need to be held until the end, if possible. With twenty children all deciding to ask questions to impress the teacher, you might never reach the end of the book.

• Don't impose interpretations of a story upon your audience. Instead, let kids talk about it themselves. The highest literacy gains occur with children who have access to discussions following a story.

And remember . . .

• Don't confuse quantity with quality. Reading to your child for ten minutes, with your full attention and enthusiasm, may very well last longer in the child's mind than two hours of solitary television viewing.

• Don't use the book as a threat ("If you don't pick up your room, no story tonight!"). No child or class should believe they have to earn the privilege and gift of a read-aloud.

Treasury of Recommended Read-Alouds

> "It's just . . . I don't think there's such a thing as
> boy books or girl books. I think there are *people*
> books."
>
> —*The Parker Inheritance* by Varian Johnson

AN essential element in reading aloud is what you choose to read. Not everyone reading this book is familiar with children's literature, either classic or contemporary. Some readers are new parents or teachers, and others are veterans to the experience; some are looking for books they remember as a child, and others are seeking new titles. To meet that diversity, I've tried to strike a balance between old and new in compiling this list.

There is a danger with any book list that only a thousand-page volume could do justice to the many titles deserving mention. Rather than being comprehensive, this list is intended as a starter and time-saver. Remember these are read-aloud titles, which eliminates some books that are difficult to read aloud or, because of the subject matter, are best read silently to oneself—like Robert Cormier's *The Chocolate War* (subject) or Christopher Paul Curtis's *The Journey of Little Charlie* (dialect).

Some of the titles included in this section have been around for a decade or more, and that's a great credential. It means these books have a lasting quality since people continue to buy or borrow them.

There are also engaging books that beg to be read aloud that have been published recently. It's difficult to determine if a book will continue to remain in print, but I've tried my best to select those I believe will have sustainability.

There are eight categories, and all books are listed alphabetically by title (the author–illustrator index at the end of *The Read-Aloud Handbook* will also help you locate books).

With each major title, I've included a listening level. Thus, when you read "K–2," that refers to the grade level at which the child could hear and understand the story; it is *not* the reading level of the book. In the book's summary section, related titles are sometimes listed.

The Treasury is organized by both types of books as well as genres. Below is an explanation of the different books included:

Wordless Books—The stories in these books are told entirely through illustrations and contain no text. They offer an excellent opportunity for you and a child to use imagination in creating your own narrative.

Predictable Books—Words or sentence patterns are repeated often enough to enable children to predict their appearance and join in the reading. There is an appealing cadence to the text that encourages children's participation. Predictable books also stimulate reading naturally because words are learned more easily. This results in matching words they are saying with those on the page.

Stories with Rhyming Verse—Rhyming is sometimes a difficult concept for young children to learn. By repeatedly hearing words that rhyme through stories, poems, and songs, young children will begin to play with language and grasp this important concept.

Picture Books—Text and illustration work in concert to create a story in picture books. These books are for all ages, not just young children.

Early Chapter Book Series—Introducing children to a chapter book series encourages their progress toward independent reading. These series have relatable characters and are heavily illustrated to make the transition to chapter books and novels easier.

Chapter Books and Novels—There are a variety of ways in which authors choose to tell stories—through narrative, graphic novel format, illustrated novel, and novel in verse. This section contains all these writing styles for a range of listening levels.

Nonfiction—The stilted language and boring illustrations of nonfiction books are long gone. In the Treasury, I have recommended nonfiction books containing narrative text or ones written in a style that makes reading aloud information pleasurable.

Poetry—Some of the most interesting and beautifully illustrated books today are those containing poetry. I've recommended some of the best.

I have limited my selections to books that are still in print. Even though obtaining out-of-print books is far less of a problem today than it was before used bookstores went online, it is still difficult, and sometimes expensive, to secure a copy of a title no longer readily available.

Happy reading!

Contents

Wordless Books

A Ball for Daisy
BY CHRIS RASCHKA
Grades PreS–1　　　　　　　　　　　　　　　*32 pages*
Schwartz & Wade, 2011; ebook
Raschka's heartwarming story begs to be read aloud. Daisy is a playful pup that loves her favorite toy—a red ball. The joy that

Daisy feels for the ball is evident as she chases it, sleeps with it, and takes it everywhere she goes. When a big dog destroys the beloved ball, Daisy's anguish is clearly understood through the expressive illustrations. This book will promote discussion with any child who has experienced the loss of a cherished toy. *Daisy Gets Lost* (2013) is a nearly wordless follow-up about Daisy being lost and the joy of being found.

Ben's Dream

BY CHRIS VAN ALLSBURG
Grades K–4   *32 pages*
Houghton Mifflin, 1982
Ben dreams that he and his house float by the monuments of the world that are half-submerged in floodwater. This book presents a wonderful opportunity to identify the various monuments and to even locate more information about them.

Chalk

BY BILL THOMSON
Grades K–3   *40 pages*
Marshall Cavendish, 2010; ebook
Who knew that a piece of chalk could not only entertain children but also generate a terrifying creature. One rainy day, three raincoat-clad children find a bag of chalk and begin to draw an image that soon comes to life—a very large dinosaur with very large teeth. What child doesn't like dinosaurs? And what adult cannot suppress their amazement when viewing the stunning illustrations?

The Farmer and the Clown

BY MARLA FRAZEE
Grades PreS–2   *32 pages*
Beach Lane Books, 2014; ebook
A farmer labors in the field but pauses when he sees a colorful train passing by. A sudden jolt sends a baby clown flying off the train and into the life of the elderly gent. Once the smiling clown makeup is washed away, the farmer realizes the baby isn't as happy as he first appeared. The farmer engages the clown in the life of the farm, and soon an unexpected loving relationship is formed between the two. When the train returns, the baby clown is reunited with his family but not without offering a final hug.

Flora and the Flamingo

BY MOLLY IDLE

Grades PreS–2   *44 pages*

Chronicle, 2013; ebook

Flora and her graceful friend, Flamingo, move from synchronized dance to a performance executed in perfect harmony. Interactive flaps reveal the twists, turns, and even a flop as the two unlikely friends explore the ups and downs of forging a new friendship. Additional Flora books include *Flora and the Peacocks* and *Flora and the Penguin*. Toddlers will enjoy the Flora board books such as *Flora and the Chicks* and *Flora and the Ostrich*.

I Got It!

BY DAVID WIESNER

Grades K–3   *32 pages*

Clarion, 2018; ebook

This nearly wordless book uses three words, *I Got It*, to capture the determination and anxiety of a young outfielder. As he steadfastly waits for a fly ball, he envisions all sorts of imaginary obstacles that could interfere with his ability to make the catch. Make sure you lift the book jacket that will reveal an additional illustration. Wiesner's other wordless books, including *Tuesday*, *The Three Pigs*, and *Flotsam* (all Caldecott Medal winners), are worth reading aloud as well.

I Walk with Vanessa: A Story About a Simple Act of Kindness

BY KERASCOËT

Grades PreS–2   *40 pages*

Schwartz & Wade, 2018; ebook

At times, a wordless book can be more powerful in conveying a message than a book with text. Such is the case with *I Walk with Vanessa*. A young girl is the newest student in her class. On the way home, she is bullied as other children stand by and do nothing. One of the girls is visibly upset and agonizes about it all night. The next day, she knocks on the door of her new classmate and walks with her to school. Soon other children join them, creating a unified group. Related books with text: *Bully* by Laura Vaccaro Seeger and *The Recess Queen* by Alexis O' Neill.

The Lion & the Mouse

BY JERRY PINKNEY
Grades PreS–2   *40 pages*
Little, Brown, 2009

This wordless adaptation of one of Aesop's most beloved fables earned Pinkney the Caldecott Medal. Set in the African Serengeti, stunning watercolors depict the ferocious lion who spares a meek mouse he had planned to eat. Mouse shows his gratitude later when he frees the lion from a poacher's net. The expressions of the characters make this a truly special retelling. Pinkney's *The Tortoise & the Hare* is virtually wordless except for "Get ready, set, go!" and equally as enjoyable and stunning.

Little Fox in the Forest

BY STEPHANIE GRAEGIN
Grades PreS–2   *40 pages*
Schwartz & Wade, 2017; ebook

A young girl plans to share her most treasured possession during tomorrow's show-and-tell. After showing her toy fox, the girl stops at a playground on her way home, only to have her plaything stolen by a real fox that runs into the nearby woods. As the girl and her classmate chase the fox, they encounter a variety of creatures as well as a world filled with personified animals. An unexpected ending is heartwarming and magical.

Pip & Pup

BY EUGENE YELCHIN
Grades PreS–2   *32 pages*
Henry Holt, 2018; ebook

Pip the chick emerges from her shell and immediately spies a potential new friend—Pup! When Pip successfully wakes the sleeping Pup, the pooch is not happy. But sometimes ingenuity overcomes anger, and soon the two become playful as they encounter new problems to solve.

The Red Book

BY BARBARA LEHMAN
Grades PreS–3   *32 pages*
Houghton Mifflin, 2004; ebook

When I read this book well over a decade ago, I immediately was drawn to the story conveyed in the art by Barbara Lehman. On her way to school, a young girl sees the cover of a red book sticking out of a snowdrift, picks it up, and stuffs it into her coat. During the school day, she continually glances at the book until she finally cannot resist and opens her treasure. What is revealed are pictures of a boy who finds a red book in the sand. This story within a story will prompt a closer look and great conversations. Other wordless books by Lehman that grab readers' attention include *Trainstop* and *The Secret Box*.

Time Flies

BY ERIC ROHMANN

Grades K–4   *32 pages*

Crown, 1994; ebook

Rohmann's wordless story is both time-travel adventure and scientific exploration. When a bird is trapped inside a dinosaur exhibit at a natural history museum one dark and stormy night, he takes flight and encounters various creatures against the backdrop of a prehistoric landscape. The stunning oil paintings will amaze children and adults alike.

Wave

BY SUZY LEE

Grades PreS–5   *40 pages*

Chronicle, 2008

Sometimes wordless books span a range of ages, and this is true for those created by Suzy Lee. In *Wave*, a child plays at the beach with the seagulls, running to where the waves break on the shore. Anyone who understands that waves are not always predictable will not be surprised the girl is drenched when water comes crashing down on her. There is so much to explore in the illustrations in *Wave* as well as other books by Lee, including *Lines*, *Shadow*, *Mirror*, and *The Zoo*. These books are excellent for older readers as their story lines are a little more complex.

Wolf in the Snow

BY MATTHEW CORDELL

Grades PreS–2   *48 pages*

Feiwel & Friends, 2017; ebook

In this 2018 Caldecott Medal book, a girl gets lost in a snowstorm as she walks home from school. Simultaneously, a wolf pup gets separated from his pack. After the girl encounters the pup, she carries it through blizzard-like conditions until she reconnects him with his pack. Unfortunately, the girl is completely exhausted and lost, but the howling wolves assist her parents in locating her. As a read-aloud, this book offers the opportunity to create a story of loss and relief felt by both child and parent.

Predictable Books

Brown Bear, Brown Bear, What Do You See?
BY BILL MARTIN JR.; ERIC CARLE, ILLUS.
Grades PreS–K   24 pages
Henry Holt, 1983; ebook
This classic predictable book follows the question through various animals and colors. Sequels include *Polar Bear, Polar Bear, What Do You Hear?* and *Panda Bear, Panda Bear, What Do You See?* Also by the author: *Barn Dance!, Chicka Chicka Boom Boom,* and *The Ghost-Eye Tree.*

Chicka Chicka Boom Boom
BY BILL MARTIN JR.; LOIS EHLERT, ILLUS.
Grades PreS–2   32 pages
Simon & Schuster, 1989; ebook
"A told B, and B told C, 'I'll meet you at the top of the coconut tree.'" In this engaging alphabet rhyme, all the letters race to the top of the coconut tree. One of the few alphabet books that contains both uppercase and lowercase letters. *Chicka Chicka ABC* and *Chicka Chicka 1, 2, 3* are also enjoyable to share with toddlers and are published in board book format.

Dinosaur vs. Bedtime
BY BOB SHEA
Grades Tod–K   40 pages
Disney-Hyperion, 2008
"ROAR!" says Little Dinosaur, "NOTHING CAN STOP ME!" as he encounters a pile of leaves, a slide, a bowl of spaghetti, and talking grown-ups. Nothing can stop him. He shouts "Dinosaur wins!" every time until he faces his biggest challenge. Predictable text will have kids joining Dinosaur as he roars with each obstacle

in his way. Other "Dinosaur vs." books by Shea include *Dinosaur vs. School*, *Dinosaur vs. Mommy*, and *Dinosaur vs. the Library*.

The Doghouse

BY JAN THOMAS

Grades Tod–1   *40 pages*

Houghton Mifflin Harcourt, 2008; ebook

Mouse, Pig, Cow, and Duck are playing when the ball gets kicked into the doghouse. As each animal is recruited to retrieve the ball, they enter the doghouse never to return. What's really going on in that doghouse? This cumulative story builds to a hilarious conclusion. *My Toothbrush Is Missing*, *What Is Chasing Duck?*, and *Is That Wise, Pig?* are other predictable books by Jan Thomas.

Duck in the Truck

BY JEZ ALBOROUGH

Grades PreS–2   *40 pages*

HarperCollins, 2000; audiobook

Duck's truck is stuck in the muck. Who will help him? Frog lends a hand and sheep helps push, but the duck's truck won't come unstuck. Is the duck out of luck in getting his truck unstuck?

If You Give a Mouse a Cookie

BY LAURA NUMEROFF; FELICIA BOND, ILLUS.

Grades PreS–1   *40 pages*

HarperCollins, 1985; audiobook

In a humorous cumulative tale that comes full circle, a little boy offers a mouse a cookie and ends up working tirelessly for the little creature. Other titles include *If You Give a Mouse a Muffin*, *If You Give a Pig a Pancake*, *If You Take a Mouse to the Movies*, *If You Give a Pig a Party*, *If You Give a Cat a Cupcake*, *If You Give a Dog a Donut*, and *If You Give a Mouse a Brownie*.

Move Over, Rover!

BY KAREN BEAUMONT; JANE DYER, ILLUS.

Grades PreS–2   *40 pages*

Houghton Mifflin Harcourt, 2006

It's raining and the animals are all trying to crowd into Rover's doghouse until one odoriferous intruder joins them. This cumulative story has rhythmic text and repetitive phrasing, concluding with a hilarious ending, which makes this an ideal read-aloud.

Pete the Cat: I Love My White Shoes
BY ERIC LITWIN; JAMES DEAN, ILLUS.
Grades PreS–2   *40 pages*
HarperCollins, 2010; ebook, audio CD
Pete the Cat loves his new white shoes and sings a catchy tune to celebrate them. Along the way his shoes change from red to white to brown to wet. Pete just keeps movin' and groovin', which is one of the things that makes this series so appealing to young children. The Pete the Cat books will engage young readers because of their simple, engaging story lines.

Shh! We Have a Plan
BY CHRIS HAUGHTON
Grades PreS–2   *40 pages*
Candlewick Press, 2014
"Ready one, ready two, ready three . . ." is a constant refrain as four friends attempt to capture a colorful bird that continually escapes their strategically positioned net. This is a perfect read-aloud with a repeatable refrain and surprising ending.

Snip Snap! What's That?
BY MARA BERGMAN; NICK MALAND, ILLUS.
Grades PreS–1   *32 pages*
Greenwillow, 2005
An alligator comes calling at the children's door. As it moves from room to room, the refrain heard is, "Were the children scared?" The response is, "You bet they were!" Finally, they muster the courage to drive him out. Was he scared? Great book for inter-action.

This Is the Nest That Robin Built
BY DENISE FLEMING
Grades PreS–2   *40 pages*
Beach Lane Books, 2018; ebook
Written in the familiar cadence of *This Is the House That Jack Built* by Simms Taback, Robin is building a nest and enlists the help of her friends. The squirrel trims the twigs, the pig mixes the mud,

and the mouse gathers weeds. A foldout shows how it all came to-gether to create a cozy nest for Robin's new babies. Another book that uses this same rhyming pattern is *This Is the Van That Dad Cleaned* by Lisa Campbell Ernst.

Two Little Monkeys
BY MEM FOX; JILL BARTON, ILLUS.
Grades PreS–2   *32 pages*
Beach Lane Books, 2012; ebook
Cheeky and Chee are trying to escape a lurking leopard by climb-ing into a tree. Fox's rhyming story encourages language develop-ment, and the repetitive phrasing invites interaction. These two clever monkey buddies will completely delight young listeners. *Where Is the Green Sheep?* is another predictable book by Mem Fox that uses a question–and–answer format.

The Very Hungry Caterpillar
BY ERIC CARLE
Grades Tod–1   *32 pages*
Philomel, 1969; ebook, audiobook
A caterpillar who becomes a butterfly is used to teach the days of the week and counting to five. Carle's signature collage illustrations are bright and colorful. As the caterpillar literally eats his way through the book, he grows bigger as do the holes he has made in the pages. Other predictable Carle books include *The Grouchy Lady-bug*, *The Very Busy Spider*, *The Very Clumsy Click Beetle*, and *The Very Lonely Firefly*.

Stories with Rhyming Verse

All Are Welcome
BY ALEXANDRA PENFOLD; SUZANNE KAUFMAN, ILLUS.
Grades PreS–2   *44 pages*
Knopf, 2018; ebook
School should be a safe and welcoming place. Children in *patkas*, hijabs, yarmulkes, and baseball caps play side by side and also learn from each other's traditions and cultures. This is a story that cele-brates diversity and provides for a meaningful, and fun, read-aloud. Pair this book with Jacqueline Woodson's *The Day You Begin*.

Be Brave, Little Penguin

BY GILES ANDREAE; GUY PARKER-REES, ILLUS.

Grades PreS–2   *32 pages*

Orchard, 2017; ebook

While the other penguins are happily swimming, little Pip-Pip plays alone. He is frightened of the water, and the other penguins call him "Scaredy-Pip-Pip." His father thinks Pip-Pip is being silly, but his mother is much more understanding. She assures him that she'll be close by. So Pip-Pip jumps into the water and joyfully begins to swim. The rhyming text reinforces the idea of having confidence and building self-esteem by tackling fears. Other stories about overcoming fears are *Courage* by Bernard Waber, *Scaredy Squirrel* by Mélanie Watt, *Max the Brave* by Ed Vere, and *Sergio Makes a Splash* by Edel Rodriguez.

Bear Snores On

BY KARMA WILSON; JANE CHAPMAN, ILLUS.

Grades PreS–1   *40 pages*

McElderry, 2005

A great brown bear is sleeping in his deep, dark lair. "The cold winds howl / and the night sounds growl. / But the bear snores on." A steady stream of animals stop by the cave to get warm, and soon a party is in full swing. But when Bear wakes up he is surprised and not too happy by what is happening. There are additional rhyming Bear books in the series including *Bear's New Friend*, *Bear Says Thanks*, *Bear Stays Up for Christmas*, *Bear Wants More*, *Bear Feels Sick*, and *Bear Feels Scared*.

Did You Eat the Parakeet?

BY MARK IACOLINA

Grades PreS–1   *32 pages*

Farrar, Straus & Giroux, 2018; ebook

A little girl cannot find her parakeet, so she accuses the cat of eating it. Rhyming text describes the dear little bird and the frustrations of the girl. What the reader knows is that the minty green parakeet is sitting on the girl's head, which she finally discovers when she looks in the mirror.

Double Take! A New Look at Opposites

BY SUSAN HOOD; JAY FLECK, ILLUS.

Grades K–2   *32 pages*

Candlewick Press, 2017

A boy, a black cat, and a blue elephant initially explore simple opposites such as *yes* and *no*, *asleep* and *awake*. Then they move to opposites whose meanings can change depending on the situation such as *near* and *far*, *big* and *small*. "Point of view (where you are) / can affect what you see." The rhyming text is playful while the digital illustrations provide visual clues to the words and their meaning.

It's Only Stanley

BY JON AGEE

Grades PreS–2   *32 pages*

Dial, 2015; ebook, audiobook

The Wimbledon family continually hears mysterious noises throughout the night. When Mr. Wimbledon checks on the sounds, he reassures his family that, "It's only Stanley." Stanley the dog seems to be quite busy as well as mechanically inclined as he fixes the oil tank, repairs the old TV, and clears the bathtub drain. What the family doesn't realize is that Stanley is turning the house into a rocket ship to zoom to outer space for an alien (that looks suspiciously like a pink poodle) encounter. This rollicking read-aloud with rhyming text is mischievously fun from beginning to surprise ending.

Llama Llama Time to Share

BY ANNA DEWDNEY

Grades PreS–2   *40 pages*

Viking, 2012; ebook, audiobook

Llama Llama's new neighbors, Nelly Gnu and her mother, stop by for a visit and a playdate. When the two children begin to build a castle made of blocks, Llama Llama decides it's not too difficult to share her toys. But when Nelly Gnu starts playing with Fuzzy Llama, a tug-of-war ensues, and soon there are two parts of the beloved toy. The rhyming text and relatable story always make the Llama Llama books perfect for reading aloud. Other titles in the series include *Llama Llama Misses Mama*, *Llama Llama Red Pajama*, *Llama Llama Loves to Read*, and *Llama Llama Gram and Granpa*.

Pretty Kitty

BY KAREN BEAUMONT; STEPHANIE LABERIS, ILLUS.

Grades PreS–1   *32 pages*

Henry Holt, 2018; ebook

An old man living in a big city is met with a kitty cat sitting at his door. "Don't you look at me like that. / I do not want a kitty cat. / SCAT!" Soon the numbers increase until ten kitties are on the mat, and the man responds the same each time: SCAT! When it begins to snow, the old man's attitude softens and he allows the cats inside where he "Loves each pretty little kitty." Part rhyming story, part counting book, *Pretty Kitty* will melt your heart, even if you aren't a cat lover.

Rosie Revere, Engineer

BY ANDREA BEATY; DAVID ROBERTS, ILLUS.

Grades K–3   *32 pages*

Abrams, 2013; ebook

Rosie Revere loves to construct inventions whether it's a hot-dog dispenser, helium pants, or python-repelling cheese. When Rosie experiences failure with one of her gizmos, she decides to invent only late at night in the attic. When her great-great-great-aunt Rose tells Rosie about her time building airplanes (a nod to Rosie the Riveter), she laments that her only thrill not realized was to fly. So Rosie gets to work on a contraption she calls the heli-o-cheese-copter to surprise her aunt. On the maiden flight, Rosie stays air-borne for a few minutes before crashing to the ground. The young girl is now convinced she will never be an engineer. Her aunt, who witnessed the flight, tells Rosie, "This great flop is over. It's time for the next!" The rhyming text reinforces that even perceived failures are only steps to the next great invention.

What About Moose?

BY COREY ROSEN SCHWARTZ; KEIKA YAMAGUCHI, ILLUS.

Grades PreS–2   *40 pages*

Atheneum, 2015; ebook

It takes teamwork to build a tree house. But what happens when a member of the team is very bossy Moose. Fox, Toad, Bear, Porcu-pine, and Skunk have plans for how to construct the tree house, but Moose decides things should be done his way. This is a lively rhyming book with colorful illustrations. A repetitive refrain, "But what about you, Moose?" will definitely get kids to join in the fun.

Picture Books

Alexander and the Terrible, Horrible, No Good, Very Bad Day

BY JUDITH VIORST; RAY CRUZ, ILLUS.
Grades K and up   *32 pages*
Atheneum, 1972; ebook, audiobook

This is a classic picture book that cuts across all ages and even resonates with adults. Everyone has a bad day once in a while, but little Alexander has the worst day of all. Follow him from a cereal box without a prize to a burned-out night-light. Sequels include *Alexander, Who Used to Be Rich Last Sunday* and *Alexander, Who's Not (Do You Hear Me? I Mean It!) Going to Move*. Also by the author: *If I Were in Charge of the World and Other Worries*. Related book: *Are You Going to Be Good?* by Cari Best.

April and Esme, Tooth Fairies

BY BOB GRAHAM
Grades PreS–K   *32 pages*
Candlewick Press, 2010

Seven-year-old April and her little sister, Esme, are the children of tooth fairies. Both are anxious to begin the exciting career of collecting those little teeth and delivering the coin rewards. They assume that excitement is years away, until April receives a call on her cell phone: her very first order! Her parents give her all the reasons why she's too young and the trip is too dangerous, but April argues a strong case until she and her sister are cautiously given permission. The excitement builds as they accomplish their goal—almost. Unfortunately, the tooth's owner awakens and sees the fairies. April, however, is a tech-savvy tooth fairy and texts her mother for instructions on what to do. Also by the author: *A Bus Called Heaven*; *How to Heal a Broken Wing*; *Jethro Byrd, Fairy Child*; *Max*; and *Rose Meets Mr. Wintergarten*. Related book: *Throw Your Tooth on the Roof: Tooth Traditions from Around the World* by Selby Beeler.

Baby Brains

BY SIMON JAMES

Grades PreS–1   *24 pages*

Candlewick Press, 2004

This is a wonderful send-up of the superbaby syndrome that afflicts too many parents, but it is also a funny story for children. Mr. and Mrs. Brains do "everything right." Before this baby is born they read to him, play music and foreign-language tapes, even watch the news with the sound turned up. Thus, days after Baby Brains is born, he's sitting up reading the newspaper when his parents come down for breakfast. After breakfast he announces he'd like to go to school tomorrow, which he does, and he heads the class! It's not long before he joins the astronauts for a trip into space, and that's where it all comes apart—but in a good way. Sequels: *Baby Brains Superstar* and *Baby Brains and Robomom*. Related books: *Boss Baby* and *Bossier Baby* by Marla Frazee; *The Wicked Big Toddlah* and *The Wicked Big Toddlah Goes to New York* by Kevin Hawkes. Also by Simon James: *The Birdwatchers, Dear Mr. Blueberry, George Flies South, Leon and Bob, Sally and the Limpet*, and *The Wild Woods*.

BE QUIET!

BY RYAN T. HIGGINS

Grades PreK–3   *40 pages*

Disney-Hyperion, 2017; ebook

Rupert wants to make a wordless book because he believes they are very artistic. When he shares the idea with his two chatty friends, they excitedly propose lots of suggestions of things to include (superheroes, kittens, and even a vegetarian). Soon the book is filled with words. The speech bubbles contain handwritten text that perfectly complements the comical illustrations. Be sure to begin the read-aloud on the endpapers and also take a peek under the book jacket. BE QUIET! will surely have kids laughing out loud. Other books worthy of laughter by Higgins are *We Don't Eat Our Classmates, Mother Bruce, Hotel Bruce*, and *Bruce's Big Move*.

Bear Came Along

BY RICHARD T. MORRIS; LEUYEN PHAM, ILLUS.

Grades PreK–3   *40 pages*

Little, Brown, 2019; ebook

The river was flowing night and day through a forest but didn't realize what it could do until a curious bear came along. Soon Frog,

Turtle, Beaver, Raccoon, and Duck are part of the adventure as they travel together with Bear downstream. When they tumble over a waterfall at one point of the river, the animals realize the joy and thrill they can experience together. This delightful picture book with watercolor illustrations by LeUyen Pham celebrates the pleasure of creating an unexpected community and the gratification of unanticipated circumstances. Other books by Richard T. Morris include *Fear the Bunny*, *Sheep 101*, and *This Is a Moose*.

Belle, the Last Mule at Gee's Bend

BY CALVIN ALEXANDER RAMSEY AND BETTYE STROUD; JOHN HOLY-FIELD, ILLUS.

Grades 1–4   *32 pages*
Candlewick Press, 2011

An old black woman sits in the shade with a young black boy, watching an old gray mule in the field across the street. In the ensuing time and pages, the woman shares the tale of that mule, from the midnight hour when Martin Luther King Jr. visited that dirt-poor Alabama community of Gee's Bend to the day three years later when that mule was asked to pull the wagon carrying Dr. King's coffin through the streets of Atlanta. In between those two events, the woman offers a moving synopsis of the civil rights movement and what it meant to the nation's poor.

    Related books: *Boycott Blues: How Rosa Parks Inspired a Nation* by Andrea Davis Pinkney; *Goin' Someplace Special* by Patricia C. McKissack; *Leon's Story* by Leon Walter Tillage; *Molly Bannaky* by Alice McGill; *More Than Anything Else* by Marie Bradby; *Freedom on the Menu: The Greensboro Sit-ins* by Carole Boston Weatherford; *My Brother Martin* by Christine King Farris; *Uncle Jed's Barbershop* and *When Grandmama Sings*, both by Margaree King Mitchell; and *White Water* by Michael S. Bandy and Eric Stein.

The Book with No Pictures

BY B. J. NOVAK

Grades K–3   *48 pages*
Dial, 2014; ebook, audiobook

A picture book with no pictures? What fun is that? As you begin to read this picture book, it becomes quite uproarious because you have to read whatever it says. Even if the words say *BLORK* or *BLUURF*. And then there's *BLAGGITY BLAGGITY* and

GLIBBITY GLOBBITY. After a few pages, you don't even realize there are no pictures because reading the text is so silly. Novak "talks" to the reader, which is a clever way to tell a story. A few other picture books that use this interactive approach: *Warning: Do Not Open This Book!* by Adam Lehrhaupt, *We Are in a Book!* by Mo Willems, and *Press Here* by Hervé Tullet.

Bully

BY LAURA VACCARO SEEGER

Grades PreS–3   *40 pages*

Roaring Brook Press, 2013; ebook

After a large bull tells him to go away, a little bull looks upset and dejected. When a rabbit, chicken, and turtle ask him if he wants to play, the little bull bellows, *NO!* Soon the little bull becomes a bully as he calls each animal a hurtful name. When he is called a bully, the little bull realizes that he is treating others as badly as he was treated by the big bull. The illustrations in *Bully* add to the story—as the little bull becomes angrier and his bullying increases, so does his size until only a portion of him is seen on a page. This book has appeal to a range of audiences and provides an opportunity to discuss bullying. Related books: *Llama Llama and the Bully Goat* by Anna Dewdney; *Bullies Never Win* by Margery Cuyler; *The Recess Queen* by Alexis O'Neill; *Henry and the Bully* by Nancy Carlson; *I Walk with Vanessa: A Story About a Simple Act of Kindness* by Kerascoët; and *Eddie the Bully* by Henry Cole.

A Bus Called Heaven

BY BOB GRAHAM

Grades PreS–1   *40 pages*

Candlewick Press, 2011

Stella is part of a crowd that is gathered around a hollowed-out bus abandoned in the middle of the street. Soon she has convinced everyone to push it into her driveway. Next step is a makeover, complete with paint, rugs, games, chairs, and mattresses. The bus is turned into a neighborhood clubhouse for all ages. Or it was—until a tow truck hauls it to the junkyard ("It's an obstruction!"). But they don't know Stella and her resourcefulness. While the small images on large pages make it difficult for a class to see the illustrations, it's a perfect book for sharing with two to three children at once. For other books by the author, see the listing for *April and Esme, Tooth Fairies.*

The Carpenter's Gift

BY DAVID RUBEL; JIM LAMARCHE, ILLUS.

Grades K–4   *44 pages*

Random House, 2011; ebook

In the early hours of the Great Depression, a very poor young boy and his father leave their rural shack and head for New York City in hopes of selling some Christmas trees they've cut. Construction workers at Rockefeller Center take pity and offer them some space for the tree sales. At the end of the day, they've turned a small profit and donate the remaining trees to the Rockefeller workmen. The next day, Christmas, the workmen return the favor. This remarkable tale is less a book about Christmas and more about giving without looking for credit, and taking without forgetting. Related books: *Pop's Bridge* by Eve Bunting and *Spuds* by Karen Hesse, which is also set during the Great Depression.

A Chair for My Mother

BY VERA B. WILLIAMS

Grades K–3   *30 pages*

Greenwillow, 1982

This is the first book in a trilogy of tender stories about a family of three women: Grandma, Mama, and daughter Rosa (all told in the first person by the child). In this book, they struggle to save their loose change in order to buy a chair for the child's mother—something she can collapse into after her waitressing job. In *Something Special for Me*, the glass jar's contents are to be spent on the child's birthday present. What an important decision for a little girl to make! After much soul-searching, she settles on a used accordion. In *Music, Music for Everyone*, the jar is empty again. With all the loose change going for Grandma's medical expenses now, little Rosa searches for a way to make money and cheer up her grandma. Related book: *Bun Bun Button* by Patricia Polacco.

Clever Jack Takes the Cake

BY CANDACE FLEMING; G. BRIAN KARAS, ILLUS.

Grades K–3   *40 pages*

Schwartz & Wade, 2010; ebook

Jack has been invited to the princess's tenth birthday party. Unfortunately, he has no money to buy her a gift. So he trades his ax for two bags of sugar, his quilt for a sack of flour, gives the hen extra seeds in exchange for two fresh eggs, and a kiss on the cow's nose for a pail of milk. Jack then gathers walnuts and searches until he finds the reddest, juiciest, most succulent strawberry in the land. Jack bakes a magnificent cake, topped with the strawberry, and sets off for the castle. Along the way, he encounters four-and-twenty blackbirds, a troll, and a gypsy woman with a dancing bear. Each one takes a portion of the cake until nothing is left. When it's Jack's turn to present his gift to the princess, he has nothing except for the tale of the cake. She exclaims that it is a fine gift and invites Jack to have the honor of cutting her birthday cake. Be sure to savor each page from the opening endpaper, to the title page, through to the final endpaper, as portions of the story are told through images only. Other picture books by Fleming: *Oh, No!*; *Tippy-Tippy-Tippy, Splash!*; *Go Sleep in Your Own Bed*; *Boxes for Katje*; and *Papa's Mechanical Fish*.

Cloudy with a Chance of Meatballs

BY JUDI BARRETT; RON BARRETT, ILLUS.
Grades PreS–5   28 pages
Atheneum, 1978

In the fantasyland of Chewandswallow, the weather changes three times a day, supplying all the residents with food out of the sky. But suddenly the weather takes a turn for the worse; instead of normal-size meatballs, it rains meatballs the size of basketballs, and pancakes and syrup smother the streets. Something must be done! Sequel: *Pickles to Pittsburgh*. Also by the author: *Animals Should Definitely Not Act Like People*, *Animals Should Definitely Not Wear Clothing*, and *Never Take a Shark to the Dentist*.

The Complete Adventures of Peter Rabbit

BY BEATRIX POTTER
Grades PreS–1   96 pages
Puffin, 1984

Here are the four original tales involving one of the most famous animals in children's literature—Peter Rabbit. Children identify with his naughty sense of adventure and then thrill at his narrow escape from the clutches of Mr. McGregor. Although all the Potter books come in a small format that is ideal because young children feel more comfortable holding that size (3″ x 5″), this larger volume is the most affordable choice and still retains the Potter illustrations.

The original story of Peter was contained in a get-well letter Potter wrote to a child; the story of that child and his letter is explored in the picture book *My Dear Noel* by Jane Johnson and can be used starting at the kindergarten level. Other studies include a children's biography, *Beatrix Potter*, by Alexandra Wallner, and *Beatrix Potter and Her Paint Box* by David McPhail. There is a wealth of Potter information on the web, beginning with www.peterrabbit.co.uk/.

Creepy Carrots!

BY AARON REYNOLDS; PETER BROWN, ILLUS.

Grades K–3   *40 pages*

Simon & Schuster, 2012; ebook, audiobook

Jasper Rabbit loves carrots. And there are plenty of fat, crispy carrots that he can munch located in Crackenhopper Field. Soon, Jasper begins to hear the *tunktunktunk* of creepy carrots coming after him. He sees them everywhere—in the shed, in the bathroom, and in his bedroom late at night. His parents reassure him it's just his imagination or a bad dream. However, Jasper isn't convinced and decides to make sure the carrots can never escape Crackenhopper Field, which is what the carrots hoped for all along. Peter Brown has written and illustrated several of his own picture books including *Mr. Tiger Goes Wild*, *The Curious Garden*, and *My Teacher Is a Monster! (No, I am Not)*.

Crown: An Ode to the Fresh Cut

BY DERRICK BARNES; GORDON C. JAMES, ILLUS.

Grades 1–5   *32 pages*

Agate Bolden, 2017; ebook

A young African American boy describes the feeling of getting a "fresh cut" at the barbershop. Rhythmic text is perfect for reading aloud as the boy imagines how others will respond to him and how he'll leave "the shop." He'll feel "Magnificent. Flawless. Like royalty." Oil paintings illustrate the successful black men in the chairs beside the boy, the intricacies of the haircuts, and the self-confidence and joy being experienced by the young boy. This award-winning picture book celebrates empowerment and feeling like a "brilliant, blazing star." Related books: *Bippity Bop Barbershop* by Natasha Anastasia Tarpley; *Uncle Jed's Barbershop* by Margaree King Mitchell; *Chocolate Me!* by Taye Diggs; and *The Barber's Cutting Edge* by Gwendolyn Battle-Lavert.

Dandy

BY AME DYCKMAN; CHARLES SANTOSO, ILLUS.

Grades PreS–2   *40 pages*

Little, Brown, 2019; ebook

Daddy lion takes pride in his perfect lawn, but then he spies a dandelion. Before he is able to get his clippers to remove it, his daughter, Sweetie, has claimed it and named it Charlotte. Every attempt to remove the weed is unsuccessful because Sweetie doesn't stray far away from it. Finally, Daddy has his chance when Sweetie leaves for swim lessons. As he makes his approach toward the dandelion, he sees a picture Sweetie has drawn of Charlotte and himself. Unfortunately, his clippers drop and damage Charlotte. The illustrations on the next few pages are hilarious as Daddy and his neighbors try to revive the damaged dandelion. If you are looking for a charming book about fathers and daughters, this one will do the trick. Related books: *Dad By My Side* by Soosh and *My Dad Thinks He's Funny* by Katrina Germein.

The Day You Begin

BY JACQUELINE WOODSON; RAFAEL LÓPEZ, ILLUS.

Grades K–3   *32 pages*

Nancy Paulsen Books, 2018; ebook

There are times when you feel you are different, whether it's the uniqueness of your name, the color of your skin, or the clothes you wear. When you begin to share your story and who you are, you might make unexpected connections with others. López's colorful and vibrant illustrations celebrate diversity and acceptance. This is an excellent read-aloud for parents and teachers to share with children. It is also available in Spanish. Related books: *All Are Welcome* by Alexandra Penfold; *Stand Tall, Molly Lou Melon* by Patty Lovell; *I Like Myself!* by Karen Beaumont; *Marvelous Me: Inside and Out* by Lisa Bullard; and *It's Okay to Be Different* by Todd Parr.

Dear Substitute

BY LIZ GARTON SCANLON AND AUDREY VERNICK; CHRIS RASCHKA, ILLUS.

Grades K-3   *40 pages*

Disney-Hyperion, 2018; ebook

A little girl is not pleased she has a substitute teacher, Miss Pelly. The substitute has no idea that it's the day to clean the turtle tank or go to the library. She also doesn't realize it's the girl's turn to be line leader and trading food with Connor at lunch is highly desirable (even though it isn't allowed because of allergies). But when Miss Pelly reads some "strange little poems" instead of the chapter book that is normally read aloud, the girl begins to consider that maybe the substitute isn't as bad as she first thought. Raschka's illustrations start with a somber scene filled with broken pencils and drooping flowers and progress to a vibrant, colorful classroom and the feeling everything is going to be fine. Even Mrs. Giordano, the regular classroom teacher, seems to be feeling much better. Liz Garton Scanlon's stories present children faced with ordinary dilemmas that are resolved through empowerment—both big and small. A classic picture book about a substitute teacher is *Miss Nelson Is Missing!* by Harry Allard and James Marshall. Other books written by Scanlon and perfect for reading aloud include *Kate, Who Tamed the Wind*; *All the World*; and *Another Way to Climb a Tree*.

Doll-E 1.0

BY SHANDA MCCLOSKEY
Grades PreS–2   *40 pages*
Little, Brown, 2018; ebook
Charlotte is quite the whiz at technology. She's able to tinker, toggle, code, and download. She even assists her parents with their own tech issues. But when she receives a doll that doesn't appear to do anything, Charlotte has no idea how to play with it. But then she discovers a battery pack inside the doll and devises a way for Dolly to speak. Related books about girls and technology are *Izzy Gizmo* by Pip Jones; *How to Code a Sandcastle* by Josh Funk; and *Rosie Revere, Engineer* by Andrea Beaty.

Don't Want to Go!

BY SHIRLEY HUGHES
Grades PreS–K   *32 pages*
Candlewick Press, 2010
Lily's mother is home sick with the flu and her dad must go off to work, which means Lily must spend the day at the home of her parents' friend. That is *not* what Lily wants. She is not big on changes or strangers. But Dad prevails and off they go, where she has a wonderful day—so good, in fact, she's not keen on returning home. Sequel: *Bobbo Goes to School*. Also by the author: *All About Alfie* and *Dogger*. Related books: *Llama Llama Home with Mama* by Anna Dewdney, *A Sick Day for Amos McGee* by Philip C. Stead, and *A Visitor for Bear* by Bonny Becker.

Cyndi's Favorite Picture Books About Reading

Again! by Emily Gravett

Baabwaa and Wooliam: A Tale of Literacy, Dental Hygiene, and Friendship by David Elliott

Book Uncle and Me by Uma Krishnaswami

Bunny's Book Club by Annie Silvestro

A Child of Books by Oliver Jeffers

Froggy Goes to the Library by Jonathan London

Give Me Back My Book! by Travis Foster

How Do Dinosaurs Learn to Read? by Jane Yolen

How Rocket Learned to Read by Tad Hills

How This Book Was Made by Mac Barnett

How to Read a Story by Kate Messner

I Am a Story by Dan Yaccarino

I Do Not Like Books Anymore! by Daisy Hirst

I Hate to Read by Rita Marshall

The Incredible Book Eating Boy by Oliver Jeffers

Let Me Finish! by Minh Lê

Lexie the Word Wrangler by Rebecca Van Slyke

Look! by Jeff Mack

Madeline Finn and the Library Dog by Lisa Papp

The Not So Quiet Library by Zachariah OHora

Open Very Carefully: A Book with Bite by Nick Bromley

This Is My Book! by Matt Pett

This Is Not a Picture Book! by Sergio Ruzzier

We Are in a Book! by Mo Willems

The Whisper by Pamela Zagarenski

Wild About Books by Judy Sierra

Wolf! by Becky Bloom

You Can Read by Helaine Becker

Drawn Together

BY MINH LÊ; DAN SANTAT, ILLUS.

Grades K–3   *40 pages*

Disney-Hyperion, 2018; ebook

A young boy reluctantly visits his grandfather, and the contrasts between the two becomes apparent immediately. They don't like to eat the same foods, use the same utensils, and, more important, they don't speak the same language. But when they sit down to draw together, something magical happens as a love of art and storytelling emerges. This stunning picture book is one that you cannot rush through as the story is told through text and illustration. Be sure to look under the book jacket at the cover and also pause to examine the endpapers. Related books: *Grandpa Green* by Lane Smith; *A Couple of Boys Have the Best Week Ever* by Marla Frazee; *The Hello, Goodbye Window* by Norton Juster.

Dreamers
BY YUYI MORALES
Grades K–3   *32 pages*
Holiday House, 2018; ebook, audiobook
This is one of the most beautifully illustrated books that will also touch your heart. In 1994, Yuyi Morales immigrated to the United States from Mexico with her two-month-old son. She did not speak English and felt that no one seemed to notice she existed. When Yuyi discovered the public library, her life was changed forever. Books taught her "to speak, to write, and to make our voices heard." Woven throughout the illustrations are the children's books that influenced and inspired her. The book concludes with Yuyi telling her story in further detail along with a listing of the books she read. This talented illustrator has received numerous awards for her work including the Pura Belpré Award for *Just a Minute: A Trickster Tale and Counting Book*; *Los Gatos Black on Halloween*; *Just in Case: A Trickster Tale and Spanish Alphabet Book*; *Niño Wrestles the World*; and *Viva Frida*.

The Everything Book
BY DENISE FLEMING
Inf–Tod   *64 pages*
Henry Holt, 2000
After Mother Goose, all new parents should have this terrific book about everything important to a child—animals, shapes, colors, rhymes, finger games, food, faces, letters, traffic, and toys. The art is a rainbow feast for the eyes but is done in a style very young children can easily absorb.

Goldilocks and the Three Bears
BY JAMES MARSHALL
Grades PreS–2   *32 pages*
Dial, 1988; audiobook
This is one of my favorite versions of this fairy tale. The blond-haired, strong-willed, "naughty little girl" takes a shortcut through

the woods on her trip to the village. Along the way, she drops into the home of the three bears and eats the porridge, breaks a chair, and takes a nap on the bed. The cartoonlike illustrations include a few sight gags and a touch of ironic wit. Something for both child and adult to enjoy. Related books: *Goldie and the Three Bears* by Diane Stanley, *Goldilocks and the Three Dinosaurs* by Mo Willems, *Goldilocks Returns* by Lisa Campbell Ernst, and *The 3 Bears and Goldilocks* by Margaret Willey.

Goodnight Moon

BY MARGARET WISE BROWN; CLEMENT HURD, ILLUS.
Inf–Tod   *30 pages*
Harper, 1947; ebook, audiobook
This classic is based on a bedtime ritual sure to be copied by every child who hears it. Also by the author: *The Important Book, The Runaway Bunny,* and *The Sailor Dog.* Related bedtime books for infants and toddlers: *Can't You Sleep, Little Bear?* and *Sleep Tight, Little Bear* by Martin Waddell; *Goodnight, Goodnight, Construction Site* by Sherri Duskey Rinker and Tom Lichtenheld; *Good Night, Gorilla* by Peggy Rathmann; *Hide and Squeak* by Heather Vogel Frederick; *Kiss Good Night* by Amy Hest; *Max's Bedtime* by Rosemary Wells; *The Napping House* by Audrey Wood; and *Tell Me the Day Backwards* by Albert Lamb.

Grow Up, David!

BY DAVID SHANNON
Grades PreK–2   *32 pages*
Scholastic, 2018; ebook, audiobook
In 1998, David Shannon's *No, David!* became an instant hit with kids as the spunky mischief maker colored on walls, tracked mud on the carpet, and smashed a vase with a baseball. Twenty years later, David is still that same energetic rascal who now taunts and tangles with his older brother in *Grow Up, David!* The cover illustration provides a clue that David is relentless in his antics as he delivers an unwelcome wake-up call to his sibling. David is told by his brother that he is too little to play ball and to stop following him. David retaliates by playing tricks on his sibling and by eating all the Halloween candy. The two go back and forth tormenting each other until both end up sitting in different corners for time-out. When David is finally invited to play football with his brother and his

friends, the youngster immediately is tackled after catching the ball. As with most siblings, the feelings they have for each other are sometimes not always exhibited through naughty behavior. This is the fourth in the David series, which also includes *No, David!*, *David Gets in Trouble*, and *It's Christmas, David!* All are enjoyable read-alouds that will prompt discussion about behavior and love.

Cyndi's Favorite Picture Books About Self-Identity

Ada Twist, Scientist by Andrea Beaty
Alma and How She Got Her Name by Juana Martinez-Neal
Be a Friend by Salina Yoon
Be Kind by Pat Zietlow Miller
Chrysanthemum by Kevin Henkes
The Day You Begin by Jacqueline Woodson
I Like Myself by Karen Beaumont

Julián Is a Mermaid by Jessica Love
A Lion Is a Lion by Polly Dunbar
Marisol McDonald Doesn't Match by Monica Brown
Mixed Me! by Taye Diggs
My Hair Is a Garden by Cozbi A. Cabrera
The Name Jar by Yangsook Choi
Ruby's Wish by Shirin Yim Bridges

Hand in Hand

BY ROSEMARY WELLS
Grades PreS–K   *32 pages*
Henry Holt, 2016; ebook

For decades, Rosemary Wells has written and illustrated exceptional stories for young children, many published in picture book and board book formats. *Hand in Hand* celebrates the bond between parent and child. "Be my teacher from day one. / Be my sky, my moon, my sun." All that parents do for and with their children from day one: talking and walking, feeding and reading, playing and dreaming, and more. This is a perfect read-aloud that will speak to both parent and child. Other recommended books by Wells: *Bunny Cakes*, *Kit & Kaboodle*, *Noisy Nora*, *Max and Ruby's Bedtime Book*, *Max's Dragon Shirt*, and *Bunny Party*.

Hello Lighthouse

BY SOPHIE BLACKALL

Grades PreK–3   *48 pages*

Little, Brown, 2018; ebook

Step inside the life of a lighthouse keeper as the days and seasons pass, as the winds blow, the fog rolls in, and the icebergs drift by. The lighthouse keeper has to be sure he records everything in his logbook. Soon, he is joined by his wife and together they tend the light. Eventually, there becomes the three of them as they welcome a child. But one day, the coast guard arrives and installs a brand-new light and a machine to run it. The lighthouse keeper and his family must say goodbye to their home. An author's note provides additional details about lighthouses and those who kept the lights burning years ago. Sophie Blackall received the 2019 Caldecott Medal for *Hello Lighthouse* and the 2016 Caldecott Medal for her picture book, *Finding Winnie: The True Story of the World's Most Famous Bear*. Related books: *Keep the Lights Burning, Abbie* by Connie Roop; *Gracie the Lighthouse Cat* by Ruth Brown; *The Lighthouse Cat* by Sue Stainton; and *Birdie's Lighthouse* by Deborah Hopkinson.

A House in the Woods

BY INGA MOORE

Grades Tod–K   *42 pages*

Candlewick Press, 2011

If there were a single book that could embody pure happiness, it would be this volume. There is no great plot here—just a group of woodland animals sharing the work of building a warm house in the woods. No calamities to overcome, no bickering, no tears; just working, sharing, creating, and peanut butter sandwiches as their reward. And how does this add up to one of the most comforting and beautifully illustrated bedtime stories ever written? Read it and see. Also illustrated by the author: *The Reluctant Dragon* by Kenneth Grahame. For other bedtime books, see the listing for *Goodnight Moon* by Margaret Wise Brown.

The House on East 88th Street

BY BERNARD WABER

Grades PreS–3   *48 pages*

Houghton Mifflin, 1962; ebook

When the Primm family discovers a gigantic crocodile in the bath-tub of their new brownstone home, it signals the beginning of a wonderful friendship (and picture book series). As soon as the Primms overcome their fright, they see him as your children will—as the most lovable and human of crocodiles. Sequels (in this order): *Lyle, Lyle, Crocodile*; *Lyle and the Birthday Party*; *Lyle Finds His Mother*; *Lovable Lyle*; *Funny, Funny Lyle*; *Lyle at the Office*; and *Lyle at Christmas*. Five Lyle books have been combined into a single volume for *Lyle, Lyle, Crocodile Storybook Treasury*. Also by the author: *Ira Sleeps Over, Courage, Evie & Margie,* and *The Mouse That Snored*.

I Am a Cat

BY GALIA BERNSTEIN
Grades PreS–2   32 *pages*
Abrams, 2018; ebook
A house cat named Simon encounters some bigger cats, all who insist he is NOT a cat. Lion, Puma, Panther, Tiger, and Cheetah describe a characteristic they each have like a mane, or spots, or stripes—none of the things that Simon has. But then Simon points out that they all don't have manes, or spots, or stripes. The other cats realize that Simon has a point and they have to agree. This is a wonderful story to read aloud because of the witty language and bold digital illustrations. Other related books with cats: *They All Saw a Cat* by Brendan Wenzel, *Kitten's First Full Moon* by Kevin Henkes, *Splat the Cat* by Rob Scotton, Cat the Cat series by Mo Willems, and the classic *Millions of Cats* by Wanda Gag.

I'm Cool!

BY KATE AND JIM MCMULLAN
Grades PreS–2   32 *pages*
HarperCollins, 2015; ebook
The McMullans give us not only an inside look at the function of a Zamboni machine but also into ice hockey. For the safety of the players, it's important to fill the dents and pits and ruts, and only one machine is designed to make the ice, well, as smooth as ice. Shazamboni! Jim McMullan's flamboyant use of colorful, blade-packing, ice-shaving, snow-eating, water-spraying typeface lends both amusement and texture to the tale. Also by the authors: *I'm Bad!, I'm Big!, I'm Dirty!, I'm Fast!, I'm Mighty!, I Stink!, I'm Smart!, I'm Brave!,* and *I'm Tough!*

If I Ran the Zoo

BY DR. SEUSS
Grades PreS–4   *54 pages*
Random House, 1950; ebook
Little Gerald McGrew finds the animals at the local zoo pretty bor-
ing compared with the zany, exotic creatures populating the zoo of
his imagination (just like a little lad imagined things while walking
to and from school in Seuss's first book for children, *And to Think
That I Saw It on Mulberry Street*). Dr. Seuss's father ran the zoo in
Springfield, Massachusetts, for thirty-one years. Seuss author studies: "Oh, the Places You've Taken Us: RT's Tribute to Dr. Seuss,"
in the May 1992 issue of the *Reading Teacher*; a children's biography,
Dr. Seuss: Young Author and Artist, by Kathleen Kudlinski (Aladdin,
2005); and two adult biographies, *The Seuss, the Whole Seuss, and
Nothing but the Seuss: A Visual Biography of Theodor Seuss Geisel*
by Charles D. Cohen and *Dr. Seuss & Mr. Geisel* by Judith and
Neil Morgan, the definitive book on his personal life. For a more
academic approach to Seuss's work, see Philip Nel's *Dr. Seuss: American Icon.*

If Wendell Had a Walrus

BY LORI MORTENSEN; MATT PHELAN, ILLUS.
Grades PreS–2   *32 pages*
Henry Holt, 2018; ebook
Wendell spies a cloud that looks exactly like a walrus, which gives
him an idea. Wouldn't it be great if he had a walrus that he could
name Roger. They could tell jokes, climb trees, build forts, fly kites,
and draw ducks. Wendell and Roger could have the most "stupen-
diferous, cosmically colossal best time of their lives." The only
problem: where to get a walrus. So Wendell writes a note, stuffs it
into a bottle, and throws it into the ocean in hopes that a walrus
somewhere will accept his invitation to come to his house. As the
bottle floats away, Wendell notices a boy who is tossing his own
bottle into the ocean in hopes of getting a whale. While the boys
wait, they decide to do all the things that Wendell had hoped to do
with the walrus, including telling jokes. The story of imagination
along with friendship makes this a wonderful read-aloud. And the
surprise ending is just perfect! More humorous picture books by
author Lori Mortensen include *Chicken Lily*, about a school-wide
poetry jam where the title character does not want to sound like a

birdbrain and must put her best claw forward, and *Cindy Moo*, about a cow who attempts to jump over the moon ("Hey Diddle Diddle").

Interrupting Chicken and the Elephant of Surprise
BY DAVID EZRA STEIN

Grades PreS–2   *40 pages*
Candlewick Press, 2018; ebook, audiobook
Little Chicken tells Papa that her teacher explained every story has an elephant of surprise. Papa questions if the teacher was talking about an *element* of surprise. Little Chicken insists it's *elephant* because that's the part in the story you didn't know was going to happen. And no one would expect an elephant in *The Ugly Duckling*, *Rapunzel*, or *The Little Mermaid*, but they appear when Papa and Little Chicken are reading the stories. This book is filled with the same humor as the first *Interrupting Chicken*. If you are searching for humorous books to read aloud, here are a few: *Stuck* by Oliver Jeffers, *We Found a Hat* by Jon Klassen, *Z is for Moose* by Kelly Bingham, and *Don't Let the Pigeon Drive the Bus!* by Mo Willems.

It Came in the Mail
BY BEN CLANTON

Grades PreS–2   *40 pages*
Simon & Schuster, 2016; ebook
Liam checks the mailbox continuously in hopes of receiving mail but finds "diddly-squat." He realizes that if he wants mail, he needs to send mail. So he writes a letter to the mailbox. What is delivered is a fire-breathing dragon that Liam loves. Since his previous attempt worked so well, he tries it again—and out pops all sorts of animals and things. A third try yields a gazillion deliveries, but what will Liam do with it all? Well, if Liam loved getting mail, wouldn't other kids feel the same? So with a little help from the mailbox, Liam begins to send things to others. Watercolor illustrations add to the enjoyment through wordplay and visual jokes that both adults and kids will enjoy. This book reminds me of some classic books about imagination and letter writing such as *Dear Mr. Blueberry* by Simon James; *I Wanna Iguana* by Karen Kaufman Orloff with hilarious illustrations by David Catrow; and *Click, Clack, Moo: Cows That Type* by Doreen Cronin and illustrated by Betsy Lewin.

The Knowing Book

BY REBECCA KAI DOTLICH; MATTHEW CORDELL, ILLUS.

Grades K and up   *32 pages*

Boyds Mills Press, 2016; ebook

"Before you forget . . . / look up. / The sky has always been above you, / is above you now. / and will always be above you. / Count on it. / It is what you will always know." Excellent advice for all of us that no matter where we go or what we do, we should rely on what we know. This book reminds me of Dr. Seuss's *Oh, the Places You'll Go!* in that it offers wisdom and advice about life's journey. Related books: *I Wish You More* by Amy Krouse Rosenthal, *Wherever You Go* by Pat Zietlow Miller, *Reach for the Stars and Other Advice for Life's Journey* by Serge Bloch, and *Be Happy!* by Monica Sheehan.

The Last Peach

BY GUS GORDON

Grades K–2   *32 pages*

Roaring Brook Press, 2019

Two bugs see the most beautiful peach of the summer. Should they eat it? And who should be the one to take the first bite? What happens if it looks gorgeous on the outside but is rotten on the inside? Maybe they could share it with their friends and be considered hungry heroes. But, it truly is the most splendid of peaches. Or was it? This charming picture book uses alternating colors for the text to show who is speaking. The collage illustrations are eye-catching and fun to examine. Two other delightful picture books by Gus Gordon are *Somewhere Else* and *Herman and Rosie*.

Last Stop on Market Street

BY MATT DE LA PEÑA; CHRISTIAN ROBINSON, ILLUS.

Grades PreS–2   *32 pages*

Putnam, 2015; ebook, audiobook

Every Sunday, CJ and his grandmother ride the bus across town. This prompts questions by CJ such as why don't they own a car like his friend Colby. Or why doesn't he have an iPod like the boys riding on the bus? And why do they get off the bus in the dirty part of town? His grandmother answers each question with a response that helps her grandson see the beauty in the world around them and to appreciate those who may not be exactly like him. This is a wonderful book that shows the loving relationship between a grandparent and her grandson as well as teaching one to appreciate diversity. Christian Robinson's radiant illustrations are eye-catching and offer a visual glimpse into communities that might be different from the one children may know. While Matt de la Peña is known for his adolescent novels, his picture books are recommended, including *Love*, *Miguel and the Grand Harmony* (inspired by the Disney Pixar film *Coco*), and *Carmela Full of Wishes*.

The Library Lion

BY MICHELLE KNUDSEN; KEVIN HAWKES, ILLUS.
Grades PreS–K   *48 pages*
Candlewick Press, 2006

When the lion walks into the library, he is too ferocious for anyone to object, and Miss Merriweather, the head librarian, thinks, "If he obeys the rules, no problem." But his roaring at the end of story time brings a sharp reprimand from her, and he gets the message. Nonetheless, the circulation assistant, Mr. McBee, doesn't like his presence, even though the lion helps out by licking envelopes and dusting shelves with his tail. Finally, McBee has enough cause to eject him—a roaring that disrupts the entire building, causing the lion to be banished. Only afterward is the cause discovered: Miss Merriweather fell and broke her arm, and the lion was roaring for help. Too late now—the embarrassed lion has departed to no-one-knows-where. Lions are no strangers to libraries: Look who's guarding the doors to the New York Public Library—lion statues Patience and Fortitude (http://www.nypl.org/help/about-nypl/library-lions). *Lost in the Library: A Story of Patience & Fortitude* by Josh Funk is a perfect companion to this book. Related books: *But Excuse Me That Is My Book* by Lauren Child, *The Day Dirk Yeller Came to Town* by Mary Casanova, *Miss Dorothy and Her Bookmobile* by Gloria Houston, *Wild About Books* by Judy Sierra, and *Words Set Me Free: The Story of Young Frederick Douglass* by Lesa Cline-Ransome.

Lilly's Purple Plastic Purse

BY KEVIN HENKES
Grades PreS–1   *32 pages*
Greenwillow, 1996

Few writers for children have as firm a grip on the pulse of childhood as does Kevin Henkes. His mice-children experience all the joys and insecurities of being a kid, but he manages to maintain a light touch throughout his stories. In this case, Lilly loves school and her teacher—until the day her antics distract the class, and the teacher temporarily confiscates her precious new plastic purse. Shattered, she's uncertain how to handle this small rebuke and seeks ways to show her hurt. With the help of her family, Lilly overcomes her embarrassment and hasty behavior, writes an apology, and soars on the good feelings that come from doing the right thing. Lilly also stars in *Lilly's Big Day*, *Chester's Way*, and *Julius, the Baby of the World*. Also by the author: *Chrysanthemum*, *A Weekend with Wendell*, and *Wemberly Worried*.

The Little House

BY VIRGINIA LEE BURTON
Grades PreS–3   *40 pages*
Houghton Mifflin, 1942

This Caldecott Medal winner uses a little turn-of-the-century house to portray the urbanization of America. With each page, the reader-listener becomes the little house and experiences the contentment, wonder, concern, anxiety, and loneliness that the passing seasons and encroaching city bring. Many of today's children who daily experience the anxieties of city life will identify with the little house's eventual triumph. Also by the author: *Katy and the Big Snow* and *Mike Mulligan and His Steam Shovel*. Related books: *Farewell to Shady Glade* and *The Wump World* by Bill Peet.

Little Mouse's Big Book of Beasts

BY EMILY GRAVETT
Grades K–2   *32 pages*
Simon & Schuster, 2016

There are several creatures that Little Mouse fears. But what can she do? Using a paint set, paper, magazine cutouts, and origami folds, Mouse tries to alter the "original" illustrations of the beasts so they are less scary. The lion now has mittens on his claws, his mouth is covered by a strip of paper with the word *Shhhh*, and a recommendation on a Post-it note is to turn the page. Accompanying each beast is a brief poem that certainly adds to the fun. This isn't a read-aloud for a group of children but one that works best side by side with an adult. There is much to be appreciated in the text and illustrations that might be missed by an emergent reader. This is a follow-up to Gravett's *Little Mouse's Big Book of Fears*, which is equally engaging.

The Little Red Cat Who Ran Away and Learned His A-B-C's (the Hard Way)

BY PATRICK MCDONNELL

Grades PreS–2   *48 pages*

Little, Brown, 2017; ebook

This hilarious, high-energy alphabetical adventure is filled with fun and frolic as a little red cat spies an open door and makes a run for it. Soon he is caught up in a wild chase with an openmouthed alligator, tree-hugging bear, and agitated chicken. McDonnell's book isn't intended to teach the letters of the alphabet, even though it's nice to have both uppercase and lowercase letters. Rather, it's to provide exuberant storytelling coupled with vibrant vocabulary (with a cheat sheet of letters/words at the end). Related fun-filled alphabet books are *Alphablock* by Christopher Franceschelli, *Chicka Chicka Boom Boom* by Bill Martin Jr., and *The Z Was Zapped: A Play in Twenty-Six Acts* by Chris Van Allsburg.

The Little Red Fort

BY BRENDA MAIER; SONIA SÁNCHEZ, ILLUS.

Grades PreS–3   *40 pages*

Scholastic, 2018; ebook

When Ruby finds some boards, she asks her three brothers, Oscar Lee, Rodrigo, and José, to help her build something. Even though Ruby doesn't know how to build a fort, she draws up the plans, gathers supplies, and cuts the boards, each time asking her brothers to help with a repeated response of "Not me," "I don't think so," and "No way." But Ruby perseveres until the fort is completed. Now the brothers are interested, but Ruby decides that since they didn't do the work, they don't get to play. In an attempt to win her over, the boys create some additions to the fort. Maier uses the familiar pattern language of *The Little Red Hen* while Sanchez's charcoal pencil, pen, and gouache illustrations depict an industrious and determined young girl. Other versions of the classic tale are *The Little Red Hen (Makes a Pizza)* by Philomen Sturges, illustrated by Amy Walrod; *Mañana, Iguana* by Ann Whitford Paul, illustrated by Ethan Long; and *Little Red Henry* by Linda Urban, illustrated by Madeline Valentine, which has a slightly different twist on the old tale.

Little Red Riding Hood

BY JERRY PINKNEY
Grades PreS–3   *40 pages*
Little, Brown, 2007
Pinkney's version of the classic fairy tale features an African American Little Red Riding Hood who is a "sweet little girl" wearing the beloved cape that her mother stitched for her. The story proceeds in the traditional way with the girl taking soup and muffins to her sick grandmother. There are no blood and guts but lots of pattern and colors in this lovely retelling. Related books: *Little Red Riding Hood* by Trina Schart Hyman, *Flossie and the Fox* by Patricia C. McKissack (African American version), *The Gunniwolf* by Wilhelmina Harper, *Lon Po Po* by Ed Young (Chinese version), and *Pretty Salma* by Niki Daly (African version). Parodies: *Betsy Red Hoodie* by Gail Carson Levine and *Little Red Riding Hood: A Newfangled Prairie Tale* by Lisa Campbell Ernst.

The Littlest Train

BY CHRIS GALL
Grades K–2   *40 pages*
Little, Brown, 2017; ebook
A little train spends his days circling the track. When Mr. Fingers arrives, he demolishes the train set and the little train finds himself in a brand-new world. There he meets all sorts of big trains who take him on a variety of adventures. But there's no place like home, and that's where the other trains help him find his way back to. Related book: *The Little Engine That Could* by Watty Piper.

Lousy Rotten Stinkin' Grapes

BY MARGIE PALATINI; BARRY MOSER, ILLUS.
Grades K–3   *32 pages*
Simon & Schuster, 2009
The title here will grab any child's attention. With that kind of title, I was prepared for an original twist on the old Aesop's fable, and I wasn't disappointed. The original tale featured only a single character—the fox—but Palatini has added six forest neighbors to the cast, each enlisted by the sly fox to help get the just-out-of-reach grapes. Each tries to explain to him that there's an easier way to reach his goal, but he won't take any advice. It's his way or no way. In the original tale, he concedes defeat by grousing that the grapes

probably were sour anyway—thus the origin of the phrase "sour grapes." The ending here is the same, but the moral of the story is entirely different: don't be a know-it-all. Related book: *Aesop's Fables* by Jerry Pinkney.

Madeline

BY LUDWIG BEMELMANS
Grades K–3   *32 pages*
Viking, 1939; ebook, audiobook
This series of six books features a daring and irrepressible girl named Madeline and her eleven friends, who all live together in a Parisian boarding school. The author's use of fast-moving verse, daring adventure, naughtiness, and glowing color keep it a favorite in early grades year after year. Other books in the series: *Madeline and the Bad Hat, Madeline and the Gypsies, Madeline in London, Madeline's Rescue*, and *Madeline's Christmas*.

Madeline Finn and the Library Dog

BY LISA PAPP
Grades K–3   *32 pages*
Peachtree, 2016; ebook, audiobook
Madeline Finn does not like to read, especially out loud. She struggles to figure out words, and sometimes her classmates giggle when she makes a mistake. When Madeline and her mother visit the public library, they discover a program has been initiated for kids to read to dogs. The librarian takes Madeline over to a big white dog, Bonnie, that appears ready to listen to a story. Bonnie doesn't giggle or even care when Madeline gets words wrong. Every Saturday thereafter, Madeline reads to Bonnie. Soon her confidence soars and she is ready to read out loud in class. Papp wrote a companion book: *Madeline Finn and the Shelter Dog*. There are a number of animal shelters, such as the Humane Society of Missouri, that have a program where kids can read to dogs. If you have a child who might need to build his reading confidence or just loves to read aloud, see if you have a similar program in your community.

Make Way for Ducklings
BY ROBERT MCCLOSKEY
Grades PreS–2   62 pages
Viking, 1941
In this Caldecott award-winning classic, we follow Mrs. Mallard and her eight ducklings as they make a traffic-stopping walk across Boston to meet Mr. Mallard on their new island home in the Public Garden. Also by the author: *Blueberries for Sal*; *Burt Dow, Deep-Water Man*; *Lentil*; and *One Morning in Maine*. Be sure to check out *Make Way for McCloskey: A Robert McCloskey Treasury*, a single-volume anthology containing six of his best works. Related books: *Chibi: A True Story from Japan* by Barbara Brenner and Julia Takaya, *John Philip Duck* by Patricia Polacco, and *Micawber* by John Lithgow.

Marisol McDonald Doesn't Match/*Marisol McDonald no combina*
BY MONICA BROWN; SARA PALACIOS, ILLUS.
Grades PreS–3   32 pages
Candlewick Press, 2012
Marisol McDonald is a Peruvian Scottish American girl with flaming red hair and nut-brown skin. She loves wearing a combination of polka dots and stripes, prefers peanut butter and jelly burritos, and sees herself as a soccer-playing pirate princess. This bilingual book is about being yourself and not allowing others to define who you are. Other books in the Marisol series: *Marisol McDonald and the Clash Bash/Marisol McDonald y la fiesta sin igual* and *Marisol McDonald and the Monster/Marisol McDonald y el monstruo*.

Marshall Armstrong Is New to Our School
BY DAVID MACKINTOSH
Grades PreS–1   32 pages
Abrams, 2011; audiobook
Marshall is the new kid at school and sits next to the story's narrator—who thinks he's weird, to say the least. He doesn't eat what everyone else eats, doesn't play their games, and certainly doesn't dress like they do. Even his skin looks weird. And then everyone in class gets invited to Marshall's house for a party. Wow! What a cool guy he turned out to be. Related books: *Odd Boy Out: Young Albert Einstein* by Don Brown, *The Recess Queen* by Alexis O'Neill, and *Somebody Loves You, Mr. Hatch* by Eileen Spinelli.

Me and Momma and Big John

BY MARA ROCKLIFF; WILLIAM LOW, ILLUS.

Grades K–3   *32 pages*

Candlewick Press, 2012

Momma is a single parent raising three children, providing for them with her new job as an apprentice stonecutter in New York City, working on the Cathedral of Saint John the Divine, one of the largest churches in the world. Its construction began in 1892, and through the years the cathedral has earned two nicknames among its neighbors: "St. John the Unfinished" and "Big John." The story's young narrator has many questions, including why the church remains unfinished and how people will know his mother's stone from all the others. It is a gorgeously illustrated tale of art, worship, family, and pride.

The Mermaid's Purse

BY PATRICIA POLACCO

Grades K–4   *48 pages*

Putnam, 2016; ebook

Patricia Polacco often draws on her family history for memorable picture books. This one, based on her grandmother, is no exception. Stella loves books. Soon they begin to overtake the farmhouse. Her pa tells her that she needs her own library so the neighbors help to build one. Stella opens the library, called the Mermaid's Purse, to her neighbors and travels around the countryside to take books to others. When a tornado destroys the building, the community rallies once again to help. Other books by the author: *Thank You, Mr. Falker; The Keeping Quilt; The Bee Tree; Chicken Sunday; Bully;* and *When Lightning Comes in a Jar.*

Mike Mulligan and His Steam Shovel

BY VIRGINIA LEE BURTON

Grades K–4   *42 pages*

Houghton Mifflin, 1939; ebook, audiobook

This is the heartwarming classic about the demise of the steam shovel and how it found a permanent home with driver Mike. Also by the author: *Choo Choo, The Emperor's New Clothes, Katy and the Big Snow,* and *The Little House.*

Mirette on the High Wire

BY EMILY ARNOLD MCCULLY
Grades K–2   *32 pages*
Putnam, 1992; ebook, audiobook

One hundred years ago in a small boardinghouse in Paris lived the Great Bellini, a daredevil tightrope walker who had lost his confidence. In the weeks that followed, the innkeeper's daughter became enchanted with rope walking and was able to restore the man's lost confidence while becoming a star herself. Winner of the Caldecott Medal, the book was followed by *Starring Mirette & Bellini* and *Mirette & Bellini Cross Niagara Falls*. Also by the author: *The Bobbin Girl*. Related books: *Brave Irene* by William Steig and *The Man Who Walked Between the Towers* by Mordicai Gerstein.

Miss Nelson Is Missing!

BY HARRY ALLARD; JAMES MARSHALL, ILLUS.
Grades PreS–4   *32 pages*
Houghton Mifflin, 1977; audiobook

Poor, sweet Miss Nelson! Kind and beautiful as she is, she cannot control her classroom—the worst-behaved children in the school. But when Miss Nelson is suddenly absent, the children begin to realize what a wonderful teacher they had in her. Her substitute is wicked-looking, strict Miss Viola Swamp, who works the class incessantly. Wherever has Miss Nelson gone and when will she return? Sequels: *Miss Nelson Is Back* and *Miss Nelson Has a Field Day*.

Naptastrophe!

BY JARRETT J. KROSOCZKA
Grades Tod–K   *40 pages*
Knopf, 2017; ebook

It's naptime and Lucy insists she is not tired. She stays awake by thinking about the fun she is missing by not playing with her toys. Finally, naptime is over and her daddy needs to run errands. As they buy groceries, Lucy continues to proclaim, "Not tired, not tired, not tired." But when daddy says no to candy, the meltdown begins—it is a naptastrophe! This picture book might be more entertaining for parents than for children, but it's definitely a fun read-aloud. Related books: *Llama Llama Red Pajama* by Anna Dewdney, *Dinosaur vs. Bedtime* by Bob Shea, *Goodnight Moon* by Margaret Wise Brown, *How Do Dinosaurs Say Good Night?* by

Jane Yolen, and *I Am Not Sleepy and I Will Not Go to Bed* by Lauren Child.

Ocean Meets Sky

BY TERRY FAN AND ERIC FAN
Grades K–3   *48 pages*
Simon & Schuster, 2018; ebook

Finn is a young boy of Asian descent. He vividly remembers the stories that his grandfather has told him about a place far away where the ocean meets sky. To honor and celebrate what would have been his grandfather's ninetieth birthday, Finn builds a boat "fit for a long journey." The sailing vessel is crafted from an old tire, driftwood, and window frames. Once complete, Finn crawls inside and takes a nap. Soon the boat is rocking gently and his journey has begun. This fantasy adventure is filled with wonders from the ocean such as submarines, a giant whale, and massive ships along with hot air balloons and dirigibles in the air. When Finn hears a familiar voice calling him, it's time to return home. Sumptuous, dreamlike illustrations stir the imagination. Don't forget to look at the illustration on the hardcover edition of the book as well as the endpapers. *The Night Gardener* is also written and illustrated by this brother duo and is equally mesmerizing. Related book: *Where the Wild Things Are* by Maurice Sendak.

Oh No, Bobo! You're in Trouble

BY PHIL GOSIER
Grades PreS–2   *32 pages*
Roaring Brook Press, 2019

Bobo is a sneaky little monkey who steals the zookeeper's flashlight. He is fascinated by the light as he clicks it on and off, on and off. That is, until it stops working. Bobo's friend, Fifi, exclaims that it's broken and the monkey is going to get into trouble. As Bobo frantically runs around the zoo trying to figure out what to do, he is followed by Fifi who tells all the animals what the monkey has done. When the zookeeper discovers the flashlight doesn't work, he merely replaces the batteries. The hilarious illustrations and riotous text make this a perfect read-aloud. Related books: *Grumpy Monkey* by Suzanne Lang, *Naughty Little Monkeys* by Jim Aylesworth, *Caps for Sale* by Esphyr Slobodkina, and *Three Little Monkeys* by Quentin Blake.

Old Hat

BY EMILY GRAVETT
Grades PreS–2   *32 pages*
Simon & Schuster, 2018; ebook
Harbet has a comfy hat that was knitted by his nana when he was little. He loves his hat. That is, until others start laughing at him. So
Harbet attempts to update his hat, but each effort is met with the same
response—laughter. He even buys a copy of *Top Hat* magazine and is
first in line at the hat shop on Hat Unveiling Day. Nothing seems to
work. So Harbet takes off his hat, and what's underneath is something
no one else can match. Other books by Gravett: *Orange Pear Apple
Bear*; *Again!*; *Wolves*; *Bear and Hare: Where's Bear?*; and *Meerkat Mail*.

Old MacDonald Had a Farm

BY GRIS GRIMLY
Grades Tod–2   *40 pages*
Orchard, 2017; ebook
A book that makes you break into song is never a bad thing. As Old
MacDonald walks around his farmyard, he greets each animal and
soon they fall into line, forming a parade. But there's one unex-
pected animal that makes the farmer say, "E-I-E-I . . . UH-OH!"
The illustrations are hilarious, which will make this book a home
and classroom favorite. Other illustrated songs: *Pete the Cat: The
Wheels on the Bus* by James Dean; *It's Raining, It's Pouring* by Kin
Eagle; *What a Wonderful World* by Bob Thiele and George David
Weiss; and *Row, Row, Row Your Boat* and *If You're Happy and You
Know It!* by Jane Cabrera.

Otis

BY LOREN LONG
Grades PreS–2   *36 pages*
Philomel, 2009; ebook, audiobook
Otis is a throwback. A small but diligent tractor, Otis is the life of
the barnyard and the best friend of a lonely calf residing in the
barn's adjoining stall. When his day's labors are done, they sit in
the shade of an apple tree to contemplate their happy lives. But their
happiness is suddenly interrupted when the farmer purchases a
brand-new yellow tractor, which quickly relegates Otis to the
scrap-heap weed patch outside the barn. He is now outdated, un-
employed, and too sad to play with his friend.

The calf, in turn, wanders down to the pond, only to get stuck in the mud. Either unable or unwilling to work herself out of the mire, she becomes the focus of a community-wide rescue effort. But neither the farmhands, the new tractor, nor the fire department can extricate her from the mud. Suddenly, Otis is seen making his way down the hillside, and soon a happy ending is in sight. Other Otis books include *Otis and the Tornado, Otis and the Puppy*, and *Otis and the Kittens*. Related books: *The Story of Ferdinand* by Munro Leaf, *The Little House* and *Mike Mulligan and His Steam Shovel* by Virginia Lee Burton, and *Smokey* by Bill Peet.

A Parade of Elephants
BY KEVIN HENKES
Grades Tod–K   *40 pages*
Greenwillow, 2018
This is a perfect book for toddlers and preschoolers. A parade of elephants go up and down, over and under, in and out. They are marching somewhere, but where are they going and what will they do when they get there? The five brightly colored elephants will delight any young child. This picture book also incorporates basic concepts such as numbers, shapes, adjectives, and adverbs along with daytime and nighttime. Other picture books by Kevin Henkes for young children: *Kitten's First Full Moon, Waiting, In the Middle of Fall*, and *When Spring Comes*.

Penguin Problems
BY JORY JOHN; LANE SMITH, ILLUS.
Grades K–3   *32 pages*
Random House, 2016; ebook
Penguin is a bit of a complainer. Nothing is right—from his beak being cold, not liking snow, and fretting that everybody looks the same. Walrus reminds him of all the beauty around him and that everyone has difficult times. And for a few moments, Penguin looks at his world differently. But then it's back to complaining again. This is a good book for those days when it seems like nothing goes right. *Giraffe Problems* by the same author and illustrator has Cyrus the giraffe questioning why his neck is so long. Other books by Jory John include *The Good Egg, Quit Calling Me a Monster!*, and *Come Home Already!*.

A Perfect Day

BY LANE SMITH
Grades Tod–2   *32 pages*
Roaring Brook Press, 2017; ebook

It's a perfect day in Bert's backyard for Cat, Dog, Chickadee, and Squirrel. The cat is lounging in the daffodils while Dog is enjoying the water in the wading pool. Chickadee is enjoying the birdseed that Bert has put in the bird feeder, and Squirrel is ready to munch on the corncob Bert has dropped. Ah yes, a perfect day. That is, until Bear comes along. He crushes the daffodils, drinks the pool water, and eats the birdseed and corncob. Now it's his perfect day. Smith's illustrations provide a texture that captures the uniqueness of each animal and their surroundings. Related books: *Waiting* by Kevin Henkes, *Move Over, Rover!* by Karen Beaumont, and *My Friend Rabbit* by Eric Rohmann.

The Pied Piper of Hamelin

BY MICHAEL MORPURGO; EMMA CHICHESTER CLARK, ILLUS.
Grades K–5   *64 pages*
Candlewick, 2011

Through the ages there have been many versions of the legend of Hamelin and the piper who led the children away when he was left unpaid. Here is yet another version, but this one has particular relevance to our times, and it comes from one of the most decorated British authors in children's literature, Michael Morpurgo. This version of Hamelin shows hundreds of neglected or abandoned children, wealthy townspeople who detest the poor, corrupt politicians, and a community overrun by garbage and refuse—which invites the invasion of rats. Enter the Pied Piper with his promise. The plot then takes the traditional path, including the lame boy who falls behind and returns to the village with the sad news. But from there, Morpurgo offers a different slant, a parable very much for our time. It is handsomely illustrated, with oversize pages. Also by the author: *Kaspar the Titanic Cat* and *Kensuke's Kingdom*.

Pink and Say

BY PATRICIA POLACCO
Grades 3 and up   *48 pages*
Philomel, 1994

Based on an incident in the life of the author-illustrator's great-great-grandfather, this is the tale of two fifteen-year-old Union soldiers—one white, one black. The former is wounded while deserting his company; the latter has been separated from his black company and stumbles upon the left-for-dead white soldier. The pages that follow trace this sad chapter in American history about as well as it's ever been told for children, beginning with a visit to the black soldier's mother, who is living on a nearby plantation ravaged by the war. There the wounded boy is nursed to both health and full courage while discovering the inhumanity of slavery. Related books: *January's Sparrow* also by Patricia Polacco; *Nurse, Soldier, Spy: The Story of Sarah Edmonds, a Civil War Hero* by Marissa Moss; and *Thunder at Gettysburg* by Patricia Lee Gauch.

Rapunzel
ADAPTED BY PAUL O. ZELINSKY
Grades 1–4   *32 pages*
Dutton, 1997
Of all the fairy-tale picture books in the marketplace, this is perhaps the most lushly illustrated and thus deserving of its Caldecott Medal. Borrowing from both the Brothers Grimm and previous versions from France and Italy, Zelinsky's retelling might make it the best of all, especially when coupled with his Italian Renaissance oil illustrations of the fair damsel locked in the tower by the evil sorceress. No other illustrator has captured as many Caldecott honors as Zelinksy, including awards for *Hansel and Gretel*, *Rumpelstiltskin*, and *Swamp Angel*. Another version of *Rapunzel* is by Rachel Isadora and set in Africa. The graphic novel *Rapunzel's Revenge* by Shannon Hale and Dean Hale is great for an older child.

The Rough-Face Girl
BY RAFE MARTIN; DAVID SHANNON, ILLUS.
Grades 1–4   *32 pages*
Puffin, 1998; ebook, audiobook
There are more than seven hundred different versions of Cinderella from various cultures. This is a retelling of the Algonquin Indian version, complete with the evil sisters who try to betray "Cinderella." In this story, she is known as the Rough-Face Girl, because sparks from the campfire have scarred her face through the years. Another retelling of Cinderella can be found in *Mufaro's Beautiful Daughters* by John Steptoe.

Stegothesaurus

BY BRIDGET HEOS; T. L. MCBETH, ILLUS.

Grades K–3   *40 pages*

Henry Holt, 2018; ebook

Once upon a time, there were three dinosaurs: a stegosaurus, another stegosaurus, and a stegothesaurus. Stegothesaurus had a great love of words and used them to describe everything. The shrubs they ate weren't just tasty; they were savory, succulent, and scrumptious. The sun wasn't just hot; it was blazing, blistering, and broiling. When the three dinosaurs see a scary-looking dinosaur, all but Stegothesaurus run away. It turns out that it wasn't an allosaurus but an allothesaurus, and the stegothesaurus is happy, thrilled, and ecstatic. But he realizes what he loves more than words: his family. This clever picture book will definitely enhance a child's vocabulary while providing a few chuckles along the way. A few other books about words: *The Word Collector* by Peter H. Reynolds, *Betty's Burgled Bakery: An Alliteration Adventure* by Travis Nichols, *Take Away the A* by Michaël Escoffier, and *Lexie the Word Wrangler* by Rebecca Van Slyke.

Strictly No Elephants

BY LISA MANTCHEV; TAEEUN YOO, ILLUS.

Grades PreS–3   *32 pages*

Simon & Schuster, 2015; ebook

It's Pet Club Day and children have brought their cats, dogs, birds, and fish. But the sign on the door clearly states Strictly No Elephants. The boy realizes that his beloved tiny elephant just doesn't fit in. When he meets a girl who was also excluded from the Pet Club meeting because she has a pet skunk, the two decide to start a club of their own. This is a story about friendship, including others, and recognizing not everyone is the same. Related books: *A Pet for Petunia* by Paul Schmid, *I Wanna Iguana* by Karen Kaufman Orloff, *The Pigeon Wants a Puppy!* by Mo Willems, *Let's Get a Pup! Said Kate* by Bob Graham, *Harry the Dirty Dog* by Gene Zion, and *How to Find an Elephant* by Kate Banks.

The Super Hungry Dinosaur

BY MARTIN WADDELL; LEONIE LORD, ILLUS.

Grades Tod–PreK   *32 pages*

Dial, 2009

A small boy and his dog are playing in the backyard when the Super Hungry Dinosaur arrives and announces he's going to eat the boy.

The ensuing simple tale details how the lad and his dog outwit and tame the dinosaur. And any damage done by the dinosaur's rampage is fixed by the exasperated creature before he can have lunch (cooked by Mom). Martin Waddell uses the same simple storytelling here that made his earlier book *Owl Babies* so successful, and illustrator Leonie Lord turns what could have been a threatening story into an exciting but nonthreatening adventure. Together they have created the perfect toddler/preschool book.

Cyndi's Favorite Sports Picture Books

All-Star!: Honus Wagner and the Most Famous Baseball Card Ever by Jane Yolen

America's Champion Swimmer: Gertrude Ederle by David A. Adler

Baseball Saved Us by Ken Mochizuki

Brothers at Bat by Audrey Vernick

Casey at the Bat by Ernest L. Thayer (C. F. Payne, illus.)

Game Changer: John McLendon and the Secret Game by John Coy

The Greatest Skating Race by Louise Borden

I Got It! by David Wiesner

The Kid from Diamond Street: The Extraordinary Story of Baseball Legend Edith Houghton by Audrey Vernick

Major Taylor: Champion Cyclist by Lesa Cline-Ransome

Miss Mary Reporting: The True Story of Sportswriter Mary Garber by Sue Macy

Mitchell Goes Bowling by Hallie Durand

A Nation's Hope: The Story of Boxing Legend Joe Louis by Matt de la Peña

Oliver's Game by Matt Tavares

Pecorino Plays Ball by Alan Madison

Randy Riley's Really Big Hit by Chris Van Dusen

Salt in His Shoes: Michael Jordan in Pursuit of a Dream by Deloris Jordan and Roslyn M. Jordan

Shoeless Joe & Black Betsy by Phil Bildner

Teammates by Peter Golenbock

There Goes Ted Williams: The Greatest Hitter Who Ever Lived by Matt Tavares

The Wildest Race Ever by Meghan McCarthy

Wilma Unlimited: How Wilma Rudolph Became the World's Fastest Woman by Kathleen Krull

Surprise!

BY CAROLINE HADILAKSONO
Grades K–3   *32 pages*
Arthur A. Levine Books, 2018; ebook

Bear, Squirrel, and Raccoon are bored. They want to make new friends to play with, but it has to be the right friends. When a family sets up their campsite in the woods, the animals decide they need to do something splendid to make them stay. They think a surprise welcome party is the answer. Squirrel will provide entertainment (juggling), Bear will create the decorations, and Raccoon will make the snacks (all using the family's food). When the family returns, they are definitely surprised, shocked, and in a hurry to leave. What else can the animals do but enjoy the surprise themselves!

Sylvester and the Magic Pebble

BY WILLIAM STEIG
Grades PreS–4   *30 pages*
Simon & Schuster, 1969; audiobook

In this contemporary fairy tale and Caldecott Medal winner, young Sylvester finds a magic pebble that will grant his every wish as long as he holds it in his hand. When a hungry lion approaches, Sylvester wishes himself into a stone. The pebble drops to the ground, and he can't reach it to wish himself normal again. The subsequent loneliness of both Sylvester and his parents is portrayed with deep sensitivity, making all the more real their joy a year later when they are happily reunited. Also by the author: *The Amazing Bone, Brave Irene, Doctor De Soto, Pete's a Pizza, The Toy Brother,* and *Zeke Pippin.*

Tap the Magic Tree

BY CHRISTIE MATHESON
Grades PreS–2   *42 pages*
Greenwillow, 2016

Who needs a screen on a tablet to make magical things happen in a book. In this innovative picture book, you tap the magic tree on the page to make a tree change with the seasons. Tap once, turn the page, and you'll see one green leaf. Tap again—one, two, three, four, and you'll see four more leaves on the tree on the next page. Pat, clap, wiggle, jiggle, and blow a kiss to see other changes. This highly interactive picture book is not only fun but also educational as it explores the seasons. Other similar books by the author: *Touch the Brightest Star* and *Plant the Tiny Seed*. Hervé Tullet's *Press Here*, *Mix It Up!*, and *Let's Play!* are equally as interactive.

Ten Little Fingers and Ten Little Toes
BY MEM FOX; HELEN OXENBURY, ILLUS.
Inf–Tod   *36 pages*
Harcourt, 2008
There are two widely accepted facts among early childhood educators: (1) children gravitate first to rhyming words (thus the success of Mother Goose and Dr. Seuss), and (2) children gravitate to images of other children, especially babies to babies. Apply those facts to the efforts of the popular Mem Fox and illustrator Helen Oxenbury, and you end up with what may become their biggest picture book success ever. With the multiethnic flavor of the book and boys and girls equally present, I can't think of a better gift for the new baby, and it is available as a board book. Also by the author: *Two Little Monkeys* and *Time for Bed*. Related books: *Gossie* by Olivier Dunrea, *Ten Little Babies* by Gyo Fujikawa, and *The Neighborhood Mother Goose* by Nina Crews.

The True Story of the Three Little Pigs!
BY JON SCIESZKA; LANE SMITH, ILLUS.
Grades K and up   *32 pages*
Viking, 1989; audiobook
For two hundred years we've taken the word of the three little pigs as gospel truth. But when the author presents the infamous wolf's side of the story, we get an implausible but entertainingly different point of view. Related books: *The Three Little Aliens and the Big Bad Robot* by Margaret McNamara, *The Three Little Wolves and the Big Bad Pig* by Eugene Trivizas, *The Three Little Pigs* by Steven Kellogg, *The Three Little Pigs: An Architectural Tale* by Steven Guarnaccia, *The Three Ninja Pigs* by Corey Rosen Schwartz, and *The Three Pigs* by David Wiesner.

When Sophie Gets Angry—Really, Really Angry . . .
BY MOLLY BANG
Grades PreS–2   *32 pages*
Scholastic, 1999; ebook, audiobook
Sophie gets angry when her sister wants a turn playing with a stuffed gorilla. Sophie gets angrier when her mother agrees. To make

matters worse, Sophie trips over a toy truck as the two sisters fight over the stuffed animal. As Sophie's anger increases, the scenes are illustrated in orange, yellow, and red. Finally, Sophie slams the door and runs, and runs, and runs outside until she can't run anymore. As she calms down she notices birds and ferns and the world around her. The colors in the illustrations have changed to blues and greens. This is a great book to talk about emotions and sharing with others. Additional Sophie books by Molly Bang: *When Sophie's Feelings Are Really, Really Hurt* and *When Sophie Thinks She Can't . . .* Related book: *Sometimes I'm Bombaloo* by Rachel Vail.

When You Are Brave

BY PAT ZIETLOW MILLER; ELIZA WHEELER, ILLUS.
Grades K–3   *40 pages*
Little, Brown, 2019
It's difficult to leave behind what you know. And that's what children do when they move to a new neighborhood. A young girl needs to say goodbye to neighbors and friends, and it all feels a little scary. What she realizes is that she must draw from the strength and power within her. This is a book about empowerment and believing that "No matter what happens, you'll be all right." Related books: *Oh the Places You'll Go!* by Dr. Seuss and *Walk On!: A Guide for Babies of All Ages* by Marla Frazee.

Where the Wild Things Are

BY MAURICE SENDAK
Grades K–3   *32 pages*
Harper, 1963; audiobook
This is the 1963 Caldecott winner that changed the course of modern children's literature. Sendak creates a fantasy about a little boy and the monsters that haunt and fascinate children. The fact that youngsters are not the least bit frightened by the story, that they love it as they would an old friend, is a credit to Sendak's insight into children's minds and hearts. Also by the author: *In the Night Kitchen*. Related books: *The Super Hungry Dinosaur* by Martin Waddell and *There's a Nightmare in My Closet* by Mercer Mayer.

The Wretched Stone

BY CHRIS VAN ALLSBURG
Grades 2–7 32 *pages*
Houghton Mifflin, 1991

When the crew members of a clipper ship sailing tropical seas discover a desert island, they also find a large gray stone, luminous and with one smooth side. When it is brought on board, an eerie change begins to envelop the ship. Fascinated by the rock, the crew members gradually desert their work and leisure activities, spending more and more time gazing in silent numbness at the rock—despite the protestations of their captain. A powerful allegory about the effects of television on society.

Van Allsburg's other books include *Ben's Dream*, *The Garden of Abdul Gasazi*, *Jumanji*, *Just a Dream*, *The Mysteries of Harris Burdick*, *The Polar Express*, *The Stranger*, *The Sweetest Fig*, *Two Bad Ants*, *The Widow's Broom*, *The Wreck of the Zephyr*, and *The Z Was Zapped* (an unusual alphabet book).

XO, OX: A Love Story

BY ADAM REX; SCOTT CAMPBELL, ILLUS.
Grades 1–4 40 *pages*
Roaring Brook Press, 2017; ebook

A simple ox professes his love for the glamorous, and graceful, gazelle. When he receives a form letter in return to his initial correspondence, he is more smitten. Soon, the back and forth letters between the hapless ox and the conceited gazelle show she is definitely not interested in an "animal that is too large, and too stout . . . and unlovable." Or is she? Scott Campbell's watercolor illustrations add to the humor. Don't overlook the endpapers, title page, and back jacket flap. Other related amusing picture books using a letter format: *The Day the Crayons Quit* by Drew Daywalt, *Meerkat Mail* by Emily Gravett, and *Diary of a Wombat* by Jackie French.

Kid's Favorite Series Books (not reviewed in the Treasury)

Big Nate by Lincoln Peirce

Goosebumps by R. L. Stine

Jasmine Toguchi by Debbi Michiko Florence

Judy Moody by Megan McDonald

Knights of the Lunch Table by Frank Cammuso

The Lost Hero: Heroes of Olympus (Percy Jackson) by Rick Riordan

Mac B., Kid Spy by Mac Barnett

The Magic School Bus Rides Again: Sink or Swim by Judy Katschke

The Spiderwick Chronicles by Tony DiTerlizzi and Holly Black

Victor Shmud, Total Expert: Night of the Living Things by Jim Benton

Early Chapter Book Series

Benny and Penny in the Big No-No! (graphic format)
BY GEOFFREY HAYES

Grades PreS–K   *30 pages*

Toon/Candlewick Press, 2009

Early easy reader books can be an important bridge to print for beginning readers, if they have plots kids care about. Toon books and their comic book style provide such stories. Equally important are characters that have similar experiences happen to them and issues kids worry about—like bullies, lying, tantrums, or broken toys. In this winner of the Theodor Seuss Geisel Award, the two mouse siblings go into forbidden territory—the new neighbors' yard! Also by the author: *Benny and Penny in Just Pretend, The Bunny's Night-Light: A Glow-in-the-Dark Search, Benny and Penny in the Toy Breaker,* and *Patrick in a Teddy Bear's Picnic and Other Stories.*

Bink & Gollie: Two for One
BY KATE DICAMILLO AND ALISON MCGHEE; TONY FUCILE, ILLUS.

Grades 1–3   *96 pages*

Candlewick Press, 2012; ebook, audiobook

Bink and Gollie are best friends and complete opposites in terms of appearance, but that's one of the many reasons why this series for younger readers is so entertaining. This time the duo goes to the state fair where Bink attempts to win a giant donut at the Whack a Duck game, Gollie enters a talent show, and both ask Madame Prunely to predict their destiny. The stories are delightfully illustrated by Tony Fucile who adds another layer to the story with his visual humor. Two additional books complete the series: *Bink and Gollie* and *Bink and Gollie: Best Friends Forever.*

Cam Jansen and the Joke House Mystery

BY DAVID A. ADLER

Grades 1–3   *64 pages*

Puffin, 2015; ebook, audiobook

Thanks to Cam Jansen's photographic memory, little escapes her notice in this easy mystery series that comprises more than thirty books. You might say she's a grade school Nancy Drew but with far fewer pages per book. In this volume, Aunt Molly has entered a joke-telling contest at a local comedy club. Cam, her best friend Eric, and Mr. Jansen are in the audience when the young sleuth realizes that one of the prizes has disappeared. Everyone in the club quickly become suspects. This is an excellent introduction to the mystery genre. Encyclopedia Brown by Donald J. Sobol is another early chapter book mystery series, starring the local police chief's ten-year-old son, who is always too smart for the crime crowd.

Dinosaurs Before Dark

BY MARY POPE OSBORNE

Grades K–2   *76 pages*

Random House, 1992; ebook, audiobook

In this first book of the popular Magic Tree House time-travel series (with three- to four-page chapters), young Annie and Jack discover a tree house that transports them back in time to the age of dinosaurs. The journey is filled with fantasy adventure while exploring scientific, cultural, or historic places and events.

Dory Fantasmagory: Head in the Clouds

BY ABBY HANLON

Grades PreS–2   *160 pages*

Dial, 2018; ebook, audiobook

This is the fourth book in the series of wildly imaginative chapter books that are just right for reading aloud. Dory has her first loose tooth and cannot stop talking about it. As usual, she drives her siblings crazy. Mrs. Gobble Gracker isn't too happy either and decides to steal the tooth fairy's job. Characters, both real and imaginary, provide hilarious plots. The books contain a bounty of black-and-white illustrations, which limits the amount of text on each page. Other books in the series: *Dory Fantasmagory, Dory Fantasmagory: Dory Dory Black Sheep,* and *Dory Fantasmagory: The Real True Friend.*

Fox + Chick: The Party and Other Stories

BY SERGIO RUZZIER

Grades PreS–2   *46 pages*
Chronicle, 2018; ebook

Fox and Chick are the most unlikely of friends, which makes this early chapter book so enjoyable. The three short stories contain a simple story line punctuated with strong vocabulary such as parsley, grasshoppers, potatoes, chipmunks, and landscape. The ink-and-watercolor illustrations add another layer of enjoyment to this appealing book that is sure to be a hit with young children. *Fox + Chick: The Quiet Boat Ride and Other Stories* is the second book in the series, with others sure to follow.

Gooney Bird Greene

BY LOIS LOWRY

Grades K–2   *88 pages*
Houghton Mifflin, 2002; ebook, audiobook

Gooney Bird Greene is the antithesis of Junie B. Jones in civil behavior but a carbon copy in uniqueness and irrepressibility. Second-grader Gooney Bird is smart, mature, kind, and in charge at all times—or at least she wants to be, which sometimes presents a challenge for her teacher. But on the first day in her new school, it's clear she is mysterious and interesting. Her clothes are unusual. Her hairstyles are unusual. Even her lunches are unusual. On her second day at school, she wears a pink ballet tutu over green stretch pants, and she has three small red grapes, an avocado, and an oatmeal cookie for lunch. Just as Gooney wins over her classmates and teacher, she'll win over her readers. Sequels: *Gooney Bird and the Room Mother, Gooney the Fabulous, Gooney Bird Is So Absurd, Gooney Bird on the Map,* and *Gooney Bird and All Her Charms.* The Newbery-winning Lowry has long been one of our most gifted writers for children, and this series proves again her great versatility.

Hello, Hedgehog! Do You Like My Bike?

BY NORM FEUTI
Grades PreS–2   *46 pages*
Scholastic, 2019; ebook

Scholastic's newest series is aimed at early readers ages four to seven. Using a graphic format with speech bubbles, protagonist Hedgehog encounters kid challenges such as riding a bike with a friend (after he finds his helmet of course). A second book in the series is *Let's Have a Sleepover!* After one or repeated read-alouds, children will become confident in reading this enjoyable series independently.

Here's Hank: A Short Tale About a Long Dog

BY HENRY WINKLER AND LIN OLIVER
Grades K–2   *128 pages*
Grosset & Dunlap, 2014; ebook

Here's Hank is a series for young readers by actor Henry Winkler. While I'm generally not a fan of celebrity books for children, this series is the exception. The reason is that Winkler is genuine in his desire to write books that appeal to children with reading difficulties, which he also experienced as a child. *A Short Tale About a Long Dog* is the second in the series about a relatable character. Hank is in second grade and desperately wants a dog. His father makes a deal with him that if he can bring up his grades, then they will go to the animal shelter to get a family dog. When his grades increase a little, Hank's father relents and off they go. Mesmerized by a little wiener dog chasing his tail, Hank decides that this is the dog for him. The new pet, Cheerio, poses some challenges especially when he gets loose in the park. But the situation gets resolved, and Hank keeps his new best friend. The books use the font Dyslexie, which was designed by a Dutch graphic designer to make the letters "more distinct from one another and to keep them tied down, so to speak, so that the reader is less likely to flip them in their minds." Hank works hard to overcome his learning disabilities, and his family is there to support him. Other books in the Here's Hank series include *Bookmarks Are People Too!* and *Stop that Frog!* Winkler has a series for older readers, Hank Zipzer, which also presents believable characters and situations.

Hilde Cracks the Case: Fire! Fire!

BY HILDE LYSIAK WITH MATTHEW LYSIAK; JOANNE LEW-VRIETHOFF, ILLUS.

Grades K–3   *96 pages*

Scholastic, 2017; ebook

Hilde Kate Lysiak is a ten-year-old American journalist and author who also publishes a local newspaper, the *Orange Street News*, in Selinsgrove, Pennsylvania. This series of books offers fast-paced action as Hilde attempts to solve a mystery of a fire on Orange Street that burns down a shop. Mrs. Brown thinks her candles started the fire and is so distraught that she won't leave her house. Can Hilde find out what or who really caused the fire? Pages from Hilde's notebook introduce new vocabulary and model questioning of who, what, when, where, why, and how. Other books in the series: *Bear on the Loose!*, *Hero Dog!*, *UFO Spotted!*, and *Tornado Hits!*

The Infamous Ratsos

BY KARA LAREAU; MATT MYERS, ILLUS.

Grades K–2   *64 pages*

Candlewick Press, 2016; ebook

Third-grader Ralphie and fifth-grader Louis want to be like their father, Big Lou, and that means being *TOUGH*. The boys' plans to show how tough they are involve pulling pranks on classmates and neighbors. However, things don't quite work out the way they envisioned. When Big Lou finds out about the good deeds that resulted from the pranks, he tells his sons that being tough all the time is really tough and it's time to change. The cartoonlike black-and-white illustrations offer a glimpse into the characters while capturing the action of the story. Other books in the series: *The Infamous Ratsos Are Not Afraid* and *The Infamous Ratsos: Project Fluffy*.

Ivy + Bean: One Big Happy Family

BY ANNIE BARROWS; SOPHIE BLACKALL, ILLUS.

Grades K–3   *124 pages*

Chronicle, 2018; ebook, audiobook

This popular series was slated to end after the tenth book, but young fans wrote so many compelling (and entertaining) letters to author Annie Barrows that she fortunately relented. Ivy is an only child, and all the books she has read point out that only children are sometimes spoiled rotten, don't share their toys, and scream and cry when they don't get their way. So how can Ivy avoid the inevitable? The perfect solution is to get a baby sister, and she knows her best friend Bean will help her find one. What makes this series such a fun read-aloud for both child and adult is that each will view the humorous predicaments of Ivy and Bean a little differently. Four previous books in the series include *Ivy + Bean: What's the Big Idea?*, *Ivy + Bean: No News Is Good News*, *Ivy + Bean Make the Rules*, and *Ivy + Bean Take the Case*.

Junie B. Jones and the Stupid Smelly Bus

BY BARBARA PARK

Grades K–1   70 pages

Random House, 1992; ebook, audiobook

Don't be put off by the title of this book, the first of a wonderfully funny series (more than thirty books to date). Junie B. is Ramona, Little Lulu, and Lucy all rolled into one determined kindergartner. The sixty-five million copies sold in the Junie B. Jones series is proof positive how popular she is. Related book: *Gooney Bird Greene* by Lois Lowry. Park's other books, like *Mick Harte Was Here* and *Skinnybones*, are aimed at older students and demonstrate why she's consistently a state award winner with children.

Mr. Monkey Bakes a Cake

BY JEFF MACK

Grades K–2   64 pages

Simon & Schuster, 2018; ebook

Mr. Monkey bakes a cake in hopes of winning a ribbon. But first he needs to carry it to the contest. What could possibly go wrong? This is an enjoyable story that will provide a fun read-aloud experience and enable young children to obtain new vocabulary. The next two books in the series, *Mr. Monkey Visits a School* and *Mr. Monkey Takes a Hike*, continue the monkey's wacky adventures.

The Notebook of Doom: Whack of the P-Rex

BY TROY CUMMINGS

Grades K–3   96 pages

Atheneum, 2014; ebook

Alexander Bopp is ready to battle Stermont's biggest monster yet, the P-Rex. This highly engaging early chapter book series has high-interest content, fast-paced plots, and illustrations on every page. Introducing young children to a series such as this as a read-aloud will foster their independent reading. There are thirteen books in the Notebook of Doom series including *Charge of the Lightning Bugs, Pop of the Bumpy Mummy, Flurry of the Snombies, Chomp of the Meat-Eating Vegetables,* and *Attack of the Shadow Smashers.*

The Princess in Black Takes a Vacation

BY SHANNON HALE AND DEAN HALE; LEUYEN PHAM, ILLUS.
Grades K–3   *96 pages*
Atheneum, 2017; ebook, audiobook
This is book four in the popular Princess in Black series. Our heroine, Princess Magnolia, is exhausted. She has been battling monsters for the fourteenth time in one week. When the masked Goat Avenger suggests she take a vacation, the Princess decides to ride her bicycle to the seashore. When a sea monster begins terrorizing the beach, the Princess in Black knows she needs to spring into action. Dual story lines of Princess Magnolia and the Goat Avenger keep the pace exciting. Illustrations by LeUyen Pham add to the fun. Other books in the series: *The Princess in Black, The Princess in Black and the Perfect Princess Party, The Princess in Black and the Hungry Bunny Horde, The Princess in Black and the Mysterious Playdate,* and *The Princess in Black and the Science Fair Scare.*

Violet Mackerel's Remarkable Recovery

BY ANNA BRANFORD; ELANNA ALLEN, ILLUS.
Grades K–2   *128 pages*
Atheneum, 2013; ebook
Seven-year-old Violet Mackerel has developed "The Theory of Giving Small Things." If someone has a problem, you give them something small like a feather, a pebble, or a purple lozenge, which may help them in a special way. This theory is put to the test when Violet develops a bad case of tonsillitis and has to have her tonsils removed. In the hospital waiting room, Violet meets an older woman, Iris MacDonald, who is there to have surgery on her arm. Violet suggests the two have tea once they both recover, and Iris agrees. Unfortunately, Violet doesn't know how to contact her new friend so she puts into action her plan for "Thinking Outside the Box About Finding Iris MacDonald." This highly readable series will introduce children to a positive protagonist through humor and plausible plots. Other Violet Mackerel books include *Violet*

Mackerel's Natural Habitat, Violet Mackerel's Brilliant Plot, Violet Mackerel's Possible Friend, and *Violet Mackerel's Pocket Protest.*

Chapter Books and Novels

Adam Canfield of the Slash

BY MICHAEL WINERIP
Grades 5–8   *326 pages*
Candlewick Press, 2005; ebook, audiobook

An African American girl named Jennifer is the bright, levelheaded coeditor of Harris Elementary/Middle School's student newspaper, *The Slash.* Coeditor Adam Canfield is a bright but not-so-levelheaded eighth grader. Together they're a veritable Woodward and Bernstein. Author Michael Winerip (a Pulitzer Prize–winning education writer for the *New York Times*) has placed his coeditors in wealthy Tremble, suburbia brimming with overscheduled kids too busy to play, school administrators and real estate agents too focused on test scores, and a husband-wife team that owns both the cable company and the local newspaper and is thus able to slant news and views as they wish. This is a superb introduction to modern journalism and some contemporary issues the author has dealt with as a reporter. Sequels: *Adam Canfield: Watch Your Back!* and *Adam Canfield: The Last Reporter.*

The Bad Beginning (series)

BY LEMONY SNICKET
Grades 2–4   *162 pages*
Harper, 1999; ebook, audiobook

Contrary to the title, this is a splendid beginning to the enormously popular A Series of Unfortunate Events thirteen-book series that follows the riches-to-rags tale of three resilient orphans who no sooner overcome one Dickensian misfortune and villain than even darker ones appear. The children must and do resist these threats with determined quick wits. Sending up the moralistic Victorian adventure tales of a century ago, as well as old-time Saturday movie serials, the author's asides to the reader-listener are humorous, helpful, and enlightening (especially with vocabulary). Since the success of this series, there has been a wave of published imitations, none of which compare even closely to its originality or humor.

Be a Perfect Person in Just Three Days!

BY STEPHEN MANES

Grades 2–5   76 pages

Yearling, 1996; ebook

If any subversive person is interested in sneaking in a little laughter among the many serious books these days about orphans, vampires, and postapocalyptic children, this is for that person. A young boy, tired of being the brunt of everyone's taunts, begins a do-it-yourself course in becoming perfect—with hilarious and unpredictable results. Conclusion: Nobody's perfect, even the popular kids.

Because of Winn-Dixie

BY KATE DICAMILLO

Grades 2–5   182 pages

Candlewick Press, 2000; ebook, audiobook

Ten-year-old India Opal Buloni is not only the new kid in town, she's also a preacher's kid. She picks up a stray dog at the neighborhood Winn-Dixie grocery (that's how it gets its name) and charms her daddy into letting her keep him. She also charms everyone she meets, collecting the weirdest assortment of cast-off grown-ups and kids you'll ever meet and grow fond of. The movie is a good translation of the book. Also by the author: *The Tale of Despereaux*. Related books: *Wish* by Barbara O'Connor, *Shiloh* by Phyllis Reynolds Taylor, *Ribsy* by Beverly Cleary, and *Almost Home* by Joan Bauer.

Bob

BY WENDY MASS AND REBECCA STEAD; NICHOLAS GANNON, ILLUS.

Grades 2–5   204 pages

Feiwel and Friends, 2018; ebook, audiobook

Livy is returning to Australia after a five-year absence. There are many things she doesn't remember from when she was a five-year-old including a short greenish creature, Bob, who has been hiding in a closet, waiting for her return. Livy's promise before leaving was that she would help Bob find his way back home. As her memory slowly unfolds, Livy realizes how Bob came into her life and what she needs to do to help him. This enjoyable chapter book with elements of both realism and fantasy will hold children's attention from beginning to the satisfying conclusion.

Bridge to Terabithia

BY KATHERINE PATERSON

Grades 4–7   *128 pages*

Crowell, 1997; ebook, audiobook

Few novels for children have dealt with so many emotions and issues so well: sports, school, peers, friendship, death, guilt, art, and family. This popular Newbery Medal winner deserves to be read or heard by everyone. Also by the author: *The Great Gilly Hopkins* and *Lyddie*.

Brown Girl Dreaming

BY JACQUELINE WOODSON

Grades 5 and up   *352 pages*

Penguin Random House, 2014; ebook, audiobook

Woodson's memoir in verse tells of her childhood growing up in Ohio, South Carolina, and New York during the 1960s and 1970s. As an African American, Woodson lived with the remnants of Jim Crow and the awareness of the civil rights movement. Each poem shares further insight into what Woodson refers to in her author's note as, "my past, my people, my memories, my story." It becomes evident how much stories matter to Woodson, then and now. The audiobook of Woodson reading *Brown Girl Dreaming* can be enjoyed as part of the read-aloud process in giving voice to both poetry and story. Pair with the picture book *Show Way*, based on Woodson's own history, which tells of African American women across generations and is beautifully illustrated by Hudson Talbott. Other books by Woodson include *After Tupac and D Foster*, *Feathers*, and *If You Come Softly*.

Bud, Not Buddy

BY CHRISTOPHER PAUL CURTIS

Grades 4–8   *243 pages*

Delacorte, 1999; ebook, audiobook

After escaping a succession of bad foster homes, ten-year-old Buddy sets out to find the man he suspects to be his father—a popular jazz musician in Grand Rapids, Michigan. Told in the first person, this engaging Newbery Medal winner brims with humor and compassion while offering a keen insight into the workings of a child's mind during the Great Depression. Also by the author: *The Watsons Go to Birmingham—1963*, *The Mighty Miss Malone*, *Elijah of Buxton*, and *The Journey of Little Charlie*. Related books: *City of Orphans* by Avi and *Roll of Thunder, Hear My Cry* by Mildred D. Taylor.

Charlotte's Web

BY E. B. WHITE; GARTH WILLIAMS, ILLUS.
Grades K–4   *192 pages*
Harper, 1952; ebook, audiobook
One of the most acclaimed books in children's literature that is loved by adults as well as children, the tale centers on the barnyard life of a young pig who is to be butchered in the fall. The animals of the yard (particularly a haughty gray spider named Charlotte) conspire with the farmer's daughter to save the pig's life. While there is much humor in the novel, the author uses wisdom and pathos in developing his theme of friendship within the cycle of life. Also by the author: *Stuart Little* and *The Trumpet of the Swan*. Melissa Sweet's *Some Writer!: The Story of E. B. White* is an excellent children's biography of the author. *A Boy, a Mouse, and a Spider: The Story of E. B. White* is a picture book biography of the author by Barbara Herkert.

The City of Ember

BY JEANNE DUPRAU
Grades 4–7   *288 pages*
Random House, 2003; ebook, audiobook
More than 240 years before the story opens, a great holocaust confronted the population of earth. To save the species, one group created a huge underground city, Ember, that would be safe from the ravages above. Because it was complete with giant storehouses of supplies and a huge generator, humanity could survive. These forefathers also conceived a means by which the inhabitants would be able to extricate themselves from their underground tomb after 200 years, estimating that by then the surface would be habitable again. Detailed instructions were given to the mayor who, in turn, would pass them to his successor. The book picks up the story almost 250 years later. Those instructions have long been misplaced and forgotten, and so has much of history. The people know only their life underground and live increasingly meager existences with dwindling supplies and energy.

But the youngest generation is chafing under the regimentation of the old order, even wondering if there might be something beyond the here and now, pondering, "What if . . . ?" Two such people are twelve-year-olds Doon and Lina. The latter has stumbled on some strange but ancient instructions in her grandmother's closet, and the former is a born rebel and questioner but sentenced to spend the rest of his life repairing the plumbing in the bowels of the city. Together they begin the journey outward and upward that will save their civilization—if they can ever get anyone to follow them. Sequels: *The People of Sparks*, *The Prophet of Yonwood*, and *The Diamond of Darkhold*. There is also a graphic novel version by Dallas Middaugh and Niklas Asker. Related book: *The Giver* by Lois Lowry.

City of Orphans

BY AVI

Grades 5–8   *350 pages*

Atheneum, 2011; ebook, audiobook

It's 1893 on the Lower East Side of New York City and the tenements are brimming with poor immigrants, most of them living lives of desperation, others dying by the wayside. In the middle of this mix we find the Geless family, including the story's main character, thirteen-year-old Maks. As a school dropout, he's earning eight cents a day selling newspapers on street corners, then turning the money over to help support his family—the same thing his older sisters do with their money. As the narrative plays out (told through the vernacular of a working-class New Yorker of that time whose English is less than perfect, not unlike the technique used in Tom Sawyer), we meet the realities of life in America—where the streets were never paved with gold, and dreams sometimes came true but most often did not—and the primal power of family bonding. Indeed, as we live through five days in the Geless household, we encounter all the hardships and indignities of poverty. The book is arranged in ninety-one two-page chapters, perfect for short readings. Related film: *Newsies*, the Disney film musical based on the 1899 newsboys strike against the newspaper barons Joseph Pulitzer and William Randolph Hearst. See also the *New York Times* article "Read All About It! Kids Vex Titans!" by Dan Barry, March 2, 2012, about the Broadway show based on the same events. A Google search for "Lewis Hine + newsboys" will give you hundreds of original newsboy images from that era, taken by the famous photographer/sociologist.

Close to Famous

BY JOAN BAUER
Grades 7–9   *250 pages*
Viking, 2011; ebook, audiobook

Twelve-year-old Foster McFee is lovable and determined, just like her mother. You get the feeling right from the get-go that things are going to work out for the two of them, but not before there are some rough spots. First, they have to start life over again in a new town, Culpepper, West Virginia, where they're hiding from Foster's mother's abusive boyfriend, an Elvis impersonator. Culpepper is struggling with the letdown from the promises that the new penitentiary would bring all kinds of jobs for the local folks. So the town is devoid of hope, which is frustrating to Foster, who envisions herself as a TV chef. How do you build a career on a hopeless town? The same goes for her new friend Macon, who has his eye set on becoming a film documentarian. And then things begin to fall into place as Foster starts a cupcake business through the local café. And true to form, the abusive boyfriend resurfaces, as do an assortment of bad guys, good guys, and as warm a collection of neighbors since Kate DiCamillo's *Because of Winn-Dixie*. If you don't bring in cupcakes while you're reading this book, you're missing a big opportunity. Also by the author: *Hope Was Here*, *Rules of the Road*, and *Soar*.

Crispin: The Cross of Lead

BY AVI
Grades 4–7   *262 pages*
Hyperion, 2002; ebook, audiobook

Set in AD 1377, a thirteen-year-old known only as Asta's son lives as a peasant in the village of Stromford in England. When his mother dies, he is left with nothing but the cross of lead that belonged to her. The village priest, Father Quinel, reveals the boy's name is Crispin and promises to tell him who is father is as well. Before he is able to do so, the steward of the manor, John Aycliffe, has him murdered. Aycliffe has also accused the boy of theft, forcing Crispin to flee the village. When Crispin is befriended by a juggler by the name of Bear, he is coerced into becoming a servant whose primary task is to think for himself. *Crispin* was the recipient of the 2003 Newbery Medal and is a tale filled with breathtaking plot twists and vivid characters. The trilogy of books includes *Crispin: At the Edge of the World*, published in 2006, and *Crispin: The End of Time*, released in 2010. Avi's books beg to be read aloud. The historical setting offers an opportunity to learn about this time period as will vocabulary words such as *portcullis, caterwauling, glaive, tonsure, solar,* and *tunic.* Other books set during medieval times include *The Book of Boy* by Catherine Gilbert Murdock; and *The Inquisitor's Tale: Or, the Three Magical Children and Their Holy Dog* by Adam Gidwitz.

The Crossover

BY KWAME ALEXANDER
Grades 5–10   *240 pages*
Houghton Mifflin Harcourt, 2014; ebook, audiobook
Twins Josh and Jordan are junior high school basketball stars due in part because of coaching by their dad, a former professional basketball player. Unfortunately, their dad had to quit playing because of health reasons that he doesn't want to discuss. The boys have a strong bond until Jordan begins dating Miss Sweet Tea. Josh struggles with his feelings of jealousy and abandonment along with knowing things are changing as they grow up. The novel is written in verse with a little hip-hop, concrete poetry, and jazz woven together. *Rebound* and *Booked* are the other two books in the author's Crossover series.

Danny the Champion of the World

BY ROALD DAHL
Grades 3–5   *196 pages*
Knopf, 1975; ebook, audiobook
In what might be Dahl's most tender book for children, a motherless boy and his father—"the most wonderful father who ever lived"—go on an adventure together. Teachers and parents should explain the custom and tradition of poaching in England before going too deep into the story (Robin Hood was a poacher). Also by the author: *James and the Giant Peach, Charlie and the Chocolate Factory,* and *Matilda.*

Darby

BY JONATHON SCOTT FUQUA
Grades 2–4   *240 pages*
Candlewick Press, 2002; ebook
To get a quick grip on this book, think of it as *To Kill a Mockingbird* for nine-year-olds—except *Darby* is told with the immediate

feelings and words of a girl who is nine and hasn't achieved the wisdom that comes with hindsight. It takes us back to 1926 and the American South, specifically Marlboro County, South Carolina. And though Darby Carmichael acts as if the world revolves around her, she is beginning to notice other forces in her small universe—some of which she can't control. She is writing the book to explain the good and terrible things that happened that year in her family and community.

Truthfulness is at the heart of this novel, from the time Darby is inspired by her best friend to become a newspaper writer. The friend, Evette, is the daughter of a black tenant farmer on her father's farm. It wasn't fashionable for a white girl to have a black best friend in that time and place, but sometimes friendships grow like wildflowers. Ever since Evette told her that newspaper writers must always write the truth, Darby has been writing short articles for the local paper and has become a little celebrity in the community. Then the Carmichaels' redneck neighbor assaults a black boy he finds stealing a chicken, a beating that results in the boy's death. This opens Darby's eyes to the unfair differences between whites and blacks in her town, and she and her friend write an essay that unsettles family, friends, and community. Readers-aloud should not be put off by the size of the book (240 pages); the page dimensions are small, and the text is double-spaced, so it's really about 140 pages in length. Related book: *The Parker Inheritance* by Varian Johnson.

Dream of Night

BY HEATHER HENSON

Grades 4–8   *218 pages*

Atheneum, 2010; ebook

Make no mistake: This is no cookie-cutter horse story. Old Jess is feeling her age these days, weary of caring for rejected horses and foster kids who inflict too much pain. So this just might be the last time around for her. First, she's boarding a former champion thoroughbred she's rescued from an abusive owner. Unless she finds a way to defuse Dream of Night's angry temperament soon, euthanasia may be the only option. And then there's Shiloh, an angry, uncommunicative twelve-year-old girl who has bounced among a series of foster homes. Unless Jess can also defuse this boarder's rage, a juvenile institution will be the next stop. Complicating matters, neither boarder wants anything to do with the other. Teens of either gender will find this a believable and riveting narrative. *New York Times* coverage of one alleged abuse case can be found online at http://www.nytimes .com/2009/04/05/sports/othersports/05horses.html. The opposite of Dream of Night's life is that of the great Triple Crown winner Seattle Slew. The black colt with the crooked leg was turned over to Paula Turner for training, and right away she sensed something special in him, although her view may have been biased by a childhood favorite book called *The Black Stallion*. She told her heartwarming story, "Training a Champion," to American Public Media's *The Story* in 2011, accessible online at http://www.thestory.org/stories/2011-05 /training-champion. Related books: *Black Beauty* by Anna Sewell, *Who Was Seabiscuit?* by James Buckley Jr. (nonfiction), *War Horse* by Michael Morpurgo, and *Riding Freedom* by Pam Muñoz Ryan.

A Drop of Hope
BY KEITH CALABRESE
Grades 3–8   *320 pages*
Scholastic, 2019; ebook

A well, a wish, and a little drop of hope—these three things are expertly woven together in this engaging and thought-provoking read-aloud. The town of Cliffs Donnelly is facing tough times, and a few miracles would help its residents. Sixth-grader Ernest Wilmette is small in stature, but large with optimism. His classmates, Ryan Hardy and Lizzy MacComber, are not quite as positive in their outlook given their family and personal challenges. And then there's bully Tommy Bricks who is feared by all. At the center of the story is Thompkins' Well where, legend has it, a miracle took place generations ago when a significant wish was granted. When Ernest and Ryan discover a hidden tunnel that leads to the bottom of the well, they also unwittingly hear the wishes of people—some whose voices they recognize and others that are unfamiliar. Ernest decides they should find a way to make the wishes come true despite Ryan's skepticism. Couple Ernest's genuine wish-granting intent with his task of cleaning his late grandfather's attic, and somehow wishes do come true. Told through various characters' perspectives, this novel is storytelling at its finest. Related books: *Hello, Universe* by Erin Entrada Kelly, *The Dreamer* by Pam Muñoz Ryan, *Louisiana's Way Home* by Kate DiCamillo, and *Walk Two Moons* by Sharon Creech.

Dugout Rivals

BY FRED BOWEN
Grades 3–5   *128 pages*
Peachtree, 2010; ebook

Twelve-year-old Jake has labored for a couple of years with a mostly losing baseball team, but this year promises to be different. First, the team is loaded with experienced players, and second, Jake will be taking over at the coveted shortstop position. To make it even better, the team has a new kid, named Adam, who is the best player Jake and his teammates have ever seen. As expected, they begin to win. The unexpected part is that Adam also plays shortstop and pitches. Jake is suddenly playing in the shadow of a superstar, something he's never had to deal with before. To complicate matters, Adam is just as nice as he is athletic. Other novels by the author: *Throwing Heat, Perfect Game, Hardcourt Comeback, Soccer Team Upset, T. J.'s Secret Pitch, The Golden Glove,* and *Touchdown Trouble.*

El Deafo (graphic novel)

BY CECE BELL
Grades 3–7   *248 pages*
Abrams, 2014; ebook

Told in a graphic novel format, Cece Bell's memoir is both humorous and poignant. At age four, she contracted meningitis, which resulted in hearing loss. When she begins school, Cece is equipped with the Phonic Ear, which amplifies her teacher's voice and actions no matter where she goes (including the bathroom). The bulky hearing aid is difficult to hide, which prompts a variety of reactions from her schoolmates. Cece just wants to fit in and find a true friend. *El Deafo* shares a compelling story not only about a child with a disability but also about the challenges of growing up.

Escape from Mr. Lemoncello's Library

BY CHRIS GRABENSTEIN
Grades 3–7   *304 pages*
Random House, 2013; ebook, audiobook

Eccentric inventor of video and board games, Luigi Lemoncello, returns to his hometown to build a library unlike any other. In honor of the grand opening, Mr. Lemoncello selects a dozen twelve-year-olds to participate in an overnight lock-in event. The kids soon discover a different and unexpected game is being waged that involves finding a way out of the library. Whoever is able to do so will earn the grand prize. Kyle Keeley wants to be the winner of this challenge, but he has to use all he can muster in regard to skill, wit, and possibly teamwork. It would also be great if he could beat his nemesis, the conniving Charles Chiltington. Avid readers will find numerous references to classic and current children's books. Other chapter books in the Mr. Lemoncello's Library series: *Mr. Lemoncello's Library Olympics*, *Mr. Lemoncello's Great Library Race*, and *Mr. Lemoncello's All-Star Breakout Game*.

Esperanza Rising

BY PAM MUÑOZ RYAN

Grades 3 and up   *272 pages*
Scholastic, 2000; ebook, audiobook

This is a powerful read-aloud that is successful with a wide range of children. In Mexico, Esperanza had fancy dresses, a home filled with servants, and family members to care for her. But a sudden tragedy forces Esperanza and her family to flee to California and settle in a Mexican farm labor camp. The young girl is hardly prepared or equipped for this change in her lifestyle. Kids are often in disbelief at the part when Esperanza does not even know how to use a broom. When her mother becomes ill and a workers' strike looms to seek better working conditions, Esperanza needs to find a way to rise above her difficult circumstances and rely on the strength and courage within herself. Other novels by the author worth reading aloud are *Echo*, *Riding Freedom*, *The Dreamer*, and *Becoming Naomi León*.

Finding Langston

BY LESA CLINE-RANSOME

Grades K–2   *112 pages*
Holiday House, 2018; ebook, audiobook

It's 1946 and eleven-year-old Langston's beloved mother has passed away. His grief-stricken father decides they should leave their rural Alabama home to travel north to Chicago. It's lonely with just the two of them in their one-room apartment without having family nearby. If that's not enough, Langston is being bullied at school. When he discovers the public library that allows him to read and check out books, unlike the white-only library in Alabama, he has found where he belongs. When he discovers another Langston, a poet by the name of Langston Hughes, the young boy realizes his mother named him after this influential individual. The story will prompt discussion about why African Americans moved from the South. *Finding Langston* is a celebration of reading and libraries and the power that each holds. This fictional chapter book will provide an opportunity to share information and stories about Langston Hughes. A good place to start is *Coming Home: From the Life of Langston Hughes* by Floyd Cooper; *That Is My Dream!* (a picture book of Langston Hughes's "Dream Variation") by Langston Hughes and Daniel Miyares; and *The Dream Keeper and Other Poems* by Langston Hughes with eye-catching illustrations by Brian Pinkney.

The First Rule of Punk

BY CELIA C. PÉREZ
Grades 4 and up   *336 pages*
Viking, 2017; ebook, audiobook
What's the first rule of punk? Be yourself. And that's exactly what twelve-year-old Malú (Maria Luisa, if you want to annoy her) intends to be. When Malú and her mother move a thousand miles away from her father, the potential to be what she wants at her new school is on full display. On her first day at Posada Middle School, she violates the dress code with her punk rock look and tries to establish her identity. She is proud of her Mexican roots as well as her passion for punk. While her mother wants to believe her daughter is just in a rebellious stage, Malú knows that this is who she is—an individual with her own sense of self. Related books: *The Blossoming Universe of Violet Diamond* by Brenda Woods, *Two Naomis* by Olugbemisola Rhuday-Perkovich and Audrey Vernick, and *Goodbye Stranger* by Rebecca Stead.

Flora & Ulysses: The Illuminated Adventures

BY KATE DICAMILLO; K. G. CAMPBELL, ILLUS.
Grades 2–5   *240 pages*
Candlewick Press, 2013; ebook, audiobook
This Newbery Medal recipient begins in the kitchen of the Tickham household when a truly unique gift is bestowed upon the lady of the house—a Ulysses Super-Suction, Multi-Terrain 2000X vacuum cleaner. A tragic accident immediately occurs and, unfortunately, Ulysses the squirrel never saw it coming. Self-described

cynic, Flora Belle Buckman, who has read every issue of the comic book *Terrible Things Can Happen to You!* is the perfect person to rescue Ulysses. The confrontation with the vacuum has rendered the squirrel with powers of strength, flight, and the ability to write poetry with numerous misspellings. The characters are quirky and memorable. The plot a bit overwhelming at times but totally engaging. And the potential connections between text and reader are phenomenal. Illustrations by K. G. Campbell only add to the hilarity and absurdity of the situations. I met a first grader who was completely enthralled with this book and even created her version of what comes next in the story. Each book by Kate DiCamillo presents a different style of storytelling. A few of her other books not included in the Treasury include *The Tale of Despereaux: Being the Story of a Mouse, A Princess, Some Soup, and a Spool of Thread*; *The Miraculous Journey of Edward Tulane*; *The Magician's Elephant*; and *The Tiger Rising*.

Freak the Mighty

BY RODMAN PHILBRICK

Grades 6–9   *165 pages*

Scholastic, 1993; ebook, audiobook

Many popular entertainment tales have involved teams—Batman and Robin, the Lone Ranger and Tonto, Luke Skywalker and Han Solo. Each member is usually of vastly different stature. In that tradition comes the team of Max and Kevin, two unlikely teenage heroes. Middle-schooler Max is gigantic, powerful, and a remedial student. The wisecracking Kevin suffers from a birth defect that limits his growth and keeps him on crutches; his body cannot grow to more than a few feet in height, but his mind has expanded to brilliant proportions. The two become fast friends and give themselves the nickname Freak the Mighty (Kevin and Max, respectively). Their adventures run the gamut from escaping street bullies and outwitting school authorities to educating Max and surviving his homicidal father. While some parts are implausible, the friendship between the two is a thing of beauty, and Max's first-person voice rings true as he painfully explores the anxieties of adolescence. Sequel: *Max the Mighty*.

Frindle

BY ANDREW CLEMENTS
Grades 3–6   105 pages
Simon & Schuster, 1996; ebook, audiobook
This book will have you laughing out loud by paragraph five, nodding in affirmation of its wisdom throughout, and wiping the tears away at its end. The story is what education, family, and relationships are supposed to be about, never mind what a good book can do for the reading appetite. And—it's fall-down funny. Oh, yes, it's about the dictionary too (so be sure to have a copy of the picture book *Noah Webster and His Words* by Jeri Chase Ferris nearby). No author rivals Clements in capturing the soul of the American classroom. Also by the author: *About Average, Extra Credit, The Jacket, The Janitor's Boy, The Landry News, The Last Holiday Concert, Lost and Found, Lunch Money, No Talking, The Report Card, Troublemaker,* and *A Week in the Woods.*

From the Mixed-up Files of Mrs. Basil E. Frankweiler

BY E. L. KONIGSBURG
Grades 4–7   62 pages
Macmillan, 1967; ebook, audiobook
A bored and brainy twelve-year-old girl talks her nine-year-old brother into running away with her. To throw everyone off their trail, Claudia chooses the Metropolitan Museum of Art in New York City as a refuge, and amid centuries-old art they sleep, dine, bathe, and pray in regal secret splendor. An exciting story of hide-and-seek and a wonderful art lesson to boot. For experienced listeners. Related runaway books: a city boy hides in the wilderness for a year in *My Side of the Mountain* by Jean Craighead George, and a city boy hides in the subway system for 121 days in *Slake's Limbo* by Felice Holman.

Full of Beans

BY JENNIFER L. HOLM
Grades 3–7   208 pages
Random House, 2016; ebook
It's 1934 and the middle of the Great Depression on Key West. Beans Curry and his family are struggling financially as are most of the families in town. One thing that Beans has learned is, adults lie to children. So when a New Deal stranger shows up one day

claiming the government sent him to make their dumpy town a tourist attraction, Beans is skeptical. But Beans has bigger issues to contend with and that includes finding ways to make money for him and his family. When Beans has a role in a tragedy, he has to step up and try to make something, right. If you are familiar with Holm's *Turtle in Paradise*, you might remember Turtle's cousin, Beans. However, this novel stands on its own. Holm weaves in family stories and historical information into this enjoyable, well-written chapter book for middle grades. Other novels set during the Great Depression are *Moon Over Manifest* by Clare Vanderpool; *Out of the Dust* by Karen Hesse; and *Bud, not Buddy* by Christopher Paul Curtis.

Ghost Boys

BY JEWELL PARKER RHODES
Grades 4–7   *224 pages*
Little, Brown, 2018; ebook, audiobook
Middle-schooler Jerome Rogers lives in a low-income Chicago neighborhood. He is constantly bullied at school, which forces him to hide during lunch in the bathroom, locker room, or supply closet. Jerome also doesn't have any friends until Carlos, a new boy in school, befriends him. When the two are discovered in the bathroom by the bullies, Carlos pulls out a gun that looks real. After the bullies retreat, Carlos gives the toy gun to Jerome who plays an imaginary game of good guy/bad guy on his way home from school. Thinking it's a real gun, a police officer shoots Jerome in the back as he is running away. The officer later claims he feared for his life. The chapters alternate between Jerome talking about his life and the events leading up to the shooting, and his death in which, as a ghost, he is able to see his grief-stricken family and follow the officer's trial. Another ghost boy, Emmett Till, tries to help Jerome understand what happened to him. *Ghost Boys* will prompt important questions and conversation which makes it an excellent book to read aloud by parents or teachers. It's a powerful story that is honest in its depiction of this all-too-frequent occurrence today that is meaningfully connected to Till's murder decades ago.

Harbor Me

BY JACQUELINE WOODSON
Grades 5–8   *192 pages*
Nancy Paulsen Books, 2018; ebook, audiobook
Six kids are sent, by themselves, to a room each Friday afternoon where they can just talk. No adults, no assigned topics, no homework—just talk. In the place they call the ARTT (A Room to Talk), the stories of each kid slowly unfolds: Esteban fears his father has been deported; Haley doesn't want to reveal the truth about her family; Holly appears to have everything since her family has money but that proves not to be the case; Tiago and his mother face discrimination because they speak primarily in Spanish; Ashton who feels on the outside of everything because he is white in a school filled with shades of brown; and Amari who is a talented artist but recognizes that being a black teenager poses risks every day. This is a powerful story about compassion, understanding, acceptance, and freedom. Woodson's writing is so compelling and her words flow easily when read aloud even if the subject matter is ripped from today's headlines. Reading aloud this book might provide an opportunity to share some of Woodson's picture books such as *The Other Side*, *Each Kindness*, and *The Day You Begin*.

Harry Potter and the Sorcerer's Stone (series)

BY J. K. ROWLING
Grades 2–8   *309 pages*
Scholastic, 1998; ebook, audiobook
Harry Potter is the best thing to happen to children's books since the invention of the paperback. While the plot of the series is surely original, it follows in the path of C. S. Lewis's dual Narnia world, George Lucas's *Star Wars* struggles with the "dark side," and Dorothy's search for the Wizard of Oz. It is also blessed with an abundance of Roald Dahl's cheeky childhood humor.

   Harry is the orphan child of two famous wizards who died mysteriously when he was very young. Rescued at age eleven from abusive relatives, he is sent to Hogwarts School of Witchcraft and Wizardry (sorcery's equivalent of an elite boarding school), where he experiences high adventure as he and his friends (boy and girl) struggle with classes in potions, charms, and broom flying, all the while battling a furtive faculty member working for the dark side.

   This is not an easy read-aloud, and the reader-aloud should be aware that the first two chapters of the first book are a bit complicated, as they set the scene for Harry's dual world. Definitely for experienced listeners, the books grow darker in content as they proceed toward the final volume. Actor Jim Dale has done a masterful job of recording (unabridged) all the Harry Potter books for Listening Library/Penguin Random House.

Other books in the series (in order): *Harry Potter and the Chamber of Secrets*, *Harry Potter and the Prisoner of Azkaban*, *Harry Potter and the Goblet of Fire*, *Harry Potter and the Order of the Phoenix*, *Harry Potter and the Half-Blood Prince*, and *Harry Potter and the Deathly Hallows*. Younger fans of Harry may also enjoy the Deltora Quest series by Emily Rodda; *The Lion, the Witch and the Wardrobe* by C. S. Lewis; and the Redwall series by Brian Jacques, beginning with *Martin the Warrior*. Older fans may be ready for *The Hobbit* by J. R. R. Tolkien.

Hatchet

BY GARY PAULSEN
Grades 6 and up   *195 pages*
Bradbury, 2007 (20th anniversary edition); ebook, audiobook
The lone survivor of a plane crash in the Canadian wilderness, thirteen-year-old Brian Robeson carries three things away from the crash: a fierce spirit, the hatchet his mother gave him as a gift, and the secret knowledge that his mother was unfaithful to his father. All play an integral part in this Newbery Honor survival story for experienced listeners. Sequels: *The River*, *Brian's Winter*, *Brian's Return*, and *Brian's Hunt*. Having received about four hundred letters a week with *Hatchet*-related queries, Paulsen has answered them in one book: *Guts*, detailing the true-life events that inspired the series. Related survival books: *The Cay* and *Ice Drift*, both by Theodore Taylor; *Incident at Hawk's Hill* by Allan W. Eckert; the Island series by Gordon Korman; *Kensuke's Kingdom* by Michael Morpurgo; and *Winter Camp* by Kirkpatrick Hill. Other books by Paulsen: *The Foxman* (a precursor to *Harris and Me*); *Mr. Tucket*; *The Rifle*; *Soldier's Heart*; *The Tent*; a survival-at-sea novel, *The Voyage of the Frog*; and *Woods Runner*. Paulsen also has written a memoir for children of his relationships with dogs, *My Life in Dog Years*. An author profile is available at www.trelease-on-reading.com/paulsen.html.

Hello, Universe

BY ERIN ENTRADA KELLY

Grades 5–8   *314 pages*

Greenwillow, 2017; ebook

Four middle school students' fates become unexpectedly inter-twined one summer in this 2018 Newbery Medal winner that tack-les bullying, disabilities, culture, and self-acceptance. Virgil Salinas is shy and rarely speaks except to his beloved guinea pig, Gulliver. Virgil also struggles with his multiplication tables, prompting class-mate and bully Chet "the Bull" Bullens to call him "retardo." Va-lencia Somerset is clever, yet stubborn, but feels like an outsider because she is deaf. Kaori Tanaka is a self-claimed psychic and fortune-teller who counsels Virgil to befriend Valencia. Alternating chapters share the four protagonists' perspectives while providing insight into their actions and behavior. When Chet throws Virgil's backpack, containing Gulliver, into an abandoned well, the uni-verse comes together as the paths of the four tweens intersect. As Virgil sits at the bottom of the well after attempting to retrieve his backpack, Valencia and Kaori sense that something is amiss and go in search of him. Believable characters and a story line that will elicit conversation make this a terrific read-aloud. Other books by the author: *You Go First, Blackbird Fly, The Land of Forgotten Girls*, and *Lalani of the Distant Sea*.

Holes

BY LOUIS SACHAR

Grades 4–8   *233 pages*

Farrar, Straus & Giroux, 1998; ebook, audiobook

Holes is an adventure tale, a mystery, a fantasy, and a quest book. (It captured a rare literary triple crown: Newbery, National Book, and Horn Book awards—among many other honors.) An important in-gredient in this success is Sachar's wit. Set in a juvenile detention station in the Texas desert, it traces the sad life of fourteen-year-old Stanley Yelnats, who has just been sentenced (mistakenly) for steal-ing a pair of sneakers. Not only has the friendless, hopeless Stanley been haunted all his life by a dark cloud of events, so has his family. Indeed, there is a family legend that his grandfather's long-ago self-ishness in Latvia has rusted every golden opportunity for the family since then. Forced by the abusive camp police to dig holes all day long in the baking desert, he experiences an epiphany, makes his first friend, and gradually discovers courage he never knew he had. In so doing, he slowly and painfully unwinds the century-old family curse. The movie based on the book was exceptionally well received by critics and families, perhaps because the author himself wrote the screenplay. Sequel: *Small Steps.* Also by the author: *Wayside School Is Falling Down, Sideways Stories from Wayside School,* and *Wayside School Gets a Little Stranger.* Related book: *Maniac Magee* by Jerry Spinelli.

The Hundred Dresses

BY ELEANOR ESTES

Grades 3–6   *78 pages*

Harcourt Brace, 1944; ebook, audiobook

Wanda Petronski comes from the wrong side of the tracks and is the object of class jokes, until her classmates sadly realize their awful mistake and cruelty. But by then it's too late. Though written more than sixty years ago, the book has a message about peer pressure that has lost none of its power or relevance in an age of bullying. Related book: *The Bears' House* by Marilyn Sachs.

Inside Out & Back Again

BY THANHHA LAI

Grades 3–8   *266 pages*

HarperCollins, 2011; ebook, audiobook

Short free verse poems tell the poignant story of Lai's personal experiences as a child refugee. Ten-year-old Hà flees Vietnam with her mother and three older brothers. Traveling by boat, the family reaches a tent city in Guam, then Florida, and finally Alabama, where they are connected with sponsors. Hà struggles with the language, customs, and dress, which prompts verbal cruelty by her classmates. She ultimately spends her lunchtime hiding in the bathroom as she deals with the anguish of not being accepted and feeling alienated by others. Eventually, she does get back at the kids bullying her and slowly adjusts to her new life. This stirring, and at times humorous, novel provides a perspective of being a refugee and what children and their families endure in building a new life in an unfamiliar country. Related books: *Nowhere Boy* by Katherine Marsh, *A Long Walk to Water* by Linda Sue Park, *The Red Pencil* by Andrea Davis Pinkney, and *Bamboo People* by Mitali Perkins.

The Invention of Hugo Cabret

BY BRIAN SELZNICK
Grades 3 and up   *536 pages*
Scholastic, 2007; ebook, audiobook

Don't let the number of pages in this Caldecott Medal–winning book deter you from reading it aloud. Told through 284 pages of original drawings, this picture book/illustrated novel will capture your attention and propel you through the story. Hugo's father has tragically lost his life, leaving the young boy alone and living in the walls of a busy Paris train station. He is determined to find the parts to the mechanical man, or automaton, his father was working on. The only problem is he has no money and resorts to stealing the needed parts from a bitter old man who owns a toy booth in the train station. The cinematic quality of the book naturally lent itself to being made into a movie by Martin Scorsese. Selznicks's website (www.theinventionofhugocabret.com) provides additional information about filmmaker Georges Méliès and the movie in 1902 that inspired this book. Similar in style are *Wonderstruck* and *The Marvels*, also by Selznick. His illustrated picture books include *The Dinosaurs of Waterhouse Hawkins* and *Walt Whitman: Words for America*, both by Barbara Kerley; and *When Marian Sang: The True Recital of Marian Anderson* by Pam Muñoz Ryan.

James and the Giant Peach

BY ROALD DAHL
Grades K–6   *120 pages*
Knopf, 1961; ebook, audiobook

Four-year-old James, newly orphaned, is sent to live with his abusive aunts and appears resigned to spending his life as their humble servant. Then a giant peach begins growing in the backyard. Waiting inside that peach is a collection of characters that will captivate your audience as they did James. Few books hold up over six grade levels as well as this one does, and few authors for children understand their world as well as Dahl did. Also by the author: *The BFG, Danny the Champion of the World, Fantastic Mr. Fox, Matilda, The Minpins, The Wonderful Story of Henry Sugar,* and *The Roald Dahl Treasury,* a collection of his best work.

Kaspar the Titanic Cat
BY MICHAEL MORPURGO; MICHAEL FOREMAN, ILLUS.
Grades 2–5   *200 pages*
Harper, 2012; ebook, audiobook
Fourteen-year-old Johnny Trott is the savvy orphan bellboy at London's swanky Savoy Hotel when he's spotted by a Russian countess and designated to care for her prized black cat, Kaspar. Soon a tragedy leaves him the sole protector of the cat, which he must hide in his room against the hotel rules. Unfortunately, Kaspar refuses to eat without his countess and is starving to death—until Lizziebeth, an eight-year-old American heiress, arrives on the scene and saves the day, though not before her dangerous impulsiveness requires her to be publicly rescued from the rooftop by Johnny. No good melodrama should be without a villain, and Morpurgo provides a dandy in Skullface, the feared head housekeeper. When it's time for Lizziebeth and her parents (and Kaspar) to depart for America, their ship is the *Titanic* (with Johnny aboard as a working stowaway). Of course, all survive, including the cat. Better yet, it's not even the end of the book. The description of the *Titanic* sinking is based on careful research and includes realistic portrayals of the crew's heroics. For other books by the author, see the entry for *Kensuke's Kingdom*.

Kensuke's Kingdom
BY MICHAEL MORPURGO
Grades 3–5   *164 pages*
Scholastic, 2003; ebook, audiobook
Because childhood can sometimes be a case of survival, children seem to gravitate to survival books, as proved by Paulsen's success with *Hatchet*. This volume ranks with the best of that genre.

Michael is twelve years old when he and his dog are washed overboard from the family's yacht and into the Coral Sea off Australia. Clinging to the dog and a soccer ball, the boy is washed up on a tropical island. While appearing uninhabited, the island has a host of animals, plants, and fish that might keep him alive. It also contains another resident—a very old and very angry Japanese man named Kensuke Ogawa, a navy doctor who has been on the island since the end of World War II. Initially, Kensuke was marooned there when his ship sank, but eventually he was there by choice, more than fifty-five years after his home in Nagasaki was bombed with one of the first atomic bombs. The rest is his story and Michael's. Entwined with the modern survival story are issues of war and peace, brotherhood, family ties, art, nature, and hope. Related books: *Baseball Saved Us* by Ken Mochizuki (a story from the Japanese internment camps); *The Cay* by Theodore Taylor; *Robinson Crusoe* by Daniel Defoe (one of the Scribner Illustrated Classics series [abridged, thank you], illustrated by N. C. Wyeth); and three books by Gary Paulsen: *The Foxman, Hatchet,* and *The Voyage of the Frog.* Also by the author: *Kaspar the Titanic Cat, The Pied Piper of Hamelin, Private Peaceful, War Horse,* and *The War of Jenkins' Ear.*

Kindred Souls

BY PATRICIA MACLACHLAN

Grades 2–5   *117 pages*

Harper, 2012; ebook

Like her famous Newbery Medal winner *Sarah, Plain and Tall,* this novella is set on the American plains but in contemporary times. It's a plain farm, populated by six people and a dog that appeared one day out of nowhere. The central characters are eighty-eight-year-old Billy, his youngest grandson, Jake, and Lucy the dog. Off on the farm's hillside are the decayed remains of the sod house that Billy grew up in, a site that brings back the happiest of memories for the old man. Gradually it's decided that young Jake will attempt to rebuild the sod house as a favor for his grandfather, something the boy feels is beyond his capabilities. When Billy needs to be temporarily hospitalized, the whole family pitches in to finish the house as a gift for him. A warm and loving portrait of what family can be and how affection works as a powerful force when decent, loving people rub against one another all day long, willing to go the extra mile for each other.

Lily's Crossing

BY PATRICIA REILLY GIFF

Grades 3–6   *180 pages*

Delacorte/Dell, 1997; ebook

This coming-of-age novel focuses on the summer of 1944 and one feisty yet frightened young girl in a Long Island beach community. With her beloved father shipped overseas and her best friend moved away, Lily befriends a Hungarian refugee, Albert. Together they experience the great fears and small triumphs that keep children afloat during the war years. Lily, reader and future writer, learns the hard way that tall tales, spun out of control, can become dangerous lies. And Albert finds in Lily a friend who will change his life forever. This is a multiple award winner, including the Newbery Honor. Related books: *Alan and Naomi* by Myron Levoy and *Because of Winn-Dixie* by Kate DiCamillo.

The Lion, the Witch and the Wardrobe (Narnia series)
BY C. S. LEWIS
Grades 3–6   *186 pages*
HarperCollins, 1950; ebook, audiobook
Four children discover that the old wardrobe closet in an empty room leads to the magical kingdom of Narnia—a kingdom filled with heroes, witches, princes, and intrigue. This is the most famous (first to be published but considered second chronically) of seven enchanting books in the Chronicles of Narnia series, which can be read as adventures or as Christian allegory. The series in chronological order: *The Magician's Nephew*; *The Lion, the Witch and the Wardrobe*; *The Horse and His Boy*; *Prince Caspian*; *The Voyage of the Dawn Treader*; *The Silver Chair*; and *The Last Battle*. *The Land of Narnia* by Brian Sibley is an excellent guide to Narnia. Many reasonable comparisons have been made between the dual world of Narnia and the Harry Potter books.

Lions & Liars
BY KATE BEASLEY; DAN SANTAT, ILLUS.
Grades 3–6   *304 pages*
Farrar, Straus and Giroux, 2018; ebook, audiobook
Frederick Frederickson has a food-chain theory about life. There are lions who are the school bullies and the gazelles who are their targets. And then there are the meerkats, and the lowest of all, the fleas that live on the butts of meerkats. Frederick is a flea. When a hurricane cancels the family's annual cruise vacation, Frederick is upset. After a fight with his friend, he takes a boat and inadvertently loses the motor and anchor. When he finally washes up on land after a night floating down the river, Frederick finds himself at a weekend disciplinary camp for troublesome boys. He's mistaken for another camper, who is legendary, and the confusion builds from there. All Frederick wants is not to be a flea and to have friends value him. Will his new fellow cabinmates—Nosebleed, Specs, the

Professor, and Ant Bite—become those friends? This humorous novel is about friendship, brotherhood, and finding your own way even when you have floated a bit far downstream in life. Related books: *Breakout* by Kate Messner and *Loser* by Jerry Spinelli.

Lone Stars

BY MIKE LUPICA

Grades 4–7   *234 pages*

Philomel, 2017; ebook, audiobook

Mike Lupica is one of the most talented children's sports novelists for middle-grade readers. Clay is an excellent receiver who can zip across the football field to catch the ball as it sails through the air and into his hands. And he idolizes Coach Cooper who was a star player for the Dallas Cowboys. As the season gets under way, Clay begins to notice some odd behavior from Coach Coop—he has lapses in his memory and mood swings. It soon becomes apparent that Coop is suffering from the side effects of the many concussions he sustained during his playing days. This touching story demonstrates Lupica's knowledge of the game while dealing with the current issue of concussive injury. Other Mike Lupica sports books: *Travel Team*, *QB1*, *The Batboy*, *True Legend*, *Million-Dollar Throw*, and *Fast Break*.

Long Way Down

BY JASON REYNOLDS

Grades 7 and up   *320 pages*

Atheneum, 2017; ebook, audiobook

This has to be one of the most powerful novels written in recent years. Told through verse we learn that fifteen-year-old Will's big brother, Shawn, has been shot and killed. In accordance with The Rules in his head: don't cry, don't snitch, and "if someone you love / gets killed / find the person / who killed / them and /kill them." Will locates Shawn's gun, leaves the family's eighth-floor apartment, and steps into the elevator. At each floor, the elevator stops and the ghost of a victim or perpetrator in a chain of violence enters. There's Shawn's best friend, Buck; Will and Shawn's uncle Mark; and finally the ghosts of Will's father and brother. Each one shares his perspective of The Rules. The final lines of the novel will take your breath away and leave you pondering Will's next steps. This book has received multiple awards which are well deserved.

It's a powerful novel in verse that will prompt conversation about guns and violence. Other novels by Reynolds for an adolescent audience: *When I Was the Greatest, The Boy in the Black Suit*, and *All American Boys*.

The Losers Club

BY ANDREW CLEMENTS
Grades 3–7   240 pages
Random House, 2017; ebook, audiobook
Who knew that a book about a boy who is a bibliophile could be so much fun! Sixth-grader Alec would rather read for pleasure than listen to his teacher. This often leads to Alec being in trouble with his parents, his teacher, and the principal. When he is forced to join a club as part of the after-school program, Alec decides to start his own—the Losers Club. No one would want to join that club, Alec reasons, and he would be able to sit and read without anyone bothering him. But the club is a huge success! Soon Alec is making new friends and reconnecting with old ones. He realizes it's great to read, but it's also good to be part of the real world. Realistic dialogue, relatable characters, and a dash of humor offer a glimpse of middle school and determining one's identity. Other books by Clements: *Frindle, No Talking, Lunch Money, The Report Card*, and *Extra Credit*.

Malcolm at Midnight

BY W. H. BECK; BRIAN LIES, ILLUS.
Grades 2–4   265 pages
Houghton Mifflin, 2012; ebook, audiobook
When the teacher purchased Malcolm from the pet shop, he thought he was just a large mouse. Wrong. And when Malcolm ended up in the fifth grade as the classroom pet, he thought he had gone to heaven. Wrong. Malcolm is a rat, a species with a particularly bad reputation, something he spends the book trying to overcome. And just in case you think the teachers run the school—wrong again. In this school, the Midnight Academy rules—a collection of all the classroom pets that meet outside their cages each midnight to debate and investigate school issues. A warm, humorous adventure with many illustrations. Related books: *Charlotte's Web* and *Stuart Little* by E. B. White, *James and the Giant Peach* by Roald Dahl, and *Poppy* by Avi.

Martin the Warrior (Redwall series)

BY BRIAN JACQUES

Grades 4–7   *376 pages*

Philomel, 1994; ebook, audiobook

The Redwall series is in the tradition of *The Hobbit* but for younger readers. Built around an endearing band of courageous animals inhabiting an old English abbey, the books describe their fierce battles against evil creatures. There is high adventure galore, cliff-hanger chapter endings, gruesome behavior by evil outsiders, and rollicking fun. For experienced listeners. *Martin the Warrior* is a prequel, going back to the founding of the abbey and should be read first, followed by *Redwall* and then the rest of the series. Related books: *Harry Potter and the Sorcerer's Stone* by J. K. Rowling and *The Lion, the Witch and the Wardrobe* by C. S. Lewis. For grades 6 and up: *The Hobbit* by J. R. R. Tolkien.

The Mighty Miss Malone

BY CHRISTOPHER PAUL CURTIS

Grades 5–8   *320 pages*

Wendy Lamb Books, 2012; ebook, audiobook

Revisiting some of the territory he made familiar to us with his Newbery-winning *Bud, Not Buddy*, the author portrays a plucky eleven-year-old African American girl narrating her family's journey through the Great Depression. A determined optimist, Deza Malone is mighty in word and thought, never to be outtalked and shining in the classroom—when there is one. And unlike her counterpart in *Buddy*, Deza is surrounded by one mighty sacrificing family that encounters in the 1930s what many families are facing in today's Great Recession. Many people were reduced to riding filthy, dangerous freight trains to get from place to place, as do the Malones en route to a shantytown. PBS's *American Experience* spotlighted that experience in the film *Riding the Rails*, accessible online at http://www.pbs.org/wgbh/americanexperience/films/rails/. As bad as the times were, they were worse for people of color. See the article "Added Obstacles for African Americans," online at http://www.pbs.org/wgbh/americanexperience/features/general-article/rails-added-obstacles/. For related books, see the listing for *Bud, Not Buddy* by the author.

Mimi

BY JOHN NEWMAN

Grades 4–8   *186 pages*

Candlewick Press, 2011; ebook, audiobook

We meet this family—a father, two teens, and one primary grader—
five months after the mother died in a traffic accident. The tale is
seen through the witty but penetrating eyes of Mimi, the youngest.
No one is finished grieving; they are all going through the motions,
especially Dad, who is on leave from his job and tuned out to everyone's needs except his own. This isn't a depressing tale but instead one about family dysfunction and humans working their way
out of the wreckage of a tragedy. The author is a classroom teacher
who has obviously met a few struggling families. In this case, it's a
supporting cast of relatives, teachers, and classmates who come to
the rescue. There are gobs of laughter as well as pure wisdom in
these pages ("'You said that with your head, love, not with your
heart—so it doesn't count,' said Dad" after an angry outburst by the
teenage daughter).

Mockingbird

BY KATHRYN ERSKINE

Grades 6 and up   *235 pages*

Putnam, 2010; ebook, audiobook

With autism cases tripling in the past several decades, this book is
long overdue. Soon-to-be eleven-year-old Caitlin has Asperger's
syndrome and tells her own story in a most compelling voice. People on the autism spectrum normally don't handle interpersonal
communication or social issues easily, and *Mockingbird* offers its
readers (and listeners) a deep insight into one girl's mind and heart,
far closer than they might ever come with an actual classmate.

Not only does Caitlin have to cope with Asperger's, she's also
struggling to understand the tragedy that recently struck her family
when her older brother was one of the victims in a fatal school
shooting. While Caitlin is loved by her widower father, her brother
was the pride of his life and she's trying to fill the family void left by
his death—not an easy task for anyone, let alone someone for whom
empathy is a foreign emotion. As the book progresses, we see the
efforts of her teachers, counselor, father, and classmates in trying to
bring closure to the struggling child, giving us an opportunity to
view all of them through the child's eyes. And while there are many

wrenching moments, the book is not without its honestly humorous moments as she struggles with literal interpretations of classmates' and teachers' words and actions.

Because of the serious nature of the book and its subjects, I would hesitate in sharing it with children as young as the narrator unless they are very mature. One cannot come away from this book without both a greater understanding of autism and a greater empathy for those suffering with social disorders. This tale will grab you by the throat, give you a good shake, and then set you cheering for the human spirit. In a related novel, *Wonder* by R. J. Palacio, a spunky boy with a deeply deformed face who has been previously homeschooled is enrolled at a neighborhood middle school. Like *Mockingbird*, his story enables readers and listeners to crawl into a "different" child's skin and soul for a more complete view of the world.

The Monster's Ring (Magic Shop series)

BY BRUCE COVILLE
Grades 2–4   *87 pages*
Pantheon, 1982; ebook

Just the thing for Halloween reading, this is the Jekyll and Hyde tale of timid Russell and the magic ring he buys that can turn him into a monster. Not a make-believe monster, but one with hairy hands, fangs, and claws, one that roams the night, one that will make short order of Eddie the bully, and one that will bring out the worst in Russell. An exciting fantasy of magic gone awry, this is part of the Magic Shop series, which includes *Jeremy Thatcher, Dragon Hatcher*; *Jennifer Murdley's Toad*; and *The Skull of Truth*.

Mostly Monty

BY JOHANNA HURWITZ
Grades K–2   *96 pages*
Candlewick Press, 2007; ebook

This is the author's latest creation in a career of gentle family stories. Monty is an asthmatic who is overly protected by his family, leaving him with few social contacts, not even pets (allergies). All of this is going to change in first grade, where he discovers not only his own talents (reading first in his class) but his first friends. Along the way, his little adventures with the school's Lost and Found section are giving him the confidence to start a hobby and a neighborhood club. Sequels: *Mighty Monty* and *Amazing Monty*.

The Mouse and the Motorcycle

BY BEVERLY CLEARY

Grades K–2   *158 pages*

Morrow, 1965; ebook, audiobook

When young Keith and his family check into a run-down motel one day, the mice in the walls are disappointed. They'd hoped for young children, messy ones who leave lots of crumbs behind. What Ralph S. Mouse gets instead is a mouse-size motorcycle. He and the boy guest become fast friends and embark on a series of hallway-to-highway escapades that make this tale a longtime favorite. Sequels: *Runaway Ralph* and *Ralph S. Mouse*. Also by the author: *Ramona the Pest*. Related books: *Malcolm at Midnight* by W. H. Beck, *Poppy* by Avi, and *Stuart Little* by E. B. White.

Mrs. Frisby and the Rats of NIMH

BY ROBERT C. O'BRIEN

Grades 4–6   *232 pages*

Atheneum, 1971; ebook, audiobook

In this unforgettable fantasy/science fiction tale, we meet a group of rats that has become superintelligent through a series of laboratory injections. Though it opens with an almost fairy-tale softness, it grows into a taut and frighteningly realistic tale. A decade after the publication of this Newbery Medal winner, the author's fiction grew closer to fact with a breakthrough in genetic engineering. Sequels: *Racso and the Rats of NIMH* and *R-T, Margaret, and the Rats of NIMH*, both by Jane Leslie Conly, one of the daughters of the late author. Also by O'Brien: *The Silver Crown*.

My Father's Dragon

BY RUTH STILES GANNETT

Grades K–2   *78 pages*

Knopf, 1948; ebook, audiobook

This is the little fantasy novel that has stood the test of time—surviving in print for more than seventy years. The three-volume series is bursting with hair-raising escapes and evil creatures. The tone is dramatic enough to be exciting for even mature preschoolers but not enough to frighten them. The narrator relates the tales as adventures that happened to his father when he was a boy. This is an excellent transition series for introducing children to longer stories with fewer pictures. The rest of the series, in order: *Elmer and the Dragon* and *The Dragons of Blueland*. Related dragon books for young readers: *The Best Pet of All* by David LaRochelle and *The Reluctant Dragon* by Kenneth Grahame.

My Side of the Mountain
BY JEAN CRAIGHEAD GEORGE
Grades 3–8   178 pages
Dutton, 1959; audiobook
A modern teenage Robinson Crusoe, city-bred Sam Gribley describes his year surviving as a runaway in a remote area of the Catskill Mountains. His diary of living off the land is marked by moving accounts of the animals, insects, plants, people, and books that helped him survive. For experienced listeners. Sequels: *On the Far Side of the Mountain* and *Frightful's Mountain*. For other survival books, see the entry for *Hatchet* by Gary Paulsen.

New Shoes (graphic novel)
BY SARA VARON
Grades 2–5   206 pages
First Second, 2018; ebook
Frances the donkey makes the best shoes possible with the help of his friends including Nigel the squirrel monkey who collects the tiger grass that is woven into fabric for his incredible designs. When he is asked to make new shoes for the famous singer Miss Manatee, he is thrilled. However, he needs to obtain the tiger grass, but Nigel is missing. As Francis embarks on a journey into the formidable jungle to locate Nigel and the desired grass, he meets a variety of animals who assist him on his quest. This engaging graphic novel uses both full-page illustrations as well as panels in telling the story. The text is large with challenging vocabulary interspersed such as *provincial, embellishment, durable, consulted,* and *stumped*. Varon's graphic novels are perfect for readers merging into this format. Also by the author: *Bake Sale* and *Robot Dreams*.

Number the Stars
BY LOIS LOWRY
Grades 4–7   137 pages
Houghton Mifflin, 1989; ebook, audiobook
In 1943, as the occupying Nazi army attempted to extricate and then exterminate the seven thousand Jews residing in Denmark, the

Danish people rose up as one in a determined and remarkably successful resistance. Against that backdrop, this Newbery winner describes a ten-year-old Danish girl joining forces with her relatives to save the lives of her best friend and her family. Related books: *Darkness over Denmark* by Ellen Levine, which is an excellent nonfiction companion to this book, with photos of Denmark and the resistance fighters; the popular novel *Snow Treasure* by Marie McSwigan, which is about Norwegian children smuggling gold past the Nazis; and *The Little Ships: The Heroic Rescue at Dunkirk in World War II* and *The Greatest Skating Race: A World War II Story from the Netherlands*, both by Louise Borden.

The One and Only Ivan

BY KATHERINE APPLEGATE

Grades 3–7   *320 pages*

HarperCollins, 2012; ebook, audiobook

Inspired by a true story, this is a heart-wrenching novel that celebrates the transformative power of unexpected friendship. Ivan the gorilla has spent twenty-seven years behind the glass walls of his enclosure in a shopping mall. It has been so long since he lived in the jungle that he rarely thinks about it anymore. He has grown impervious to the stares of the humans who view him every day. He does have his television as well as friends Stella and Bob. And then there's his painting. When Ruby, a baby elephant captured in the wild, becomes part of his environment, he is forced to see his life and art through new eyes. The Newbery Medal recipient blends humor and poignancy while providing a message of hope. Other novels by the author: *Wishtree* and *Crenshaw*.

The Parker Inheritance

BY VARIAN JOHNSON

Grades 5 and up   *352 pages*

Scholastic, 2018; ebook, audiobook

Candice Miller discovers a letter in a book, in a box, in the attic of her late grandmother's house in Lambert, South Carolina. The letter is not addressed to Candice but rather to her grandmother, Abigail Caldwell, who left the small southern town in a cloud of shame. What follows is a story laden with an unsolved mystery, intricate puzzles, engaging characters, and a range of social issues such as racism, segregation, gender and racial identity, friendship, and divorce.

The well-written narrative alters between past and present and is filled with twists and turns that perplex Candice and her neighborhood peer, Brandon Jones. There is much to discuss as the story unfolds. Following multiple stories might be a bit challenging but definitely well worth it. Ellen Raskin's classic *The Westing Game* plays a role in the story and would be a good introduction or follow-up read-aloud novel. *The Lions of Little Rock* by Kristin Levine set in 1958 also focuses on integration of public schools and the portrayal of a young black girl who poses as a white student. *Game Changer: John McLendon and the Secret Game* by John Coy is an excellent picture book to read aloud that is referenced in the author's notes about a secret basketball game in 1944 between the North Carolina College of Negroes and the Duke University Medical School team.

The Penderwicks: A Summer Tale of Four Sisters, Two Rabbits, and a Very Interesting Boy

BY JEANNE BIRDSALL

Grades 3–7   *262 pages*

Knopf, 2005; ebook, audiobook

The Penderwicks series is extremely popular and with good reason. In the first novel, a National Book Award winner, the Penderwick sisters are spending the summer on a beautiful estate called Arundel. There they discover sprawling gardens, tame rabbits, and a treasure-filled attic. In addition, there is a cook who makes the best gingerbread in Massachusetts. The greatest discovery of all is Jeffrey Tifton, son of Arundel's owner, who joins the girls on their wonderful adventures. Too bad Jeffrey's mother isn't quite as thrilled with the girls' presence. There is a nostalgic feel to the series, but friendship has no time frame. Other books in the series: *The Penderwicks on Gardam Street*; *The Penderwicks at Point Mouette*; *The Penderwicks in Spring*; and the finale, *The Penderwicks at Last*.

Peter & Ernesto: A Tale of Two Sloths (graphic novel)

BY GRAHAM ANNABLE

Grades 1–5   *128 pages*

First Second, 2018; ebook

Peter and Ernesto are sloths and best friends but complete opposites. Peter is content to live in their tree and observe the world immediately around him. Ernesto has an intense desire to see the sky from other places on earth. So the adventurous sloth embarks on a journey and views the sky from the ocean, the desert, and the Arctic. Meanwhile, Peter becomes worried about his friend and decides he needs to bring him back to the tree. Along the way, both are assisted by other animals that help them in being reunited. The illustrations are charming and actually make sloths look lovable. Be sure to look under the book jacket for an illustration of the endearing twosome. The next book in the series is *Peter & Ernesto: The Lost Sloths*.

Poppy
BY AVI; BRIAN FLOCA, ILLUS.
Grades K–4   *160 pages*
Orchard, 1995; ebook, audiobook
Like an evil dictator, a great horned owl keeps the growing deer mouse population in Dimwood Forest under his fierce control, eating those who disobey his orders. When he kills her boyfriend, little Poppy dares to go where no mouse has gone before—to the world beyond Dimwood. Indeed, she uncovers the hoax the evil owl has perpetrated through the years and leads her frightened family to the promised land. Told with wit and high drama, this is an excellent introduction to the tales from Dimwood Forest. While *Poppy* was the first in the series to be published, it actually falls second chronologically. The six books in the series in narrative order: *Ragweed*, *Poppy*, *Poppy & Rye*, *Ereth's Birthday*, *Poppy's Return*, and *Poppy and Ereth*. Older fans of this series will enjoy *Martin the Warrior* by Brian Jacques; younger fans, *Charlotte's Web* by E. B. White.

Princess Cora and the Crocodile
BY LAURA AMY SCHLITZ; BRIAN FLOCA, ILLUS.
Grades K–3   *74 pages*
Candlewick Press, 2017; audiobook
When Princess Cora was born, her parents decided they must teach and train her to someday serve as Queen. This results in her mother having Cora read books about how to run the kingdom; her father has her engaging in calisthenics in the dungeon turned gym, and the hired nanny entrusted to ensure Cora is always tidy means she takes three baths a day. Cora is clearly overscheduled with absolutely no time to engage in the activities she wants to do. She also wishes for a big golden dog with a fluffy tail for a pet. When a

special wish sent to her fairy godmother results in a crocodile instead of a dog, Cora tries to make the best of the situation. The two decide to change places, and the fun begins. Fortunately, the King and Queen realize they are being a bit overbearing and allow their daughter to be a child who gets dirty, plays outside, and owns a dog. The language used will challenge young listeners, but the story is certainly one they can easily comprehend. An excellent read-aloud for older readers is Schlitz's *The Hired Girl* and the Newbery Medal–winning *Good Masters! Sweet Ladies!: Voices from a Medieval Village*, which is a book of narrative poetry.

Ramona the Pest
BY BEVERLY CLEARY
Grades K–4   *144 pages*
Morrow, 1968; ebook, audiobook
Not all of Beverly Cleary's books make good read-alouds, though children love to read her silently. Some of her books move too slowly to hold read-aloud interest, but that's not the case with the Ramona series, which begins with *Beezus and Ramona*, published in 1955, and concludes with *Ramona's World* in 1999. The second book, *Ramona the Pest*, follows this outspoken young lady, a forerunner of Junie B. Jones with a better grasp of grammar, through her early months in kindergarten. Children will smile in recognition of Ramona's encounters with the first day of school, show-and-tell, seat work, a substitute teacher, Halloween, young love—and dropping out of kindergarten. Long chapters can easily be divided. Early grades should have some experience with short novels before trying this eight-book series. The sequels follow Ramona as she grows older and, with her family, experiences the challenges of modern life: *Ramona the Brave*; *Ramona and Her Father*; *Ramona and Her Mother*; *Ramona Quimby, Age 8*; *Ramona Forever*; and *Ramona's World*. Also by the author: *Dear Mr. Henshaw*; *The Mouse and the Motorcycle*; *Henry Huggins*; and for preschoolers, *Two Times the Fun*.

Raymie Nightingale
BY KATE DICAMILLO
Grades 3–7   *272 pages*
Candlewick Press, 2016; ebook, audiobook
Raymie Clarke has arrived at Miss Ida Nee's for the sole purpose of learning how to twirl a baton so she can win the Little Miss Central

Florida Tire competition. If she does, her picture will be in the paper, which she is sure will bring home her father, who left town two days ago with a dental hygienist. Raymie didn't plan on two other girls with their own mission—the frequently fainting Louisiana Elefante, who also desperately wants to win the contest, and Beverly Tapinski, whose intent is to sabotage it. Friendship for the three seems highly unlikely, but sometimes loneliness and loss bring people together in unexpected ways. *Louisiana's Way Home* is the sequel to this highly readable book with short chapters and engaging characters. Louisiana has been spirited away from town by her grandmother who believes that someone is watching them. When they leave in the middle of the night, it's because they have a "date with destiny." Louisiana misses Raymie and Beverly and doesn't understand why they have to leave. Sometimes things, and people, aren't quite what they seem, and the truth impacts Louisiana's life forever. DiCamillo's books always lend themselves to be read aloud, and these two books are no exception.

The Real McCoys

BY MATTHEW SWANSON AND ROBBI BEHR
Grades 3–6   336 pages
Macmillan, 2017; ebook

Here are a few things to know before launching into *The Real McCoys*. Moxie McCoy, a fourth grader at Tiddlywhump Elementary School, avows that she is a highly skilled detective and is quite proud of the fact that her entomologist mother named an insect after her, the *Moximaxus*. Her brainy first-grade brother, Milton, is quiet, cautious, and "boring as a butter knife." Fellow detective and best friend Maude has moved to California so Moxie is now interviewing for a replacement who hates soup, loves slugs, and is adept on the unicycle. In this humorous illustrated chapter book, the beloved school mascot, Eddie the Owl, has gone missing, prompting the principal to cancel the much-anticipated school assembly. Moxie is absolutely positive she is destined to receive the Eddie Award that is given to the student who has exemplified courage, patience, and wisdom, which means she must find that owl. Her four suspects all seem to have had opportunity, but apparently they also had an alibi, which Moxie discovers from the principal. The illustrations are a perfect complement to this riotous mystery that is definitely a page-turner. Sequel: *The Real McCoys: Two's a Crowd*.

The Reluctant Dragon

BY KENNETH GRAHAME; ERNEST H. SHEPARD, ILLUS.
Grades 2–4   57 pages
Holiday House, 1989; ebook, audiobook
The author of the classic *Wind in the Willows* wrote this simple boy-and-dragon story in 1938. The dragon is not a devouring dragon but a reluctant one who wants nothing to do with violence. The boy is a scholar, well versed in dragon lore and torn between his desire to view a battle between the dragon and Saint George and the desire to protect his dragon friend. Related books: *My Father's Dragon* by Ruth Stiles Gannett; *Saint George and the Dragon*, retold by Margaret Hodges; and *The Story of Ferdinand* by Munro Leaf.

Roll of Thunder, Hear My Cry

BY MILDRED D. TAYLOR
Grades 5 and up   276 pages
Dial, 1976; ebook, audiobook
Filled with the lifeblood of a black Mississippi family during the Depression, this Newbery winner depicts the pride of people who refuse to give in to threats and harassments from white neighbors. The story is narrated by daughter Cassie Logan, age nine, who experiences her first taste of social injustice and refuses to swallow it. Along with her family, her classmates, and neighbors, she will stir listeners' hearts and awaken many children to the tragedy of prejudice and discrimination. For experienced listeners. Caution: There are several racial epithets used in the dialogue. Other books in the Logan Family Saga series: *The Land* (a prequel to *Roll of Thunder*), *Let the Circle Be Unbroken*, *The Road to Memphis*, and four short novels, *The Friendship*, *Mississippi Bridge*, *Song of the Trees*, and *The Well*. Also by the author: *The Gold Cadillac*.

Related nonfiction titles: *Getting Away with Murder: The True Story of the Emmett Till Case* by Chris Crowe, *Heart and Soul: The Story of America and African Americans* by Kadir Nelson, *More Than Anything Else* (Booker T. Washington learns to read) by Marie Bradby, *Rosa Parks: My Story* by Rosa Parks with Jim Haskins, and *Words Set Me Free: The Story of Young Frederick Douglass* by Lesa Cline-Ransome.

Roll of Thunder, Hear My Cry is an excellent introduction to the American civil rights movement, something that now can be turned into a multimedia experience. Consider the wide array of options available for expanding on the book:

Video recommendations: *Once Upon a Time . . . When We Were Colored* is an affectionate look back at life in a black Mississippi neighborhood from the mid-1940s to the dawn of the civil rights movement, based on the autobiographical novel by Clifton L. Taulbert. See also *4 Little Girls*, Spike Lee's acclaimed 1997 documentary about the turning point in the civil rights movement—the bombing of the 16th Street Baptist Church (for grades 7 and up); and *The Untold Story of Emmett Louis Till*, Keith A. Beauchamp's documentary film about one of the most horrific murders in the civil rights era (for grades 7 and up).

Audio recommendations: Listen to "Behind the Veil," Duke University's oral history project composed of the memories of those who lived in the segregated South, accessible online at https://library.duke .edu/digitalcollections/behindtheveil/. Different portions of that collection can be heard on the internet at American RadioWorks, in the documentary *Remembering Jim Crow*. The RadioWorks site also includes excellent slideshows of images taken during the period; see http://americanradioworks.publicradio.org/features/remembering/; also see American RadioWorks, americanradioworks.publicradio .org/features/sayitplain/links.html. American Public Media's radio program *The Story*, with Dick Gordon, which went off the air in 2013, featured interviews with nonfamous people who have lived in and behind the headlines. Most of the program's civil rights interviews can be found at www.thestory.org/.

Roller Girl (graphic novel)
BY VICTORIA JAMIESON
Grades 4–7   *240 pages*
Dial, 2015; ebook, audiobook
This graphic novel debut by real-life derby girl Victoria Jamieson contains realistic characters and a relatable story. Twelve-year-old Astrid and her best friend, Nicole, do pretty much everything together. When Astrid's mom takes the two girls to a roller derby for "an evening of cultural enlightenment," Astrid decides that she wants to sign up for derby camp. However, Nicole has her own plans to attend dance camp. Though disappointed, Astrid rolls on through the summer, learning how to do crossovers, plow stops, and how to fall. She also knows the positions of the players, defensive and offensive techniques, and how to score points. At the same time, Astrid realizes that her friendship with Nicole is slipping away

as interests change and new friends emerge. Girl power is alive and well in this engaging story. Who wouldn't enjoy reading about roller derby players named Napoleon Blownapart, Braidy Punch, and Heidi Go Seek! Also by Jamieson: *All's Faire in Middle School*.

Rosetown

BY CYNTHIA RYLANT
Grades 2–5   *149 pages*
Beach Lane Books, 2018; ebook, audio CD

It's 1972 in Rosetown, Indiana. Flora Smallwood has recently lost her beloved dog, Laurence, and is trying to cope with the recent separation of her parents. Flora is also entering fourth grade and is surprised at the sudden confidence of her classmates who also happen to look taller, sound louder, and appear stronger. Flora does have a best friend in third grade and has made a new friend, Yury, who has moved to Rosetown from the Ukraine. Flora enjoys going to the Wings and a Chair bookstore three days a week where her mother has a part-time job. She also has a wonderful relationship with her photographer father. There's a feeling of nostalgia with this well-written chapter book, but children will relate to Flora's concerns about friends, family, and the desire for things not to change. Rylant's *Missing May* is also an excellent read-aloud.

Saving Winslow

BY SHARON CREECH
Grades 2–5   *165 pages*
Harper, 2018; ebook

Louie doesn't have much luck when it comes to nurturing small creatures, not even worms, goldfish, or lightning bugs. When his father brings home a sickly, newborn minidonkey, no one expects it to live through the night. Everyone except for Louie, who is determined to save this feeble animal he has named Winslow. As he tends to the donkey, he befriends a quirky new classmate, Nora, who seems to have dealt with loss as well. Part of Louie's resolve to save Winslow aligns with the longing for his brother, Gus, who is serving in the military. This short chapter book weaves together themes of friendship, determination, and perseverance. *Saving Winslow* would pair nicely with Creech's *Moo*, which addresses similar issues.

Scorpions

BY WALTER DEAN MYERS

Grades 7 and up 216 pages

Harper, 1988; ebook, audiobook

This award-winning novelist has drawn upon his childhood in Harlem to give us a revealing and poignant look at an African American family facing the daily pressures of urban poverty. While seventh-grader Jamal Hicks struggles to resist the pressures to join a neighborhood gang, he is watching his family being torn apart by the crimes of an older brother and a wayward father. Moreover, his relationship with school is disintegrating under a combination of his own irresponsibility and an antagonistic principal. Unable to resist the peer pressure, Jamal makes a tragic decision involving a handgun. Readers-aloud should be aware that some of the book's dialogue is written in black dialect.

In 1993, National Public Radio (NPR) gave a tape recorder to two boys living in Chicago public housing and allowed them to produce a documentary eventually called *Ghetto Life 101*. Several years later, the two boys again recorded their life in the projects, this time after a five-year-old had been hurled to his death from a fourteenth-floor window by two other young children. If ever there was audio to add another dimension to Myers's urban novel *Scorpions*, these two NPR programs are it. They can still be heard online at https://archive.org/details/GhettoLife101RadioDocumentary.

Also by the author: *Bad Boy: A Memoir*. Related books: Sheila P. Moses offers a moving, inspiring, more contemporary tale of urban black life in her novels *Joseph* and *Joseph's Grace*, in which we follow a teenager as he battles to stay safe and sane while his mother disintegrates and he tries to figure out whom to trust in his family and peer group; also *Ghetto Cowboy* by G. Neri.

Myers's *Monster* won the Michael L. Printz Award for Young Adult literature in 2000 but may not be a suitable read-aloud for all adolescents and public classrooms. Written in the form of a screenplay and diary, the story focuses on a young black male charged with murder in a Harlem drugstore. The scenes, which shift between the courtroom and detention center, are unflinching and visceral in their descriptions. Any collection of urban teens (or older) will find much to discuss in this docudrama. For an NPR interview with the late Walter Dean Myers, see "To Do Well in Life, You Have to 'Read Well,'" *Morning Edition*, January 10, 2012, online at

http://www.npr.org/2012/01/10/144944598/to-do-well-in-life-you
-have-to-read-well.

The Secret Garden

BY FRANCES HODGSON BURNETT; INGA MOORE, ILLUS.
Grades 2–5   278 pages
Candlewick Press, 2007; ebook, audiobook
Few books spin such a web of magic around their audiences as does
this 1911 children's classic about the sulky orphan who comes to
live with her cold, unfeeling uncle on the windswept English
moors. Wandering the grounds of his immense manor house one
day, she discovers a secret garden, locked and abandoned. This leads
her to discover her uncle's invalid child hidden within the mansion,
her first friendship, and her own true self. While this is definitely
for experienced listeners, try to avoid the abridged versions, since
too much of the book's flavor is lost in those. The Inga Moore illustrated version is by far the best full edition to date. Also by the
author: *Little Lord Fauntleroy, A Little Princess,* and *The Lost Prince.*

Sideways Stories from Wayside School

BY LOUIS SACHAR
Grades 2–5   124 pages
Random House, 1990; ebook, audiobook
Thirty chapters about the wacky students who inhabit the thirtieth
floor of Wayside School, the school that was supposed to be built
one story high and thirty classes wide, until the contractor made a
mistake and made it thirty stories high! If you think the building is
bizarre, wait until you meet the kids who inhabit it. Sequels: *Wayside School Is Falling Down* and *Wayside School Gets a Little Stranger.*
Also by the author: *Holes, Johnny's in the Basement,* and *There's a Boy
in the Girls' Bathroom.*

Smile (graphic novel)

BY RAINA TELGEMEIER
Grades 4–8   224 pages
Scholastic, 2010; ebook
This memoir in graphic novel format begins just as Raina is ready to
get braces. Unfortunately, she falls one night and knocks out her two
front teeth. She just wants to be a normal sixth grader but is now
faced with not only getting braces on but also surgery, embarrassing

headgear (every adolescent's nightmare!), and even a retainer with fake teeth attached. And of course there is the angst of entering middle school and dealing with what relationships—both girlfriend and (potential) boyfriend—have to offer. The graphic format and easy-to-follow story line make this a great read-aloud. Other graphic novels by the author include *Drama*, *Sisters*, and *Ghosts*. Telgemeier has also adapted and illustrated graphic novel versions of Ann M. Martin's Baby-sitters Club series including *The Truth About Stacey*, *Dawn and the Impossible Three*, and *Kristy's Big Day*.

Soof: A Novel
BY SARAH WEEKS
Grades 3–7 *208 pages*
Scholastic, 2018; ebook, audiobook
Aurora Franklin calls herself weird. She appears to be on the autism spectrum, but a wise doctor refuses to identify her with that label. Aurora has a few oddities such as tapping her forehead, counting things, and wearing clothing inside out because she doesn't like tags, but she also has a genuine and profound love for her dog, Duck. For years, Aurora has heard stories about Heidi, a woman who lived with her parents as a young girl and is now all grown up and expecting her first child. Heidi is also coming to visit, which causes Aurora great anxiety. When tragedy strikes, the relationship between Aurora and her mother is put to the test. *Soof* is a companion to the author's *So B. It*, which is a remarkable read-aloud and even a movie. However, *Soof* stands on its own through excellent writing, a delightful protagonist, a relatable story, and brilliant foreshadowing. And what is *soof*? It can best be described as an emotional bond. Author Sarah Weeks is known for her poignant and often humorous stories that focus on family dynamics, coming-of-age, and emotional journeys. Other books by Weeks for this listening range include *Pie*, *Save Me a Seat*, *As Simple as It Seems*, and *Honey*.

Stella Díaz Has Something to Say
BY ANGELA DOMINGUEZ
Grades 1–4 *208 pages*
Roaring Brook Press, 2018; ebook
Dominguez draws on her own childhood experiences in this engaging novel about a girl struggling to find her voice as she attempts

to find a cultural balance between home and school. Stella was a baby when her family moved from Mexico City to Arlington Heights, a suburb of Chicago. She often has difficulty in pronouncing words in English and isn't confident in her Spanish-language skills either. When confronted by a class bully, a spelling bee, and an oral presentation in class, Stella discovers she does have something to say. Spanish words are sprinkled through this illustrated novel. The relationships she has with her loving mother and frequently absent father (her parents are divorced) are realistic and adds another layer to the complexities of family circumstances. Related book: *Cilla Lee-Jenkins: Future Author Extraordinaire* by Susan Tan.

Stone Fox

BY JOHN REYNOLDS GARDINER
Grades 1–7   *96 pages*
Crowell, 1980; ebook, audiobook

A multimillion-copy bestseller in its nearly forty years, this is a story that, like its ten-year-old orphan hero, never stands still. Based on a Rocky Mountain legend, the classic action-packed adventure recounts the valiant efforts of young Willy to save his grandfather's farm by attempting to win the purse in a local bobsled race. Pushing the plot is a big dose of loyalty: grandson to grandfather, dog to his young master. Related books: *Because of Winn-Dixie* by Kate DiCamillo and *Shiloh* by Phyllis Reynolds Naylor.

Stormbreaker (Alex Rider series)

BY ANTHONY HOROWITZ
Grades 5–8   *234 pages*
Philomel, 2000; ebook, audiobook

When fourteen-year-old Alex Rider is informed that his bachelor uncle/guardian has died in an auto accident, he's understandably distressed. But he's also perplexed by the news that he wasn't wearing his seat belt—something he was fanatical about. He's even more confused when two men show up at the funeral wearing loaded shoulder holsters under their jackets. Why guns at a bank manager's funeral? Before long, his questions bring him into Britain's top-secret intelligence agency, and he may not make it out alive. If James Bond had a kid relative, it would have been Alex Rider. This first book in the fast-paced, increasingly popular series by Horowitz has, like most thrillers, a certain amount of violence, though none of it is gratuitous. Books like this are very likely to produce a kid who likes to read at least as much as he likes to play video games. Sequels in order: *Point Blanc, Skeleton Key, Eagle Strike, Scorpia, Ark Angel, Snakehead, Crocodile Tears, Scorpia Rising, Yassen,* and *Never Say Die.*

Stuart Little

BY E. B. WHITE
Grades K–3   *130 pages*
Harper, 1945; ebook, audiobook
Stuart is a very, very small boy (two inches) who looks exactly like a mouse. This leaves him at a decided disadvantage living in a house where everyone else is normal size, including the family cat. White's first book for children, it is filled with beautiful language and lots of adventures as Stuart struggles to find his way in the world—an important job for all children, even if they don't look like a mouse. Also by the author: *Charlotte's Web.* Related books: *The Mouse and the Motorcycle* by Beverly Cleary and *Poppy* and the rest of the Tales from Dimwood Forest series by Avi.

Tales of a Fourth Grade Nothing

BY JUDY BLUME
Grades 3–5   *120 pages*
Dutton, 1972; ebook, audiobook
A perennial favorite among schoolchildren, this novel deals with the irksome problem of a kid brother whose hilarious antics complicate the life of his fourth-grade brother, Peter. Sequels: *Superfudge* (caution: *Superfudge* deals with the question, "Is there a Santa Claus?"), *Fudge-a-Mania,* and *Double Fudge.* Also by the author: *Freckle Juice* and *Otherwise Known as Sheila the Great.*

Tintin in Tibet (graphic novel)

BY HERGÉ
Grades 2–4   *62 pages*
Little, Brown, 1975
When you've been in print for nearly ninety years, translated into eighty languages, praised by presidential advisers (Arthur Schlesinger Jr.), and made into movies by Peter Jackson and Steven Spielberg, you must be special. Tintin is just that. He's the boy detective/reporter who hopscotches the globe in pursuit of thieves and smugglers. Loaded with humor, adventure, and marvelous artwork (seven

hundred pictures in each issue), *Tintin* has special appeal for parents who want to assist their child in reading: Each *Tintin* contains more than eight thousand words. Having heard *Tintin* read aloud, children will want to obtain his other adventures and read them by themselves, oblivious to the fact that they are reading so many words in the process. Because of the size of the pictures, *Tintin* is best read aloud to no more than two children at a time. Furthermore, a comic book should be read aloud to children only a few times—to show how comic books work so that then they can read them on their own.

Beginning in 1994, *Tintin*'s American publisher began issuing the comics in hardcover, three to a volume. Related books in comic format: the BONE series by Jeff Smith; and the Little Lit series, an excellent collection of stories told in comic format, selected and edited by Art Spiegelman and Françoise Mouly: *Little Lit: Folklore & Fairy Tale Funnies*, *Little Lit: Strange Stories for Strange Kids*, and *Little Lit: It Was a Dark and Silly Night*.

Tree of Dreams

BY LAURA RESAU
Grades 4 and up   *336 pages*
Scholastic, 2019

Coco loves chocolate. When she's not helping her mother at their chocolate shop, El Corazón, Coco is busy creating new recipes to entice customers. Unfortunately, the donut shop across the street is attracting customers to their door, and Coco's mother is considering closing the candy shop when revenue falls. After a series of dreams about a ceiba tree, the young girl is convinced the answer (and treasure) lays at its roots. But how is Coco going to travel to the Amazon rain forest where the wondrous tree is found? And once she is there, how can she stop the destruction of the rain forest that is destroying the environment and harming the people who live in the region? *Tree of Dreams* addresses the ugly realities of what is occurring in the rain forest and the total disregard for its annihilation. There is also information about various types of chocolate woven throughout the story. Other novels by Resau include *The Lightning Queen* and *What the Moon Saw*.

The True Confessions of Charlotte Doyle
BY AVI
Grades 4 and up   *215 pages*
Orchard, 1990
Winner of a Newbery Honor medal, this is the exciting tale of an
obstinate thirteen-year-old girl who is the lone passenger aboard a
merchant ship sailing from England to the United States in 1832.
The crew is bent on mutiny, the captain is a murderer, and within
weeks the girl is accused of murder, tried by captain and crew, and
sentenced to hang at sea. Avi is at his finest with this first-person
adventure, exploring history, racism, feminism, and mob psychology. Other books by the author: *City of Orphans*, *Crispin: The Cross
of Lead*, *The Good Dog*, *Nothing but the Truth*, *Poppy*, and *Wolf Rider:
A Tale of Terror.*

Tumble & Blue
BY CASSIE BEASLEY
Grades 4–7   *400 pages*
Dial, 2017; ebook, audiobook
In 1817, Walcott Montgomery and Almira Wilson scrambled to be
the first to reach the golden gator deep in the Okefenokee Swamp.
The fate of whoever was successful would be forever changed.
When the two arrived simultaneously, they were forced to split the
mysterious gift, which resulted in decades of descendants being
cursed or blessed with the talents they possessed. Blue Montgomery
and Tumble Wilson vow to reverse the curse on the night when the
moon runs bloodred, which happens only once a century. This
engaging middle-grade novel is a mix of tall tale, comedic may-
hem, and magical realism. It also speaks to the power of friendship
and family and what it means to be a hero. Related books: *Holes*
by Louis Sachar, *Savvy* by Ingrid Law, and *A Snicker of Magic* by
Natalie Lloyd.

Two Times the Fun
BY BEVERLY CLEARY
Grades PreS–K   *92 pages*
Harper, 2005; ebook
Beverly Cleary raised a set of twins, so she knows the breed well.
Couple that with her witty insight into the workings of family life,
and you've got everything that makes this collection of four stories

work so well. Jimmy and Janet are four-year-olds with two distinct approaches to things like dog biscuits, new boots, holes in the ground, and personal possessions. Originally separate picture books, these four tales (*Two Dog Biscuits*, *The Growing-Up Feet*, *The Real Hole*, and *Janet's Thingamajigs*) work perfectly in the short novel category for preschoolers. Other chapter books by the author: *The Mouse and the Motorcycle*; *Ramona Quimby, Age 8*; *Henry Huggins*; *Ramona the Pest*; and *Muggie Maggie*.

The Vanderbeekers of 141st Street

BY KARINA YAN GLASER
Grades 3–6   *304 pages*
Houghton Mifflin Harcourt, 2017; ebook
The Vanderbeekers are a biracial family living in Harlem. Their life revolves around neighbors and friends but is soon to be disrupted when the curmudgeonly landlord, Mr. Beiderman, decides not to renew their lease. Oliver and his four sisters, Isa, Jessie, Laney, and Hyacinth, have eleven days to try to find a way to convince Mr. Beiderman to let them stay in their beloved home. This well-written novel provides a relatable story through engaging text sprinkled with humor. The sequel, *The Vanderbeekers and the Hidden Garden*, focuses on the children's desire to plant a garden in an abandoned lot in order to surprise their ailing neighbor. The third book in the series, *The Vanderbeekers to the Rescue*, finds the siblings racing to save their mother's baking business from being shut down by the city.

The War That Saved My Life

BY KIMBERLY BRUBAKER BRADLEY
Grades 4–7   *320 pages*
Dial, 2015; ebook, audiobook
This historical novel is set during World War II and explores the themes of family, acceptance, and survival. Ada was born with a clubfoot, and her abusive mother uses this disability to confine her to their third-floor one-bedroom apartment. Jamie, Ada's younger brother, is free to go to school and roam the neighborhood. When preparations are made to ship Jamie to the countryside with other children being evacuated from London, Ada sneaks out to join him. Unfortunately, none of the villagers want to take them in. The woman in charge forces recluse Susan Smith to care for the two

children. Susan does her best but has difficulty understanding why Ada flinches whenever she makes a mistake. Susan has no idea the physical and emotional abuse Ada suffered at the hands of her mother. Ada's strong voice, the vivid setting, the humor, and the heartbreak come together to create a story that is worthy of being read aloud and discussed. Related books: *Lily's Crossing* by Patricia Reilly Giff, *Milkweed* by Jerry Spinelli, *Number the Stars* by Lois Lowry, and *When My Name Was Keoko* by Linda Sue Park.

When the Whistle Blows

BY FRAN CANNON SLAYTON
Grades 6 and up   *162 pages*
Philomel, 2009; ebook, audiobook

This fine first novel traces one family's life in a small West Virginia town that is so dependent upon its trains and steam engines that it literally lives and dies by them. And there is some of both in this volume. Each of the book's chapters is set on Halloween night for seven successive years, 1943 through 1949. Each episode finds the protagonist, Jimmy Cannon, a little older and a little wiser but still yearning to work the rails—much to his rail machinist father's dismay. The railroad's days are coming to an end, declares the father, but Jimmy turns a deaf ear. By novel's end, however, the father's prescience is clearly evident. In this respect, the changing times of the 1940s are reflected in the employment ruptures today in American industry.

As the book spans the years, Jimmy's Halloween adventures move from giggly preteen stuff to sobering adult, from a cemetery prank to a gut-wrenching high school football contest and, finally, to Jimmy's father's death. This is a pulsating slice of small-town America as it used to be (and still is in parts of rural America).

Where the Red Fern Grows

BY WILSON RAWLS
Grades 3 and up   *212 pages*
Doubleday, 1961; ebook, audiobook

A ten-year-old boy growing up in the Ozark Mountains, praying and saving for a pair of hounds, finally achieves his wish. He then begins the task of turning the hounds into first-class hunting dogs. It would be difficult to find a book that speaks more definitively about perseverance, courage, family, sacrifice, work, life, and death.

The long chapters are easily divided, but have a box of tissues nearby for the final ones. Wilson Rawls wrote only one other book, another delightful re-creation of his childhood in the Ozarks: *Summer of the Monkeys*. The author's recitation of the story of his life ("Dreams Can Come True") is available on CD; for details, see www.trelease-on-reading.com/rawls.html.

The Whipping Boy

BY SID FLEISCHMAN
Grades 3–6   90 pages
Greenwillow, 1986; audio CD

The brattish medieval prince is too spoiled ever to be spanked, so the king regularly vents his anger on Jeremy, a peasant "whipping boy." When circumstances lead the two boys to reverse roles à la *The Prince and the Pauper*, each learns much about friendship and sacrifice. Painted with Fleischman's broad humor, this is a fast-paced Newbery-winning melodrama with short cliff-hanger chapters. Also by the author, who is known for injecting the perfect amount of humor into his historic novels: *The Ghost in the Noonday Sun*, *By the Great Horn Spoon!*, *Jim Ugly*, and *Humbug Mountain* (my favorite).

The Wild Robot

BY PETER BROWN
Grades 3–7   288 pages
Little, Brown, 2016; ebook, audiobook

After a violent storm decimates a cargo ship, a few crates drift toward the coastline of an isolated island. Only one crate is left intact. When a gang of sea otters scamper to see what is inside, they inadvertently activate the robot, Roz, inside. Roz has no idea where she is but quickly realizes that in order to survive she will need to adapt to her surroundings, including learning the language of the animal inhabitants. Understandably, the animals are suspicious of her until she parents an orphaned gosling. Life on the island becomes idyllic for Roz until the RECOs come in search of her. The sequel, *The Wild Robot Escapes*, follows Roz as she attempts to return to the island after having been captured from the island and sent to a farm as a robot servant. The plot is unique, but Roz is believable because of the human qualities she possesses. Interspersed with black-and-white illustrations, both novels will prompt conversations about the world we might encounter in the not-so-far-distant future. Pair these novels with David Lucas's picture book, *The Robot and the Bluebird*.

Willie & Me
BY DAN GUTMAN
Grades 3–7   *181 pages*
Harper, 2015; ebook, audiobook
This is the twelfth and final book in the Baseball Card Adventures series by Dan Gutman. Thirteen-year-old Joe Stoshak, or Stosh, is able to travel back in time using baseball cards. Stosh thinks he's done time-traveling, but Ralph Branca shows up needing help. In 1951, Branca pitched a ball to Bobby Thomson that became the "Shot Heard Round the World," a home run that won the National League pennant for the New York Giants. Branca insists the Giants were cheating, and he needs Stosh to travel back in time to make it right. But when you change one thing in history, it may forever change the life of a young rookie by the name of Willie Mays. Gutman weaves black-and-white photographs and statistics throughout the story. Back matter offers additional information. If you want to begin with the first book in the series, then read *Honus and Me*. Other baseball players in the series include Roberto Clemente, Mickey Mantle, Babe Ruth, Ted Williams, Jackie Robinson, Shoeless Joe Jackson, Satchel Paige, Jim Thorpe, and Ray Chapman. One book in the series, *Abner and Me*, investigates whether Civil War general Abner Doubleday really invented the game of baseball.

Wish
BY BARBARA O'CONNOR
Grades 4–7   *240 pages*
Farrar, Straus & Giroux, 2016; ebook, audiobook
Eleven-year-old Charlie Reese has a dad, Scrappy, who is in jail getting "corrected" and a mom who can't get up off the couch to take care of her. So Charlie is sent to live with an aunt and uncle in North Carolina she doesn't know. But she does have a wish and does whatever she can to make it happen, like blowing on an eyelash or hearing a bird singing in the rain. When she develops a connection with a stray dog, "Wishbone," Charlie begins to realize what being home means. This middle-grade novel has strong, believable characters that make it a heartfelt tale of wishes coming true in unexpected ways. Related chapter books about kids and

dogs: *Because of Winn-Dixie* by Kate DiCamillo; *Rain Reign* by Ann M. Martin; and *How to Steal a Dog*, also by Barbara O'Connor.

Wishtree

BY KATHERINE APPLEGATE

Grades 3–6   *224 pages*

Feiwel and Friends, 2017; ebook, audiobook

Red is an old tree that has seen a lot of changes over many decades. Told from the perspective of an ancient oak tree, Red has seen it all. Now there is a new family who has moved in and a boy uses the tree to leave hateful messages. Red's status of being a "wishtree," where people write their wishes on pieces of cloth and tie them to the tree's branches, is also now in jeopardy. Other novels by Applegate: *The One and Only Ivan*; *Crenshaw*; and her novel in verse for older readers, *Home of the Brave*.

Wonderland

BY BARBARA O'CONNOR

Grades 3–7   *288 pages*

Farrar, Straus & Giroux, 2018; ebook, audiobook

Mavis Jeeter's mother has accepted a new job as a housekeeper in another town. Mother and daughter have never stayed in one place for very long, which has impacted Mavis's ability to find herself a best friend. But now she has met Rose Tully, who is a worrier and doesn't fit in with other girls in her neighborhood. Rose also has a special relationship with Mr. Duffy, the gatekeeper at Magnolia Estates where she lives. Unfortunately, Mr. Duffy hasn't been the same since his dog, Queenie, died. Chapters alternate between Rose's and Mavis's perspectives along with Henry, the dog who has escaped from the local shelter and is trying to survive in the wooded area near Magnolia Estates. Mavis takes it upon herself to make Rose her best friend and to rectify the situation for Mr. Duffy. The brief chapters present a heartwarming story that celebrates friendship and the role that pets play in our lives. Also by O'Connor: *Wish* and *How to Steal a Dog*.

Cyndi's Favorite Biographies

Amelia Lost: The Life and Disappearance of Amelia Earhart by Candace Fleming

Between the Lines: How Ernie Barnes Went from the Football Field to the Art Gallery by Sandra Neil Wallace

Bill Peet: An Autobiography by Bill Peet

Boy: Tales of Childhood by Roald Dahl

The Boy Who Invented TV: The Story of Philo Farnsworth by Kathleen Krull

The Day-Glo Brothers: The True Story of Bob and Joe Switzer's Bright Ideas and Brand-New Colors by Chris Barton

Emmanuel's Dream: The True Story of Emmanuel Ofosu Yeboah by Laurie Ann Thompson

I Dissent: Ruth Bader Ginsburg Makes Her Mark by Debbie Levy

The Librarian of Basra: A True Story from Iraq by Jeanette Winter

Lincoln: A Photobiography by Russell Freedman

Martin's Big Words: The Life of Dr. Martin Luther King, Jr. by Doreen Rappaport

Me . . . Jane by Patrick McDonnell (Jane Goodall)

A Splash of Red: The Life and Art of Horace Pippin by Jen Bryant

Nonfiction

Ada Lovelace, Poet of Science: The First Computer Programmer

BY DIANE STANLEY; JESSIE HARTLAND, ILLUS.

Grades 1–4   *40 pages*

Simon & Schuster, 2016; ebook

Two hundred years ago, a daughter was born to the famous poet Lord Byron and his mathematical wife, Annabella. Ada had a vivid imagination and a gift for connecting ideas in original ways. She also had a passion for science, mathematics, and machines. A chance meeting with Charles Babbage and Ada's curiosity along with her meticulous eye for detail led to her becoming the first computer programmer. Other biographies about Lovelace include *Ada Byron Lovelace and the Thinking Machine* by Laurie Wallmark; *Ada's Ideas: The Story of Ada Lovelace, the World's First Computer Programmer* by Fiona Robinson;

Who Says Women Can't Be Computer Programmers?: The Story of Ada Lovelace by Tanya Lee Stone; and *Dreaming in Code: Ada Byron Lovelace, Computer Pioneer* by Emily Arnold McCully. Related book: *Grace Hopper: Queen of Computer Code* by Laurie Wallmark.

Animals by the Numbers: A Book of Animal Infographics

BY STEVE JENKINS

Grades 1–4   *48 pages*

Houghton Mifflin Harcourt, 2016; ebook

Jenkins uses numbers to highlight amazing feats and features of the animal kingdom. Animal size, speed, sound, and factual curiosities are presented through compelling charts and graphs. Sometimes it's fun to explore a book through read-aloud that is not written in a narrative format. Jenkins's books will pique kids' interests in the world around them. Other nonfiction books by the author to explore: *Actual Size*; *Creature Features: Twenty-Five Animals Explain Why They Look the Way They Do*; *What Do You Do with a Tail Like This?*; *Eye to Eye: How Animals See the World*; and *Down, Down, Down: A Journey to the Bottom of the Sea*.

Attucks!: Oscar Robertson and the Basketball Team That Awakened a City

BY PHILLIP HOOSE

Grades 6 and up   *224 pages*

Farrar, Straus & Giroux, 2018; ebook, audio CD

Future collegiate star and NBA Hall of Famer Oscar Robertson and his Crispus Attucks Tiger teammates became the first all-black team to win a state championship in 1955. Crispus Attucks High School opened in 1927 as a segregated African American high school intended to serve the entire city of Indianapolis. High school basketball had been woven into Indiana's fabric since 1911, the year the annual statewide postseason tournament was initiated. Spawned by the tournament, Hoosier Hysteria saw towns building large gyms hoping to win tournament games to put their school on the map. When Ray Crowe became the head coach at Attucks in 1950, he had his team play at a much faster freestyle pace. Success was immediate as the Tigers made it to the semifinals in the state tournament before losing. In the semifinals again in 1954 with sophomore Oscar Robertson, Attucks lost to the eventual champion, tiny Milan High of the movie *Hoosiers* fame. Back-to-back state championships followed, the first ever for a squad from Indianapolis. Other books for older readers by Hoose: *The Boys Who Challenged Hitler: Knud Pedersen and the Churchill Club*; *Claudette Colvin: Twice Toward Justice*; and *We Were There, Too!: Young People in U.S. History*.

Balloons over Broadway: The True Story of the Puppeteer of Macy's Parade
BY MELISSA SWEET
Grades PreS–4
Houghton Mifflin Harcourt, 2011; ebook, audiobook   *32 pages*
Tony Sarg loved making marionettes and performing on Broadway in New York City. When Macy's department store heard about Tony and his puppets, they hired him to design a puppet display for the store's holiday windows. The Wondertown window was such a success that Macy's asked Tony to create puppets for the parade they were planning for their employees who were primarily immigrants. Initial efforts of creating large puppets made out of rubber and held up by sticks were eye-catching but only visible to the first few rows of people watching the parade on the street. Soon Tony devised a way for the animal balloons to be larger and filled with helium. On Thanksgiving Day in 1928, Tony's helium-filled balloons floated higher above the streets and have been a part of the Macy's parade ever since. Another story about this famous parade held each year on Thanksgiving Day is *Milly and the Macy's Parade* by Shana Corey.

Boys of Steel: The Creators of Superman
BY MARC TYLER NOBLEMAN; ROSS MACDONALD, ILLUS.
Grades 3–7   *32 pages*
Knopf, 2008; ebook
Jerry and Joe, two nerdy bespectacled teenagers in Cleveland, spend their high school years writing and drawing things that can't be seen or experienced except in their own imaginations. Their peers avoid them, and their teachers berate them. The country is mired in the Depression, and families are struggling to put bread on the table. Why can't these two kids "get real"? What they were about to create would very soon become "real"—a real supercultural hit, known the world over, that would bring daily relief from the pain of reality. Jerry Siegel would write and Joe Shuster would draw a fictional character named Clark Kent, aka Superman. This is the story behind the creation of the fictional saga.

Brave Girl: Clara and the Shirtwaist Makers' Strike of 1909

BY MICHELLE MARKEL; MELISSA SWEET, ILLUS.

Grades K–2   *32 pages*

Balzer & Bray, 2013; ebook, audiobook

In 1909, Clara Lemlich arrived in America with hundreds of immigrants from eastern Europe. Clara's father is unable to obtain a job, but the garment factories are hiring young girls for the shirtwaist factories. From dawn to dusk, Clara is locked up in a factory along with rows and rows of other young women, stitching collars, sleeves, and cuffs as fast as they can. If you're a few minutes late, you lose half a day's pay. If you prick your finger and bleed on the cloth, you're fined. The working conditions are horrendous, prompting Clara and others to strategically develop a plan to strike. All winter long, the girls continue to picket and soon begin to catch the attention of news reporters, wealthy women, and finally hundreds of bosses. The workweek was shortened and salaries were increased. Another story about early immigration is *All the Way to America: The Story of a Big Italian Family and a Little Shovel* by Dan Yaccarino.

The Brilliant Deep: Rebuilding the World's Coral Reefs (The Story of Ken Nedimyer and the Coral Restoration Foundation)

BY KATE MESSNER; MATTHEW FORSYTHE, ILLUS.

Grades K–3   *48 pages*

Chronicle, 2018; ebook

As a child, Ken Nedimyer loved the ocean, and his favorite place was always out on the reef. One summer, Ken realized the corals were losing their color and there weren't as many fish. Were the reefs dying, and if so, what could be done? As a grown-up, Ken operated a live rock farm in the Florida Keys. Using these rocks, a coral colony was generated in the ocean. If a coral colony was planted on a dying reef, would it grow? This fascinating book gives a glimpse into an environmental concern that is still present today. Related books: *Coral Reefs* by Jason Chin; *Coral Reefs* by Gail Gibbons; *Explore My World: Coral Reefs* by Jill Esbaum; *Life in the Ocean: The Story of Oceanographer Sylvia Earle* by Claire A. Nivola.

Claudette Colvin: Twice Toward Justice

BY PHILLIP HOOSE

Grades 7 and up   *124 pages*

Macmillan, 2009; ebook, audiobook

One can safely say no revolution of any size was ever neat and tidy. There are always misunderstandings, infighting, and backbiting, along with eventual triumph. Such is the case in this highly honored (National Book Award and Newbery Honor) nonfiction chronicle of Claudette Colvin's pivotal role in the great Montgomery bus boycott. Rosa Parks got all the attention and fame nine months later, but Colvin was there first—a fifteen-year-old in 1955 who refused to move for a white woman bus passenger. She was promptly arrested and manhandled by police. And even though it was Colvin's courageous and articulate testimony before the federal court (quickly affirmed by the Supreme Court) that broke the back of the Montgomery bus company, Colvin spent the next thirty-five years in obscurity, tending to elderly nursing home patients in New York City, while the fame and glory went to people like Medgar Evers, Martin Luther King Jr., and Rosa Parks. What went wrong for the young girl? Why was her courage ignored by the movement and scorned by her classmates and neighbors? This is a brilliant young adult volume on adolescence, race, politics, and American history—and every page is documented truth. Related book: *Roll of Thunder, Hear My Cry* by Mildred D. Taylor.

A Computer Called Katherine: How Katherine Johnson Helped Put America on the Moon

BY SUZANNE SLADE; VERONICA MILLER JAMISON, ILLUS.

Grades 1 and up   *40 pages*

Little, Brown, 2019; ebook

As a child, Katherine counted everything—the steps to church, the plates on the dinner table, the stars in the sky. When she began school, her teacher realized Katherine could read and also add numbers "at the speed of light" so the young girl skipped first grade. Later, Katherine would skip fifth grade as well. As she grew up, Katherine's love for math grew exponentially. After graduating from college, she became a teacher and later worked as a "human computer" for Langley Aeronautical Laboratory. When her mathematical expertise was finally recognized by male engineers, she was invited to assist with the calculations for the first space flight.

Katherine went on to be instrumental in calculating other space missions including John Glenn's first orbit of the Earth. Katherine's story as well as those of other black women who provided important contributions to America's early space missions were chronicled in the movie *Hidden Figures*. Additional books about Katherine Johnson include *Counting on Katherine: How Katherine Johnson Saved Apollo 13* by Helaine Becker and *Hidden Figures: The True Story of Four Black Women and the Space Race* by Margot Lee Shetterly.

The Dinosaurs of Waterhouse Hawkins
BY BARBARA KERLEY; BRIAN SELZNICK, ILLUS.
Grades 1 and up   48 pages
Scholastic, 2001; audiobook
In 1856, artist and naturalist Waterhouse Hawkins, collaborating with a leading scientist, earned an extraordinary commission: to build a dinosaur park. Think Jurassic Park in Queen Victoria's time. On an island outside London, Hawkins began building his giant models. And giants they were. Just one of the creatures required thirty tons of clay, six hundred bricks, fifteen hundred tiles, and thirty-eight casks of cement. The finished product would astonish Victorian England and lead him to the United States, where he was invited to build more models, this time in Central Park. Unfortunately, in the middle of his work, the henchmen of the infamous (and jealous) Boss Tweed vandalized the project beyond recovery. To this day, shattered pieces from the original models are still buried beneath the soil in Central Park. The illustrator won the 2008 Caldecott Medal for his novel/picture book *The Invention of Hugo Cabret*.

Esquivel!: Space-Age Sound Artist
BY SUSAN WOOD; DUNCAN TONATIUH, ILLUS.
Grades 1–4   32 pages
Charlesbridge, 2016; ebook, audiobook
Probably few children, and even adults, have heard of Juan García Esquivel. *Esquivel!* is known for combining Latin rhythms, jazz, human voices, and unusual instruments in order to create unique musical textures and effects. Locate his music on the internet and play a little of it to set the mood and tone for reading aloud this book. Other biographies of musicians: *Duke Ellington: The Piano Prince and His Orchestra* by Andrea Davis Pinkney; *Trombone Shorty* by Troy

Andrews; *Before John Was a Jazz Giant: A Song of John Coltrane* by Carole Boston Weatherford; *Little Melba and Her Big Trombone* by Katheryn Russell-Brown; and *The Little Piano Girl: The Story of Mary Lou Williams, Jazz Legend* by Ann Ingalls and Maryann Macdonald.

Franklin and Winston: A Christmas That Changed the World

BY DOUGLAS WOOD; BARRY MOSER, ILLUS.
Grades 4 and up   *36 pages*
Candlewick, 2011
In the first month of World War II and just after Pearl Harbor, the two leaders of the free world, Winston Churchill and Franklin D. Roosevelt, met for the Christmas holidays at the White House, where they planned a war and partnership that would save the world. One was the victim of polio, the other the victim of childhood neglect, both rising well above their prescribed stations. This book looks beyond the somber history pages to show the warm friendship between them, as well as Churchill's personal foibles (two hot baths a day, *no* noise in the hallway outside his room).

Free as a Bird: The Story of Malala

BY LINA MASLO
Grades 1 and up   *56 pages*
Balzer & Bray, 2018
"When the whole world is silent, even one voice becomes powerful." These are the words of Malala Yousafzai, the youngest recipient of the Nobel Peace Prize. People shook their heads when Malala was born because girls were considered bad luck. But her father felt differently and encouraged his daughter to get an education. As the presence of the Taliban strengthened in Pakistan, Malala's father spoke out against them. Malala did the same until one day the Taliban stopped the bus she was riding in and shot her. After Malala recovered, she knew she could not be silent and needed to advocate for education, especially for girls. This inspiring picture book demonstrates that one person can make a difference. Other picture books about Malala: *Malala's Magic Pencil* by Malala Yousafzai and Kerascoët; *For the Right to Learn: Malala Yousafzai's Story* by Rebecca Langston-George; and *Malala, a Brave Girl from Pakistan/Iqbal, a Brave Boy from Pakistan: Two Stories of Bravery* by Jeanette Winter.

There is also a young readers' edition of her book, *I Am Malala: How One Girl Stood Up for Education and Changed the World.*

Giant Squid

BY CANDACE FLEMING; ERIC ROHMANN, ILLUS.

Grades K–4   *32 pages*

Roaring Brook Press, 2016; ebook

One of the things unique about nonfiction today is the various forms of writing used to convey information. Candace Fleming's lyrical, poetic text takes readers into the cold, dark depths of the ocean to discover a strange and fearsome creature that, until 2012, had never been photographed in its natural habitat. The giant squid possesses two long curling tentacles, eight coiling arms, a parrotlike beak, and an eye as big as a soccer ball. Eric Rohmann's stunning illustrations illuminate both the movement and size of this incredible creature. A stunning double-page foldout provides a complete look at the squid . . . and then it's gone. Fleming and Rohmann have also collaborated on *Strongheart: Wonder Dog of the Silver Screen*, a middle-grade historical novel. Rohmann's eye-catching illustrations can also be found in his Caldecott Honor book *Time Flies*, a time-travel wordless picture book when dinosaur's come to life; *The Cinder-Eyed Cats*, about a boy's journey to a tropical dream world; and his Caldecott Medal–winning wordless picture book, *My Friend Rabbit.*

Harvesting Hope: The Story of Cesar Chavez

BY KATHLEEN KRULL; YUYI MORALES, ILLUS.

Grades 1–4   *48 pages*

Harcourt Brace, 2003; audiobook

This is a stunning biography of the man who made some of the richest people in America listen to some of the poorest. Despite the limitations of a picture book, the author and illustrator are able to create a multidimensional image of a man who walked so proudly in the footsteps of Gandhi and Martin Luther King Jr., faced down the rich and powerful, and changed America. The book spans his childhood in the Arizona desert and the bitter loss of his family's farm to the backbreaking harvest years and the blossoming of his labor movement for indigent farmworkers. Related book: *Separate Is Never Equal: Sylvia Mendez and Her Family's Fight for Desegregation* by Duncan Tonatiuh.

Henry's Freedom Box: A True Story from the Underground Railroad

BY ELLEN LEVINE; KADIR NELSON, ILLUS.

Grades 2 and up   *40 pages*

Scholastic, 2007; ebook, audiobook

By the start of the Civil War, more than sixty thousand of the four million slaves in the United States had escaped to freedom, most via the Underground Railroad. But the most unusual route was that chosen by Henry Brown. Brown had just seen his wife and three children sold in the slave market and figured he had nothing left to lose. With the help of a white doctor and a black friend, he had himself stuffed into a wooden crate and then mailed 350 miles from Richmond to Philadelphia. This extraordinary journey, during which he could not stretch, sneeze, or even cough, took twenty-seven hours. Related books: *Belle, the Last Mule at Gee's Bend* by Calvin Alexander Ramsey; *Heart and Soul: The Story of America and African Americans* by Kadir Nelson; and *Unspoken: A Story from the Underground Railroad* by Henry Cole.

Mighty Jackie: The Strike-Out Queen

BY MARISSA MOSS; C. F. PAYNE, ILLUS.

Grades 1–4   *36 pages*

Simon & Schuster, 2004

On April 2, 1931, Jackie Mitchell's dream was finally going to come true: She would get a chance to show the world's greatest hitters that a seventeen-year-old could throw a mighty mean curveball. All those barnyard practice throws would finally come to something, and not just against any team—but against the mighty New York Yankees, led by Babe Ruth and Lou Gehrig, coming through Tennessee on a spring barnstorming tour. So when Jackie Mitchell struck out the Babe and Gehrig in succession while pitching for the Chattanooga Lookouts, there was considerable excitement—and not just because Jackie was only seventeen years old. The bigger story was that Jackie Mitchell was a girl! In this wonderful retelling, Moss and Payne bring to life a little-known but true story in American sports. Also by the author: *The Bravest Woman in America* and *Nurse, Soldier, Spy: The Story of Sarah Edmonds, a Civil War Hero.* Related books: *Girl Wonder: A Baseball Story in Nine Innings* by Deborah Hopkinson; *Mama Played Baseball* by David A. Adler; *Players in Pigtails* by Shana Corey; *She Loved Baseball: The Effa Manley Story* and *Brothers at Bat*, both by Audrey Vernick.

Mr. Ferris and His Wheel

BY KATHRYN GIBBS DAVIS; GILBERT FORD, ILLUS.

Grades K–4   *40 pages*

Houghton Mifflin Harcourt, 2014; ebook

It's ten months before the 1893 World's Fair in Chicago, and there is no spectacular centerpiece such as the Eiffel Tower that graced the previous World's Fair in Paris. Fortunately, young George Ferris had a vision for a very large structure that could move. Consider the challenge of creating such a structure with limited funding and time, a hundred thousand various parts, and a newfangled metal called steel. Any child, or adult, will enjoy hearing how the Ferris wheel came to be. Related book: *The Fantastic Ferris Wheel: The Story of Inventor George Ferris* by Betsy Harvey Kraft.

Nurse, Soldier, Spy: The Story of Sarah Edmonds, a Civil War Hero

BY MARISSA MOSS; JOHN HENDRIX, ILLUS.

Grades 3–5   *48 pages*

Abrams, 2011; ebook

Under any circumstances, Frank Thompson—nurse, soldier, and spy—would have been an extraordinary Civil War soldier. When you discover that Frank was not Frank—that "he" was a nineteen-year-old girl named Sarah Edmonds, the story goes beyond extraordinary. Sarah had begun dressing as a man to escape Canada and an arranged marriage, and she loved the newfound freedoms that came with her disguise. With the start of the Civil War and the need for soldiers, Sarah joined the Union army. Although hundreds of other women joined in disguises, Edmonds is the only one to have accomplished so much, come so close to being both shot and discovered, and finally to be voted by Congress as the only official woman veteran of the Civil War. This book offers a striking contrast with the headlines of today, when women serve as battlefield equals on the sands of the Middle East. Also by the author: *The Bravest Woman in America* and *Mighty Jackie: The Strike-Out Queen*. Related books: *Independent Dames: What You Never Knew About the Women and Girls of the American Revolution* by Laurie Halse Anderson, *The Librarian of Basra: A True Story from Iraq* by Jeanette Winter, and *Mama Played Baseball* by David A. Adler.

Odd Boy Out: Young Albert Einstein

BY DON BROWN

Grades 2–7   32 pages

Houghton Mifflin, 2004; ebook

In this simple but insightful biographical picture book on the life of the great scientist, the author offers hope for every child who marches to a different drum, who doesn't blossom on time, who isn't good at sports, who believes in daydreaming about things that no one else can even imagine, and who is the class outsider. And for those who think they know the story already, that Einstein worked on the atom bomb—wrong! He was barred from working on it because his pacifist leanings prevented him from receiving a security clearance. This is picture-book biography at its very best, from an author-illustrator whose work places him at the very front of the field. Related book: *Marshall Armstrong Is New to Our School* by David Mackintosh. Also by the author: *American Boy: The Adventures of Mark Twain*; *Uncommon Traveler: Mary Kingsley in Africa*; *Rare Treasure: Mary Anning and Her Remarkable Discoveries*; *Alice Ramsey's Grand Adventure*; *Ruth Law Thrills a Nation*; and *Teedie: The Story of Young Teddy Roosevelt*.

Pop!: The Invention of Bubble Gum

BY MEGHAN MCCARTHY

Grades K–2   32 pages

Simon & Schuster, 2010; ebook

Back in the 1920s, a young accountant, Walter Diemer, went to work in a Philadelphia gum and candy factory. Shortly thereafter, he found an experimental laboratory set up in the adjoining office, a lab where they were trying to produce a new kind of gum. When Walter was asked to keep an eye on one of the lab kettles, he found the temptation to experiment on his own too much to resist. What follows is the evolution of bubble gum, complete with a history of gum that goes all the way back to the Greeks. Also by the author: *Earmuffs for Everyone!: How Chester Greenwood Became Known as the Inventor of Earmuffs*, *City Hawk: The Story of Pale Male*, *The Incredible Life of Balto*, *Seabiscuit the Wonder Horse*, and *Strong Man: The Story of Charles Atlas*. Related book: *The Kid Who Invented the Popsicle: And Other Surprising Stories About Inventions* by Don L. Wulffson.

Separate Is Never Equal: Sylvia Mendez and Her Family's Fight for Desegregation

BY DUNCAN TONATIUH

Grades 2–5   *40 pages*

Abrams, 2014; ebook

In the summer of 1944, Sylvia Mendez, her parents, and two brothers moved to Westminster, California, where her father was leasing a farm. The local public school was close to their house and contained spacious and clean hallways along with a playground with monkey bars and a red swing. But Sylvia and her brothers were told they had to go to the "Mexican School," Hoover Elementary, that was surrounded by cow pastures and had no playground. Sylvia was an American who spoke perfect English, her father was a U.S. citizen, and her mother was from Puerto Rico, which is a U.S. territory. The principal and superintendent stood firm in their response that the Mendez children could not attend the "Whites only" Westminster School. Mr. Mendez was determined his children would not be discriminated against and found an attorney who would file a lawsuit against the school district. On April 14, 1947, a judge ruled in their favor—seven years before the historic *Brown v. Board of Education* case that desegregated schools in the entire country. This is a little-known story that shares how segregation was occurring across the country. Deborah Wiles's *Freedom Summer* is set in the South in 1964 when African American children were not allowed to swim in public swimming pools. *The Story of Ruby Bridges*, by Robert Coles, relates the experience of the six-year-old who was the first African American child to integrate a school in New Orleans in 1960.

Some Writer!: The Story of E. B. White

BY MELISSA SWEET

Grades 1–5   *176 pages*

Houghton Mifflin Harcourt, 2016; ebook

This is an excellent biography of E. B. White that is perfect to pair with *Charlotte's Web*. Insights about White's childhood and his love of writing are shared through letters, manuscripts, essays, and poetry. The innovative format for a biography along with awesome collage illustrations makes this a book that begs to be read aloud with children. *A Boy, a Mouse, and a Spider: The Story of E. B. White* by Barbara Herkert is a picture-book biography that can be shared as well. Other books by E. B. White include *Stuart Little* and *The Trumpet of the Swan*.

Step Right Up: How Doc and Jim Key Taught the World About Kindness

BY DONNA JANELL BOWMAN; DANIEL MINTER, ILLUS.

Grades 1–3   *48 pages*

Lee & Low Books, 2016; ebook, audiobook

Doc Key's message was "that each of us should step right up and choose kindness." Born into slavery, William "Doc" Key became a successful freeman who taught the world about the power of education and of kindness. Jim Key was his beautiful, exceptional horse that Doc taught to answer questions, do math, spell words, and write letters on a blackboard. What's not to love about a story like this! *Abraham Lincoln's Dueling Words* is also written by Bowman.

We Are the Ship: The Story of Negro League Baseball

BY KADIR NELSON

Grades 4 and up   *96 pages*

Jump at the Sun/Hyperion, 2008; audiobook

Negro League baseball produced famous players such as Satchel Paige and Josh Gibson. There were also many other equally talented players. Baseball and segregation for many years went hand in hand, which Nelson explores through readable text and stunning paintings. This is a book that will be enjoyed by kids and adults. Visit the Negro Leagues Baseball Museum in Kansas City, Missouri, if you are in the area. Related books: *Satch and Me* by Dan Gutman, *A Negro League Scrapbook* by Carole Boston Weatherford, and *Negro Leagues: All-Black Baseball* by Laura Driscoll.

Who Was Steve Jobs?

BY PAM POLLACK AND MEG BELVISO; JOHN O'BRIEN, ILLUS.

Grades 3–7   *100 pages*

Grosset & Dunlap, 2012; ebook, audiobook

After nonfiction picture books, one of the best pathways for children into deeper nonfiction is biography. Too often, however, biographies for children are top-heavy with detail. In the Who Was? series, children can taste the worlds of science, art, music, and history without drowning in detail. Each of the volumes is one hundred pages. If that seems too long for young readers, nearly every page has an illustration on it, reducing the text to about fifty full pages. As here with *Who Was Steve Jobs?*, the book offers an overview of the person's entire life, along with notes on contemporary figures and events that affected him (in this case, his biggest rival, Bill Gates, and Jobs's connection to the Beatles and *Star Wars*). With more than 150 titles to date, the series' subjects run the gamut from King Tut and Marco Polo to Helen Keller and Walt Disney.

The World Is Not a Rectangle: A Portrait of Architect Zaha Hadid

BY JEANETTE WINTER

Grades K–4   *56 pages*

Beach Lane Books, 2017; ebook

Born in Baghdad, Zaha Hadid saw the world differently. She observed how the shapes and colors flowed into each other. She did not see corners in dunes or rivers or marshes. In London, she studied to be an architect and found others who shared in her vision. Her unusual designs were initially met with skepticism, but soon she began to design buildings that are located all around the world. Winter's acrylic illustrations are colorful and attention grabbing. Her other picture-book biographies include *Henri's Scissors*, *Wangari's Trees of Peace: A True Story from Africa*, *The Watcher: Jane Goodall's Life with the Chimps*, *Nasreen's Secret School: A True Story from Afghanistan*, and *The Librarian of Basra: A True Story from Iraq*.

Poetry

Bookjoy, Wordjoy

BY PAT MORA; RAUL COLÓN, ILLUS.

Grades 2 and up   *32 pages*

Wordsong, 2018

"We belong / together / books and me, / like toast and jelly / *o queso y tortillas*." Pat Mora's poems celebrate the fun of collecting words, reading books, and writing poetry. In her note at the conclusion of *Bookjoy, Wordjoy*, Mora writes, "But this book is about creative writing: wordplay. . . . Too often our young readers and writers experience the work and not the play, the wordjoy." This book of poetry is punctuated with Colón's joyful illustrations and is excellent for reading aloud. Pair this book with *BookSpeak!: Poems About Books* by Laura Purdie Salas and *Read! Read! Read!* by Amy Ludwig VanDerwater. And, of course, share other books of Mora's poetry including *Confetti: Poems for Children*.

A Bunch of Punctuation

POEMS SELECTED BY LEE BENNETT HOPKINS; SERGE BLOCH, ILLUS.

Grades 3 and up   *32 pages*
Wordsong, 2018

Who knew that the exclamation mark was such a superhero who makes you want to shout or that the period brings you to a full stop (unless you want the Grammar Police to get you). Lee Bennett Hopkins has been recognized by Guinness World Records as the world's most prolific anthologist of poetry for children. This collection of poetry features punctuation from a unique and approachable perspective written by well-known poets for children. The engaging poems are perfectly complemented by inventive illustrations by Serge Bloch. A few other poetry anthologies by Hopkins include *School People*; *Got Geography!*; *Jumping Off Library Shelves*; *Spectacular Science*; and *Wonderful Words: Poems About Reading, Writing, Speaking, and Listening*.

The Cremation of Sam McGee

BY ROBERT W. SERVICE; TED HARRISON, ILLUS.

Grades 4 and up   *32 pages*
Kids Can Press, 1987; ebook

Once one of the most recited poems in North America and among the author's most popular, this remains the best description of the sun's strange spell over the men who once toiled in the North for gold. Also by the author and illustrator: *The Shooting of Dan Mc-Grew*. Two excellent collections of Service's poetry: *Best Tales of the Yukon* (ebook) and *Collected Poems of Robert Service*.

Cricket in the Thicket: Poems About Bugs

BY CAROL MURRAY; MELISSA SWEET, ILLUS.

Grades K–3   *40 pages*
Henry Holt, 2017; ebook

Delightful poems offer insights into the world of insects from bumblebees to the praying mantis, dung beetle to termites. Each poem is coupled with a box containing additional facts. The collage illustrations by Melissa Sweet add another layer of enjoyment. The final pages include more information about each insect. Related books: *Insect Soup: Bug Poems* by Barry Louis Polisar and *Insectlopedia* by Douglas Florian.

Every Month Is a New Year

BY MARILYN SINGER; SUSAN L. ROTH, ILLUS.

Grades 1–7   56 pages

Lee & Low Books, 2018

New year celebrations, both secular and religious, from around the world are commemorated in this collection of sixteen poems. The book is formatted like a calendar you hold vertically rather than horizontally. We learn about Hogmanay in Scotland, which is the last day of the old year and the first day of the new year. The Chinese New Year, celebrated in January or February, originally marked the start of the agricultural year and honored gods and ancestors. And there is the Thai New Year, Songkran, observed in April. Each poem is accented with collage illustrations using paper sourced from across the globe. Information at the end of the book about each celebration along with a glossary and pronunciation guide provides an appreciation of global uniqueness. Other poetry books by Singer: *Feel the Beat: Dance Poems That Zing from Salsa to Swing*; *A Stick Is an Excellent Thing: Poems Celebrating Outdoor Play*; *Rutherford B., Who Was He?: Poems About Our Presidents*; and *Every Day's a Dog's Day: A Year in Poems.*

Follow Follow: A Book of Reverso Poems

BY MARILYN SINGER; JOSÉE MASSE, ILLUS.

Grades 3 and up   32 pages

Dial, 2013; ebook

This clever book contains reverso poems that are read from top to bottom and then bottom to top. Each features a classic fairy tale so knowledge of "The Princess and the Pea," "The Three Pigs," "The Tortoise and the Hare," and others is necessary in order to fully appreciate the new perspective these poems offer. *Follow Follow*, a follow-up to *Mirror Mirror: A Book of Reverso Poems*, contains fourteen pairs of reverso poems of fairy tales. *Echo Echo: Reverso Poems About Greek Myths* is the third collection of highly imaginative poetry. These poems have a wide range of audience from intermediate grades through high school.

Friends and Foes: Poems About Us All

BY DOUGLAS FLORIAN

Grades 3 and up   *32 pages*

Beach Lane Books, 2018; ebook

In a collection of twenty-five poems, Florian explores the topic of friendship. From best friends, to imaginary friends, to friends who move away, each poem depicts some aspect of being friends. Even those times when you are no longer friends. A few of the poems are ones to be read by two people, which provides a wonderful opportunity to read side by side with your child. The childlike illustrations in crayon and colored pencil perfectly complement the poems. You can't go wrong with Florian's other books of poetry: *Beast Feast: Poems and Paintings*, *Autumnblings*, *Poetrees*, and *UnBEElievables: Honeybee Poems and Paintings*.

Gone Camping: A Novel in Verse

BY TAMERA WILL WISSINGER; MATTHEW CORDELL, ILLUS.

Grades 2 and up   *106 pages*

Houghton Mifflin Harcourt, 2017; ebook

It might appear, based on the title, that this book should be included along with the chapter books and novels. What is truly unique about *Gone Camping* is the range of poetic forms that tell the story of two children who go camping with their grandpa. Lucy and Sam are excited to embark on a camping trip with Dad. Unfortunately, he becomes ill and Grandpa becomes the replacement camper. Each verse of the story is labeled: blessing poem, cinquain, concrete poem, couplet, haiku, lament, narrative poem, parody poem, and on and on. The back matter defines each poetic form as well as some rhyming basics. *Gone Fishing: A Novel in Verse* by the dynamic duo preceded this book but is equally humorous and poetic. Related books: *Falling Down the Page: A Book of List Poems* and *The Arrow Finds Its Mark: A Book of Found Poems*, both by Georgia Heard, are perfect for pairing with these novels in verse.

I'm Just No Good at Rhyming and Other Nonsense for Mischievous Kids and Immature Grown-Ups

BY CHRIS HARRIS; LANE SMITH, ILLUS.

Grades 3 and up   *192 pages*

Little, Brown, 2017; ebook, audiobook

There's a little bit of everything in this hilarious book of poetry. Harris provides a perspective on a range of everyday activities as well as a few implausible situations. The poet employs wit, word-play, nonsense, and even a few poems that do rhyme. A good example is "The Gecko": "If ever I find myself holding a gecko . . . / I'll lecko." Lane Smith's illustrations add another layer of slapstick. Don't overlook the book jacket, the page numbers, dedication, or acknowledgments. From start to finish, this is one that will entertain both kids and adults.

I've Lost My Hippopotamus

BY JACK PRELUTSKY; JACKIE URBANOVIC, ILLUS.
Grades K–4   *140 pages*
Greenwillow, 2012

Jack Prelutsky was deservedly the nation's first children's poet laureate, with more than forty books to his credit. With Jackie Urbanovic's witty ink drawings on every page, this is among his best collections of short poems. The subject matter includes great wordplay (as always) and some of the most whimsical creatures you've never met: wiguanas, penguinchworms, buffalocusts, kangarulers, and flemingoats. Among the more than one hundred subjects, there are the silly improbables: it's raining in my bedroom, the troll's not at the bridge today, my pencil will not write, and my weasels have the measles—all with Prelutsky twists, including one poem about the plight of a child whose *u*'s all come out upside down (they look like *n*'s). Also by the author: *The Dragons Are Singing Tonight, The New Kid on the Block, A Pizza the Size of the Sun, The Random House Book of Poetry for Children*, and *Read-Aloud Rhymes for the Very Young*. Prelutsky fans are almost always Shel Silverstein fans—see the listing for *Where the Sidewalk Ends*.

Jazz Day: The Making of a Famous Photograph

BY ROXANE ORGILL; FRANCIS VALLEJO, ILLUS.
Grades 3 and up   *66 pages*
Candlewick Press, 2016; audiobook

The poems in *Jazz Day* are as striking and memorable as the vibrant, acrylic and pastel paintings by Vallejo. In 1958, Art Kane pitched an idea to *Esquire* magazine to take a photo of as many jazz musicians as he could gather together. The word was put out to the local musicians' union, but Kane had no idea if anyone would show up for the photo shoot scheduled for August 12 in Harlem. Fifty-seven musicians did come that day, and it was as much about a reunion of musicians as it was about the iconic photograph that was taken. The actual photograph appears in a double-page spread, and an identification key is provided a few pages later. Short biographies of some of the well-known jazz musicians that the poems focus on are also included. Pair this book with others about jazz musicians: *Duke Ellington: The Piano Prince and His Orchestra* by Andrea Davis Pinkney; *Before John Was a Jazz Giant: A Song of John Coltrane* by Carole Boston Weatherford; *Charlie Parker Played Be Bop* by Chris Raschka; *Dizzy* by Jonah Winter; *Trombone Shorty* by Troy Andrews; and *The Little Piano Girl: The Story of Mary Lou Williams, Jazz Legend* by Ann Ingalls and Maryann Macdonald. Related books: *Jazz on a Saturday Night* by Leo and Diane Dillon and *Jazz* by Walter Dean Myers.

Lion of the Sky: Haiku for All Seasons
BY LAURA PURDIE SALAS; MERCÈ LÓPEZ, ILLUS.
Grades 4 and up   *32 pages*
Millbrook, 2019; ebook
Haiku, or what Salas calls "riddle-ku," abounds in this delightful exploration of the seasons. Twenty poems feature a riddle about a common object, whether it's a puddle, dandelion, jack-o'-lantern, or mittens. Colorful illustrations will help discover the answer. And if you can't figure it out, a key at the end of the book provides the solution. Another book of poems by Salas, *Snowman – Cold = Puddle: Spring Equations*, intermingles math, nature, and poetry in equation poems. Sidebars offer additional science information. Other poetry books by Salas include *In the Middle of the Night: Poems from a Wide-Awake House, Water Can Be . . . , A Leaf Can Be . . .* , and *BookSpeak!: Poems About Books.*

Martin Rising: Requiem for a King
BY ANDREA DAVIS PINKNEY; BRIAN PINKNEY, ILLUS.
Grades 4 and up   *128 pages*
Scholastic, 2018; ebook, audiobook
Written in a narrative form that Pinkney calls "docu-poems," this collection of vignettes highlights the events as they unfolded during the days and weeks leading up to Martin Luther King Jr.'s death. The poems are as stirring as the watercolor paintings by Brian Pinkney. Poetry is meant to be read aloud to hear the flow of language as well as the emotional impact of the writing. Related books: *I Have a Dream* by Dr. Martin Luther King Jr. and Kadir Nelson; *As Good as*

Anybody: Martin Luther King Jr. and Abraham Joshua Heschel's Amazing March Toward Freedom by Richard Michelson; *The Cart That Carried Martin* by Eve Bunting; *Who Was Martin Luther King, Jr.* by Bonnie Bader; *What Was the March on Washington?* by Kathleen Krull; and *My Brother Martin: A Sister Remembers Growing Up with the Rev. Dr. Martin Luther King Jr.* by Christine Farris.

The Neighborhood Sing-Along
PHOTOGRAPHED BY NINA CREWS
Grades Tod–K   *64 pages*
HarperCollins, 2011
Those favorite childhood singsongs from the classroom, bedroom, and playground ("Do Your Ears Hang Low?" or "The Wheels on the Bus") are all illustrated in glorious color with children of every hue from every kind of neighborhood. What Crews did for nursery rhymes with *The Neighborhood Mother Goose* she's done equally well with song. Every home and classroom should own this.

Oh, How Sylvester Can Pester!: And Other Poems More or Less About Manners
BY ROBERT KINERK; DRAZEN KOZJAN, ILLUS.
Grades K–3   *26 pages*
Simon & Schuster, 2011; ebook
One of the casualties of the modern age is manners, among young and old. Since demonstrations work better than lectures, these twenty poems have just enough humor and logic to work with the young (and maybe their elders too). Detailed here are our failings at the table and theater, with our hands, our tongues, and even our clothes. Related books: *Dude, That's Rude! (Get Some Manners)* by Pamela Espeland and Elizabeth Verdick and *This Is Just to Say: Poems of Apology and Forgiveness* by Joyce Sidman and Pamela Zagarenski.

Poems I Wrote When No One Was Looking
BY ALAN KATZ; EDWARD KOREN, ILLUS.
Grades 1–5   *145 pages*
McElderry, 2011; ebook
From the poet who gave us the series of song parodies (*Take Me Out of the Bathtub and Other Silly Dilly Songs*) comes more laughter in short rhyming verse. Everything is fair game here, from parents to peers, language, snow days, and even dad's GPS. Also by the author: *Oops!*

The Random House Book of Poetry for Children

SELECTED BY JACK PRELUTSKY; ARNOLD LOBEL, ILLUS.
Grades K–5   *248 pages*
Random House, 1983
One of the best children's poetry anthologies ever, showing that poet Jack Prelutsky recognizes the common language of children. The 572 selected poems (from both traditional and contemporary poets) are short on words but long on laughter, imagery, and rhyme. They are grouped into fourteen categories that include food, goblins, nonsense, home, children, animals, and seasons.

Read-Aloud Rhymes for the Very Young

COLLECTED BY JACK PRELUTSKY; MARC BROWN, ILLUS.
Grades Tod–K   *88 pages*
Knopf, 1986
This anthology includes more than two hundred little poems (with full-color illustrations) for little people with little attention spans, to help both to grow. More than one hundred of the best-known poets of the twentieth century are represented. Related book: *A Little Bitty Man and Other Poems for the Very Young* by Halfdan Rasmussen.

Shaking Things Up: 14 Young Women Who Changed the World

BY SUSAN HOOD; THIRTEEN WOMEN ILLUSTRATORS
Grades 1–5   *40 pages*
HarperCollins, 2018
Fourteen revolutionary women, from activists to artists, secret agents to storytellers, are celebrated in poetry. You'll meet six-year-old Ruby Bridges, who attended an all-white school in the fight to end segregation; architect and sculptor Maya Lin, who designed the Vietnam Veterans Memorial in Washington, DC; and the first known female firefighter in the United States, Molly Williams, who cooked and fought fires in the early 1800s. Each fearless female's poem is accompanied by an equally inspiring illustration by Melissa Sweet, Sophie Blackall, Shadra Strickland, Isabel Roxas, Emily Winfield Martin, LeUyen Pham, Oge Mora, Julie Morstad, Lisa Brown, Selina Alko, Hadley Hooper, Erin Robinson, and Sara Palacios. A timeline featuring the noteworthy women, a brief biographical sketch, and additional sources complete the book. Related poetry books: *Bravo!: Poems About Amazing Hispanics* by Margarita

Engle and *Out of Wonder: Poems Celebrating Poets* by Kwame Alexander.

Vivid: Poems and Notes About Color
BY JULIE PASCHKIS
Grades PreS–3   *32 pages*
Henry Holt, 2018; ebook
Yellow is described as "Loudly, rowdy / daffodils yell hello. / Hot yellow." The poet joyfully celebrates the world of color through expressive language and eye-catching illustrations. Accompanying each poem are some colorful facts and questions. In her author's note about the book, Paschkis writes, "I hope it inspires you to explore the art and science of color." Picture books about color to pair with this book: *Green* and *Blue*, both by Laura Vaccaro Seeger; *I Feel Teal* by Lauren Rille; and *Red Sings from Treetops: A Year in Colors* by Joyce Sidman.

When Green Becomes Tomatoes: Poems for All Seasons
BY JULIE FOGLIANO; JULIE MORSTAD, ILLUS.
Grades 1–5   *56 pages*
Roaring Brook Press, 2016; ebook
The four seasons are celebrated through free verse and inviting illustrations. Starting and ending on March 20, the vernal equinox, brief poems express wonder about nature through thoughtful observations about randomly chosen days like March 22: "just like a tiny, blue hello / a crocus blooming / in the snow." The gouache and colored pencil illustrations feature a multiracial cast of children savoring the unique seasonal changes and activities. This charming book of poetry can be read throughout the year or in a few readings. Peek under the book jacket for a visual treat, and consider it along with the color of the endpapers. Free verse is wonderful to share with children so they recognize that not all poetry has to rhyme. Other poetry about seasons include *Red Sings from Treetops: A Year in Colors* by Joyce Sidman, with imaginative illustrations by Pamela Zagarenski; *Hi, Koo!: A Year of Seasons* by Jon J. Muth; *Sharing the Seasons: A Book of Poems* compiled by Lee Bennett Hopkins and illustrated by David Diaz.

Where the Sidewalk Ends

BY SHEL SILVERSTEIN

Grades K–8   *166 pages*

Harper, 1974; audio CD

Without question, this is the best-loved collection of poetry for children, selling more than ten million hardcover copies in forty-five years. When it comes to knowing children's appetites, Silverstein was pure genius. The titles alone are enough to capture children's attention: "Band-Aids," "Boa Constrictor," "The Crocodile's Toothache," "The Dirtiest Man in the World," "Me and My Giant," and "Recipe for a Hippopotamus Sandwich." Here are 130 poems that will either touch children's hearts or tickle their funny bones. Also by the author: *A Light in the Attic* and the short novel *Lafcadio, the Lion Who Shot Back*. Silverstein fans are usually fans of Jack Prelutsky—see the listing for *I've Lost My Hippopotamus*.

Cyndi's Favorite Poetry Books

All the World a Poem by Gilles Tibo

Bravo!: Poems About Amazing Hispanics by Margarita Engle

Cat Says Meow and Other An•i•mal•o•poe•ia by Michael Arndt

Flutter and Hum: Animal Poems/ Aleteo y Zumbido: Poemas de Animales by Julie Paschkis

Guyku: A Year of Haiku for Boys by Bob Raczka

Hip Hop Speaks to Children: A Celebration of Poetry with a Beat by Nikki Giovanni

Home Run, Touchdown, Basket, Goal!: Sports Poems for Little Athletes by Leo Landry

The Llama Who Had No Pajama: 100 Favorite Poems by Mary Ann Hoberman

One Leaf Rides the Wind by Celeste Mannis

Poem-Mobiles: Crazy Car Poems by J. Patrick Lewis

Ubiquitous: Celebrating Nature's Survivors by Joyce Sidman

Voices in the Air: Poems for Listeners by Naomi Shihab Nye

Wet Cement: A Mix of Concrete Poems by Bob Raczka

Won Ton: A Cat Tale Told in Haiku by Lee Wardlaw

Notes

Introduction

1. Natalie Wexler, "If We Want to Boost Reading Scores, We Need to Change Reading Tests," *Forbes*, April 15, 2018, https://www.forbes.com/sites/nataliewexler/2018/04/15/if-we-want-to-boost-reading-scores-we-need-to-change-reading-tests/#24df6e7c495a.
2. Trevon Milliard, "How One Reno Student Landed Perfect SAT and ACT Scores," *Reno Gazette Journal*, June 8, 2015, https://www.rgj.com/story/news/education/2015/06/08/one-reno-student-landed-perfect-sat-act-scores/28683039/.
3. Michael Hout and Stuart W. Elliott, eds., *Incentives and Test-Based Accountability in Education*, National Research Council, National Academies Press, 2011, Washington, DC. See also Jonathan Kantrowitz, "Current Test-Based Incentive Programs Have Not Consistently Raised Student Achievement," May 26, 2011, http://educationresearchreport.blogspot.com/2011/05/current-test-based-incentive-programs.html; and Valerie Strauss, "Report: Test-Based Incentives Don't Produce Real Student Achievement," *The Answer Sheet* (blog), *Washington Post*, May 28, 2011, https://www.washingtonpost.com/blogs/answer-sheet/post/report-test-based-incentives-dont-produce-real-student-achievement/2011/05/28/AG39wXDH_blog.html.
4. The State of Obesity, "Obesity Rates & Trend Data," https://stateofobesity.org/data/.
5. Katie Reilly, "Is Recess Important for Kids or a Waste of Time? Here's What the Research Says," *Time*, October 23, 2017, http://time.com/4982061/recess-benefits-research/debate/.
6. Jay Mathews, "Let's Have a 9-Hour School Day," *Washington Post*, August 16, 2005.
7. Using weekdays, weekends, and summers, the KIPP charter schools extend the school day by 70 percent. See Jay Mathews, "Study Finds Big Gains for KIPP; Charter Schools Exceed Average," *Washington Post*, August 11, 2005.
8. Mikaela J. Dufur, Toby L. Parcel, and Kelly P. Troutman, "Does Capital at Home Matter More than Capital at School? Social Capital Effects on Academic Achievement," *Research in Social Stratification and Mobility*, 2012, https://10.1016/j.rssm.2012.08.002.

9. Dufur, Parcel, and Troutman, "Capital at Home."

10. William Johnson, "Confessions of a 'Bad' Teacher," *New York Times*, March 4, 2012; Michael Winerip, "Hard-Working Teachers, Sabotaged When Student Test Scores Slip," *New York Times*, March 5, 2012.

11. Renée Casbergue and April Bedford, "Research Round-Up: Journal of Research in Childhood Education, Volume 26, No. 4," *Childhood Education* 89, no. 5 (2013): 340–44.

12. Centers for Disease Control and Prevention, https://www.cdc.gov /media/releases/2018/p0118-smoking-rates-declining.html.

13. The brochures can be found online at http://www.trelease-on -reading.com/brochures.html; they are intended for use by nonprofit groups only.

14. Adriana Lleras-Muney, "The Relationship Between Education and Adult Mortality in the United States," *Review of Economic Studies* 72, no. 1 (2005), https://doi.org/10.1111/0034-6527.00329; Gina Kolata, "A Surprising Secret to a Long Life: Stay in School," *New York Times*, January 3, 2007.

15. Mary A. Foertsch, *Reading In and Out of School*, Educational Testing Service (Washington, DC: U.S. Department of Education, May 1992); Keith E. Stanovich, "Does Reading Make You Smarter? Literacy and the Development of Verbal Intelligence," *Advances in Child Development and Behavior* 24 (1993): 133–80, http://www.ncbi .nlm.nih.gov/pubmed/8447247; and Anne Cunningham and Keith Stanovich, "Reading Can Make You Smarter!" *Principal* 83, no. 2 (November/December 2003): 34–39.

16. Richard C. Anderson, Elfrieda H. Hiebert, Judith A. Scott, and Ian A. G. Wilkinson, *Becoming a Nation of Readers: The Report of the Commission on Reading*, U.S. Department of Education (Champaign-Urbana, IL: Center for the Study of Reading, 1985). See also Diane Ravitch and Chester Finn, *What Do Our 17-Year-Olds Know?* (New York: Harper & Row, 1987).

17. Associated Press, "Reasons Why Students Drop Out," *New York Times*, September 14, 1994.

18. Michael Greenstone and Adam Looney, "Where Is the Best Place to Invest $102,000—In Stocks, Bonds, or a College Degree?" The Hamilton Project/Brookings Institution, November 9, 2011, https://www.brookings.edu/research/where-is-the-best-place -to-invest-102000-in-stocks-bonds-or-a-college-degree/. http://www .brookings.edu/papers/2011/0625_education_greenstone_looney .aspx. See also Melissa Lee, "When It Comes to Salary, It's Academic," *Washington Post*, July 22, 1994.

19. "Trends in Reading Scores by Parents' Highest Level of Education," in M. Perie, R. Moran, and A. D. Lutkus, *NAEP 2004 Trends in Academic Progress: Three Decades of Student Performance in Reading and Mathematics*, U.S. Department of Education, Institute of Education Sciences, National Center for Education Statistics (Washington, DC: U.S. Government Printing Office, 2005): 36–37.

20. Kolata, "A Surprising Secret to a Long Life." See also James P. Martin, "The Impact of Socioeconomic Status on Health over the Life-Course," *Journal of Human Resources* 42, no. 4 (Fall 2007): 739–64; Katherine Bouton, "Eighty Years Along, a Longevity Study Still Has Ground to Cover," *New York Times*, April 19, 2011; Howard S. Friedman and Leslie R. Martin, *The Longevity Project: Surprising Discoveries for Health and Long Life from the Landmark Eight-Decade Study* (New York: Hudson Street Press, 2011); Eugene Rogot, Paul D. Sorlie, and Norman J. Johnson, "Life Expectancy by Employment Status, Income, and Education in the National Longitudinal Mortality Study," *Public Health Reports* 107, no. 4 (1992): 457–61; Jack M. Guralnik et al., "Educational Status and Active Life Expectancy Among Older Blacks and Whites," *New England Journal of Medicine* 329, vol. 2 (1993): 110–16; and E. Pamuk et al., *Health, United States, 1998: Socioeconomic Status and Health Chartbook* (Hyattsville, MD: National Center for Health Statistics, 1998).

21. Students scoring As, Bs, or Cs don't drop out. The ones who cannot read well enough to achieve those grades are the most likely to withdraw. It is the very rare performer who quits while still hitting home runs.

22. Jake Cronin, *The Path to Successful Reentry: The Relationship Between Correctional Education, Employment and Recidivism*, University of Missouri Columbia, Institute of Public Policy, Report 15-2011. Also Paul E. Barton and Richard J. Coley, "Captive Students: Education and Training in America's Prisons," Educational Testing Service (Princeton, NJ: ETS Policy Information Center, 1996); Ian Buruma, "What Teaching a College-Level Class at a Maximum-Security Correctional Facility Did for the Inmates—and for Me," *New York Times Magazine*, February 20, 2005.

23. Matthew Lynch, "High School Dropout Rates: Causes and Costs," May 30, 2014, https://www.huffingtonpost.com/matthew-lynch-edd/high-school-dropout-rate_b_5421778.html.

24. Michael Sainato, "U.S. Prison System Plagued by High Illiteracy Rates," Observer, July 18, 2017, https://observer.com/2017/07/prison-illiteracy-criminal-justice-reform/.

Chapter 1: Why Read Aloud?

1. Kate DiCamillo, Facebook post, March 8, 2018. https://m.facebook.com/story.php?story_fbid=2048957161786886&id=139485862734035.

2. Richard C. Anderson, Elfrieda H. Hiebert, Judith A. Scott, and Ian A. G. Wilkinson, *Becoming a Nation of Readers: The Report of the Commission on Reading*, U.S. Department of Education (Champaign-Urbana, IL: Center for the Study of Reading, 1985), p. 23.

3. Anderson et al., p. 51.

4. *Kids & Family Reading Report*, Scholastic, 2016, http://www.scholas tic.com/readingreport/.

5. Lea M. McGee and Donald J. Richgels, *Designing Early Literacy Programs: Strategies for At-Risk Preschoolers and Kindergarten Children* (New York: Guilford Press, 2003).

6. Warwick B. Elley, "Vocabulary Acquisition from Listening to Stories," *Reading Research Quarterly* 24 (Spring 1989): 174–87.

7. Organisation for Economic Co-operation and Development, *PISA 2009 Results: Overcoming Social Background: Equity in Learning Opportunities and Outcomes, Vol. II, PISA* (Paris: OECD Publishing, 2010), p. 95, https://doi.org/10.1787/9789264091504-en.

8. Dominic W. Massaro, "Two Different Communication Genres and Implications for Vocabulary Development and Learning to Read," *Journal of Literacy Research*, 47, no. 4 (2015).

9. Betty Hart and Todd R. Risley, *Meaningful Differences in the Everyday Experience of Young American Children* (Baltimore: Brookes Publishing, 1996). For a downloadable six-page condensation of the book: Betty Hart and Todd R. Risley, "The Early Catastrophe: The 30 Million Word Gap by Age 3," *American Educator* (American Federation of Teachers), Spring 2003, http://www.aft.org/pdfs/ameri caneducator/spring2003/TheEarlyCatastrophe.pdf. This can be freely disseminated to parents, according to the AFT website. See also Ginia Bellafante, "Before a Test, a Poverty of Words," *New York Times*, October 7, 2012, p. MB; and Paul Chance, "Speaking of Differences," *Phi Delta Kappan* 78, no. 7 (March 1997):506–7.

10. This is printed at the bottom of the article: "Articles may be reproduced for noncommercial personal or educational use only; additional permission is required for any other reprinting of the documents." That entire spring issue is an easy-to-understand treasure of research on children's language and reading comprehension, free for downloading at http://www.aft.org/pdfs/americaneducator/spring2003 /TheEarlyCatastrophe.pdf.

11. George Farkas and Kurt Beron, "Family Linguistic Culture and Social Reproduction: Verbal Skill from Parent to Child in the Preschool and School Years," paper delivered March 31, 2001, to annual meetings of the Population Association of America, Washington, DC, https://eric.ed.gov/?id=ED453910. Also Karen S. Peterson, "Moms' Poor Vocabulary Hurts Kids' Future," *USA Today*, April 12, 2001.

12. Donald P. Hayes and Margaret G. Ahrens, "Vocabulary Simplification for Children: A Special Case for 'Motherese,'" *Journal of Child Language* 15 (1988): 395–410. One departure from the Hayes-Ahrens study is the deterioration of television's vocabulary since their original study. Tom Shachtman, in a thirty-year study of the *CBS Evening News*, found its language level had dropped from complex sentences with abstract words in 1963 to simple declarative sentences with few abstractions or rare words in 1993; in other words, from post–high school level down to junior high school level. His study also found daytime talk shows to be on the language level of ten-year-olds. See Tom Shachtman, *The Inarticulate Society: Eloquence and Culture in America* (New York: Free Press, 1995), 115–42.

13. Jessica L. Montag, Michael N. Jones, and Linda B. Smith, "The Words Children Hear: Picture Books and the Statistics for Language Learning," *Psychological Science* 26, no. 9 (September 2015): 1489–96.

14. Nathan Collins, "Read—Don't Just Talk—To Your Kids," *Pacific Standard*, August 2015, https://psmag.com/social-justice/picture-books-improve-vocabularies-or-how-i-justify-reading-berenstain-bears-alone-every-night-to-fall-asleep.

15. Caroline Hendrie, "Chicago Data Show Mixed Summer Gain," *Education Week*, September 10, 1999, pp. 1, 14. See also Diane Ravitch, "Summer School Isn't a Solution," *New York Times*, March 3, 2000.

16. *The Nation's Report Card: NAEP Reading Report Card*, U.S. Department of Education, Institute of Education Sciences, National Center for Education Statistics, 2010, https://nces.ed.gov/nationsreportcard/reading/.

17. Victoria J. Rideout, Ulla G. Foehr, and Donald F. Roberts, *Generation M2: Media in the Lives of 8- to 18-Year-Olds* (Menlo Park, CA: The Henry J. Kaiser Family Foundation Study, publication #8010, 2010), p. 30, http://www.kff.org/entmedia/8010.cfm.

18. "American Time Use Survey—2017 Results," Table 11A, Bureau of Labor Statistics (Washington, DC: U.S. Department of Labor, June 28, 2018), https://www.bls.gov/news.release/atus.nr0.htm/.

19. National Endowment for the Arts, *Results from the Annual Arts Basic Survey (2013–2015)*,(Washington, DC: U.S. Census Bureau, 2016), https://www.arts.gov/artistic-fields/research-analysis/arts-data-profiles/arts-data-profile-10.

20. Maria Stephens, Ebru Erberber, Yemurai Tsokodayi, Teresa Kroeger, and Sharlyn Ferguson, "Is Reading Contagious? Examining Parents' and Children's Reading Attitudes and Behaviors," American Institutes for Research brief. January 2016, https://www.air.org/resource/reading-contagious-examining-parents-and-children-s-reading-attitudes-and-behaviors.

21. Jeanne S. Chall and Vicki A. Jacobs, "The Classic Study on Poor Children's Fourth-Grade Slump," *American Educator* 27, no. 1 (2003), http://www.aft.org/newspubs/periodicals/ae/spring2003/hirschsb classic.cfm.

22. Gordon Rattray Taylor, *The Natural History of the Mind* (New York: Dutton, 1979), 59–60.

23. Neil Gaiman, BrainyQuote.com.

24. Keith E. Stanovich, "Matthew Effects in Reading: Some Consequences of Individual Differences in the Acquisition of Literacy," *Reading Research Quarterly* 21, no. 4 (Fall 1986): 360–407; Richard

Anderson, Linda Fielding, and Paul Wilson, "Growth in Reading and How Children Spend Their Time Outside of School," *Reading Research Quarterly* 23, no. 3 (Summer 1988): 285–303; Richard L. Allington, "Oral Reading," in *Handbook of Reading Research*, P. David Pearson, ed. (New York: Longman, 1984), 829–64; Warwick B. Elley and Francis Mangubhai, "The Impact of Reading on Second Language Learning," Reading *Research Quarterly* 19, no. 1 (Fall 1983): 53–67; Chase Young, Corinne Valadez, Cori Gandara, "Using Performance Methods to Enhance Students' Reading Fluency," *Journal of Educational Research* 109 no. 6 (November 2016): 624–30.

25. Stanovich, "Matthew Effects in Reading."; Anderson, Fielding, and Wilson, "Growth in Reading."

26. *The Nation's Report Card: 2015 Reading Assessment,* Institute of Education Sciences, U.S. Department of Education, fourth-grade results, https://www.nationsreportcard.gov/reading_math_2015/#reading /groups?grade=4.

27. *The Nation's Report Card*, eighth-grade results, https://www.nations reportcard.gov/reading_math_2015/#reading/groups?grade=8.

28. Elley, *How in the World Do Students Read?*

29. Ina V. S. Mullis, Michael O. Martin, Eugenio J. Gonzalez, and Ann M. Kennedy, *PIRLS 2001 International Report: IEA's Study of Reading Literacy Achievement in Primary School in 35 Countries* (Chestnut Hill, MA: International Association for the Evaluation of Educational Achievement/International Study Center, Boston College, 2003), 95.

30. Kristen Denton and Jerry West, *Children's Reading and Mathematics Achievement in Kindergarten and First Grade* (Washington, DC: U.S. Department of Education, National Center for Education Statistics, 2002), pp. 16, 20, https://nces.ed.gov/pubs2002/2002125.pdf.

31. Allan Wigfield, Jessica R. Gladstone, and Laura Turci, "Beyond Cognition: Reading Motivation and Reading Comprehension," *Child Development Perspectives* 10, no. 3 (September 2016): 190–95.

32. Wigfield et al.

33. Kristen D. Ritchey, Kimberly Palombo, Rebecca D. Silverman, and Deborah L. Speece, "Effects of an Informational Text Reading Comprehension Intervention for Fifth-Grade Students," *Learning Disability Quarterly* 40, no. 2 (May 2017): 68–80.

34. Sam Dillon, "Schools Cut Back Subjects to Push Reading and Math," *New York Times*, March 26, 2006.

35. Jerry West, Kristin Denton, and Elvira Germino-Hausken, *America's Kindergartners: Findings from the Early Childhood Longitudinal Study, Kindergarten Class of 1998–99, Fall 1998*, National Center for Education Statistics NCES 2000-070 (Washington, DC: U.S. Department of Education, 2000). The narrow background knowledge of the poor is explored movingly by Samuel G. Freedman as he follows a group of former inmates, now group-home residents, on a trip to a bookstore, a first-time experience for many; see Samuel G. Freedman, "Tasting

Freedom's Simple Joys in the Barnes & Noble," *New York Times*, August 2, 2006, https://www.nytimes.com/2006/08/04/learning/featuredarticle/20060804friday.html.

36. David Snowdon, *Aging with Grace: What the Nun Study Teaches Us About Leading Longer, Healthier, and More Meaningful Lives* (New York: Bantam, 2001), 117–18; and Kathryn P. Riley, David A. Snowdon, Mark F. Desrosiers, and William R. Markesbery, "Early Life Linguistic Ability, Late Life Cognitive Function, and Neuropathology: Findings from the Nun Study," *Neurobiology of Aging* 26, no. 3 (March 2005): 341–47. See also Pam Belluck, "Nuns Offer Clues to Alzheimer's and Aging," *New York Times*, May 7, 2001.

Chapter 2: When to Begin (and End) Read-Aloud

1. E. B. White, *Charlotte's Web,* Harper & Brothers, 1952.
2. Quote by Laura Bush appeared in a U.S. Department of Education document, "Helping Your Child Become a Reader," p. 5, 2005.
3. *Kids & Family Reading Report*, Scholastic, 2016, http://www.scholastic.com/readingreport/reading-aloud.htm.
4. Megan McCoy Dellecese, "The Benefits of Reading to Your Unborn Child, March 2018, https://www.greenchildmagazine.com/reading-to-unborn-baby/.
5. "Study Shows Language Developments Starts in the Womb," *KU Today* (University of Kansas), https://news.ku.edu/2017/07/13/study-shows-language-development-starts-womb.
6. Jeanne W. Holland, "Reading Aloud with Infants: The Controversy, the Myth, and a Case Study," *Early Childhood Education Journal* 35, no. 4 (September 2007): 383–85, https://link.springer.com/article/10.1007%2Fs10643-007-0203-6.
7. Alice Sterling Honig and Meera Shin, "Read Aloud with Infants and Toddlers in Child Care Settings: An Observational Study, *Early Childhood Education Journal* 28, no. 3 (September 2001): 193–97.
8. Andrew Biemiller, "Oral Comprehension Sets the Ceiling on Reading Comprehension," *American Educator* 27, no. 1 (Spring 2003), http://www.aft.org/newspubs/periodicals/ae/spring2003/hirschsboral.cfm.
9. Nell K. Duke, "For the Rich It's Richer: Print Experiences and Environments Offered to Children in Very Low- and Very High-Socioeconomic Status First-Grade Classrooms," *American Educational Research Journal* 37, no. 2 (2000): 441–78.
10. Dominic W. Massaro, "Two Different Communication Genres and Implications for Vocabulary Development and Learning to Read," *Journal of Literacy Research* 47, no. 4 (2015), https://doi.org/10.1177%2F1086296X15627528.
11. Alice Ozma, *The Reading Promise: My Father and the Books We Shared* (New York: Grand Central Publishing, 2011). You can find book recommendations for creating your own streak at Ozma's website,

http://www.makeareadingpromise.com/streak.html. See also Michael Winerip, "A Father-Daughter Bond, Page by Page," *New York Times*, March 21, 2010; and "Father-Daughter Reading Streak Lasts Nearly 9 Years," *Weekend Edition Saturday*, National Public Radio, June 18, 2011, http://www.npr.org/2011/06/18/137223191/father-daughter-reading-streak-lasts-nearly-9-years.

12. Debi Silverman, "Reading Tips for Children with Special Needs," posted September 16, 2011, http://www.first5coco.org/blog/2011/09/16/reading-tips-for-children-with-special-needs/.

13. Jerome Kagan, "The Child: His Struggle for Identity," *Saturday Review* 51 (December 1968): 82. See also Steven R. Tulkin and Jerome Kagan, "Mother-Child Interaction in the First Year of Life," *Child Development* 43, no. 1 (March 1972): 31–41.

14. Further examples of "concept-attention span" can be found in Kagan, "The Child: His Struggle for Identity," p. 82.

15. Norman Herr, "Internet Resources to Accompany *The Sourcebook for Teaching Science*: Television and Health," California State University, Northridge, http://www.csun.edu/science/health/docs/tv&health.html.

16. National Center for Education Statistics, "Home Literacy Activities with Young Children," chapter 1, section Preprimary Education, in *The Condition of Education*, (Washington, DC: U.S. Department of Education), accessed September 9, 2018, https://nces.ed.gov/programs/coe/pdf/coe_sfa.pdf.

17. *Kids & Family Reading Report*, Scholastic, 201,. http://www.scholastic.com/readingreport/reading-aloud.htm.

18. *Kids & Family Reading Report*.

19. Biemiller, "Oral Comprehension." See also Thomas G. Devine, "Listening: What Do We Know After Fifty Years of Research and Theorizing?" *Journal of Reading* 21, no. 4 (January 1978): 296–304.

20. The original dust jacket copy for *The Cat in the Hat* included the words "Many children . . . will discover for the first time that they don't need to be read to anymore," as noted in Judith and Neil Morgan's *Dr. Seuss and Mr. Geisel* (New York: Random House, 1995), 155.

21. Elissa Gershowitz, "An Interview with Kate DiCamillo," *Horn Book Magazine*, 91, no. 6 (November/December 2015): 15.

22. David Denby, "Do Teens Read Seriously Anymore?" *New Yorker*, February 23, 2016, https://www.newyorker.com/culture/cultural-comment/books-smell-like-old-people-the-decline-of-teen-reading.

Chapter 3: The Stages of Read-Aloud

1. Judith Viorst, *Alexander and the Terrible, Horrible, No Good, Very Bad Day* (New York: Aladdin, 1972).

2. "Three Core Concepts in Early Development," three-part video series, Center on the Developing Child, Harvard University, and

the National Scientific Council on the Developing Child, 2011, https://developingchild.harvard.edu/resources/three-core-concepts -in-early-development/.

3. "Early Childhood Adversity, Toxic Stress, and the Role of the Pediatrician: Translating Developmental Science into Lifelong Health," policy statement from the American Academy of Pediatrics, January 2012, http://pediatrics.aappublications.org/content/129/1/e224. See also Nicholas D. Kristof, "A Poverty Solution That Starts with a Hug," op-ed, *New York Times* Sunday Review, January 7, 2012; L. Alan Sroufe, "Ritalin Gone Wrong," *New York Times* Sunday Review, January 29, 2012; Paul Tough, "The Poverty Clinic," *New Yorker*, March 21, 2011, 25–32.

4. Dr. Shonkoff's lecture video on this subject for the state of Washington in 2010, "Leveraging an Integrated Science of Development to Strengthen the Foundations of Health, Learning, and Behavior," can be found online at https://www.youtube.com/watch?v=Dwy8 UWx2_UE.

5. Peter W. Jusczyk and Elizabeth A. Hohne, "Infants' Memory for Spoken Words," *Science* 277, no. 5334 (September 26, 1997): 1984–85.

6. National Institutes of Health, "How Does Reading Work?" (Washington, DC: U.S. Department of Health and Human Services), https://www .nichd.nih.gov/health/topics/reading/conditioninfo/work.

7. "The Experience of Touch: Research Points to a Critical Role," *New York Times* Science Times, February 2, 1988.

8. Jessica S. Horst, Kelly L. Parsons, and Natasha M. Bryan, "Get the Story Straight: Contextual Repetition Promotes Word Learning from Storybooks," *Frontiers in Psychology* 2 (2011), https://www .ncbi.nlm.nih.gov/pmc/articles/PMC3111254/.

9. Foertsch, *Reading In and Out of School*.

10. Anderson, Fielding, and Wilson, "Growth in Reading."

11. Robertson Davies, *One Half of Robertson Davies* (New York: Viking, 1977), 1.

12. Linda Jacobson, "Teachers Find Many Reasons to Use Picture Books with Middle and High School Students," *School Library Journal* (September 9, 2015), https://www.slj.com/2015/09/books-media /teachers-find-many-reasons-to-use-picture-books-with-middle-and -high-school-students/.

13. Nancy Pearl, *Book Lust: Recommended Reading for Every Mood, Moment, and Reason* (Seattle: Sasquatch Books, 2003); and Nancy Pearl, *More Book Lust: Recommended Reading for Every Mood, Moment, and Reason* (Seattle: Sasquatch Books, 2005).

14. Personal email correspondence.

15. Personal email correspondence.

Chapter 4: Sustained Silent Reading and Reading for Pleasure

1. Roald Dahl, *Matilda (New York:* Puffin, 1998).
2. National Reading Panel report, *Teaching Children to Read: An Evidence-Based Assessment of the Scientific Research Literature on Reading and Its Implications for Reading Instruction—the Summary Report* (Washington, DC: National Institute of Child Health and Human Development, NIH, Publication 00-4754, 2000), p. 13, https://files.eric .ed.gov/fulltext/ED444126.pdf.
3. The NRP's own scientific standards have come under severe attack since the report was issued, the most notable being Steven L. Strauss, "Challenging the NICHD Reading Research Agenda," *Phi Delta Kappan* 84, no. 6 (February 2003): 438–42. See also Joanne Yatvin, "Babes in the Woods: The Wanderings of the National Reading Panel," *Phi Delta Kappan* 83, no. 5 (January 2002): 364–69; and James Cunningham, "The National Reading Panel Report," *Reading Research Quarterly* 36, no. 3 (2001): 326–35.
4. Stephen Krashen, "More Smoke and Mirrors: A Critique of the National Reading Panel Report on Fluency," *Phi Delta Kappan* 83, no. 2 (October 2001): 119–23. See also Stephen Krashen, "Is In-School Free Reading Good for Children? Why the National Reading Panel Report Is (Still) Wrong," *Phi Delta Kappan* 86, no. 6 (February 2005): 444–47; Cunningham, "The National Reading Panel Report"; Elaine M. Garan, *Resisting Reading Mandates: How to Triumph with the Truth* (Portsmouth, NH: Heinemann, 2002), 22–24; Stephen Krashen, *Free Voluntary Reading* (Santa Barbara, CA: Libraries Unlimited, 2011); and Elfrieda H. Hiebert and D. Ray Reutzel, eds., *Revisiting Silent Reading: New Directions for Teachers and Researchers* (Newark, DE: International Reading Association, 2010).
5. Stanovich, "Matthew Effects in Reading." See also Richard L. Allington, "Oral Reading," in *Handbook of Reading Research*, P. David Pearson, ed. (New York: Longman, 1984), 829–64; Elley and Mangubhai, "The Impact of Reading on Second Language Learning"; and Foertsch, *Reading In and Out of School*.
6. Irwin Kirsch, John de Jong, Dominique Lafontaine, Joy McQueen, Juliette Mendelovits, and Christian Monseur, *Reading for Change: Performance and Engagement Across Countries—Results from PISA 2000* (Paris: Organisation for Economic Co-operation and Development, 2002), http://www.oecd.org/dataoecd/43/54/33690904.pdf.
7. Warwick Elley, *How in the World Do Students Read?* (Hamburg: International Association for the Evaluation of Educational Achievement, July 1992).
8. Patricia L. Donahue, Kristin E. Voelki, Jay R. Campbell, and John Mazzeo, *NAEP 1998 Reading Report Card for the Nation and the States* (Washington, DC: U.S. Department of Education, Office of Educational Research and Improvement, National Center for Education Statistics, 1999). See also Ina V. S. Mullis, John A. Dossey, Jay R.

Campbell, Claudia A. Gentile, Christine O'Sullivan, and Andrew S. Latham, *NAEP 1992 Trends in Academic Progress* (Princeton, NJ: Educational Testing Service and Washington, DC: Office of Educational Research and Improvement, July 1994, http://www.eric.ed .gov/PDFS/ED378237.pdf; also found in *The Family: America's Smallest School* (Princeton, NJ: Educational Testing Service, 1992), https://www.ets.org/Media/Education_Topics/pdf/5678_PER CReport_School.pdf.

9. Sarah Knutson, "Statistics on the Scores of Middle School Students Who Read," *Classroom*, September 26, 2017, https://classroom.syn onym.com/statistics-scores-middle-school-students-read-15916 .html.

10. D. Ray Reutzel and Stephanie Juth, "Supporting the Development of Silent Reading Fluency: An Evidence-Based Framework for the Intermediate Grades (3–6)," *International Electronic Journal of Elementary Education*, 7, no. 1 (October 2014): 27–46.

11. Nancie Atwell, *The Reading Zone: How to Help Kids Become Skilled, Passionate, Habitual, Critical Readers* (New York: Scholastic, 2007), 107.

12. Richard Allington, "If They Don't Read Much, How They Gonna Get Good?" *Journal of Reading* 21 (1977): 57–61.

13. Anderson, Fielding, and Wilson, "Growth in Reading," p. 152.

14. Timothy A. Keller and Marcel Adam Just, "Altering Cortical Connectivity: Remediation-Induced Changes in the White Matter of Poor Readers," *Neuron* 64, no. 5 (2009): 624–31. See also Jon Hamilton, "Reading Practice Can Strengthen Brain 'Highways,'" *All Things Considered*, National Public Radio, December 9, 2009, http://www.npr.org/templates/story/story.php?storyId=121253104.

15. Elfrieda H. Hiebert and D. Ray Reutzel, eds., *Revisiting Silent Reading: New Directions for Teachers and Researchers* (Newark, DE: International Reading Association, 2010).

16. Several research studies over the years have made the claim that children are not actually reading during SSR. Sonya Lee-Daniels and Bruce Murray, "DEAR Me: What Does It Take to Get Children Reading?" *Reading Teacher* 54, no. 2 (October 2000): 15455. Jodi Crum Marshall, *Are They Really Reading? Expanding SSR in the Middle Grades* (Portland, Maine: Stenhouse Publishers, 2002); and Michelle Kelley and Nicki Clausen-Grace, "R^5: The Sustained Silent Reading Makeover That Transformed Readers," *Reading Teacher* 60, no. 2 (October 2006): 148–56.

17. Stephen Krashen, "Non-Engagement in Sustained Silent Reading: How Extensive Is It? What Can It Teach Us?" *Colorado Reading Council Journal* vol. 22 (2011): 5-10.

18. Krashen, "Non-Engagement in Sustained Silent Reading."

19. Krashen, *The Power of Reading: Insights from the Research* (Westport, CT: Libraries Unlimited, 1993).

20. Barbara Heyns, *Summer Learning and the Effects of Schooling* (New York: Academic Press, 1978). See also Doris R. Entwisle and Karl L. Alexander, "Summer Setback: Race, Poverty, School Composition, and Mathematics Achievement in the First Two Years of School," *American Sociological Review* 57, no. 1 (February 1992): 72–84; Barbara Heyns, "Schooling and Cognitive Development: Is There a Season for Learning?" *Child Development* 58, no. 5 (October 1987): 1151–60; Larry J. Mikulecky, "Stopping Summer Learning Loss Among At-Risk Youth," *Journal of Reading* 33, no. 7 (April 1990): 516–21; Harris Cooper, Barbara Nye, Kelly Charlton, James Lindsay, and Scott Greathouse, "The Effects of Summer Vacation on Achievement Test Scores: A Narrative and Meta-Analytic Review," *Review of Educational Research* 66, no. 3 (September 1996): 227–68; Richard L. Allington and Anne McGill-Franzen, "The Impact of Summer Setback on the Reading Achievement Gap," *Phi Delta Kappan* 85, no. 1 (September 2003): 68–75; Richard L. Allington, Anne McGill-Franzen, Gregory Camilli, Lunetta Williams, Jennifer Graff, Jacqueline Zeig, Courtney Zmach, and Rhonda Nowak, "Addressing Summer Reading Setback Among Economically Disadvantaged Elementary Students," *Reading Psychology* 31, no. 5 (2010): 1–17; Richard Allington and Anne McGill-Franzen, "Got Books?" *Educational Leadership* 65, no. 7 (April 2008): 20–23; James S. Kim and Thomas G. White, "Teacher and Parent Scaffolding of Voluntary Summer Reading," *Reading Teacher* 62, no. 2 (October 2008): 116–25. The "summer slide" was explored by American RadioWorks (American Public Media) in its podcast of May 27, 2011, http://download.publicradio.org/podcast/americanradioworks/podcast/arw_4_48_summerslide.mp3.
21. Collaborative Summer Library Program Summer Reading White Paper, December 29, 2014, https://cde.state.co.us/cdelib/summerslide.
22. Ariel Goldberg, "What Summer Slide Actually Means—and 5 Ways to Fight It," July 12, 2018, accessed September 18, 2018, https://www.edsurge.com/news/2018-07-12-what-summer-slide-actually-means-and-5-ways-to-fight-it.
23. Jimmy Kim, "Summer Reading and the Ethnic Achievement Gap," *Journal of Education for Students Placed at Risk* 9, no. 2 (2004): 169–88. See also Debra Viadero, "Reading Books Is Found to Ward Off 'Summer Slump,'" *Education Week*, May 5, 2004.
24. Jay R. Campbell, Catherine M. Hombo, and John Mazzeo, *NAEP 1999 Trends in Academic Progress: Three Decades of Student Performance*, U.S. Department of Education (Washington, DC: National Center for Education Statistics, 2000), http://nces.ed.gov/nationsreportcard/pubs/main1999/2000469.asp. For international comparison, see Kirsch et al., *Reading for Change*.
25. Nancy Padak and Timothy Rasinski, "Is Being Wild About Harry Enough? Encouraging Independent Reading at Home," *Reading Teacher* 61, no. 4 (December/January 2007): 350–53.

26. *Kids & Family Reading Report*, Scholastic, 2016.
27. National Endowment for the Arts, "Results from the Annual Arts Basic Survey, August 2016, https://www.arts.gov/artistic-fields/research-analysis/arts-data-profiles/arts-data-profile-10.
28. Stephen Krashen, "Does Accelerated Reader Work?" *Journal of Children's Literature* 29, no. 2 (2003): 16–30, http://www.sdkrashen.com/content/articles/does_accelerated_reader_work.pdf. See also Krashen, *Free Voluntary Reading*, pp. 45–52; and Steven Ross, John Nunnery, and Elizabeth Goldfeder, "A Randomized Experiment on the Effects of Accelerated Reader/Reading Renaissance in an Urban School District: Preliminary Evaluation Report" (Memphis, TN: University of Memphis, Center for Research in Educational Policy, 2004), http://doc.renlearn.com/KMNet/R004076723GH55D8.pdf; and John Nunnery and Steven Ross, "The Effects of the School Renaissance Program on Student Achievement in Reading and Mathematics," *Research in the Schools* 14, no. 1 (Spring 2007): 40–59.
29. Susan Straight, "Reading by the Numbers," *New York Times Book Review*, August 30, 2009.
30. Blaine Greteman, "Federal Bureaucrats Declare 'Hunger Games' More Complex Than 'The Grapes of Wrath,'" *New Republic*, October 29, 2013, https://newrepublic.com/article/115393/common-core-standards-make-mockery-novels-complexity.
31. Donalynn Miller, "Guess My Lexile," *Education Week Teacher*, July 25, 2012, http://blogs.edweek.org/teachers/book_whisperer/2012/07/guess_my_lexile.html.
32. Nancy J. Johnson and Cyndi Giorgis, *The Wonder of It All: When Literature and Literacy Intersect* (Portsmouth, NH: Heinemann, 2007).
33. G. Robert Carlsen and Anne Sherrill, *Voices of Readers: How We Come to Love Books* (Urbana, IL: National Council of Teachers of English, 1988); and Krashen, *The Power of Reading*, pp. 91–110.
34. D. T. Max, "The Oprah Effect," *New York Times Magazine*, December 26, 1999.
35. Lawrence and Nancy Goldstone, *Deconstructing Penguins: Parents, Kids, and the Bond of Reading* (New York City, NY: Ballantine Books, 2005), 191.

Chapter 5: The Importance of Fathers

1. Soosh, *Dad by My Side* (New York: Little, Brown Books for Young Readers, 2018).
2. Tom Loveless, *The 2015 Brown Center Report on American Education: How Well Are American Students Learning*, Part 1: Girls, Boys, and Reading (Brown Center on Education Policy at Brookings Institute, 2015), https://www.brookings.edu/research/2015-brown-center-report-on-american-education-how-well-are-american-students-learning/.

3. I. V. S. Mullis, M. O. Martin, P. Foy, M. Hooper, *PIRLS 2016 International Results in Reading*, "Trends in Reading Achievement by Gender," retrieved from Boston College, TIMSS & PIRLS International Study Center website, http://timssandpirls.bc.edu/pirls2016 /international-results/pirls/student-achievement/trends-in -reading-achievement-by-gender/.

4. Organisation for Economic Co-operation and Development (OECD), Reading performance (PISA) (indicator), 2018, doi: 10.1787/79913c69-en (accessed on September 11, 2018), https:// data.oecd.org/pisa/reading-performance-pisa.htm.

5. Kids & Family Reading Report, 5th ed., Scholastic, 2016, https:// www.scholastic.com/readingreport/past-reports.html.

6. Applerouth.com, "Troubling Gender Gaps in Education," by Jed Applerouth, posted August 15, 2017, https://www.applerouth.com /blog/2017/08/15/troubling-gender-gaps-in-education/.

7. Lester Holt, "Men Falling Behind Women," *NBC News* report, "America at the Crossroads," March 5, 2011, reported that 70 percent of high school valedictorians were female. http://www.nbc news.com/id/41928806/ns/business-us_business/t/men-falling -behind-women/#.W5gDl-hKg2x; and David Kohn, "The Gender Gap: Boys Lagging," *60 Minutes*, October 31, 2002, http://www .cbsnews.com/stories/2002/10/31/60minutes/main527678.shtml. See also Kevin Wack and Beth Quimby, "Boys in Jeopardy at School," *Portland Press Herald*, March 18, 2010.

8. National Center for Education Statistics, Fast Facts, https://nces.ed .gov/fastfacts/display.asp?id=98.

9. Tom Chiarella, "The Problem with Boys . . . Is Actually a Problem with Men," *Esquire*, July 1, 2006, https://www.esquire.com/features /ESQ0706SOTAMBOYS_94.

10. Jay Mathews, "Are Boys Really in Trouble?" *Washington Post*, June 27, 2006, https://www.washingtonpost.com/archive/business/tech nology/2006/06/27/are-boys-really-in-trouble/6749464c-4e64 -4149-8f3d-7123310ee399/?utm_term=.6982fe3008ca.

11. Wack and Quimby, "Boys in Jeopardy at School," *Portland Press Herald*, March 26, 2006.

12. "Closing the Literacy Gender Gap: Top Tips for Motivating Boys to Read," April 17, 2017, https://www.lexialearning.com/blog/closing -literacy-gender-gap-top-tips-motivating-boys-read.

13. Nola Alloway, "Swimming Against the Tide: Boys, Literacies, and Schooling," *Canadian Journal of Education* 30, no. 2 (Fall 2007): 582–605.

14. Frank Furedi, "Let's Scotch the Myth That Boys Don't Read," *The Telegraph*, October 24, 2015, https://www.telegraph.co.uk/education /educationopinion/11948122/Lets-scotch-the-myth-that-boys -dont-read.html?fb_ref=Default.

15. Matt de la Peña, "2016 Newbery Acceptance," *Horn Book Magazine* 92, no. 4 (July/August 2016): 56–64, https://www.hbook.com

/2016/06/news/awards/2016-newbery-acceptance-by-matt-de
-la-pena/.

16. Frank Serafini, "Supporting Boys as Readers," *Reading Teacher* 67, no. 1 (September 2003): 40–42.

17. Christina Clark, *Why Fathers Matter to Their Children's Literacy* (London: National Literacy Trust, June 2009).

18. Anna Sarkadi, Robert Kristiansson, Frank Oberklaid, and Sven Bremberg, "Fathers' Involvement and Children's Developmental Outcomes: A Systematic Review of Longitudinal Studies," *Acta Paediatrica* 97, no. 2 (February 2008): 153–58. See also Joseph H. Pleck and Brian P. Masciadrelli,"Paternal Involvement by U.S. Residential Fathers: Levels, Sources, and Consequences," in M. E. Lamb, ed., *The Role of the Father in Child Development*, 4th ed. (Hoboken, NJ: John Wiley & Sons, 2004).

19. Darcy Hango, "Parental Investment in Childhood and Educational Qualifications: Can Greater Parental Involvement Mediate the Effects of Socioeconomic Disadvantage," *Social Science Research* 36, no. 4 (2007): 1371–90.

20. Linda Jacobson, "Why Boys Don't Read," GreatSchools, December 2, 2018, https://www.greatschools.org/gk/articles/why-so-many
-boys-do-not-read/.

21. Diane Karther, "Fathers with Low Literacy and Their Young Children, *Reading Teacher* 56, no. 2 (2002), 184–93.

22. Rob Kemp, "Five Reasons Why Dads Should Read to Their Children More," *The Telegraph*, September 26, 2015, https://www.telegraph
.co.uk/men/fatherhood/five-reasons-why-dads-should-read-to-their
-children-more/.

23. Kemp, "Five Reasons."

24. Elisabeth Duursma, "The Effects of Fathers' and Mothers' Reading to Their Children on Language Outcomes of Children Participating in Early Head Start in the United States," *Fathering* 12, no. 3 (December 2014): 283–302.

25. United Through Reading, www.unitedthroughreading.org.

26. Sharon Tylor, "Dads and Kids Reunite by Turning Pages Together," Baltimore County News, June 14, 2017, https://www.baltimore
countymd.gov/News/BaltimoreCountyNow/dads-and-kids
-reunite-by-turning-pages-together.

27. Rob Kemp, "How Imprisoned Dads are Using Bedtime Stories to Connect with Their Kids," *The Telegraph*, April 21, 2015, https://
www.telegraph.co.uk/men/relationships/fatherhood/11549551
/How-imprisoned-dads-are-using-bedtime-stories-to-connect
-with-their-kids.html.

28. Clyde C. Robinson, Jean M. Larsen, and Julia H. Haupt, "Picture Book Reading at Home: A Comparison of Head Start and Middle-Class Preschoolers," *Early Education and Development* 6, no. 3 (1995): 241–52.

29. Janelle M. Gray, "Reading Achievement and Autonomy as a Function of Father-to-Son Reading" (master's thesis, California State

University, Stanislaus, CA, 1991). See also the study of thirty men from blue-collar families. Half stayed blue-collar when they grew up, and the other half became college professors; fathering made the difference: Virginia Olga Beattie Emery and Mihaly Csikszentmihalyi, "The Socialization Effects of Cultural Role Models in Ontogenetic Development and Upward Mobility," *Child Psychiatry and Human Development* 12, no. 1 (February 1981): 3–18.

30. David Lubar, "Kid Appeal," quoted from Jon Scieszka, ed., *Guys Read: Funny Business* (New York: Walden Pond Press, 2010).

Chapter 6: The Print Climate in the Home, School, and Library

1. Pat Mora, *Tomás and the Library Lady* (New York: Knopf, 1997).
2. Every Student Succeeds Act (ESSA), U.S. Department of Education, https://www.ed.gov/essa.
3. David E. Sanger, "The Price of Lost Chances" *New York Times* special section "The Reckoning: America and the World a Decade after 9/11," September 11, 2011.
4. Susan B. Neuman and Donna Celano, "Access to Print in Low-Income and Middle-Income Communities: An Ecological Study of Four Neighborhoods," *Reading Research Quarterly*, no. 1 (January 2001): 8–26; and Susan B. Neuman, Donna C. Celano, Albert N. Greco, and Pamela Shue, *Access for All: Closing the Book Gap for Children in Early Education* (Newark, DE: International Reading Association, 2001).
5. Nell K. Duke, "For the Rich It's Richer: Print Experiences and Environments Offered to Children in Very Low- and Very High-Socioeconomic Status First-Grade," *American Educational Research Journal* 37, no. 2 (June 2000): 441–78.
6. Krashen, *The Power of Reading*. See also Stephen Krashen, "Our Schools Are Not Broken: The Problem Is Poverty," commencement address, Lewis and Clark Graduate School of Education and Counseling, Portland, OR, June 5, 2011; video for the speech, http://graduate.lclark.edu/live/news/12363-commencement-speaker-stephen-krashen-questions.
7. Richard Allington, Sherry Guice, Kim Baker, Nancy Michaelson, and Shouming Li, "Access to Books: Variations in Schools and Classrooms," *Language and Literacy Spectrum* 5 (Spring 1995): 23–25. Also Richard L. Allington and Sherry Guice, "Something to Read: Putting Books in Their Desks, Backpacks, and Bedrooms," in Phillip Dreyer, ed., *Vision and Realities in Literacy: Sixtieth Yearbook of the Claremont Reading Conference* (Claremont, CA: Claremont Reading Conference, 1996), 5.
8. Keith Curry Lance, Marcia J. Rodney, and Christine Hamilton-Pennell, *How School Librarians Help Kids Achieve Standards: The Second Colorado Study* (Denver: Colorado State Library, Colorado

Department of Education, 2000); Keith Curry Lance, Lynda Welborn, and Christine Hamilton-Pennell, *The Impact of School Media Centers on Academic Achievement* (Denver: Colorado Department of Education, 1992). See also Christine Hamilton-Pennell, Keith Curry Lance, Marcia J. Rodney, and Eugene Hainer, "Dick and Jane Go to the Head of the Class," *School Library Journal* 46, no. 4 (April 2000): 44–47.

9. Sarah Sullivan, Bonnie Nichols, Tom Bradshaw, and Kelli Rogowski, *To Read or Not to Read: A Question of National Consequence*, Research Report No. 47 (Washington. DC: National Endowment for the Arts, 2007), 72–74, https://www.arts.gov/sites/default/files/ToRead.pdf. See also Campbell, Hombo, and Mazzeo, *NAEP 1999 Trends in Academic Progress.*

10. Ina V. S. Mullis, Michael O. Martin, Pierre Foy, and Martin Hooper, *PIRLS 2016 International Results in Reading*, retrieved from Boston College, TIMSS & PIRLS International Study Center website, http://timssandpirls.bc.edu/pirls2016/international-results/.

11. M. D. R. Evans, Jonathan Kelley, and Joanna Sikora, "Scholarly Culture and Academic Performance in 42 Nations," *Social Forces* 92, no. 4 (June 2014): 1573–605.

12. James C. Baughman, "School Libraries and MCAS Scores," paper presented at a symposium sponsored by the Graduate School of Library and Information Science, Simmons College, Boston, MA, October 26, 2000, http://web.simmons.edu/~baughman/mcas-school-libraries/. Another study found "access to books in school and public libraries was a significant predictor of 2007 fourth-grade NAEP reading scores, as well as the difference between grade 4 and grade 8 2007 NAEP reading scores": Stephen Krashen, Syying Lee, and Jeff McQuillan, "Is the Library Important? Multivariate Studies at the National and International Level," *Journal of Language and Literacy Education* 8, no. 1 (Spring 2012): 26–38, http://jolle.coe.uga.edu/wp-content/uploads/2012/06/Is-the-Library-Important.pdf.

13. David M. Quinn and Morgan Polikoff, "Summer Learning Loss: What Is It, and What Can We Do About It?" report, Brookings Institute, September 14, 2017, https://www.brookings.edu/research/summer-learning-loss-what-is-it-and-what-can-we-do-about-it.

14. Allington et al., "Addressing Summer Reading Setback." See also Allington and McGill-Franzen, "Got Books?" pp. 20–23; Cooper et al., "The Effects of Summer Vacation on Achievement Test Scores"; and Kim and White, "Teacher and Parent Scaffolding of Voluntary Summer Reading." The "summer slide" was explored by American RadioWorks (American Public Media) in its podcast of May 27, 2011, http://download.publicradio.org/podcast/american radioworks/podcast/arw_4_48_summerslide.mp3.

15. Newspapers Fact Sheet, Pew Research Center, June 13, 2018, http://www.journalism.org/fact-sheet/newspapers/.

16. Sara Guaglione, "Visitors to 'Reader's Digest' Site Soar 179% Year-to-Year," *Publishers Daily*, March 28, 2018, https://www.mediapost.com /publications/article/316756/visitors-to-readers-digest-site-soar-179 -year-.html.

17. Noam Cohen, "The Final Bell Rings for *Weekly Reader*, a Classroom Staple," *Media Decoder* (blog), *New York Times*, July 24, 2012, http:// mediadecoder.blogs.nytimes.com/2012/07/24/the-final-bell-rings -for-weekly-reader-a-classroom-staple/.

18. David Carr, "The Lonely Newspaper Reader," *New York Times*, January 1, 2007, http://www.nytimes.com/2007/01/01/business/media /01carr.html.

19. Jeffrey Gottfried and Elisa Shearer, "Americans Online News Use Is Closing In on TV News Use," Pew Research Center, Fact Tank, September 7, 2017, http://www.pewresearch.org/fact-tank/2017/09 /07/americans-online-news-use-vs-tv-news-use/.

20. Ted Widmer, "Lincoln's Other Mother," *Opinionator* (blog), *New York Times*, January 29, 2011, http://opinionator.blogs.nytimes .com/2011/01/29/lincolns-other-mother/. Widmer is a former speechwriter for President Bill Clinton and director and librarian of the John Carter Brown Library at Brown University. His essay details Lincoln's eighteen-hour journey to say goodbye to his stepmother before departing for Washington to begin his first term as president. Four years after his assassination, she was buried in an unmarked grave in the black dress he brought her on that farewell visit. Fifty-five years later a local Lions Club put a marker on the grave, something Widmer noted was more than due—"for if Lincoln saved the Union, she saved him, and for that alone she's entitled to a decent respect. Measured by the usual yardsticks of wealth and distinction, her own life may not have made much of a dent in the historical record. But at just the right moment, she encountered a small motherless boy, and helped him to become Abraham Lincoln."

21. M. D. R. Evans, Jonathan Kelley, Joanna Sikora, and Donald J. Treiman, "Family Scholarly Culture and Educational Success: Books and Schooling in 27 Nations," *Research in Social Stratification and Mobility* 28, no. 2 (June 2010): 171–97. This study was published in 2010 and then updated in 2014 to include 42 nations.

22. Selamawit Tadesse and Patsy Washington, "Book Ownership and Young Children's Learning," *Childhood Education* 89, no. 3 (April 2013): 165–72.

23. Sadie Trombetta, "7 Reasons Why Libraries Are Essential, Now More Than Ever," *Bustle*, March 20, 2017, https://www.bustle.com /p/7-reasons-libraries-are-essential-now-more-than-ever -43901.

24. Kendra Ralston, "Live Chat with Author Gary Paulsen," transcript of an IM chat, July 10, 2003, https://www.nypl.org/blog/2016/08 /31/live-chat-author-gary-paulsen.

25. Leo Burnett Worldwide, "Save the Troy Library: Adventures in Reverse Psychology," YouTube video, 2:53, November 15, 2011, https://www.youtube.com/watch?v=nw3zNNO5gX0. See also "Leo Burnett Worldwide Takes Home 23 Awards on the First Day of Cannes," PR Newswire, June 19, 2012, http://www.prnewswire.com /news-releases/leo-burnett-worldwide-takes-home-23-awards -on-the-first-day-of-cannes-159605035.html.

26. Statistics About California School Libraries, California Department of Education, accessed September 5, 2018, https://www.cde.ca.gov/ci /cr/lb/schoollibrstats08.asp.

27. Statistics About California School Libraries.

28. Statistics About California School Libraries.

29. James Ricci, "A Saving Grace in the Face of Our School Library Scandal," *Los Angeles Times Magazine*, November 12, 2000. See also Douglas L. Achterman, "Haves, Halves, and Have-Nots: School Libraries and Student Achievement in California" (PhD diss., University of North Texas, Denton, December 2008), http://digital.library.unt.edu /ark:/67531/metadc9800/.

30. Mike Szymanski, "Are School Libraries Headed Toward Extinction? LAUSD Principals Are Choosing Other Ways to Spend Limited Budgets, but Some Board Members Want to Change That," *LA School Report*, April 16, 2017, http://laschoolreport.com/are-school -libraries-headed-toward-extinction-lausd-principals-are-choosing -other-ways-to-spend-limited-budgets-but-some-board-members -want-to-change-that/.

31. Héctor Tobar, "The Disgraceful Interrogation of L.A. School Librarians," *Los Angeles Times*, May 13, 2011, http://articles.latimes .com/2011/may/13/local/la-me-0513-tobar-20110513.

32. Debra E. Kachel and Keith Curry Lance, "Changing Times: School Librarian Staffing Status." *Teacher Librarian: The Journal for School Library Professionals* 45, no. 4 (April 2018): 14–19.

33. Keith Curry Lance and Debra E. Kachel, "Why School Librarians Matter: What Years of Research Tell Us," *Phi Delta Kappan*, March 26, 2018, https://www.kappanonline.org/lance-kachel-school -librarians-matter-years-research/.

34. Keith Curry Lance and L. Hofschire, "Something to Shout About: New Research Shows That More Librarians Means Higher Reading Scores," *School Library Journal* 57, no. 9 (September 2011): 28–33.

35. National Council of Teachers of English, "Statement on Classroom Libraries," May 31, 2017, http://www2.ncte.org/statement/classroom -libraries/.

36. American Association of School Librarians, "Position Statement on Labeling Books with Reading Levels," accessed September 18, 2018, http://www.ala.org/aasl/advocacy/resources/statements/labeling.

37. David A. Bell, "The Bookless Library," *New Republic*, August 2, 2012, www.tnr.com/article/books-and-arts/magazine/david-bell-future -bookless-library.

38. Seth Godin, "The Future of the Library," *Seth Godin's Blog*, May 16, 2011, http://sethgodin.typepad.com/seths_blog/2011/05/the-future -of-the-library.html.

39. Jason Boog, "eBook Revenues Top Hardcover," *Galleycat* (blog), Mediabistro, June 15, 2012.

40. Barbara Hoffert, "What's Hot Now: Materials Survey 2018," *Library Journal*, February 6, 2018, https://www.libraryjournal.com /?detailStory=whats-hot-now-materials-survey-2018.

41. Paul Fletcher, "Reading Public Still Prefers Printed Books over E-Books," *Forbes*, September 29, 2016, https://www.forbes.com/sites /paulfletcher/2016/09/29/reading-public-still-prefers-printed -books-over-e-books/#d0db11a2a877.

42. David Guion, "What's a Library Without Books? Some Bookless Libraries," May 24, 2017, https://www.allpurposeguru.com/2017/05 /whats-library-without-books.

43. Mark Melchior, "Reintroducing Printed Books to the Cushing Academy Library," Massachusetts School Library Association Forum Newsletter, October 15, 2016, https://www.maschoollibraries .org/forum-newsletter/reintroducing-printed-books-to-the -cushing-academy-library.

44. Melchior, "Reintroducing Printed Books."

45. Julie Bosman, "After 244 Years, *Encyclopaedia Britannica* Stops the Presses," *Media Decoder* (blog), *New York Times*, March 13, 2012, http://mediadecoder.blogs.nytimes.com/2012/03/13/after-244 -years-encyclopaedia-britannica-stops-the-presses/.

46. Jim Giles, "Special Report: Internet Encyclopaedias Go Head to Head," *Nature* 438 (December 15, 2005), https://www.nature.com/ar ticles/438900a. See also Dan Goodin, "'Nature': Wikipedia Is Accurate," Associated Press, *USA Today*, December 14, 2005; and Rebecca J. Rosen, "Does Wikipedia Have an Accuracy Problem?" *The Atlantic*, February 16, 2012, http://www.theatlantic.com/technology/archive /2012/02/does-wikipedia-have-an-accuracy-problem/253216/.

47. Drew DeSilver, "Few Students Likely to Use Print Resources for Research," Pew Research Center, Fact Tank, July 30, 2013, http:// www.pewresearch.org/fact-tank/2013/07/30/few-students -likely-to-use-print-books-for-research/.

48. Bill Keller, "Steal This Column," op-ed, *New York Times*, February 6, 2012.

Chapter 7: The Impact of Electronic Media on Reading

1. Madeleine L'Engle, *A Wrinkle in Time* (New York: Farrar, Straus & Giroux, 1962).

2. Jenny Radesky, *Kids and Digital Media*, May 2017, https://www .mottchildren.org/posts/your-child/kids-and-digital-media.

3. Kaiser Family Foundation, *Daily Media Use Among Children and Teens Up Dramatically from Five Years Ago*, January 20, 2010, https://

www.kff.org/disparities-policy/press-release/daily-media-use
-among-children-and-teens-up-dramatically-from-five-years-ago/.

4. American Academy of Pediatrics, "American Academy of Pediatrics Announces New Recommendations for Children's Media Use," October 21, 2016, https://www.aap.org/en-us/about-the-aap/aap -press-room/Pages/American-Academy-of-Pediatrics-Announces -New-Recommendations-for-Childrens-Media-Use.aspx.

5. Jenny Radesky, "Digital Media and Symptoms of Attention-Deficit/ Hyperactivity Disorder in Adolescents," *Journal of the American Medical Association* 32, no. 3 (July 2018): 237–39.

6. Chaelin K. Ra, Junhan Cho, Matthew D. Stone, et. al., "Association of Digital Media Use with Subsequent Symptoms of Attention-Deficit/Hyperactivity Disorder Among Adolescents," *Journal of the American Medical Association* 320, no. 3 (2018): 255–63.

7. Radesky, "Digital Media."

8. Kelli Anderson, "Teens & Texting: Setting Boundaries," *RN Remedies* (blog), Children's Hospital Los Angeles, https://www.chla .org/blog/rn-remedies/teens-texting-setting-boundaries.

9. Radesky, "Digital Media."

10. Common Sense Media, "Children, Teens, and Reading: A Common Sense Media Research Brief," May 12, 2014.

11. American Academy of Pediatrics.

12. Anya Kamenetz, "American Academy of Pediatrics Lifts 'No Screens Under 2' Rule," October 21, 2016, https://www.npr.org /sections/ed/2016/10/21/498550475/american-academy-of-pediatrics -lifts-no-screens-under-2-rule.

13. Weerasak Chonchaiya and Chandhita Pruksananonda, "Television viewing associates with delayed language development," *Acta Paediatrica* 97, no. 7 (July 2008): 977–82, http://dx.doi.org/10.1111/j.1651 -2227.2008.00831.x.

14. Ling-Yi Lin, Rong-Ju Cherng, Yung-Jung Chen, Yi-Jen Chen, and Hei-Mei Yang, "Effects of Television Exposure on Developmental Skills Among Young Children," *Infant Behavior and Development* 38 (February 2015): 20–26.

15. Kamenetz, "American Academy."

16. World Health Organization, "Obesity and Overweight: Key Facts," February 16, 2018, www.who.int/news-room/fact-sheets/detail /obesity-and-overweight.

17. Kaiser Family Foundation, *Daily Media Use.*

18. Alan L. Mendelsohn, Samantha B. Berkule, Suzy Tomopoulos, Catherine S. Tamis-LeMonda, Harris S. Huberman, Jose Alvir, and Benard P. Dreyer, "Infant Television and Video Exposure Associated with Limited Parent-Child Verbal Interactions in Low Socioeconomic Status Households," *Archives of Pediatrics and Adolescent Medicine* 162, no. 5 (May 2008): 411–17.

19. Dimitri A. Christakis, Frederick J. Zimmerman, David L. DiGiuseppe, and Carolyn A. McCarty, "Early Television Exposure and

Subsequent Attentional Problems in Children," *Pediatrics* 113, no. 4 (April 2004): 708–13, http://pediatrics.aappublications.org/content /113/4/708.short. See also Joseph Shapiro, "Study Links TV, Attention Disorders in Kids," *Morning Edition*, National Public Radio, April 5, 2004, http://www.npr.org/templates/story/story.php?storyId =1812501.

20. Dina L. G. Borzekowski and Thomas N. Robinson, "The Remote, the Mouse, and the No. 2 Pencil," *Archives of Pediatrics and Adolescent Medicine* 159, no. 7 (August 2005): 607–13.

21. Rideout et al., *Generation M2*, 15–16.

22. Rideout et al., *Generation M2*.

23. Elijah Wolfson, "Can TV Help Minority Children Achieve? New Studies Raise Concerns That Low-Income Parents Overvalue Media-Based Education," *Huffington Post* (blog), August 20, 2013, https://www.huffingtonpost.com/elijah-wolfson-/childhood -obesity_b_3455478.html.

24. Wolfson, "Can TV Help?"

25. Stuart Webb and Michael P. H. Rodgers, "Vocabulary Demands of Television Programs," *Language Learning* 59, no. 2 (June 2009): 335–66.

26. Kristina Birdsong, "This Is Your Child's Brain on TV," *Scientific Learning* (blog), March 22, 2016, https://www.scilearn.com/blog /your-childs-brain-tv.

27. National Captioning Institute, "The Educational Value of Reading Captions," www.ncicap.org/viewer-resources/educational-uses/.

28. Susan B. Neuman and Patricia Koskinen, "Captioned Television as 'Comprehensible Input': Effects of Incidental Word Learning from Context for Language Minority Students," *Reading Research Quarterly* 27, no. 1 (Winter 1992): 95–106; P. S. Koskinen, R. M. Wilson, C. J. Jensema, "Using Closed-Captioned Television in the Teaching of Reading to Deaf Students," *American Annals of the Deaf* 131, no. 1 (March 1986): 43–46; Patricia S. Koskinen, Robert M. Wilson, Linda B. Gambrell, and Susan B. Neuman, "Captioned Video and Vocabulary Learning: An Innovative Practice in Literacy Instruction," *Reading Teacher* 47, no. 1 (September 1993): 36–43; Robert J. Rickelman, William A. Henk, and Kent Layton, "Closed-Captioned Television: A Viable Technology for the Reading Teacher," *Reading Teacher* 44, no. 8 (April 1991): 598–99.

29. Radesky, *Kids and Digital Media*.

30. "Textbook Weight in California: Analysis and Recommendations," California State Board of Education (2004), http://www2.cde.ca.gov /be/ag/ag/may04item21.pdf.

31. Chris Zook, "Infographic: Textbook costs skyrocket 812% in 35 years," Applied Educational Systems, September 7, 2017, https:// www.aeseducation.com/blog/infographic-the-skyrocketing -cost-of-textbooks-for-schools-students.

32. Mikael Ricknas, "Average Tablet Price Drops to $386, Says IMS Research," www.computerworld.com, June 8, 2012; see the

average price of consumer tablets in the United States from 2017 to 2022 at https://www.statista.com/statistics/619505/tablets-average -price-in-the-us/.

33. Use this link for many clips from the show: http://www.pbs.org /wgbh/americanexperience/films/freedomriders/.

34. Khan Academy is an extremely popular online free tutoring service consisting of more than 3,300 math, science, and history tutorials. See Clive Thompson, "How Khan Academy Is Changing the Rules of Education," *Wired*, August 2011. See also Steve Kolowich, "The Problem Solvers," *Inside Higher Ed* (blog), December 7, 2011, http:// www.insidehighered.com/news/2011/12/07/khan-academy -ponders-what-it-can-teach-higher-education-establishment; "Khan Academy: The Future of Education?" *60 Minutes*, video, 13 minutes, March 11, 2012, https://www.youtube.com/watch?v= zxJgPHM5NYI; and Salman Khan, founder of Khan Academy, in-terview by Charlie Rose, *Charlie Rose*, video, 21 minutes, May 4, 2011, https://www.youtube.com/watch?v=fJFKE8kyz7w.

35. Jim Sadwith, "Meeting Salinger," interview by Dick Gordon, *The Story*, video, 31 minutes, American Public Media, July 9, 2009, http://www.thestory.org/stories/2009-07/meeting-salinger.

36. Kara Yorio, "eBooks: Author Signings Are Going Digital," *The Re-cord*, June 3, 2012.

37. Adina Shamir, Ofra Korat, and Renat Fellah, "Promoting Vocabu-lary, Phonological Awareness and Concept About Print Among Children At-Risk for Learning Disability: Can E-books Help?" *Reading and Writing* 25, no. 1 (January 2012): 45–69.

38. Amelia K. Moody, Laura M. Justice, and Sonia Q. Cabell, "Elec-tronic Versus Traditional Storybooks: Relative Influence on Pre-school Children's Engagement and Communication," *Journal of Early Childhood Literacy* 10, no. 3 (October 2010): 294–313.

39. Julia Parish-Morris, Neha Mahajan, Kathy Hirsh-Pasek, Roberta Michnick Golinkoff, and Molly Fuller Collins, "Once Upon a Time: Parent-Child Dialogue and Storybook Reading in the Elec-tronic Era," *Mind, Brain, and Education* 7, no. 3 (2013): 200–11.

40. Parish-Morris et al.

41. Andrew Perrin, "Book Reading 2016," Pew Research Center, Sep-tember 1, 2016, www.pewinternet.org/2016/09/01.

42. Margaret K. Merga and Saiyidi Mat Roni, "Children Prefer to Read Books on Paper Rather Than Screens," *The Conversation*, March 9, 2017.

43. Jan M. Noyes and Kate J. Garland, "Computer- vs. Paper-Based Tasks: Are They Equivalent?" *Ergonomics* 51, no. 9 (September 2008): 1352–75, http://www.princeton.edu/~sswang/noyes_Gar land_computer_vs_paper.pdf.

44. "Download Free Books from Gutenberg.org to Kindle on iPad," YouTube video, 2 minutes, January 21, 2011, https://www.youtube .com/watch?v=NHonEWPN2x8.

45. Storyline Online, https://www.storylineonline.net/?gclid=EAIaI
QobChMIwJbInZyE3QIVAcBkCh2r6Q8FEAAYASAAEgLa
__D_BwE.

46. "Story Time from Space: In-Orbit Readings and Science to Encourage STEM in the Classroom," March 9, 2018, https://www
.nasa.gov/mission_pages/station/research/news/story_time_from
_space.

47. Melissa N. Callaghan and Stephanie M. Reich, "Are Educational
Preschool Apps Designed to Teach? An Analysis of the App Market," *Learning, Media and Technology* 43, no. 3 (2018): 280–293.

48. SuHua Huang, Nicole Clark, and Whitney Wedel, "The Use of an
iPad to Promote Preschoolers Alphabet Recognition and Letter
Sound Correspondence," *Practically Primary* 18, no. 1 (April 2013):
24–26; Guy Merchant, "Keep Taking the Tablets: iPads, Story
Apps, and Early Literacy," *Australian Journal of Language and Literacy*
38, no. 1 (February 2015):3–11.

49. Michelle M. Neumann, "Using Tablets and Apps to Enhance Emergent Literacy Skills in Young Children," *Early Childhood Research
Quarterly* 42 (2018):239–46.

50. Hannah Natanson, "Yes, Teens are Texting and Using Social Media
Instead of Reading Books, Researchers Say," *Washington Post*, August, 20, 2018.

51. Hayley Tsukayama, "Teens Spend Nearly Nine Hours Every Day
Consuming Media," *Washington Post*, November 3, 2015.

52. William Deresiewicz, "The End of Solitude," *Chronicle of Higher
Education*, January 30, 2009, http://chronicle.com/article/The-End
-of-Solitude/3708.

53. M. Csikszentmihalyi and K. Sawyer, "Creative Insight: The Social
Dimension of a Solitary Moment," in Robert Sternberg and Janet
Davidson, eds., *The Nature of Insight* (Cambridge, MA: MIT Press,
1996), 329–61.

54. Jonah Lehrer, "The Virtues of Daydreaming," *Frontal Cortex* (blog),
New Yorker, June 5, 2012, http://www.newyorker.com/online/blogs
/frontal-cortex/2012/06/the-virtues-of-daydreaming.html.

55. Marc Berman, Stephen Kaplan, and John Jonides, "The Cognitive
Benefits of Interacting with Nature," *Psychological Science* 19, no. 12
(December 2008): 1207–12. See also Eric Jaffe, "This Side of Para-
dise: Discovering Why the Human Mind Needs Nature," *Observer*,
May/June 2010, https://selfsustain.com/blog/this-side-of-paradise
-discovering-why-the-human-mind-needs-nature/.

56. Matt Richtel, "Digital Devices Deprive Brain of Needed Downtime," *New York Times*, August 24, 2010, http://www.nytimes.com
/2010/08/25/technology/25brain.html. See also Loren Frank, one
of the neuroscientists doing research on downtime and learning
among rats who can be heard in an interview on the *Brian Lehrer
Show* August 26, 2010, WNYC, at https://www.wnyc.org/story
/92581-open-phones-mental-down-time/.

Chapter 8: Visual Literacy and Reading Aloud

1. Lewis Carroll, *Alice's Adventures in Wonderland* (London: Macmillan, 1865).
2. Kevin Henkes, "The Artist at Work," *Horn Book Magazine*, 68, no. 1 (January 1992): 48–57.
3. Angela Eckhoff, "Using games to explore visual art with young children," *Young Children* 65, no. 1 (January 2010): 18–22.
4. Common Core State Standards Initiative, www.corestandards.org.
5. Common Core State Standards Initiative.
6. Common Core State Standards English Language Arts Standards—Reading: Literature—Kindergarten, www.corestandards.org/ELA-Literacy/RL/K/.
7. Common Core State Standards, English Language Arts Standards—Reading: Literature—Grade 5, www.corestandards.org/ELA-Literacy/RL/5/.
8. Allie Bidwell, "The History of Common Core State Standards," *U.S. News & World Report*, February 27, 2014, https://www.usnews.com/news/special-reports/articles/2014/02/27/the-history-of-common-core-state-standards.
9. Two South Dakota parents filed a lawsuit arguing that South Dakota's involvement in a multistate assessment group aligned with Common Core State Standards was illegal. The circuit court determined that the state had not violated any federal or state laws. Former Louisiana governor, Bobby Jindal, filed a lawsuit against President Barack Obama and his administration over the Common Core State Standards that cost the state over $450,000. Governor John Bel Edwards, elected in 2016, dropped the lawsuit.
10. Todd Finley, "Common Core in Action: 10 Visual Literacy Strategies," *Edutopia*, February 19, 2014, https://www.edutopia.org/blog/ccia-10-visual-literacy-strategies-todd-finley.
11. Philip Yenawine, *Visual Thinking Strategies: Using Art to Deepen Learning Across School Disciplines* (Cambridge, MA: Harvard Education Press, 2013).
12. Yenawine, *Visual Thinking Strategies*.
13. The Learning Network, "What's Going On in This Picture? *New York Times*, February 10, 2014, https://learning.blogs.nytimes.com/2014/02/10/whats-going-on-in-this-picture-feb-10-2014/.
14. Cyndi Giorgis, "Illustrations in Picture Books: The Art of Reading Images," in *Children's Literature in the Reading Program: Engaging Young Readers in the 21st Century*, ed. Deborah A. Wooten and Bernice E. Cullinan, 4th ed. (Newark, DE: International Reading Association, 2015): 71–82.
15. Roger Sutton and Martha V. Parravano, *A Family of Readers: The Book Lover's Guide to Children's and Young Adult Literature* (Somerville, MA: Candlewick Press, 2010).
16. Frank Serafini and Lindsey Moses, "Considering Design Features," *Reading Teacher* 69, no. 3 (August 2015): 307–9.

17. Giorgis, "Illustrations in Picture Books."
18. Frank Serafini, "Exploring Wordless Picture Books," *Reading Teacher* 68, no. 1 (September 2014): 24–26.
19. Graphic Novel/Comic Terms and Concepts, http://www.readwrite think.org/files/resources/lesson_images/lesson1102/terms.pdf.
20. Barbara Ward and Terrell A. Young, "Reading Graphically: Comics and Graphic Novels for Readers from Kindergarten Through High School," *Reading Horizons* 50, no. 4 (January/February 2011): 283–95.
21. Jacquelyn McTaggart, "Graphic Novels: The Good, the Bad, and the Ugly," in *Teaching Visual Literacy: Using Comic Books, Graphic Novels, Anime, Cartoons, and More to Develop Comprehension and Thinking Skills*, ed. Nancy Frey and Douglas Fisher (Thousand Oaks, CA: Corwin Press, 2008): 27–46.
22. Tom Burns, "Graphic Language: How to Read Comic Books with Your Kids," https://www.readbrightly.com/how-to-read-comic -books-with-your-kid/.
23. "Thinking Outside the Picture Book Box: Graphic Novels for Reading Aloud," Colorado Libraries for Early Literacy, March 12, 2018, https://www.clel.org/single-post/2018/03/12/Thinking-Outside -the-Picture-Book-Box-Graphic-Novels-for-Reading-Aloud.
24. "Tips for Reading—and Loving—Graphic Novels with Your Kids," Hachette Book Group, https://www.hachettebookgroup.com/2017 /09/25/reading-graphic-novels-with-kids/.
25. Arthur Schlesinger Jr., "Advice from a Reader-Aloud-to-Children," *New York Times Book Review*, November 25, 1979. For the most up-to-date summary of the Tintin experience, see Charles McGrath, "An Innocent in America," *New York Times*, January 2, 2012.

Chapter 9: The Significance of the Read-Aloud Experience

1. Kate DiCamillo, *Because of Winn-Dixie* (Somerville, MA: Candlewick Press, 2000).
2. Pam Allyn, "Read Aloud. Change the World," *Huffington Post*, May 3, 2014, https://www.huffingtonpost.com/pam-allyn/read -aloud-change-the-wor_b_4892116.html.
3. LitWorld International, http://www.litworld.org/.
4. Dominic W. Massaro, "Two Different Communication Genres," 2015.
5. Massaro, "Two Different Communication Genres."
6. Carl B. Smith and Gary M. Ingersoll, "Written Vocabulary of Elementary School Pupils, Ages 6–14," ERIC document ED323564, pp. 3–4, https://eric.ed.gov/?id=ED323564.
7. John Holt treated this concept at length in "How Teachers Make Children Hate Reading," *Redbook*, November 1967.
8. The Nation's Report Card, 2017 NAEP Mathematics and Reading Assessments, https://www.nationsreportcard.gov/reading_math _2017_highlights/. See also Dana Gioia, ed., *To Read or Not to Read:*

A Question of National Consequence: Executive Summary, Research Report No. 47 (Washington, DC: National Endowment for the Arts, 2007), p. 13.

9. Lois Bridges, *Open a World of Possible: Real Stories About the Joy and Power of Reading* (New York: Scholastic, 2014).

10. Jacques Barzun, *Begin Here* (Chicago: University of Chicago Press, 1991), 114–16. Barzun is one of the grand old men of American letters (author of thirty books, including a National Book Award finalist, *From Dawn to Decadence: 500 Years of Western Cultural Life*, at age ninety-two) and former dean of graduate faculty and provost of Columbia University. He is a renowned authority in education and philosophy, to say nothing of detective fiction and baseball, whose advice should never be taken lightly.

11. Eric R. Kandel, James H. Schwartz, and Thomas M. Jessell, eds., *Principles of Neural Science*, 3rd ed., Center for Neurobiology and Behavior, College of Physicians and Surgeons of Columbia University and the Howard Hughes Medical Institute (East Norwalk, CT: Appleton & Lange, 1991): "The visual system is the most complex of all the sensory systems. The auditory nerve contains about 30,000 fibers, but the optic nerve (visual) contains one million, more than all the dorsal root fibers entering the entire spinal cord!"

12. Dolores Durkin, *Children Who Read Early* (New York: Teachers College Press, 1966); Margaret M. Clark, *Young Fluent Readers* (London: Heinemann, 1976). See also Anne D. Forester, "What Teachers Can Learn from 'Natural Readers,'" *Reading Teacher* 31, no. 2 (1977): 160–66.

13. I. V. S. Mullis, M. O. Martin, P. Foy, and M. Hooper (2017), *PIRLS 2016 International Results in Reading*. Retrieved from Boston College, TIMSS & PIRLS International Study Center website, http://timssandpirls.bc.edu/pirls2016/international-results/.

14. National Center for Education Statistics, "Home Literacy Activities with Young Children," chapter 1, section Preprimary Education, accessed September 9, 2018, https://nces.ed.gov/programs/coe/pdf/coe_sfa.pdf.

15. Mullis, *PIRLS 2016*.

16. "Benefits of Asking Young Kids Open-Ended Questions,"https://www.under5s.co.nz/shop/Hot+Topics+Articles/Child+Development/Benefits+of+asking+young+kids+open-ended+questions.html.

17. Dillon, "Schools Cut Back Subjects."

18. Daniel Goleman, *Emotional Intelligence: Why It Can Matter More Than IQ* (New York: Bantam, 1995).

19. Irwin Kirsch, John de Jong, Dominique Lafontaine, Joy McQueen, Juliette Mendelovits, and Christian Monseur, *Reading for Change: Performance and Engagement Across Countries—Results from PISA 2000* (Paris: Organisation for Economic Co-operation and Development, 2000), pp. 106–10, http://www.oecd.org/dataoecd/43/54/33690904.pdf.

20. Annie Murphy Paul, "Your Brain on Fiction," *New York Times* Sunday Review, March 18, 2012. See also Maja Djikic, Keith Oatley, Sara Zoeterman, and Jordan B. Peterson, "On Being Moved by Art: How Reading Fiction Transforms the Self," *Creativity Research Journal* 21, no. 1 (2009): 24–29, http://dx.doi.org/10.1080/10400410802633392; and Raymond A. Mar, Keith Oatley, Jacob B. Hirsh, Jennifer de la Paz, and Jordan B. Peterson, "Bookworms Versus Nerds: Exposure to Fiction Versus Non-Fiction, Divergent Associations with Social Ability, and the Simulation of Fictional Social Worlds," *Journal of Research in Personality* 40, no. 5 (December 2006): 694–712.

21. Lester L. Laminack, *Unwrapping the Read Aloud: Making Every Read Aloud Intentional and Instructional* (New York: Scholastic, 2009): 93–95.

Chapter 10: The Dos and Don'ts of Reading Aloud

1. Mem Fox, *Koala Lou* (Boston: Houghton Mifflin, 1994).

2. Mem Fox, *Reading Magic: Why Reading Aloud to Our Children Will Change Their Lives Forever* (New York: Harcourt, 2008), p. 10.

Bibliography

Adams, Marilyn Jager. *Beginning to Read: Thinking and Learning About Print—A Summary*. Champaign-Urbana: University of Illinois, Center for the Study of Reading, 1990.

Allington, Richard. *Big Brother and the National Reading Curriculum: How Ideology Trumped Evidence*. Portsmouth, NH: Heinemann, 2002.

Anderson, Richard C., Elfrieda H. Hiebert, Judith A. Scott, and Ian A. G. Wilkinson. *Becoming a Nation of Readers: The Report of the Commission on Reading*. Champaign-Urbana: University of Illinois, Center for the Study of Reading, 1985.

Applebee, Arthur N., Judith A. Langer, Ina V. S. Mullis, Andrew S. Latham, and Claudia A. Gentile. *NAEP 1992 Writing Report Card*. Educational Testing Service. Washington, DC: U.S. Department of Education, June 1994. https://files.eric.ed.gov/fulltext/ED370119.pdf.

Bae, Yupin, Susan Choy, Claire Geddes, Jennifer Sable, and Thomas Snyder. *Trends in Educational Equity of Girls and Women*. Washington, DC: U.S. Government Printing Office, 2000.

Bang, Molly. *Picture This: How Pictures Work*. 25th anniversary edition. San Francisco: Chronicle Books, 1991/2016.

Barton, Paul E. *Parsing the Achievement Gap: Baselines for Tracking Progress*. Princeton, NJ: Educational Testing Service, 2003.

Barton, Paul E., and Richard J. Coley. *The Family: America's Smallest School*. Princeton, NJ: Educational Testing Service, 1992. http://www.ets.org/Media/Education_Topics/pdf/5678_PERCReport_School.pdf.

———. *Captive Students: Education and Training in America's Prisons*. Princeton, NJ: Educational Testing Service, Policy Information Center, 1996.

Barzun, Jacques. *Begin Here: The Forgotten Conditions of Teaching and Learning*. Chicago: University of Chicago Press, 1991.

Beatty, Alexandra S., Clyde M. Reese, Hilary R. Persky, and Peggy Carr. *NAEP 1994 U.S. History Report Card*. Washington, DC: U.S. Department of Education, Office of Educational Research and Improvement, 1996.

Berliner, David C., and Bruce J. Biddle. *The Manufactured Crisis: Myths, Fraud, and the Attack on America's Public Schools*. Reading, MA: Addison-Wesley, 1996.

Bradshaw, Tom, Bonnie Nichols, Kelly Hill, and Mark Bauerlein. *Reading at Risk: A Survey of Literary Reading in America*. Washington, DC:

National Endowment for the Arts, Research Division, Report No. 46, 2004.

Bridges, Lois. *Open a World of Possible: Real Stories About the Joy and Power of Reading.* New York: Scholastic, 2014.

Bruer, John T. *The Myth of the First Three Years: A New Understanding of Early Brain Development and Lifelong Learning.* New York: Free Press, 1999.

Bruner, Jerome S., Alison Jolly, and Kathy Sylva, eds. *Play: Its Role in Development and Evolution.* New York: Penguin, 1976.

Cain, Susan. *Quiet: The Power of Introverts in a World That Can't Stop Talking.* New York: Crown, 2012.

Campbell, Jay R., Catherine M. Hombo, and John Mazzeo. *NAEP 1999 Trends in Academic Progress: Three Decades of Student Performance.* U.S. Department of Education. Washington, DC: National Center for Education Statistics,2000. https://nces.ed.gov/nationsreportcard/pdf /main1999/2000469.pdf.

Carlsen, G. Robert, and Anne Sherrill. *Voices of Readers: How We Come to Love Books.* Urbana, IL: National Council of Teachers of English, 1988. https://files.eric.ed.gov/fulltext/ED295136.pdf.

Carr, Nicholas. *The Shallows: What the Internet Is Doing to Our Brains.* New York: W. W. Norton, 2010.

Cazden, Courtney B. *Child Language and Education.* New York: Holt, Rinehart and Winston, 1972.

Clark, Margaret M. *Young Fluent Readers.* London: Heinemann, 1976.

Coley, Richard J. *An Uneven Start: Indicators of Inequality in School Readiness.* Princeton, NJ: Educational Testing Service, Policy Information Center, 2002.

Davidson, Cathy N. *Now You See It: How the Brain Science of Attention Will Transform the Way We Live, Work, and Learn.* New York: Viking, 2011.

Davies, Robertson. *One Half of Robertson Davies.* New York: Viking, 1977.

Davis, Sampson, George Jenkins, Rameck Hunt, and Lisa Frazier Page. *The Pact: Three Young Men Make a Promise and Fulfill a Dream.* New York: Riverhead, 2003.

Denton, Kristin, and Jerry West. *Children's Reading and Mathematics Achievement in Kindergarten and First Grade.* Washington, DC: U.S. Department of Education, NCES, 2002. https://nces.ed.gov/pubs2002 /2002125.pdf.

Donahue, Patricia L., Kristin E. Voelki, Jay R. Campbell, and John Mazzeo. *NAEP 1998 Reading Report Card for the Nation and the States.* Washington, DC: U.S. Department of Education, National Center for Education Statistics, 1999.

Dreyer, Philip, ed. *Vision and Realities in Literacy: Sixtieth Yearbook of the Claremont Reading Conference.* Claremont, CA: Claremont Reading Conference, 1996.

Durkin, Dolores. *Children Who Read Early.* New York: Teachers College Press, 1966.

Dynarski, Mark, Roberto Agodini, Sheila Heaviside, Timothy Novak, Nancy Carey, Larissa Campuzano, Barbara M. Means et al. *Effectiveness of Reading and Mathematics Software Products: Findings from the First Student Cohort*. Washington, DC: U.S. Department of Education, Institute of Education Sciences, 2007.

Elkind, David. *The Hurried Child: Growing Up Too Fast Too Soon*. 3rd ed. Cambridge, MA: DaCapo Press, 2001.

Elley, Warwick B. *How in the World Do Students Read?* Hamburg: International Association for the Evaluation of Educational Achievement, July 1992. https://files.eric.ed.gov/fulltext/ED360613.pdf.

Ferguson, Ronald F. *What Doesn't Meet the Eye: Understanding and Addressing Racial Disparities in High-Achieving Suburban Schools*. Oak Brook, IL: North Central Regional Educational Laboratory, 2002.

Foertsch, Mary A. *Reading In and Out of School*. Educational Testing Service/Education Information Office. Washington, DC: U.S. Department of Education, 1992.

Fox, Mem. *Reading Magic: Why Reading Aloud to Our Children Will Change Their Lives Forever*. Orlando, FL: Harcourt, 2008.

Friedman, Howard S., and Leslie R. Martin. *The Longevity Project: Surprising Discoveries for Health and Long Life from the Landmark Eight-Decade Study*. New York: Hudson Street Press, 2011.

Friedman, Thomas L. *The World Is Flat: A Brief History of the Twenty-First Century*. New York: Farrar, Straus & Giroux, 2005.

Garan, Elaine M. *In Defense of Our Children: When Politics, Profit, and Education Collide*. Portsmouth, NH: Heinemann, 2004.

———. *Resisting Reading Mandates: How to Triumph with the Truth*. Portsmouth, NH: Heinemann, 2002.

Gawande, Atul. *The Checklist Manifesto: How to Get Things Right*. New York: Metropolitan Books, 2009.

Goleman, Daniel. *Emotional Intelligence: Why It Can Matter More Than IQ*. New York: Bantam, 1995.

Goodman, Kenneth S., Patrick Shannon, Yvonne S. Freeman, and Sharon Murphy. *Report Card on Basal Readers*. New York: Richard C. Owen Publishers, 1988.

Gopnik, Alison, Andrew N. Meltzoff, and Patricia K. Kuhl. *The Scientist in the Crib: Minds, Brains, and How Children Learn*. New York: Morrow, 1999.

Graff, Harvey. *The Literacy Myth*. San Diego, CA: Academic, 1979.

Hart, Betty, and Todd R. Risley. *Meaningful Differences in the Everyday Experience of Young American Children*. Baltimore, MD: Brookes Publishing, 1996.

Heyns, Barbara. *Summer Learning and the Effects of Schooling*. New York: Academic Press, 1978.

Hodgkinson, Harold L. *The Same Client: The Demographics of Education and Service Delivery Systems*. Washington, DC: Institute for Educational Leadership, 1989.

Hout, Michael, and Stuart W. Elliott. *Incentives and Test-Based Accountability in Education.* National Research Council. Washington, DC: National Academies Press, 2011.

Institute of Education Sciences, U.S. Department of Education. *The Nation's Report Card: Reading 2011* (NCES 2012–457). Washington, DC: National Center for Education Statistics, 2011.

Isaacson, Walter. *Steve Jobs.* New York: Simon & Schuster, 2011.

Johnson, Nancy J., and Cyndi Giorgis. *The Wonder of It All: When Literature and Literacy Intersect.* Portsmouth, NH: Heinemann, 2007.

Kamil, Michael L., Peter B. Mosenthal, P. David Pearson, and Rebecca Barr, eds. *Handbook of Reading Research.* Vol. 3. New York: Erlbaum, 2000.

Kandel, Eric R., James H. Schwartz, and Thomas M. Jessell, eds. *Principles of Neural Science.* 3rd ed. Center for Neurobiology and Behavior, College of Physicians and Surgeons of Columbia University and the Howard Hughes Medical Institute. East Norwalk, CT: Appleton & Lange, 1991.

Kirsch, Irwin, John de Jong, Dominique Lafontaine, Joy McQueen, Juliette Mendelovits, and Christian Monseur. *Reading for Change: Performance and Engagement Across Countries—Results from Pisa 2000.* Paris: Organisation for Economic Co-operation and Development (OECD), 2002. http://www.oecd.org/dataoecd/43/54/33690904.pdf.

Klingberg, Torkel. *The Overflowing Brain: Information Overload and the Limits of Working Memory.* Oxford: Oxford University Press, 2009.

Kohn, Alfie. *Punished by Rewards: The Trouble with Gold Stars, Incentive Plans, A's, Praise, and Other Bribes.* Boston: Houghton Mifflin, 1993.

Krashen, Stephen D. *Free Voluntary Reading.* Santa Barbara, CA: Libraries Unlimited, 2011.

———. *The Power of Reading: Insights from the Research.* 2nd ed. Westport, CT: Libraries Unlimited and Portsmouth, NH: Heinemann, 2004.

———. *Writing: Research, Theory, and Applications.* Torrance, CA: Laredo Publishing Company, 1984.

Kubey, Robert, and Mihaly Csikszentmihalyi. *Television and the Quality of Life: How Viewing Shapes Everyday Experience.* Hillsdale, NJ: Erlbaum, 1990.

Lambert, Megan Dowd. *Reading Picture Books with Children: How to Shake Up Storytime and Get Kids Talking About What They See.* Watertown, MA: Charlesbridge, 2015.

Laminack, Lester L. *Unwrapping the Read Aloud: Making Every Read Aloud Intentional and Instructional.* New York: Scholastic Teaching Sources, 2009.

Lance, Keith Curry, Lynda Welborn, and Christine Hamilton-Pennell. *The Impact of School Library Media Centers on Academic Achievement.* Castle Rock, CO: Hi Willow Research and Publishing, 1993.

Lance, Keith Curry, Marcia J. Rodney, and Christine Hamilton-Pennell. *How School Librarians Help Kids Achieve Standards: The Second Colorado Study.* Denver: Colorado State Library, 2000.

Lee, Valerie E., and David T. Burkam. *Inequality at the Starting Gate: Social Background Differences in Achievement as Children Begin School.* Washington, DC: Economic Policy Institute, 2002.

Marmot, Michael. *The Status Syndrome: How Social Standing Affects Our Health and Longevity.* New York: Times Books, 2004.

McQuillan, Jeff. *The Literacy Crisis: False Claims, Real Solutions.* Portsmouth, NH: Heinemann, 1998.

Mogel, Wendy. *The Blessings of a B Minus: Using Jewish Teachings to Raise Resilient Teenagers.* New York: Scribner, 2010.

Mormino, Gary R., and George E. Pozzetta. *The Immigrant World of Ybor City: Italians and Their Latin Neighbors in Tampa, 1885–1985.* Gainesville: University Press of Florida, 1998.

Mullis, Ina V. S., J. R. Campbell, and A. E. Farstrup. *NAEP 1992 Reading Report Card for the Nation and the States.* Washington, DC: National Center for Education Statistics, U.S. Government Printing Office, 1993. https://files.eric.ed.gov/fulltext/ED369067.pdf.

Mullis, Ina V. S., John A. Dossey, Jay R. Campbell, Claudia A. Gentile, Christine O'Sullivan, and Andrew S. Latham. *NAEP 1992 Trends in Academic Progress.* Washington, DC: Office of Educational Research and Improvement, U.S. Department of Education, July 1994.

Mullis, Ina V. S., Michael O. Martin, Eugenio J. Gonzalez, and Ann M. Kennedy. *PIRLS 2001 International Report: IEA's Study of Reading Literacy Achievement in Primary School in 35 Countries.* Chestnut Hill, MA: International Association for the Evaluation of Educational Achievement/International Study Center, Boston College, 2003. https://pirls.bc.edu/pirls2001i/pdf/p1_IR_book.pdf.

National Assessment of Educational Progress. *Literacy: Profiles of America's Young Adults.* Princeton, NJ: Educational Testing Service, 1986.

National Center for Education Statistics. *National Household Education Surveys.* Washington, DC: U.S. Government Printing Office, 1999.

National Commission on Excellence in Education. *A Nation at Risk: The Imperative for Educational Reform.* Washington, DC: U.S. Government Printing Office, 1983.

National Reading Panel. *Teaching Children to Read: An Evidence-Based Assessment of the Scientific Research Literature on Reading and Its Implications for Reading Instruction; Reports of the Subgroups.* Washington, DC: National Institute of Child Health and Human Development, NIH, Publication 00-4754, 2000.

National Survey of Student Engagement. *Fostering Student Engagement Campuswide—Annual Results 2011.* Bloomington: Indiana University Center for Postsecondary Research, 2011. http://nsse.iub.edu/nSSE_2011_Results/pdf/nSSE_2011_AnnualResults.pdf.

Neuman, Susan B., Donna C. Celano, Albert N. Greco, and Pamela Shue. *Access for All: Closing the Book Gap for Children in Early Education.* Newark, DE: International Reading Association, 2001.

Nielsen Media Research. *2000 Report on Television: The First 50 Years.* New York: Nielsen Media Research, 2000.

Niles, J. A., and L. A. Harris. *New Inquiries in Reading: Research and Instruction.* Rochester, NY: National Reading Conference, 1982.

Organisation for Economic Co-operation and Development. *PISA 2009 Results: Overcoming Social Background: Equity in Learning Opportunities and Outcomes (Volume II).* Programme for International Student Assessment Paris: OECD Publishing, 2010. http://dx.doi.org/10.1787/9789264091504-en.

Ogbu, John U. *Black American Students in an Affluent Suburb: A Study of Academic Disengagement.* Mahwah, NJ: Erlbaum, 2003.

Ozma, Alice. *The Reading Promise: My Father and the Books We Shared.* New York: Grand Central Publishing, 2011.

Pamuk, E., D. Makuc, K. Heck, C. Reuben, and K. Lochner. *Health, United States, 1998: Socioeconomic Status and Health Chartbook.* Hyattsville, MD: National Center for Health Statistics, 1998.

Pearl, Nancy. *Book Lust: Recommended Reading for Every Mood, Moment, and Reason.* Seattle: Sasquatch Books, 2003.

———. *More Book Lust: Recommended Reading for Every Mood, Moment, and Reason.* Seattle: Sasquatch Books, 2005.

Pearson, P. David, ed. *Handbook of Reading Research.* New York: Longman, 1984.

Perie, Marianne, Rebecca Moran, and Anthony D. Lutkus. *NAEP 2004 Trends in Academic Progress: Three Decades of Student Performance in Reading and Mathematics* (NCES 2005–464). U.S. Department of Education, Institute of Education Sciences, National Center for Education Statistics. Washington, DC: U.S. Government Printing Office, 2005.

Rampey, B. D., G. S. Dion, and P. L. Donahue. *NAEP 2008 Trends in Academic Progress* (NCES 2009–479). U.S. Department of Education, Institute of Education Sciences, National Center for Education Statistics. Washington, DC: U.S. Government Printing Office, 2009.

Ravitch, Diane. *The Death and Life of the Great American School System: How Testing and Choice Are Undermining Education.* New York: Basic Books, 2010.

Rideout, Victoria J., Elizabeth A. Vandewater, and Ellen A. Wartella. *Zero to Six: Electronic Media in the Lives of Infants, Toddlers and Preschoolers.* Menlo Park, CA: The Henry J. Kaiser Family Foundation, 2003. https://kaiserfamilyfoundation.files.wordpress.com/2013/01/zero-to-six-electronic-media-in-the-lives-of-infants-toddlers-and-preschoolers-pdf.pdf.

Rideout, Victoria J., Ulla G. Foehr, and Donald F. Roberts. *Generation M2: Media in the Lives of 8- to 18-Year-Olds.* Menlo Park, CA: The Henry J. Kaiser Family Foundation, 2010. https://kaiserfamilyfoundation.files.wordpress.com/2013/01/8010.pdf.

Roberts, Donald F., Ulla G. Foehr, and Victoria Rideout. *Generation M: Media in the Lives of 8–18Year-Olds.* Menlo Park, CA: The Henry J. Kaiser Family Foundation, 2005. https://kaiserfamilyfoundation.files

.wordpress.com/2013/01/generation-m-media-in-the-lives-of-8-18
-year-olds-report.pdf.

Roberts, Donald F., Ulla G. Foehr, Victoria J. Rideout, and Mollyann Brodie. *Kids and Media @ the New Millennium.* Menlo Park, CA: The Henry J. Kaiser Family Foundation, 1999. https://kaiser familyfoundation.files.wordpress.com/2013/01/kids-media-the-new -millennium-report.pdf.

Schlesinger, Arthur M. Jr. *A Life in the Twentieth Century: Innocent Beginnings, 1917–1950.* Boston: Houghton Mifflin, 2000.

Schramm, Wilbur, ed. *The Process and Effects of Mass Communication.* 6th ed. Urbana: University of Illinois Press, 1965.

Shachtman, Tom. *The Inarticulate Society: Eloquence and Culture in America.* New York: Free Press, 1995.

Snow, Catherine E., M. Susan Burns, and Peg Griffin, eds. *Preventing Reading Difficulties in Young Children.* Washington, DC: National Academies Press, 1998.

Snowdon, David. *Aging with Grace: What the Nun Study Teaches Us About Leading Longer, Healthier, and More Meaningful Lives.* New York: Bantam, 2001.

Stewig, John Warren. *Looking at Picture Books.* Fort Atkinson, WI: Highsmith, 1995.

Sum, Andrew, Neeta Fogg, Ishwar Khatiwada, Joseph McLaughlin, Sheila Palma, Jacqui Motroni, and Paulo Tobar. *Getting to the Finish Line: College Enrollment and Graduation, A Seven Year Longitudinal Study of the Boston Public Schools Class of 2000.* Center for Labor Market Studies. Boston: Northeastern University Press, 2008.

Suskind, Ron. *A Hope in the Unseen: An American Odyssey from the Inner City to the Ivy League.* New York: Broadway Books, 1999.

Sutton, Roger, and Martha V. Parravano. *A Family of Readers: The Book Lover's Guide to Children's and Young Adult Literature.* Somerville, MA: Candlewick Press, 2010.

Taylor, Gordon Rattray. *The Natural History of the Mind.* New York: Dutton, 1979.

Thernstrom, Abigail, and Stephan Thernstrom. *No Excuses: Closing the Racial Gap in Learning.* New York: Simon & Schuster, 2004.

Underhill, Paco. *Why We Buy: The Science of Shopping.* New York: Simon & Schuster, 1999.

U.S. Department of Education. *The Condition of Education 2000* (NCES 2000–062), Washington, DC: National Center for Education Statistics, 2000.

U.S. Department of Education. *Trends in Educational Equity of Girls and Women.* Washington, DC: National Center for Education Statistics, 2000.

Vernez, Georges, Richard A. Krop, and C. Peter Rydell. *Closing the Education Gap: Benefits and Costs.* Santa Monica, CA: RAND Corporation, 1999.

West, Jerry, Kristin Denton, and Elvira Germino-Hausken. *America's Kindergartners: Findings from the Early Childhood Longitudinal Study, Kindergarten Class of 1998–99, Fall 1998.* Washington, DC: U.S. Department of Education, National Center for Education Statistics, 2000. https://nces.ed.gov/pubs2000/2000070.pdf.

Yardley, Jonathan. *Our Kind of People: The Story of an American Family.* New York: Weidenfeld & Nicolson, 1989.

Zill, Nicholas, and Marianne Winglee. *Who Reads Literature? The Future of the United States as a Nation of Readers.* Cabin John, MD: Seven Locks Press, 1990. https://files.eric.ed.gov/fulltext/ED324633.pdf.

Subject Index for the Text

Page numbers in **bold** indicate sections devoted to a subject. Page numbers in *italics* indicate photographs, illustrations, and captions. For books listed in the Treasury, see the Author-Illustrator Index, pp. 353.

Author-Illustrator Index
for the Treasury

Italics are for illustrator only; ★ after page number gives location of a group of books by an author or illustrator.

Photograph credits

Unless otherwise indicated, photos are by Cyndi Giorgis.

Page vi: Photo courtesy of Charity Delach
Page xviii: Photo courtesy of Marie LeJeune
Page xxi: Photo courtesy of Diane Crawford
Page 13: Photo courtesy of Diane Crawford
Page 24: Photo courtesy of Clara Lackey
Page 31: Photo courtesy of Peter Delach
Page 37: Photo courtesy of Scott Riley
Page 42: Photo courtesy of Charity Delach
Page 55: Photo courtesy of Melissa Olans Antinoff
Page 90: Photo courtesy of Charity Delach
Page 91: Photo courtesy of Mark Lackey
Page 96: Photo courtesy of Elysha O'Brien
Page 110: Photo courtesy of Megan Sloan
Page 140: Photo courtesy of Melissa Olans Antinoff
Page 146: Photo courtesy of Diane Crawford
Page 155: Photo courtesy of Diane Crawford
Page 160: Photo courtesy of James Kim
Page 170: Photo courtesy of Elysha O'Brien